Edition **DETAIL**

Staib
Dörrhöfer
Rosenthal

COMPONENTS AND SYSTEMS

MODULAR CONSTRUCTION

DESIGN STRUCTURE
NEW TECHNOLOGIES

Edition DETAIL – Institut für internationale
Architektur-Dokumentation GmbH & Co. KG
München

Birkhäuser
Basel · Boston · Berlin

Imprint

Authors

Gerald Staib, architect
Prof. Dipl.-Ing.
Department for Building Construction and Design
at the Technical University Dresden

Andreas Dörrhöfer
Dipl.-Ing. Arch.
Department for Building Construction and Design
at the Technical University Dresden

Markus Rosenthal
Dipl.-Ing. Arch.
Department for Building Construction and Design
at the Technical University Dresden

Technical essay:

Jan Knippers, Prof. Dr.-Ing.
Institute for Construction and Design, University of
Stuttgart

Thorsten Helbig, Dipl.-Ing.

Editorial services

Project management:
Steffi Lenzen

Editorial services and copy editing:
Cornelia Hellstern

Editorial services:
Carola Jacob-Ritz, Michaela Linder, Eva Schönbrunner,
Cosima Strobl, Melanie Weber

Drawings:
Marion Griese, Caroline Hörger, Emese Köszegi,
Nicola Kollmann, Simon Kramer, Elisabeth Krammer,
Martin Hämmel, Daniel Hajduk

Cover design:
Josef A. Grillmeier

DTP:
Simone Soesters

Reproduction:
Martin Härtl OHG, Martinsried

Printing and binding:
Kösel GmbH & Co. KG, Altusried-Krugzell

A specialist publication from Redaktion DETAIL.
This book is a cooperation between
DETAIL – Review of Architecture and
Birkhäuser Verlag AG

© 2008, 1st edition Institut für internationale
Architektur-Dokumentation GmbH & Co. KG,
P.O. Box 33 06 60, D-80066 Munich, Germany and
Birkhäuser Verlag AG, Basel • Boston • Berlin,
P.O. Box 133, CH-4010 Basel, Switzerland

ISBN: 978-3-7643-8656-6

This book is also available in a German language edition
(ISBN: 978-3-7643-8655-9).

Preface

"Unitised building" and "system building" are concepts that are often considered to conflict with the idea of "creative design". But are these really incompatible opposites? Shouldn't they rather complement each other, or even effectively sustain each other?

Nowadays it is not unusual for prefabricated building to encounter strong resistance; an understandable response when one considers recent history. The origins of these prejudices often lie in the ill-considered employment and application of building with prefabricated elements and systems. One is confronted with the "architectural" consequences of this approach everywhere, for example in the shape of countless prefabricated panel construction buildings in Eastern Europe; no-one wants to repeat these, but, strictly speaking, they do not represent the true purpose of prefabricated building. But with the continuously growing ecological and economical challenges facing the construction industry today, structures based on building systems and prefabricated production techniques are becoming increasingly important.

With this publication we would like to pave the way for a sensible approach to the use of prefabricated elements and systems: away from a view of prefabrication as an end in itself, and seeing it more as an instrument capable of enhancing comprehensive design concepts. Prefabrication doesn't necessarily mean off-the-peg architecture or universally usable elements; quite the opposite in fact: modern systems promote the customised prefabrication of discrete units with high levels of differentiation. This can actively encourage designers' creativity rather than curtail it. The questions to be posed are: What can contemporary prefabrication techniques enable us to do? How do they work? How can we utilised and apply them most effectively?

"Components + Systems" is subdivided into five main sections focussing on the following topics:

A comprehensive introduction to the history of this subject is presented in part A. Although the construction of the nomadic shelters of early history indicate first attempts in this direction, the concept of prefabrication reached its climax in the 1960's with the diverse urban and architectural utopias of that era. The monotonous designs of the architecture of this period, however, also heralded the "demise" of these ideas. It was not until the present time – almost a quarter of a century later – that, faced with a growing necessity for resource-conserving techniques and the desire to increase design flexibility continuously, thoughts again began to turn increasingly to the concepts of systems.

Part B describes the technical and constructional foundation of unitised building. Relevant terms – such as level of prefabrication, type standardisation, module and modular system – are defined and explained for architects within the context of integrated planning. In addition to descriptive presentations of the relevant assembly methods, planning strategies facilitate an initial understanding of this topic.

Part C comprises the applications of various systems in the construction of load-bearing structures and the materials used in such systems. The essential construction principles for unitised building are presented; frame systems, panel systems and room module systems. In this context the level of prefabrication of the elements selected for these methods of building plays an enormously important role for the construction of the individual buildings.

Prefabricated facade systems are dealt with separately in part D. Systems for office and administration buildings often include frames, glazing, supporting construction and sunshading in a single element. These systems are, however, not only to be found in present-day high-rise building envelopes, but increasingly in everyday architecture also.

Finally, part E discusses contemporary trends in the field of computer-based design methods and fabrication techniques. A discussion of potential developments for system building presents new impulses and allows us to look toward the future with great anticipation. Is there a future for system building? If so, what could it look like? Is it possible for us to learn from the mistakes of the past, and to transform them into something positive?

Each chapter is supported by comprehensive detailed examples which present ideas for the successful translation of theory into practice, far removed from the standard "mishmash" and dismal repetition of industrially produced modules. The examples prove, once again, that high levels of prefabrication, functionality and high quality design are not mutually exclusive.

Knowledge of the interdependence and constraints of various organisational systems and building methods, as well as of the assembly of different building elements and of contemporary fabrication techniques, encourages the responsible deployment of prefabricated systems and will enable good quality architecture to benefit from unitised and system building.

Publisher and editorial department, Munich, May 2008

Contents

Imprint	4	Module	44
		Grid	44
Preface	5	Dimensional coordination	45
		Geometrical positioning of	
Introduction	8	structural and fit-out elements	45
		Transport	45
		Assembly	47
		Jointing	47
Part A History of prefabrication	12	Tolerances	47

Nomads and settled dwellers	14		
Brickwork	14		
Stone	14	**Part C Structural systems**	**48**
Timber	15		
The military and colonial expansion	17	**Materials in system building**	
Iron – the first systems	18	Steel	50
Prefabricated concrete construction	21	Timber	51
Rationalisation, serial production,		Concrete	51
type standardisation and mass			
housing construction	22	**Frame systems**	
The prefabricated house –		Steel frame systems	55
the modular building system	25	Timber frame systems	61
Large span structural systems	31	Concrete frame systems	68
Mega-structures and visions	31		
Industrial fabrication – "synonym		**Built examples in detail**	
for progress"	33	Temporary House, Paris (F)	72
Open structures	34	House, Rotenburg (D)	76
		House, Phoenix (USA)	78
		Demonstration house, Tosu-City (J)	82
		House, Sakurajosui (J)	86
		Extension, Preding (A)	90
		House, Andelsbuch (A)	92
Part B Fundamentals	**38**	House, Gams (CH)	96
		Fashion center, Fukuoka (J)	100
Industrial prefabrication	40	Universitiy institute, Grenoble (F)	102
Site prefabrication and		Housing and office block, Kassel (D)	106
mobile production plants	41		
Building methods	41		
Elements	42	**Panel systems**	
Type standardisation	42	Building with steel panels	111
System – building system	42	Building with timber panels	114
Closed systems	42	Building with concrete panels	119
Modular building systems	43	Building with masonry panels and	
Open systems	43	brickwork elements	124
Semi-finished elements	43		

Built examples in detail

House, Sumvitg (CH)	126
House, Dalaas (A)	128
Weekend house, Tokyo (J)	132
Weekend house, Northport (USA)	134
House, Münchenbuchsee (CH)	136
Carpentry works, Feldkirch (A)	140
Technology centre, Munich (D)	144
Advertising agency, Munich (D)	148
Winery, Fläsch (CH)	152
Hotel management and catering school,	
Nivilliers (F)	156

Room module systems

Steel room module systems	160
Timber room module systems	162
Concrete room module systems	163

Built examples in detail

Office block, Fellbach (D)	164
Residential and commercial block,	
Rathenow (D)	168
Office building, Munich (D)	172
Tomihiro Art Museum, Azuma (J)	174
Pavilion, Venice (I)	176
Loft, New York (USA)	178
Café, Helsinki (FIN)	180
Hotel extension, Bezau (A)	182
Prefabricated house from Denmark (DK)	186
Transportable living unit (D)	190
Nakagin Capsule Tower, Tokyo (J)	192

Part D   Building envelopes   **194**

Structural facades	196
Non-structural facades	196
Glass facade systems	197
Multi-layer glass facade	
and window systems	198
Metal facade systems	201
Timber facade systems	203

Concrete facade systems	204
Brickwork facade systems	205
Natural stonework facade systems	205
Plastic facade systems	206

Glazed grid shells   **208**

Changes in the	
planning process	208
Glazed single-skin steel grid shells	209

Built examples in detail

Westhafen Tower,	
Frankfurt/Main (D)	214
Office block, London (GB)	216
Uptown Munich (D)	218
Hotel, Tokyo (J)	220
Museum of Contemporary Art,	
Chicago (USA)	222

Part E   Developments   **224**

From industrial mass production	
to customised prefabrication	226
Computer-assisted design	226
Computer-assisted	
production processes	227
Construction robots	228
User-specific customisation	228
Digital construction systems	229

Appendices   **230**

Authors	230
Statutory instruments, directives,	
standards	231
Bibliography	232
Illustration credits	234
Index of persons	237
Index	238

Introduction

"Components" and "Systems" – these terms evoke – not only for architects – associations with industrial production, serial fabrication and assembly lines; more precisely, post-war construction techniques. That is, images dominated by technology, uniformity, indeed even monotony.

Although serial production on assembly lines in automotive production plants is accepted as standard procedure, a comparable approach in architecture is widely considered undesirable, burdened as it is by examples from more recent architectural history. Surely, however, this reaction has nothing to do with the concept of "repeating" similar components in architecture as such, but rather with the use of industrially prefabricated elements dominated by technical concerns.

That is, of course, the first emotional reaction. If we allow ourselves to address this issue pragmatically and consider the history of architecture, specifically this particular aspect, we can in fact find many excellent examples of "system building". A fascinating, diverse, multi-facetted aspect of the "making of architecture" is revealed; the relationship between architecture, manual skills and industry, the significance of construction within architecture and the way in which architecture is created. The hopes and expectations that are projected onto industry and technology in the expectation of an architectural revitalisation are revealed. But we also see just how often one-dimensional technical developments have led to dead-ends.

In principle, every building is a composition of walls, floors and roof. Independent systems have been developed for each and every discrete section of a building

over the years. For example, the system "wall": studs with infill panels, courses of brickwork in a masonry bond, or modern prefabricated facades which no longer incorporate load-bearing functions but merely enclose an interior space. In this sense construction with elements or systems can be considered to be the very essence of building.

The subject of this book is the development of system building techniques throughout the history of architecture and, more importantly, how they are applied today. It will be demonstrated how these processes of development reflect a tireless search and experimentation that aimed at improving building and construction techniques, initially using traditional materials, later on employing the new materials iron, steel and concrete. This book focuses on the presentation of the various options available today for building with prefabricated elements in building systems, and, additionally, examines the potential and trends in the development of different construction techniques. Frame, panel and room module systems are looked at under the headings of the building materials steel, timber and concrete.

The history of architecture is also one of an extended process of differentiation. The entire classification "structure" has resolved itself into a multi-layered composition of differentiated systems due to shifting demands and increasingly complex energy-related, materials-related, technical and functional expectations. Nowadays individual elements are developed, manufactured and assembled according to highly specific demands.

Two examples that significantly demon-

House, Overijse (B) 2004,
Buelens Vanderlinden Architects

9

strate this change are the Pompidou Centre in Paris by Renzo Piano/Richard Rogers (1977) and the Hong Kong & Shanghai Bank by Norman Foster (1986). Not only do these buildings show how they function at the highest technical level of their time, but the role played by each building part is also individually legible. Nowadays every larger building can be viewed as a construction consisting of various systems, without, however, each of them being recognisable as independent design elements.

The typically closed systems of the 1960s that determined the design of a building up to and including the internal fit-out no longer exist in this sense. Buildings have developed into compositions that use a variety of specific systems. Standards based on technological typologies have developed for standard elements such as load-bearing systems, facade construction and partition walling, which simultaneously serve as the bases for a wide range of systems. Industrially manufactured building elements have thus become a fundamental component of architecture today.

The production of individual components within a system no longer inevitably means the production of an entire series of identical elements, as was previously the case for technical and economic reasons. Modern, computerised planning and production techniques are now capable of developing, producing and assembling distinct elements within interconnected systems.

Thus, it is now possible to determine the most appropriate system for each and every constructional or technical part of a building – from prefabricated, lightweight concrete wall elements with factory-fitted service runs, to technically complex, multi-layered prefabricated facades. This differentiation of construction systems also affects the structure of the manufacturing companies. The firms generally no longer offer everything, even smaller and middle-sized producers can now secure a niche in the market by developing and offering optimal solutions for specific areas.

The desire to bring architecture and industry closer together and to take advantage of the resultant opportunities has encouraged the development of systems as an important part of modern, industrialised building. From the very beginning of industrialisation, architects have seen the serial fabrication of components, their interconnection within systems and the associated rationalisation of the construction process as an opportunity to bring about a long overdue revitalisation.

Post-war industrialisation of the construction process, however, led rather to disillusionment regarding building systems. It became clear that deterministic, closed systems are incapable of leading to acceptable solutions.

The range and variety of systems will continue to increase firstly because systems generally develop as direct responses toparticular tasks and secondly because existing systems are continually being further improved and optimised.

This means that the architect's responsibility will increasingly be to minimise the constangly growing discrepancies between knowledge and technical possibilities in the construction industry and developments in other areas such as technology, industry and science. Only in this way can solutions be found that respond to contemporary conditions and requirements.

Frei Otto examined the methods and principles of nature in order to develop solutions for maximum performance with minimal outlay. Joseph Paxton, working as an experimental gardener in association with engineers and manufacturers, arrived at answers many aspects of which, even today, are still regarded as modern achievements. R. Buckminster Fuller applied the technical possibilities of the automotive and aeronautical industries to the construction industry. Similarly, widely used modern facade techniques, for example structural glazing and point-fixed construction systems, have been based upon technology transferred from these industries to the building industry by present-day architects and constructors, such as Peter Rice and Norman Foster.

This means that those working in architecture must once again focus on the exchange of knowledge and competence, they must remain open to unusual solutions, cultivate a view that extends beyond aspects of building, and take a delight in trying out something new, in experimentation. Collaboration with scientists, developers and engineers from various specialised areas must and will play an important role in these new responsibilities. The interdisciplinary transfer of information, ideas and solutions is an indispensable aspect of architects' work in order to develop a form of building, capable of anticipating and meeting the technical, ecological and social demands that will be made upon it.

The "System Building", this composition of countless individual components and systems, is becoming more and more

complex, systems are growing more closely linked, and the differentiation of the individual elements and systems is increasing.

Technical solutions, while certainly vital, are just one of many aspects that define architecture. Technology is therefore not the principle impulse in architectural design. At the beginning of the last century, Le Corbusier described it roughly so; building is always a composition of building elements, everything is available, but it is the architect who makes the choice and is therefore responsible for the architecture. He or she selects the elements and decides how they will be combined to create an architectural entity.

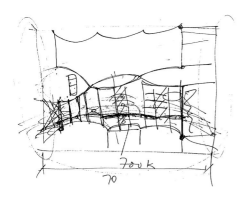

La Grande Arche, Paris (F) 1989;
Johann Otto von Spreckelsen and Paul Andreu;
freehand sketch: Peter Rice

Part A History of prefabrication

Nomads and settled dwellers   14
Brickwork   14
Stone   14
Timber   15
    American frame construction
    Balloon and platform framing
    Timber framed construction
    The traditional Japanese house
The military and colonial expansion   17
Iron – the first systems   18
    Iron frame construction
    The glasshouses
    High-rise iron construction
Prefabricated concrete construction   21
Rationalisation, serial production,
type standardisation and mass
housing construction   22
The prefabricated house –
the modular building system   25
    Modular building systems
    in America
Large span structural systems   31
Mega-structures and visions   31
Industrial fabrication – "synonym
for progress"   33
Open structures   34

figure A

History of prefabrication

Nomads and settled dwellers

The prototypes of prefabricated and unitised buildings were first developed many
thousands of years ago. While nomadic
peoples were predominantly on the move
searching for new habitats, they also
required shelters or huts, in order to dwell
temporarily in one location (fig. A 1). They
made these dwellings out of tree trunks,
branches, twigs, leaves, animal furs and
skins. Archaeologists have been able to
date the finds of these constructions as
originating some 400,000 years B.C.

To avoid having to search for the required
building materials after each and every
change of location, the nomads collected
materials which could be quickly and
easily assembled, after a time dismantled
and simply taken with them. It was important that the prefabricated building materials be lightweight, easy to handle and
not consist of too many individual pieces.
Each piece was deliberately selected to
fulfil the desired function, roughly worked
and shaped. Lightweight, textile methods
of shelter were developed to suit different
regions, climates and traditions, and
some of them are still in existence today.
The first tentative steps of systemised
building are recognisable in these unitised nomadic dwellings.

With the advent of crop production and
animal husbandry, humankind became
independent of hunting and gathering for
his livelihood, settled and erected permanent dwellings. Handwork skills were
refined and tools were improved upon,
allowing a tradition of masonry, stonework
and timber constructions to develop over
a period of many centuries.

Brickwork

Clay was available nearly everywhere in
the fertile alluvial regions of the Near East.
Mesopotamians and Egyptians used
wooden forms to mould flat, rectangular
blocks, thus creating the first artificial
building block – the sun-baked brick –
which could be manufactured en masse,
and enabled entire cities and monuments
to be built.

The temple constructions of the Sumeri-
ans (3500 B.C.), for example the temple
terrace in Uruk, were constructed entirely
of clay bricks, including the foundations
(fig. A 4). These Ziggurats – named after
the Sumerian term for "to be high up" –
were considered to be "where heaven
and earth met and formed the epicentre
of Sumerian religion and, as such, urban
life" [1].

Making clay bricks dimensionally stable
and weatherproof by means of firing and
glazing, created a conveniently sized
building unit that could be combined in
numerous ways, which has retained its
importance in manual building down to
the present day. The shape and size of
the bricks was determined by the behaviour of the material when drying and
firing; the ease of putting the units
together and the stability of the brickwork
was ensured by the particular system of
bonding.

Stone

In building their temples, the Greeks per-
fected the use of stone to such a level
that the individual finished blocks could
be put together with razor-sharp accuracy. To fix the blocks they employed

A 3

A 4

clamps and pins of bronze and iron. The principles of the floor plans and elevations were exactly determined mathematically, on the basis of strict rules of order.

The Romans can be credited with collecting, documenting and spreading a multitude of technical developments throughout the various regions of their empire. *The Ten Books on Architecture* by Vitruvius, from the first century B.C. established themselves as the foundation for the development of construction and contained instructions for modular building systems employing stone elements, which could be used to build temples in farflung colonies.

The Gothic cathedrals of the Middle Ages were a highpoint of prefabricated and unitised stone construction. In the cathedral masonry lodges highly specialised stonemasons planned magnificent filigree church constructions, in which stone was loaded to its structural limits. The basis for the stonework was provided by precise, geometric drawings (without dimensions) which enabled a number of stone

masons working together to produce the required quantity of complicated elements. The stonemasons passed on their skills and experience to selected apprentices who in turn carried their knowledge out into the world during the obligatory period that they spent wandering throughout Europe.

Timber

The development of timber constructions began with very simple systems. One of the earliest methods was to lean wooden posts against each other at an angle, bind them together and cover them with straw. Another variation was to sink posts into the ground, fill the gap between with loam-coated wattling and to cover the entire result with a simple roof structure. These were the first post constructions – the forerunners of frame buildings. Each individual element was sized and shaped to fulfil its particular task. Different elements were used to carry loads or to enclose space. The next step was to set the posts on large stones or on a kind of base or sill plate to prevent them sinking

into the earth and decomposing. This combination of sill plates, posts and top-rails formed a constructional entity – a timber frame (fig. A 5). These framed compartments were filled with planks, generally horizontal, less frequently vertical. The consistent development of this technique led to the refinement of half-timbering in which the posts were built closer to each other than in timber frameworks (figs. A 6 and A 7, p.16). The spaces between these narrow frames were filled with wattle, daub or clay bricks.

Another possibility of constructing buildings with timber elements was the log, or block, construction method. In this form of construction the beams are placed on top of each other, and the walls fulfil both load-bearing and partitioning functions. The timbers – round, squared or half-round – are notched or cut 15 to 20 cm from the end and connected at right-angles to form block corner junctions. The timbers are nailed together vertically and sealed with moss. The weight of the stacked timbers produces a solid, dense wall.

A   Yurt: view of what is called the "crown" from below
A 1   Yurt (from the Turkish for housing) Structural system: criss-cross willow lattice, covered by a roof structure of 81 curved rods which run together at a wooden wheel, known as the crown.
A 2   This form of tent developed as a result of climatic conditions, lifestyles and the economic situation of the nomadic shepherd peoples of the central Asian steppes. They can still be found in the region between the Black Sea and Mongolia.
A 3   "The first structure" by Viollet-le-Duc
A 4   Ziggurat of Urnammu in Ur, approx. 2100 B.C.
A 5   Simplified timber frame construction

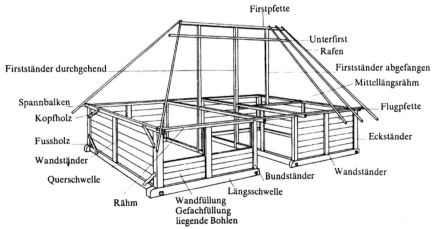

A 5

A 6   Farmhouses, open-air museum,
      Bad Windsheim, Germany
A 7   Timber frame construction
A 8   Balloon frame
      a braced or eastern frame
      b balloon frame
      c platform frame
A 9   Floor plan of a house in Atami, Japan
A 10 Shogakuin Villa in Kyoto, Japan

A 6

American frame construction

During the settlement of the North American prairies in the 1860's, the immense demand for easily transportable housing and the local wooden house traditions led to the rapid growth of the industrial processing of timber, which was available in large quantities. A simplified construction method was developed that could be manufactured in large series and is still widely used today.

Balloon and platform framing

The geodesist George W. Snow created the "balloon frame" in 1832, a construction still found in housing construction in the USA today (fig. A 8b). It was a further development of the early timber framework structures, the difference being that, instead of posts and beams, timber studs at close spacing were employed. These studs were connected to each other by industrially manufactured nails, were of standardised cross-sections, could be easily produced with circular saws and gang saws, and after a comparatively short drying period could be easily stored and transported. The vertical elements, at centres between 30 and 40 cm, extended the entire height of the buildings; the external walls were clad both internally and externally, while only the upper surface of the intermediate floors was covered with boards. The walls in this type of structure act structurally as plates and openings can therefore be made at almost any desired location. It thus became possible to provide comparable buildings at considerably lower cost and with less labour than required by traditional building construction techniques.

The essential difference between balloon framing and platform framing is that the latter system uses uprights that are just

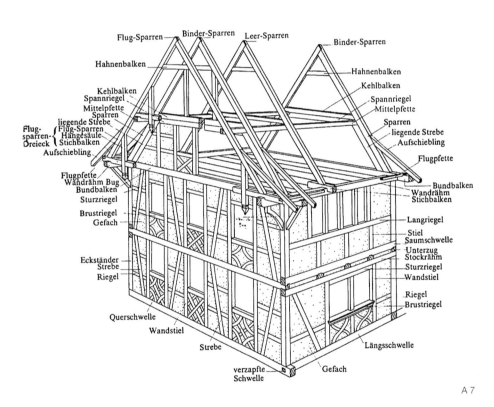

A 7

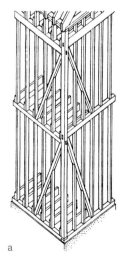
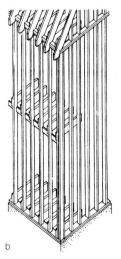
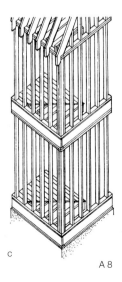

a   b   c   A 8

16

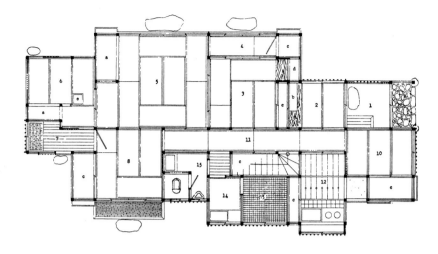

one-storey high. Therefore new studs must be erected on each successive floor level (fig. A 8c).

Timber framed construction

Timber framed construction was developed from these American building systems. The standard spacing between the studs is usually 62.5 cm. By creating multiple layers of a timber section, different elements such as studs, sill plates, beams and top plates can be produced. Individual wall elements are prefabricated with external cladding, quickly connected on site to form a building, and then clad internally with panels.

The advantage common to all timber construction methods was that industrial fabrication techniques allowed more effective exploitation of the tree trunk as well as the acceleration of the building process. The cross-sections were standardised and cut to provide the structurally and constructionally necessary sizes, and thanks to the introduction of iron connections could be technically rationalised rather than remaining masterpieces of traditional carpentry skills.

The traditional Japanese house

Among the various types of timber construction, the traditional Japanese house holds a unique position as a single-storey timber frame construction (fig. A 9). Due to their basic dimensional order and the design and construction of the building elements, these exemplary structures provide inspiration for countless modern architects.

The construction techniques, building elements, organisation, form and size of the rooms were determined and rationalised many centuries ago. The basic module is the "shaku", which originated in China, a unit of measurement approxi-

mately the same length as an English foot i.e. 30.48 cm. All building elements are based on this fundamental unit which thus determines the layout of the structure, the room dimensions and the relationship of the elements to each other. The distance between the columns is dimensioned using a different unit, called the "ken", which was introduced in the Japanese Middle Ages. There are regional differences in the length of the ken; in Kyoto it is equal to 6.5 shaku and in Tokyo 6. The spaces between the columns can be filled, according to the individual requirements of the users and, depending upon the time of day and the season, with wall elements, translucent or opaque sliding doors or even bamboo curtains (fig. A 10). The timber elements are prefabricated with great skill and craftsmanship, without the use of additional connection materials and have flexible joints so that they cannot be damaged by tremors and earthquakes. The Japanese house is an early example of a basic modular arrangement, and of standardisation and unitisation in timber construction.

The military and colonial expansion

Unitised modular construction systems were of paramount importance in two specific areas: the military and colonial expansion. Many developments in the building industry sprang from these needs. Mobile military forces required accommodation and storage facilities. Tents were lightweight, transportable structures that could be quickly erected and dismantled and had proven their worth over the centuries. In the 18th century, however, routes and transport methods improved dramatically within Europe.

The needs and demands of the military increased at the same time, leading to the development of larger, demountable buildings constructed of boarded timber frames. During the Austro-Ottoman War (1788–1791) entire mobile military hospital buildings, stables and accommodation facilities for troops were transported across the Danube into the war zone. However, in the procedure of speedily erecting and dismantling temporary structures (later to be called barracks) fixing the board cladding by hand proved to be too time-consuming. The invention of corrugated iron sheeting in 1837 made the entire process simpler and more efficient. The cladding for a building with a ground-floor area of 4.1 by 6.1 m could be packed into two crates measuring 31 by 62 by 275 cm. The corrugated panels were screwed to cast iron substructures and the outside face was galvanised in order to reflect sunlight, the internal walls were clad with wooden panels.

The company Christoph & Unmack, founded in 1892 by the steam engine constructor Christoph and located in Niesky, was the first to offer similar construction sets in Germany. In 1882 Christoph purchased a patent from the Dane Doecker for a construction system for military hospital barracks that was based on a timber structure and clad with felt boarding and sailcloth. He subsequently expanded this system for export to the tropics, for example by using a double layer roof.

Simply fitted-out shelters for the early settlers in the British colonies were initially manufactured in England and subsequently prefabricated; they were then dismantled into small, lightweight elements and shipped overseas in the form of com-

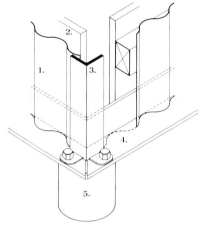

A 11   A 12

THE
South Australian Record.

No. 4.]   SATURDAY, JANUARY 13, 1838.   [PRICE 5d.

WARRANTED FIRST SHIP.

Under engagement with Her Majesty's Colonization Commissioners, to sail the 15th of January, for SOUTH AUSTRALIA.

THE splendid fast-sailing, River-built Ship EDEN, A 1, 523 tons per Register. Lying in the St. Katharine Docks.

Has a lofty and commodious Poop, with superior accommodations for Passengers, carries a Surgeon, and has room for about 150 tons goods only.

For Freight or Passage, apply to
WADDELL, BECK, & Co.
No. 5, Leadenhall-street.

FOR SOUTH AUSTRALIA.

To sail the 20th instant,

THE Colonization Commissioners' Brig RAPID.
Lieut. FIELD, R.N. Commander.
Lying in the St. Katharine Docks.

The well-known sailing qualities of this Vessel present a favourable opportunity to any Gentleman wishing for an immediate and expeditious passage. Has room for two Passengers only. Apply to

TINKLER and HANCOCK,
5, Harp Lane, Tower Street.

Under engagement for SOUTH AUSTRALIA.

THE fine Ship HENRY PORCHER, A 1, burthen 480 tons. JOHN HART, Commander.
Lying in the St. Katharine Docks.

Has a Poop, and superior accommodation for Passengers.

For Freight or Passage, apply to N. GRIFFITHS, White Hart Court, Gracechurch Street; or to

J. H. ARNOLD & WOOLLETT,
3, Clement's Lane, Lombard-street.

EMIGRANTS' HOUSES.

THE Advertiser having designed and prepared, complete for exportation, the undermentioned Public Buildings and Private Dwellings for South Australia and other Colonies), with many others for distinguished individuals, too numerous to mention within the limits of an advertisement, sees to draw the attention of Gentlemen, Emigrants, and others, to his superior method of providing Houses complete, which, for utility, elegance, and convenience, with economy combined, he flatters himself, from his experience a building, cannot be surpassed.

ADELAIDE CHURCH,

City of Adelaide, South Australia. This Church was designed and prepared for the South Australian Church Commissioners.

SOUTH AUSTRALIAN BANK.

This Banking House was designed and prepared for the Directors of the South Australian Company.

RESIDENCE OF OSMUND GILLES, Esq. COLONIAL TREASURER.
This Villa Residence is 80 feet by 32.

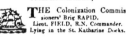

RESIDENCE OF J. H. FISHER, Esq. COLONIAL COMMISSIONER.
This spacious Dwelling, 80 feet by 40, is replete with every convenience, containing sixteen Rooms.

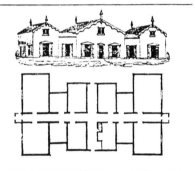

Three-roomed Cottages of this plan prepared complete, and delivered at the Docks from £30.

Four-roomed Cottages of this style, complete, from £40.

Models and Plans to be seen at No. 3, Ornaburgh-place, New Road. Regent's Park.

Models and Designs made to Order.

A 13

pact building kits. One of the first such kit houses exported to Australia in 1788 was erected within the space of a week. Over the course of time a huge market developed for systems used for different building types (fig. A 13). For example towards the end of the 18th century a hospital, a warehouse and various smaller dwellings were shipped from England to Sydney. Initially these "portable cottages" were still built by hand of timber and were often decorated according to the taste of the time; however, due to increasing insurance premiums for wooden houses and the wide range of areas where iron could be used, it eventually became the predominant building material in the 1840's.

Iron – the first systems

At the beginning of the industrial revolution high quality iron became readily available in great quantities. By using coke instead of coal in the foundries, it was possible to manufacture better quality iron at higher temperatures. Cast iron, and later wrought iron and steel introduced new possibilities for building. Iron established new standards of architectural quality, with regard to both construction techniques and the external appearances of the buildings. The dimensions of the buildings could be increased, and the sections of structural elements reduced. The development of systems based on as many identical prefabricated elements as possible resulted from the fact that the cast and rolled materials were readily available as semi-finished products in the factory. It had become possible to calculate and dimension the building elements according to the actual loads applied and, particularly with cast iron products, to design them in accordance with the

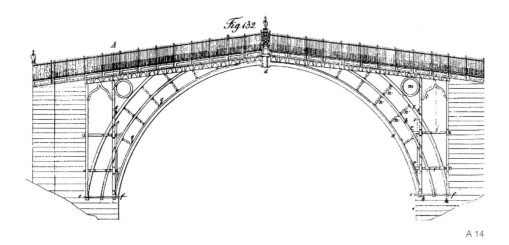

fashions of the era. The high performance building material that we know today could only be produced after the Englishmen Henry Bessemer (in 1855) and Sidney Gilchrist Thomas (in 1879) – among others – refined the process of manufacturing low carbon steel from pig iron. This material, in the form of rolled sections, became the fundamental element of later frame structures. According to Christian Schädlich, "the iron industry (…) performed the function of a pacemaker for the general industrialisation of the building industry. It developed those elements of industrial technologies relevant to building: from the dismantling of the product into large elements, their prefabrication in the factory and mechanised assembly, to the standardisation of dimensions and forms for the purpose of serial production, and on to new organisational structures of the construction business." [2]

The possibilities of prefabrication were particularly useful for bridge construction in the early years of industrialisation. The arched bridge over the River Severn in Coalbrookdale is one surviving (fig. A 14). The Darby brothers who built the bridge between 1775 and 1779 were, with their family company the Coalbrookdale Company, instrumental in guiding the development of iron production and processing for generations. Five cast-iron arches, with crown heights of 13 m, span approximately 30.5 m across the river. Each of the half-arches arches was cast in one piece and connected according to the principles of timber construction. The arched form, under compression, was ideal for cast iron, although the cross-sections of such members could not yet be accurately calculated at that time. This structure, built entirely of iron, was a

first step on the road to industrialised construction.

Iron frame construction
The flax mill built in 1796/97 by Charles Bage, for the company Benyon, Bage & Marshall in Castle Forgate in Shrewsbury, is considered one of the first buildings where the internal frame was constructed entirely of serial-fabricated cast iron columns and joists, although the external walls and floors were built of solid masonry. The columns could be easily erected at large centres, and were ornamented in the popular architectural style of the era.

The progress of prefabricated iron construction was heterogeneous; the structural, technical and therefore also architectural developments occurred at several different locations in a multitude of building projects.

The first important developments on the path towards pure iron frame structures occurred in the construction of greenhouses. With the colonisation of far off lands, many exotic plants were transported to Europe. Light-drenched palm houses and conservatories became highly desirable. Unfettered by questions of style and architectural meaning, those designing such buildings could concentrate on rational solutions to structural, technical and climatic problems. This was how the first unitised systems – later to be transferred to other building types – were designed.

The glasshouses
Based upon his experience with glasshouses, gardener Joseph Paxton developed the Crystal Palace for the World Exhibition of 1851 in London in collaboration with the engineers Fox and Hender-

A 11   Cottage, South Melbourne (AUS) 1853
A 12   Detail of footing, connection of the corrugated iron to the external steel construction, cottage, South-Melbourne (AUS) 1853
A 13   Advertisement in the "South Australian Record" of January 13,1838, Peter Thompson Emigrants Houses (AUS) 1838
A 14   Bridge over the Severn near Coalbrookdale (GB) 1779, Thomas F. Pritchard/John Wilkinson/Abraham Darby
A 15   Crystal Palace, Hyde Park, London (GB) 1851, Joseph Paxton
A 16   Glass Palace, Munich (D) 1854, August Voit Inspired by English models, this iron and glass structure has a number of small further structural developments.The main difference to the English predecessors is the differentiation between load-bearing and non-load-bearing elements in the facade.

A15

A 16

A 17

A 17   Crystal Palace, Hyde Park, London (GB) 1851,
       Joseph Paxton
A 18   Frame structure Crystal Palace, London
A 19   Bogardus Factory, New York (USA) 1848,
       James Bogardus
A 20   Section through a corn mill for Turkey (GB)
       1840, William Fairbairn
       This building is considered England's first
       building entirely constructed of cast and
       wrought iron; prefabricated in England,
       shipped to Turkey and erected in Istanbul.
A 21   Chocolate factory, Noisel-sur-Marne (F) 1872,
       Jules Saulnier
       The construction is reminiscent of timber fram-
       ing and has infill elements of glazed bricks,
       some of which are coloured.
A 22   Cast iron arched elements, Bibliothèque
       St.-Geneviève, Paris (F) 1850, Henri Labrouste
A 23   Bibliothèque St.-Geneviève

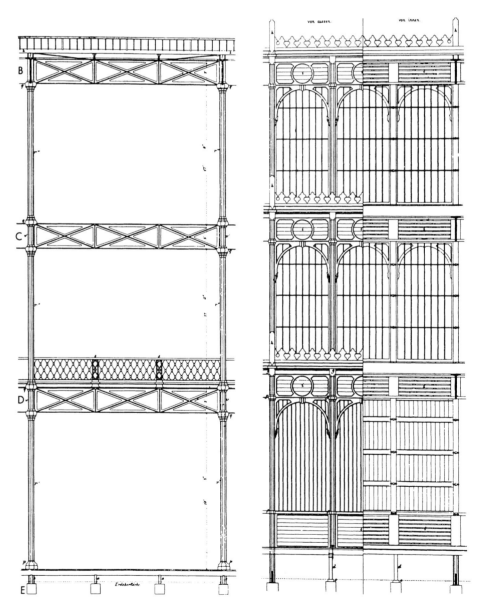

A 18

son in an extremely short period of time –
a consummate building system, both
architecturally and technically (figs. A 15
p. 19, A 17 and A 18). A minimum
number of different standardised units
were connected to create a frame based
upon the principles of modular arrangement. Thereby the "production and connection of the prefabricated parts"
should, in Paxton's own words, "function
like a machine." [3]. Although the Crystal
Palace measured 564 m by 124 m with
an overall height of 40 m, there were only
two different forms of column for the
ground floor and two for the first floor, and
the trusses were of consistent depth
despite the different distances apart. The
folded "ridge and furrow" roof – a stable
roof construction with a high level of light
transmission that rested upon a structure
of timber sections and valley beams –
was designed using countless identical
elements. The basic module for the frame
was derived from the maximum size of
glass pane that could be mass-produced
at that time. The architect and constructor
Konrad Wachsmann described the Crystal Palace as a "visible turning point (...),
through which the entire development of
building history started on a new course."
[4]. The glass palace demonstrated not
only the possibilities of industrialised,
rationalised building through the fabrication of building elements, but also the
development of the building process as
flow production. It showed how designers, engineers and production companies
could work together as a team, and initiated new discussions in architecture as a
result of its structural clarity and
unbounded space.

High-rise iron construction

James Bogardus, an American businessman and constructor, erected a four-sto-

A 19

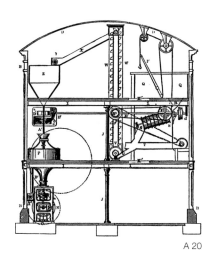

A 20

rey company headquarters (fig. A 19), in New York in 1848, after being inspired by a visit to England where he most likely saw Fairbairns corn mill (fig. A 20). The facade was constructed entirely of prefabricated cast iron elements, and was therefore a precursor of the later curtain wall facades. The goals were firstly to create a permanent, economical and fire-resistant construction and secondly to imitate the classical forms of stonework "in the Italian style", in a more cost effective and less massive manner.

Both James Bogardus and his competitor Daniel Badger produced and assembled cast iron external walling for four to six storey business premises, warehouses and office buildings. The prefabricated elements could be selected from a catalogue. The system was designed to be dismantled and rebuilt in other locations when and as desired. The building's load-bearing system was initially constructed of masonry with a timber beam floor, but was later built entirely of cast iron. This form of architecture reached its zenith in the mid 19th century.

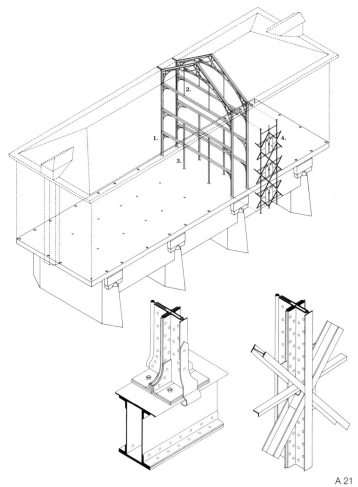

A 21

Prefabricated concrete construction

Alongside iron another new building material appeared at this time. The gardener Joseph Monier managed to make cement flowerpots more stable by inserting wire in them. He continued to experiment with this technique, in this way developing the first reinforced concrete elements. An additional high-performance building material became available to the building industry; one suitable for mono-lithic constructions of great stability. In erecting the casino in Biarritz in 1891, the French businessman E. Coignet was the

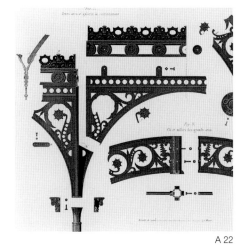

A 22

A 23

A 24

A 25

A 24 House in Letchworth Gardencity (GB) 1904, John Brodie
The prefabricated storey-height, room-sized concrete panels were assembled on site by crane.
A 25 Placing a Hennebique House in position, 1896
A 26 "Unit Structural Concrete Method", 1916, John E. Conzelmann;
Pre-cast frame system with wall, floor and roof panels of reinforced concrete, originally used for industrial and railway buildings, later for housing.
A 27 Reinforced pre-cast concrete element, France, 1854, François Coignet
A 28 "System Dom-ino", 1914, Le Corbusier

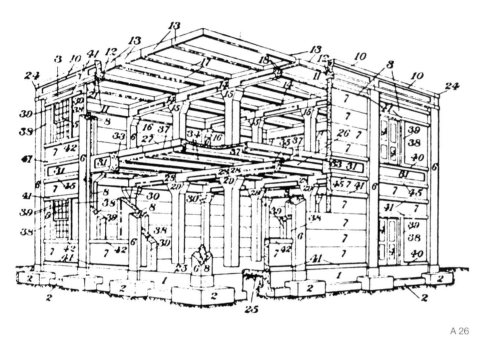

A 26

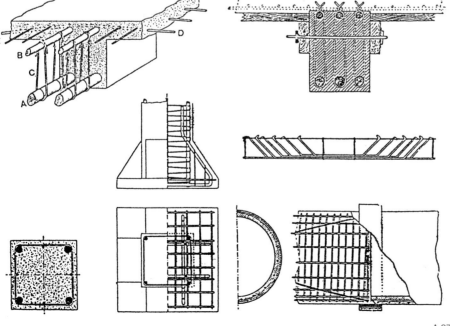

A 27

first to use prefabricated concrete elements (fig. A 27). Another businessman and constructor, François Hennebique, developed gatekeepers lodges for the French national railways five years later – these structures were the first concrete modular units (fig. A 25).

Rationalisation, serial production, type standardisation and mass housing construction

Under the influence of industrialisation new standards of quality were established in the building industry with regard to construction, space and form. There were now new, faster ways of using machines to manufacture products industrially in large series, which were therefore no longer the individual results of manual labour. The forms of industrialised products – machines, ocean liners or automobiles – and the simple, unadorned engineered structures that had been created in the 19th century greatly influenced the thinking and action of the architects of the day. Architecture, it was believed, needed to be fundamentally renewed in formal, social and economic terms, with the assistance of industry. Buildings should be produced in series in factories, standardised and prefabricated, so that they could be assembled on site according to the principles of modular construction.

It was hoped that these new production methods would help solve the pressing problems facing the housing industry. The flow of people to the larger European cities, especially in France, Germany and England, grew continuously throughout the 19th century. The increasing housing shortage, particularly for the poorer working classes, and the appalling conditions

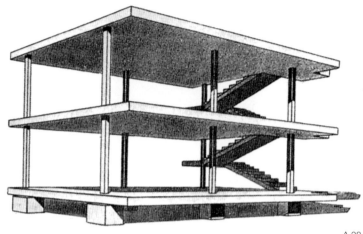

in the ghettos, demanded immediate solutions and new, economical building methods. The demand for better organised housing estates and affordable, well-ventilated and well-lit housing became more and more insistent. A number of politicians and designers, influenced by the industrial developments in America, recognised that quantity and quality in housing construction could only be achieved by employing the appropriate production techniques. Industrially manufactured building elements and faster assembly techniques, in addition to properly, rationally organised building sites, had to replace the conventional, manual building process.

The United States, with its unadorned silos and technical buildings, free of all architectural input, and its rationally organised industries became the example for Europe. Frederick Winslow Taylor, born in 1856, developed what was known as "Scientific Management", also called Taylorism. This was a scientific approach to management based on breaking down work processes into their individual elements and analysing these in detail in order to then reorganise the production so that it became faster, more rationalised, more efficient and more economical. Henry Ford introduced assembly line production into the automotive industry in 1913, based on this principle. His concept of the modern production of automobiles also revolutionised modern culture. The architects of the avant-garde were also greatly influenced by mass production in the automotive industry. The notion of producing houses in much the same way as cars became an ideal. Rationalisation and standardisation were to become decisive concepts within the field of architecture.

In his work *Vom sparsamen Bauen* (Economical Building) of 1918, architect Peter Behrens demanded the mechanisation of the building process, and said that "the industrialisation of building elements (by these he meant windows, doors, etc.) must be undertaken in a far more wide-ranging and generous way" [5]. By using the standardised dimensions and forms of fabricated products for building small houses, Behrens believed that the foundations could be laid for industrialised mass production, which in turn could pave the way for a general decrease in the cost of a small house [6]. In order to reduce costs further, he also called for the introduction of the principles of Taylorism in the area of small house construction.

In 1928 in the Declaration of La Sarraz, the Congrès Internationaux d'Architecture Moderne, otherwise known as CIAM, spoke out in favour of rationalisation and standardisation as necessary economical methods of production.

Le Corbusier quickly incorporated technical and formal developments from industry, thereby influencing a great number of architects. In *Towards a New Architecture* he wrote in the chapter "Houses Produced in Series" that: "a new era has begun; a new spirit is abroad in the world. Industry, as forceful as a river surging towards its destiny, gives us the new solutions appropriate to the new era. The law of economy dictates our actions. The problem of housing is a problem of our times; the balance of our social order depends upon solving it. Re-evaluation of existing values is the re-evaluation of the essential elements of the house. Serial construction relies on analysis and experimental research. Large industry must

address building and produce individual building elements in series. The intellectual requisites for serial production must be created." [7] In 1914 he developed the "Dom-ino House Project" (fig. A 28), a system based on concrete columns and flat slabs. Prefabricated, serially produced windows, doors and walk-in closets could be put together individually by the users. This house, in which the frame basically consists of columns (pilotis) and cantilevering floor slabs, was to revolutionise building construction. He named another house type that he designed in 1921 the "Citrohan", "in other words a house like a car, designed and constructed in much the same way as a bus or ship cabin" [8].

The driving forces for the reform of housing construction in Germany at the time were Martin Wagner, Ernst May and Walter Gropius. Martin Wagner, the director of city planning in Berlin, had been calling for the rationalisation of building and standardisation of dwelling types since 1918. Construction costs, he said, must be reduced in order to provide affordable accommodation. Traditional building companies should be taken over by rationalised industrial companies with organised trade unions, and manual labour replaced by machines. Because in building the "Britz" and "Uncle Tom's Cabin" housing estates in Berlin the construction process was improved by the use of conveyor belts and excavators, and rationalised by the restriction to only four dwelling types, costs could be reduced, but the construction methods employed were still traditional. The housing estate at Berlin-Friedrichsfelde is an exception, however. There, in 1926, storey-height concrete panels were used according to the "occi-

A 29   Aerial view of Westhausen housing estate,
       Ernst May, 1932
A 30   Panel construction system "System Stadtrat
       Ernst May" from the Ernst May house construc-
       tion factory, Frankfurt/Main (D) 1926
A 31   Fabrication hall, Ernst May house construction
       factory, Frankfurt/Main (D) 1926
A 32   Exhibition Stuttgart 1927, single family house
       no. 17, Walter Gropius, steel frame
A 33   House no. 17, ground floor plan
A 34   House no. 17, first floor plan

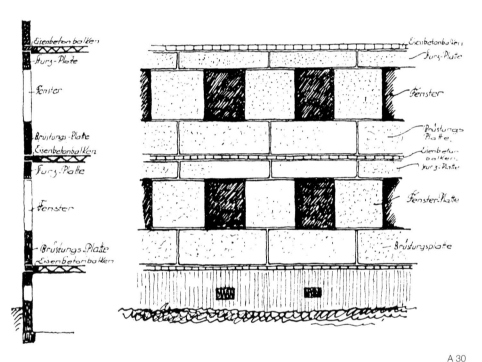

A 30

dent process". This was a large-panel construction system that had been patented in Holland and had been previously used in a garden city development in Amsterdam. Panels 25 cm thick and measuring between 25 and 40 square metres, with maximum dimensions of 10 by 4 m had to be manufactured on site due to their immense size and were then erected by cranes. The external panels consisted of three layers; aggregate concrete on the outside, slag concrete on the inside and slag in the cavity between. The internal wall panels were of slag concrete both sides. Manufacturing these elements was a highly complex process and over time serious building defects appeared.

Frankfurt am Main was an important pioneer in the field of rationalised and industrialised construction. Ernst May, the director of city planning in Frankfurt, wrote in 1929 in an article entitled *The Apartment for Minimum Existence* that "apartments should be built in adequate numbers, where the rents do not exceed the weekly wages of the workers." Similarly in his *Guidelines for Rationalisation of Housing Construction for the Minimum Existence*, he wrote with respect to the process of dwelling production, that "the production of dwellings should be organised in much the same way as the production of all other mass produced articles in the economy, that is exemplary well-worked out models (or types) should be fabricated in series, concentrated in a minimum of different locations. The mechanisation of the housing industry in particular should be encouraged. The goal must remain the factory produced dwelling – including internal fittings – that can be delivered as a complete product, and assembled in a few days." [9]

A 31

24

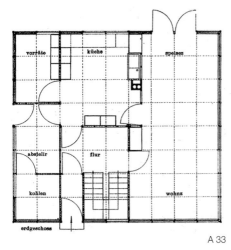

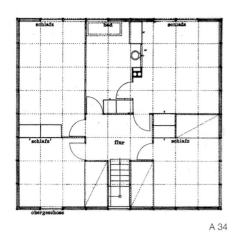

A 32

A 33

A 34

The Frankfurter Häuserfabrik (fig. A 31), founded by Ernst May, manufactured the first industrially produced building panels in Germany in 1926; they were given the name "System Stadrat Ernst May" (fig. A 30). The difference between this system and the "occident process" was that the windows and doors were not already integrated. The wall consisted of three layers of lightweight concrete – pumice aggregate, fine pumice sand and Portland cement – the window panel, the non-reinforced spandrel panel measuring 3.0 by 1.1 by 0.2 m, and the reinforced lintel panel measuring 3.0 by 0.4 by 0.2 m. These elements were placed in position in a pumice mortar bed by means of a tower crane, and the butt joints filled. The floor and roof slabs were constructed of pre-fabricated hollow reinforced concrete beams. To erect the building shell only one and a half days were required per house. Thanks to their size the panels could be used for different house types. Doors, windows, metal fittings, iron doorframes and stoves were produced in large series according to standard specification sheets. After a construction period of only 26 days the dwelling was ready for occupation. These housing developments and apartments were intended to demonstrate the new principles of production and construction. This form of housing construction was, however, the exception – traditional methods remained the rule.

In view of the rationalisation and industrialisation taking place in America, Walter Gropius also addressed the issue of standardisation of building elements while working in Behren's practice in 1909–10. It was not until 1922, however, inspired by the "Dom-ino House" and writings of Le Corbusier, that Gropius once again con-

sidered these construction techniques and called for a large "construction kit where, dependent upon the number and individual needs of the occupants, different living machines can be put together" and "a house of variable elements that are manufactured in advance and can be combined and joined together much in the manner of a large construction kit" [10]. This construction kit was in fact developed in 1922 for a Bauhaus housing project. His call, formulated in 1923, for individual, ready to assemble elements "like machines that (...) can be assembled in a dry-construction process" on the building site, was in fact realised much later [11]. A great admirer of both Ford and Taylor, it seems that Gropius' aim was to become the "Housing-Ford". [12]

The prefabricated house – the modular building system

Alongside mass housing construction in housing estates, there was a great demand for single-family houses. The housing shortage and the lack of standard building materials after the First World War led to experimentation with new construction methods. The inactive former armaments industry – inspired by the steel architecture of America and England – took on the role of developing new systems for housing construction after 1925. By 1932 a multitude of building systems in timber and steel had been created (e.g. the Copper House by Walter Gropius), although compared with England, relatively few steel dwellings were built in Germany. An important area of research opened up for the steel and timber industries, as well as for the architects; offering single houses in catalogues as complete "construction kits".

When the economic situation improved after the First World War, the steel industry dedicated itself to steel housing construction from the mid 1920's on. These houses used either frames or storey-height panels, a system that had already been successful in England.

Walter Gropius wanted to demonstrate "new solutions for industrialised building" in two houses in the 1927 exhibition "The Apartment" in Weißenhof in Stuttgart [13]. House no. 16 in Bruckmannstraße was a traditionally constructed solid masonry building, while house no. 17 was constructed of individual, industrially prefabricated elements in a dry-construction assembly process (figs. A 32 – A 34). A concrete slab was cast on site and a steel frame of Z-sections – with a basic module dimension of 1.06 m – was erected on top of it; the cavities were filled with 8 cm thick cork panels. The frame was clad externally with 6 mm Eternit shingles and lined internally with Lignat panels, which were subsequently finished in different ways (Celeotox, sugar cane or asbestos panels) depending upon the function of the room. The desire to live in the countryside and the shortage of building materials such as steel, bricks and concrete after the First World War led to a great demand for ready-made timber houses. Leading companies in this area were Christoph & Unmack, already mentioned above, and the German workshops Hellerau in Munich. From the 1880s onwards Christoph & Unmack no longer offered just factory produced barracks but also private houses, school buildings etc. in panel and block construction systems, and exported them worldwide. In the 1920's this company was the leader in its field in Europe with Konrad Wachsmann acting as head architect.

25

A 35

A 36

A 37

Even within the rather traditionally-oriented Stuttgart School, Paul Schmitthenner examined cost-effective construction and developed "factory manufactured-half-timbering", the so-called Schmitthenner System for both dry and partially dry construction techniques (figs. A 35 – A 37). The intention was to modernise the traditional frame by the use of serially prefabricated four-sided, closed frames with integrated doors and windows. The modules, made of timber sections, measured 110 or 165 by 280 cm, and were screwed together on site. Horizontal timber boarding was fitted internally to provide bracing, and gypsum fibreboard cladding or render was then applied. The infill elements were 12 cm thick lightweight hollow concrete panels, that projected beyond the frame and were covered with wire mesh. 55 cm wide plasterboard panels were nailed to the exterior and the cavities between filled with insulation material. The weight of the external walls was 152 kg/m², and the construction time from ground breaking to occupation was ten weeks.

The economic crisis at the end of the 1920's, and the advent of National Social-

ism put an end to industrial construction based on prefabricated systems in Germany.

Modular building systems in America
In America in the last quarter of the 19th century the steel frames of the "Chicago School" represented the start of a long process of development that continued up until the creation of the post-war skyscrapers in New York and Chicago. On the other hand, there was also a booming industry of individually built, single family homes which, both as fixed and mobile homes, could be self-built by the residents thereby realising countless variations of the American dream of building one's own home. The prosperity of the succeeding decades led to a growth in demand for individuality, and it was not until the Great Crash of 1929 that the prefabricated housing industry in America enjoyed a revival. The focus then shifted to low budget housing rather than representative, individually designed dwellings.

The ingenious inventor, philosopher and visionary Richard Buckminster Fuller was

one of the driving forces behind the development of transportable prefabricated houses. Since his childhood, he had been fascinated by ship building and by forms that were reduced to a minimum and designed solely for their specific function. His many inventions include an airship and a great variety of different machines. In the 1920's he became aware of "the chaos in the building industry", to correct which "physically effective and lasting technology is required." [14] His first "living machine" was developed in 1927 in pursuit of this goal. The "Dymaxion House" was a hexagonal construction suspended from a mast. The name is derived from dy(namic) max(imum) (tens)ion (figs. A 38 and A 39). The principle was to use lightweight materials to create a maximum of space with a minimum surface area. Thus the construction system and all materials used were designed to take tension forces. The house weighed a total of 2720 kg and could be crated up for transport within a single day. Technical services, two standardised bathrooms and a lift were located at the centre of the house. The external walls were a double-

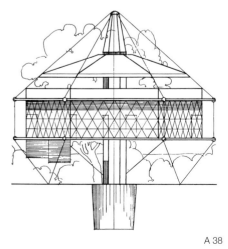

A 38

A 39

A 35 System of fabricated frame (Fafa), wall frame infilled with hollow light-weight pumice block panels, Paul Schmitthenner
A 36 Sander house constructed using the Fafa technique, one day prior to completion, Stuttgart (D) 1927/28, Paul Schmitthenner
A 37 Sander house
A 38 Elevation "Dymaxion House", project phase 1927, Buckminster Fuller
A 39 Floor plan "Dymaxion House"
A 40 Prefabricated house by "General Panel Corporation", 1945, Konrad Wachsmann
A 41 "Packaged House", 1944, Konrad Wachsmann
A 42 Beech Aircraft Company, Wichita/Kansas (USA) 1945
A 43 Prototype "Wichita House", Wichita/Kansas (USA) 1946, Buckminster Fuller in cooperation with the Beech Aircraft Company
A 44 Floor plan "Wichita House"

A 40

A 41

layered construction of "translucent, transparent and opaque material" with a vacuum "as ideal insulation against heat and noise". [15] The floors were constructed of two membranes with air cushions, while the internal fittings were standardised and prefabricated. There was sufficient space available for cars, airplanes etc. under this suspended, hovering house. The prefabricated lightweight house, constructed of steel and aluminium was intended to demonstrate how the materials and production techniques of the automotive industry could be successfully applied to the housing industry. It was an experiment with new ideas which, regrettably, could not be fully applied in the building industry due to the technological limitations of the day. In 1940, in the expectation of German bombing attacks on English cities, Buckminster Fuller was commissioned to develop emergency housing. Inspired by the stable, cylindrical form of a corrugated iron granary, he designed the "Dymaxion Development Unit" that could be used for both civil and military purposes. This product was quickly acquired by the US Signal Corps and served as

emergency accommodation for radar groups.

For the "Wichita House" (figs. A 42 – A 44), produced in 1944–46 in cooperation with the Beech Aircraft Company in Wichita, Kansas, Buckminster Fuller used Duraluminium, a material that came from the aeronautical industry. The circular building with a floor area of 74 m^2 weighed only 3500 kg. The primary construction consisted of a mast, from which anchor cables were spanned, a bracing compression ring and a floor construction of aluminium sections arranged like the spokes of a wheel with plywood panels clamped on top. The roof cladding was constructed of lightly curved metal sheeting similar to the skin of an aircraft. The vertical external wall in the parapet zone beneath the windows and around the Plexiglas windows consisted of two layers. Like in the "Dymaxion House", all services such as heating, air-conditioning, kitchen and bathroom, were located at the centre of the building. Fresh air was introduced under the floor, led through the mast and into the dwelling; similarly exhaust air was removed through the floor construction. Not a single ele-

ment in this house weighed more than 5 kg, thus six men could erect the house in a single day – or one man in six days. It was originally intended to erect 200 of these houses daily. Only two prototypes, however, could be realised due to the high investment costs involved for the Beech Aircraft Company, the advent of the Cold War which meant the withdrawal of the military from civil building projects, and, last but not least, Buckminster Fuller's own difficult personality.

Konrad Wachsmann, who was by now living in exile in the USA, developed the "Packaged House System" (fig. A 41) in collaboration with Walter Gropius with whom he had established a partnership in 1941. This was based on his previous work on load-bearing panel construction systems with Christoph & Unmack. The "Packaged House System" was a three-dimensional modular timber construction system for small buildings in which the elements were connected by way of hooks and cotters. This system was further developed in 1943/44 to form the so-called General Panel System (fig. A 40), which had fewer elements and improved connection techniques; it was

A 42

A 43

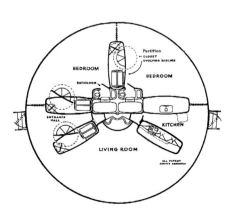

A 44

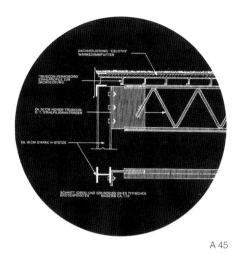

A 45

A 46

A 45 Constructional detail Case Study Eames House, Pacific Palisades (USA) 1949, Charles and Ray Eames
A 46 Exterior of the Eames house
A 47 Prefabricated house type "Central Column", Jean Prouvé
A 48 Square Mozart, Paris (F) 1954, Jean Prouvé
A 49 and 50 MAN ready-built house
The MAN ready-built house was a steel-panel construction made of load-bearing, 1 mm-thick steel panels, measuring 1.00×2.51 m. The 20 cm thick wall construction was clad internally with particle board panels; the cavities were filled with glass wool insulation mats.
A 51 and A 52 "Dornier-Heim" ready-built houses, Lochham (D) 1947, aircraft company Dornier
A 53 Title page of the catalogue for a ready-built house exhibition in Stuttgart (D) 1947

MONTAGE

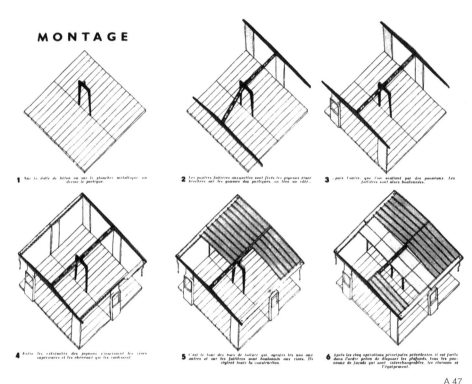

A 47

A 48

sold as "General Panel Units" somewhere between 150 and 200 times. The intention was to develop "the most complete prefabricated construction system possible, which could be simply assembled on site by untrained workers, who had no previous knowledge or skills, to create any kind of single or double storey building required" [16].

Timber was, in this case, the most economic building material available with regard to both quality and quantity. The elements, which already contained the electrical wiring, were connected to one another by means of standardised hook closures. Despite the short construction time required of only 36 hours, the "General Panel System" was unsuccessful due to the higher costs in comparison to classic timber frame systems, and the manufacturing company, General Panel Corporation, was forced to terminate production.

The French businessman, engineer and constructor, Jean Prouvé, played a key role in industrial fabrication from the 1930's on. He was fascinated by aircraft, ships, automobiles and therefore also by the modern materials metal sheeting, aluminium and plastics, their properties, their structural potential and the ways in which they could be processed. Applications suited to the materials, efficient construction and the production process, rather than formal aspects, were decisive for Prouvé. His solutions were the result of a long process starting with hand-made models, through prototypes and on to industrial serialisation. The "Maison du Peuple" in Clichy, which was developed with the architects Eugène Beaudoin and Marcel Lods in 1936–39, consisted mostly of prefabricated elements 1.04 m

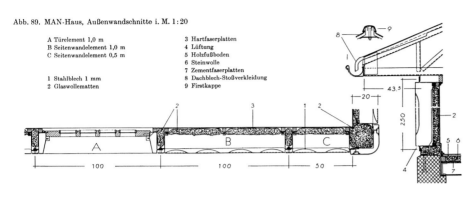

Abb. 89. MAN-Haus, Außenwandschnitte i. M. 1:20

A Türelement 1,0 m
B Seitenwandelement 1,0 m
C Seitenwandelement 0,5 m

1 Stahlblech 1 mm
2 Glaswollematten

3 Hartfaserplatten
4 Lüftung
5 Holzfußboden
6 Steinwolle
7 Zementfaserplatten
8 Dachblech-Stoßverkleidung
9 Firstkappe

A 49

A 50

A 51

A 52

wide. The roof, floor slabs and partition walls could be moved. The facade panels were made of two steel sheets, with folded edges, spot-welded together. These panels were braced with springs from bed frames he had produced himself and the cavity was filled with mineral wool insulation. The facade construction – patented in 1950 – of load-bearing posts, infill elements, sealing profiles and screw-mounted fixing strips, forms the basis for all present-day post-and-rail construction systems. Many of his products and modular construction systems for schools, military and emergency accommodation are considered as belonging to the classic structures of the last century. Like Buckminster Fuller, Prouvé played a key role in 20th century architecture and inspired architects like Renzo Piano and Le Corbusier, with whom he collaborated on a project in 1939/40 entitled "The Flying Schools".

John Entenza, the editor of the journal *Arts & Architecture*, initiated the "Case Study House Programme" in 1945, which looked for designs for economical, industrially fabricated prototypical houses. He commissioned eight architects, including Charles and Ray Eames and Eero Saarinen, as well as Richard Neutra. As a result of this programme, 36 buildings were completed that set new standards in housing construction. Charles and Ray Eames had already garnered experience with industrial fabrication in their work as laminated furniture designers. Thus it was not surprising that they used mostly industrial products to build their own house in Santa Monica near Los Angeles (figs. A 45 and A 46). The simple steel construction was exposed internally and consisted of 30.5 cm deep trusses with spans of 6.01 m, and universal col-

umns measuring approximately 10 cm. The facade, articulated by the columns at centres of 2.35 m, is made of transparent and translucent glazing panels in addition to opening elements and coloured panels. The longitudinal bracing is provided by wind braces. It was only the opening elements that were not prefabricated – they were manufactured in the Eames atelier and fitted by the construction company. The living and working areas were separated by an internal courtyard and derived their ambience from the spatial diversity and relationship to the outdoors. The combination of lightweight structure, internal fittings, materials, colours and furniture in this house erected in 1949, meant that it, like the "Case Study Houses", came to symbolise the concept of modern living and design in the post-war years.

In badly damaged post-war Germany the currency reform was followed by a surge in the development of prefabricated and ready-built housing systems. Examples of this are the panel construction systems by the company "Holig-Homogen-Holzwerk" in Baiersbronn and the gas concrete element houses by J. Hebel. The Hebel gas concrete panels measured 50 cm in width and 200 or 250 cm in length, with a thickness of 15+10 cm for external and internal walling. Willy Messerschmidt, better known as an aircraft constructor, was interested in incorporating the industrial achievements of the day into the building industry; he had the gas concrete panels encased in metal sheeting, this was, however, omitted at a later date.

Based on its experience in the construction of temporary housing the aircraft manufacturer, Dornier, produced small

A 53

A 54   IBM travelling pavilion, 1984, Renzo Piano/
       Peter Rice
A 55   Principle of the MAXI modular construction
       system, (D) 1961, Fritz Haller
A 56   Detail of the MAXI modular construction sys-
       tem, (D) 1964, Fritz Haller
A 57   Maxi modules construction system (construc-
       tion elements), isometric, no scale
A 58   Company building, Münsingen (CH)
       1962/1994, Fritz Haller
A 59   MERO-System standard units, (D) 1940, Max
       Mengeringhausen
A 60   Hall built using the two-dimensional directional
       construction system "Mobilar Structure" made
       of steel tubes, (D) 1945, Konrad Wachsmann
A 61   US-Pavilion at the World Expo in Montreal
       (CDN) 1967, Richard Buckminster Fuller

A 54

A 55

Fixed-base columns

Main lattice girders

Intermediate lattice girders

A 56

Roof (aerated concrete planks/steel trapezoidal profile sheeting)

Wall posts,
floor guide,
roof verge

External wall elements
(basic frame with fixed or
movable infills)

A 57

two-storey ready-built houses,which had primary load-bearing structures of light-weight folded steel sections (figs. A 51 and A 52, p. 29). They were factory-built in two parts on the assembly line as "internal houses", complete with internal fit-out, and were put together and clad on site with gas concrete and then rendered. But when the company started to manu-facture aircraft once again this production process was terminated.

On a considerably larger scale Fritz Haller developed modular systems for a rationalised, minimised, steel construc-tion, primarily intended for industrial buildings (figs. A 55 – A 58). He wanted to create buildings capable of responding to continuous functional and technical changes.
Layout, building shell and structure were to be reduced to as few elements as pos-sible. Between 1961 and 1964 he devel-oped different steel construction systems based on simple, modular geometry sys-tems that could easily be dismantled and moved to other locations. He regarded the integration of the technical services as fundamentally important. Depending on the size and desired span of the build-ings and halls, either the MINI, MIDI or MAXI system could be used.

In the 1980's Renzo Piano demonstrated just how a system of materials that are completely different to each other but have complementary properties can form a structure that is convincing both in aes-thetic and constructional terms. Between 1982 and 1984, in conjunction with Peter Rice, he developed the IBM travelling pavilion, reminiscent of the demountable greenhouses or the Crystal Palace of the 19th century (fig. A 54). It was in this pavilion that the new world of computers

A 58

A 59

A 60

A 61

was presented in large European cities over a period of some years. The building, 48 m long, consisted of 34 arched segments built of laminated timber struts with cast aluminium connections and polycarbonate pyramids. Five articulated trucks transported the parts; it took 15 days to erect the pavilion.

Large span structural systems

In the course of dematerialising traditional structures subject to bending and compression loads, designers arrived, via planar framework trusses and space frames, at the network domes of Frei Otto and Jörg Schlaich. The once massive, load-bearing beam was dissolved into a multitude of – ideally identical – rod or strut-like elements that were calculated and shaped according to their individual structural tasks.

On the roof of the Carl-Zeiss-Werke in Jena Walter Bauersfeld erected a hemispherical steel lattice as the reinforcement for an experimental reinforced concrete shell. The construction of this planetarium dome consisted of a network of flat irons with an average length of 60 cm. The basic geometry for the composition of rods was an icosahedron projected onto the inner side of the dome; the surface was made up of 20 equilateral triangles and, as a polyhedron, enclosed the maximum of space with a minimum surface area. These curved areas were in turn subdivided with a triangulated network of rods. By subsequently spraying this structure with a 3 cm thick layer of concrete a reinforced concrete shell was formed.
Max Mengeringhausen, inspired by the constructions of nature, also examined

spatial structures made up of rods. He recognised from the "example of the crystal [that] regular bodies have equally long edges. When one arranges the nodes and rods as elementary forms together, following the example of the crystal, one can compose space frames of any desired size with rods of a single length" [17]. MERO nodes and rods (MEngeringhausens ROhrbauweise – Mengeringhausen's tubular structures) have been produced in series since 1940 (fig. A 59). The nodes are based on a sphere with threaded holes into which the tubular rods can be simply screwed. The rods have threaded attachments at both ends. After the first presentation of structural system at the Interbau Exhibition "The City of Tomorrow" in 1957, MERO Systems has enjoyed continuous success.

When developing his modular panel systems Konrad Wachsmann was particularly interested in the jointing of standardised elements. While searching for large-scale, lightweight, wide-span structures, his so-called "space structures", Wachsmann created the system "Mobilar Structure" for the aeronautical industry; a "two-dimensional directional construction system made up of tubes and used to build large halls", in 1944/45 (fig. A 60). In the early 1950's the space frames built for large aircraft hangars were based on universal nodes and tubes that allowed adaptable space frames to be created. It was "a building system of standardised elements which, in the context of flexible, anonymous building methods, allowed every possible combination of construction method, geometrical system, building type and span sizes." [18]
The guiding light of large space-frame structures, and therefore the inspiration for many visionary architectural designs

and lifestyles, was Buckminster Fuller. Since the 1940's he had conducted many structural studies during his search for a geometry "which nature herself uses" [19]. One such study was his examination of the sphere; for example the two-dimensional developed drawing of the globe, and, subsequently, the subdivision of the earth into a geodetic network. A geodetic line is the shortest connection between two points on a surface. Buckminster Fuller's developed his "geodesic domes" in the 1950's. The aim was to enclose a maximum of space with a minimum of material. Between 1954 and 1971 numerous constructions of this type were built for a variety of events.

The most famous of these is the US pavilion for the World Expo in Montreal in 1967. The structure was based on a double-layer tubular structural system, the inner layer was made up of hexagonal arrangements of rods, the outer layer of triangles (fig. A 61). The external skin of the building was made of acrylic glass panels. Fuller's vision was to create a large-scale "Garden of Eden" of geodesic domes; an enormous, artificially air-conditioned environment.

Mega-structures and visions

Buckminster's fascinating visions and constructions, and the expected population explosion with all the associated problems of expanding cities led to the design of new, futuristic habitats. The goal was that flexible construction systems, which could grow to become enormous, high-density spatial living structures with exchangeable and variable elements, cells and capsules, should offer an alternative concept to the conventional, traditional urban housing model.

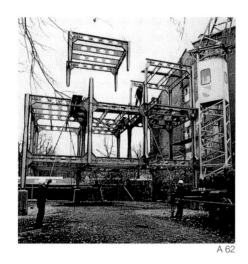

A 62   A 63   A 64

The city as a process: nothing is fixed, everything can be changed.

Kiyonoru Kikutake and Kisho Kurokawa, who, with other architects and designers, founded the metabolist movement in Japan in 1960, had worked on capsule agglomerations since 1959. Prefabricated capsules were slotted into the load-bearing, serviced primary structure by means of a crane. Kurokawa's Nakagin Tower was completed in Tokyo in 1972 – the individual capsules could be exchanged as desired and are fixed with only eight screws at four points (see pp. 192–193).

The Habitat housing development by Moshe Safdie, built as part of the World Expo in Montreal in 1967, was another attempt to create an alternative to standard housing. This "spatial sculpture" made up of many prefabricated concrete apartments cost approximately ten times more than conventional housing (fig. C 4.14 p. 163).

The Metastadt (meta-city) project by Richard Dietrich, which was started at the end of the 1960s, was an attempt to offer new urban solutions, for which a new range of technical construction instruments had to be invented and developed. Meta-cities are created through the regeneration and intensification of existing cities. To achieve this goal an element building system for flexible, multi-functional, multi-storey buildings, in which, essentially, all the components can be varied was created.

The steel frame primary structure of the meta-city Wulfen (figs. A 62–64) was based on a grid of 4.2 m horizontally and 3.3, 3.6 and 3.9 m vertically. The mega-structure was intended to offer the users individual options, but regrettably, making constructional alterations was far too

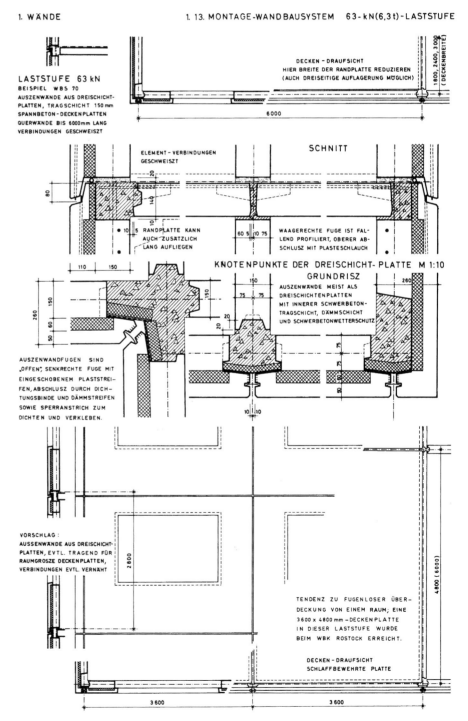

A 65

plans and facades, as well as simplified building forms. In the former GDR industrialisation of the building industry was a political programme. "Better, cheaper and faster" was the motto for the housing programme; firstly in large block construction, later using large-format panel construction methods. Basic modular units of 120 cm were laid down for all "housing and social buildings". While large block construction was based upon block-like wall elements of lightweight or aerated concrete that were not laid in bond and connections to the floor slabs and cross-walls were made by means of ring-beam elements at slab level, large panel construction was based on room-sized elements. The Housing Construction Series 70 (WBS 70) consisted of elements with finished surfaces and built-in windows (fig. A 65, p. 32). Decorative ceramic tiles were often used. Compared with the huge range and variety of systems available in Western Europe, later there was really only one system for the whole of the GDR.

This large panel construction system determined the appearance not only of the new housing developments in the GDR, but also of residential areas such as the "grands ensembles" and "villes nouvelles" around Paris, the Märkische Viertel in Berlin and the suburb of Neuperlach in Munich.

Many architects (just like Le Corbusier and Gropius some years before) saw the rationalisation of design and construction processes, modern fabrication techniques and the influence of unitisation and type standardisation on the organisation of building sites and the appearance of buildings as an opportunity to create a new form of architecture – one capable of throwing off the shackles of the past and liberating itself from the traditional "definition of beauty".

Günter Behnisch developed his own prefabricated concrete prototypes, such as the "System Behnisch", with various production companies. In 1959–63 he built, in collaboration with the engineering school in Ulm (fig. 67, p. 33), "the first large-element, fully prefabricated building in Germany" where the visual expression of the industrial fabrication method was restrained [22]. In 1964/65, he wrote that "these building methods (…) when consistently applied, lead to a very clear form; their purity is comparable with the older, entirely hand-produced houses." [23] "The use of these standardised elements and systems brings us exceptional advantages, so that in the future we will be liberated from the work that, up until now, has overwhelmed our offices." [24] "The architect will be free for major new undertakings." [25]

Architecture was, nevertheless, shaped by the additive use of identical elements. Ways out of this dilemma were difficult to find, particularly in large-scale housing developments, but some attempts in this direction were made at an urban scale by means of spatial differentiation, the use of colour or the special design of the panels.

The French architect Emile Aillaud was an avowed follower of industrialised building but also attempted to elevate serially produced elements above purely technical considerations by means of various designs. He used facade panels that were flat, concave and convex, and that were articulated with various differently sized, freely positioned openings. But this external design could do nothing to alter the public rejection of the apartments on account of the problematic floor plans, substandard finishes, insufficient light and the general urban situation. Ricardo Bofill introduced an even more distinctive design treatment of serially produced elements (fig. A 68). He had concrete facade elements cast in forms derived from the ornament of historic facades in an attempt to reduce the banality and monotony of the enormous housing blocks in Marne-la-Vallée and Cergy-Pontoise near Paris.

The students' residence at the University of St. Andrew's in Edinburgh, built by James Stirling in 1964 is a further example from the 1960s of the use of prefabricated wall and floor elements (fig. A 69). For the construction of the Olivetti Training Centre in Haslemere Stirling used – in a reference to the industrial design of the Olivetti typewriters – prefabricated glass-fibre reinforced polyester facades and prefabricated roof elements for the external skin of the classroom wings.

Open structures

The urban planning and architectural design of housing developments, with their inflexible attitudes towards the residents, met with great criticism and alternatives were called for. Improved architectural solutions were wanted, specifically, more open concepts that could meet the individual requirements of the users and would allow alterations to be made. Closed building systems where nothing can be removed or added were no longer acceptable, instead what was needed was the chance to combine the existing/unchangeable with the individually flexible/changeable, order with free-

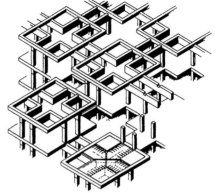

A 70

A 71

dom. Le Corbusier had suggested this type of openness in 1930 with his "plan d'obus d'alger".

In England, from the beginning of the 1960's onwards, countless rigid systems were developed. In political terms the need to develop new building methods was recognised in the form of "industrialised building". But these systems vanished as quickly as they had appeared – mostly due to their inadequate flexibility in terms of the users' changing demands.

Based on these experiences, Ezra Ehrenkrantz founded the SCSD programme (School Construction Systems Development) in California in 1961 (fig. A 72). This programme focused on building new types of schools. It was a very progressive and internationally much admired steel building system (for the construction of schools) that deeply influenced the work of many different architects, for example Norman Foster, Richard Rogers and Renzo Piano. It was not a system designed by an architect; but was based on requirements and rules that determined what the individual subsys-

tems should provide – not which materials should be used or how the buildings should look. Thus companies that specialised in producing the respective subsystems were invited to take part in developmental work by means of a competition. What was important was that the constraints laid down by SCSD should be observed, these stated that the building elements should be compatible with elements from other manufacturers. In this way part constructions were produced by independent companies that could be combined to create new building systems. And, as they were universally applicable, some of them were soon released onto the market as industrially mass produced elements. This is what ensured the success of the system. This cooperation of different manufacturing companies was one of the first truly convincing demonstrations of the efficiency of open building systems. [26]

For Aldo van Eyck and Hermann Hertzberger it was not the technical aspect of a system that was important but a structure of regularly arranged elements that was open to different uses. The two

Dutchmen exercised great influence both through their architecture and their criticism of functionalistic urban planning. In the design of his experimental "Diagoon" houses between 1967 and 1971 in Delft, Hertzberger's concern was "that the house should be adaptable. What has been designed should be considered as an empty framework. It is a half-product, that everyone can complete, according to his or her needs." [27]

This approach is clearly legible in the Central Beheer insurance company office building, built in 1970–72 (figs. A 70 and A 71). It is based on the geometry of a square band grid and allows the different areas to be used individually. The precast concrete load-bearing structure, its spandrel elements and concrete block walls were left exposed and without surface treatment. We must "offer an opportunity for personal interpretation by designing things in such a way that they are truly interpretable." [28]

Dutch architect Nicolaas Habraken founded the S.A.R. Stiftung Architekten Research (Foundation for Architects'

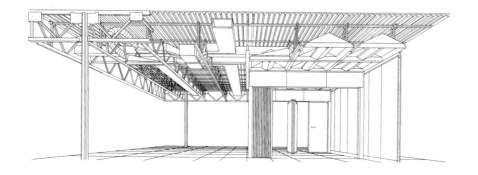

A 68   Les Arcades du Lac Housing Development, Saint-Quentin-en-Yvelines (F) 1975–1982, Ricardo Bofill
A 69   Bedroom levels with promenade deck, student housing St. Andrew's University (GB) 1964, James Stirling
A 70   Office building Centraal Beheer, Apeldoorn (NL) 1970–1972, Herman Hertzberger
A 71   Office building Centraal Beheer, schematic structural sketch
A 72   SCSD in Palo Alto (USA) 1965, Ezra Ehrenkrantz

A 72

A 73   Housing experiment Genter Straße, Munich (D)
           1972, Otto Steidle
A 74   Construction system shell for the housing ex-
           periment Genter Straße
A 75   Centre Georges Pompidou, Paris (F) 1977,
           Renzo Piano and Richard Rogers

A 73

Research) in order to "research possibilities in the design and production of frame structures and built-in fixtures" [29]. The foundation was less concerned with developing a technical system, and more with building structures that allow the users a maximum of participation in the organisation and design of the floor plans. The building was to be divided into load-bearing (frame) structure and (internal built-in) fixtures. The layouts were to be open-plan, with only kitchen and bathroom locations being fixed; the remaining areas could be individually designed by the users.

Building with large, prefabricated element systems was also promoted in the post-war years in Scandinavia. The Danish system "Jespersen", which was based on relatively large elements, was particularly widely used.

Danish architect Jorn Utzon developed his "Additive Architecture" in the 1960's, inspired by both the American "Case Study Houses" and traditional Japanese dwellings. The individual elements were room types that could be freely combined, thus creating a structure that can be constantly changed.

Otto Steidle's experimental housing in Genter Strasse in Munich (built 1970–72) employs an open pre-cast concrete element system that allows flexibility and variation; it encourages residents to fit-out, use and alter their housing (figs. A 73 and A 74). Rectangular concrete columns with supporting brackets, and floor slabs with downstand beams provide the primary structure, while the prefabricated and movable partition and facade elements could be positioned differently within the structure. In 1985 Steidle said: "Thus I (…) grasped the idea of erecting

A 74

A 75

frameworks that allow the free integration and arrangement of dwellings and encourage the gradual establishment of life within these open structures." [30]

In California in the 1970's Helmut C. Schulitz conducted research with the T.E.S.T. Group on the further development of building systems for housing. The aim was to find a system based on finite construction kits that "does not start out from the development of new building elements, but rather represents a coordination system for elements already available on the market". In this case, system means finding rules "according to which building elements already in mass production can be put together." [31] Additionally a catalogue was to be produced that would give the users an overview of which elements can be used to fulfil their individual requirements, within the range of products available in the building centre. Schulitz' own house, which he built in 1975/76, was an experiment that tested the results of his research work.

In his publication *Die Unwirtlichkeit unserer Städte. Thesen zur Stadt der Zukunft* (The Inhospitality of Our Cities. Theses on the City of the Future) Munich-born critic and author Alexander Mitscherlich criticised the destruction of existing, organically developed structures by the urban development of the post-war era". Industrialised building, however, continued to be considered by many a "synonym for progress" up until the1970's.
In 1967 Günter Behnisch turned his back on industrialised building; architecture should once again be a product of place, materials and functions.

In 1973 Helmut Schulitz described "the dead-end of industrialised processes"

[32] as a problem resulting from the self-contained nature of the systems used. The "limits of progress" (1972), the oil crisis in 1973 and the resultant environmental consciousness dramatically reduced the former euphoria for technology.

The Pompidou Centre in Paris (fig. A 75), stemming from a competition in 1967 and finally completed in 1977 by Renzo Piano and Richard Rogers, that looks like a "building as a machine" or a "building as a construction kit" [33], seems like an icon of the 1960's, the time of Buckminster Fuller and the British group of architects, Archigram. The foci of architecture shifted; technology and industry no longer determined the visual appearance of buildings. A few architects such as Foster, Rogers and others, committed to the great English tradition of iron and glass, continue to show how a building functions by clearly exposing its structural system and technical equipment.

Architecture is no longer dominated by a single system, but rather by a collection of systems with different technical standards that are combined to produce the built form. Each of these system develops continuously in response to architectural, technical and functional demands. Present-day systems have little in common with earlier ones; back then the principle was to produce as many identical elements as possible. Now – in response to numerous different influences and requirements (energy, cooling, material efficiency etc.), and the newest technical possibilities in the areas of design, production and assembly – systems are no longer discrete individuals but rather individualisation is continued within a system. The building has become a complex arrangement of different systems.

Notes
[1] Klotz, Heinrich: Von der Urhütte zum Wolkenkratzer. Munich 1991, p. 55
[2] Schädlich, Christian: Das Eisen in der Architektur des 19. Jahrhunderts. Ein Beitrag zur Geschichte eines neuen Baustoffs. Habilschrift, Weimar 1966, p. 319
[3] Kohlmaier, Georg, Barna von Sartory: Das Glashaus – ein Bautyp des 19. Jahrhunderts. Munich 1988, p. 415
[4] Wachsmann, Konrad: Wendepunkt im Bauen. Stuttgart 1989, p. 14
[5] Behrens, Peter: Vom sparsamen Bauen. Ein Beitrag zur Siedlungsfrage. Berlin 1918, p. 59
[6] ibid. [5], p. 60
[7] after Le Corbusier: Ausblick auf eine Architektur. Gütersloh 1969, p. 166
[8] ibid, p. 179
[9] Hirdina, Heinz (Ed.): Neues Bauen, neues Gestalten. Das neue Frankfurt. Dresden 1984 Issue 11/1929, p. 29
[10] Nerdinger: Walter Gropius, Frankfurt 1985/1996, p. 15
[11] ibid. [10], p. 16
[12] ibid. [10], p. 20
[13] Deutscher Werkbund (Ed.): Bau und Wohnung, Stuttgart 1927, p. 59
[14] after Fuller, Buckminster: Bedienungsanleitung für das Raumschiff Erde, Dresden 1998, p. 195
[15] Krausse, Joachim, Lichtenstein, Claude (Ed): Your Private Sky. R. Buckminster Fuller, Baden 1999, p. 135
[16] ibid. [4], p. 140
[17] Klotz, Heinrich: Vision der Moderne. Das Prinzip Konstruktion. Frankfurt 1986, p. 280
[18] ibid. [13], p.170
[19] ibid. [12], p. 286
[20] Diedrith, Richard: Metastadt – Idee und Wirklichkeit. In: db 8/1975, p. 29
[21] Nerdinger, Winfried: Konstruktion und Raum in der Architektur des 20. Jahrhunderts. Munich 2002, p. 122
[22] Spieker, Elisabeth: Günter Behnisch – Die Entwicklung des architektonischen Werkes. Diss. 2005 TU Stuttgart, p. 70
[23] ibid. [17], p. 75
[24] ibid. [17], p. 83
[25] ibid. [17], p. 76
[26] Schulitz; Helmut: Stahlkonstruktionen für den Wohnungsbau. In: Das Bauzentrum, 1/1999, p. 29
[27] Lüchinger, Arnulf: Hertzberger, Herrmann: Bauten und Projekte 1959–1986. The Hague 1987, p. 72
[28] Frampton, Kennenth: Modern Architecture: A Critical History, Stuttgart 1983, p. 247
[29] Schulitz, Helmut: Bauen mit Systemen. In: db 3/1973, p. 262
[30] Sack, Manfred: Otto Steidle. Braunschweig 1985, p. 11
[31] Schulitz, Helmut; Bauen mit Systemen. In: db 3/1973, p. 254
[32] ibid. [27], p. 251
[33] Buchanan, Peter: Renzo Piano Building Workshop. Volume 1. Stuttgart 1994, p. 52

Part B   Basic Principles

Industrial prefabrication   40
Site prefabrication and
mobile production plants   41
Building methods   41
Elements   42
Type standardisation   42
System – building system   42
Closed systems   42
Modular building systems   43
Open systems   43
Semi-finished elements   43
Module   44
Grid   44
Dimensional coordination   45
Geometrical positioning of
structural and fit-out elements   45
Transport   45
Assembly   47
Jointing   47
Tolerances   47

figure B

B 1

Basic principles

Industrial prefabrication

Industrial prefabrication of building elements has been possible since the beginning of the 19th century, with the advent of industrialisation (fig. B 1). The serial prefabrication of structural steel elements aided the development of building systems, for example frame construction systems.

Today, industrial prefabrication for building means the production of building products by way of industrial techniques. Site work is transferred to a specialised plant, where building elements can be manufactured independently of the weather and under optimal production conditions (fig. B 3). In the building industry there are numerous high-tech production plants in which building materials are processed to produce building elements. Even building methods traditionally based on manual skills, such as masonry and bricklaying, can now be carried out in the plant using the most modern factory processes. The proportion of industrially manufactured products in onventionally constructed buildings nowadays is usually around 50–60%. The application of systems based on prefabricated building components is increasing – for both building envelopes and interior fit-out. A major advantage of building with prefabricated elements compared with traditional construction techniques is the constant quality level achieved by production in plants. This reduces the construction time on site and, with it, costs. Current standard practice is to combine industrially prefabricated building units with elements produced in situ to form complex building elements. As conditions on site are often less than optimal and cannot match industrial production standards this can lead to construction delays and loss of quality.

The continually increasing demand for better quality and the efforts to shorten the design and construction periods encourages to the development of industrial prefabrication in the building industry.

Computerised, automated production techniques and equipment, for example CNC milling and specialised robots, enable the manufacture of highly complex building elements.

The level of prefabrication of the building

Type of building	Level of prefabrication [%]
Rationalised housing	25–35
Industrial building site processes	20–30
Standard ready-built (rein. conc., steel, timber)	40–60
Ready-built housing (timber panel system)	50–80
Modular units/sanitary blocks (rein. conc., steel, timber)	60–90
Mobile modular units (steel, timber)	95–100
Automobiles (for purposes of comparison)	100

B 2

B 3

B   Prefabrication of a timber framed wall panel
B 1 Industrial steel production in the 19th century
B 2 Level of prefabrication (%) in different areas of
     the building industry
B 3 Production of a steel framed wall panel
B 4 Steel frame construction, Lake Shore Drive
     Apartments, Chicago (USA) 1951,
     Ludwig Mies van der Rohe
B 5 Solid masonry construction,
     Roman Art Museum, Merida, 1985
     architect: José Rafael Moneo
B 6 High-rise office block in Kawasaki after five
     months construction time
B 7 Internal view of a work platform
B 8 Assembly process using construction robots

B 4

B 5

parts is decisive for a building project, as this helps define the – proportion of prefabricated construction with respect to the overall construction – the greater the level of prefabrication, the lower the amount of assembly work on site and, subsequent, the shorter the construction time. Panel construction systems have prefabrication levels of approximately 60 % and modular systems approximately 85 % (fig. B 2). Fully equipped, fitted-out room modules have a level of prefabrication of up to 95 % [1].

Site prefabrication and mobile production plants

Production plants for the prefabrication of building elements are seldom near the relevant building sites, which often means that elements must be transported long distances to the location where they are assembled and erected. When finances and time allow, building elements can now be produced in mobile factories that are temporarily set up in close proximity to the building site for the duration of the production.

For these, however, fully automated, specially developed production techniques are a prerequisite. These techniques are supported by the use of robots that can carry out the assembly work autonomously.

Japan boasts a particularly high level of development in the area of computer-operated assembly and finishing plants which are considered standard procedure for construction sites there. Such fully automated assembly systems are used even in the construction of high-rise buildings. The system is based upon travelling platforms that construct the building as they rise vertically (fig. B 6). A steel frame construction forms the framework for the scaffolding and simultaneously serves as the guide rail for the work platform, which is equipped with cranes, building robots and hydraulic presses, all under a weatherproof cover (figs. B 7 and B 8). The prefabricated construction elements are moved to the required position and fitted in place by the computer-operated cranes. The first stage of the building process is the construction of the ground floor; the work platform travels upwards automatically on four steel jacks

in order to construct the next level – including fit-out. The entire construction process is computer-operated and is supervised from a control room. The construction workers are responsible for operating the completely automated high-rise construction system. However, difficulties still arise with programming of the robots and the punctual delivery of building elements. In this system all the building elements are prefabricated, with only the sealing and insulating of joints and some of the service installation work still being carried out manually [2].

Building methods

Within the building industry a basic distinction is made between solid construction methods, such as masonry and concrete structures, and frame constructions, such as steel and timber frame structures (figs. B 4 and B 5). These systems provide the guidelines for the combination of building components and greatly influence the design and form of a building. Traditional building methods based on the skills of craftsmen, for example half-

B 6

B 7

B 8

A 62 Assembly of the test building for the "Meta-stadt" in Munich (D) 1961, Richard Dietrich
A 63 Metastadt Wulfen (D) 1965
A 64 Model Metastadt Wulfen
A 65 Assembly wall construction system, Series 70, former GDR, 1970
A 66 Staatliche Fachhochschule für Technik, Ulm (D) 1963, Günther Behnisch
A 67 Schedule of pre-cast concrete elements for the Haigerloch school centre (D) 1965, Günther Behnisch

A 66

1. Stützen

Pos.	Skizze	Bezeichnung	Progymn. Stück	Volkssch. Stück
1.1a 1.1b		Flurrahmen Träger 30/38 l = 3,65 Stütze 30/30 h = 3,82 Mit Konsole Ohne Konsole	85 6	
1.2a 1.2b		Stütze 30/30 h = 3,32 h = 4,12	74 7	
1.3a 1.3b		Stütze 30/30 eingespannt 70 cm h = 4,02 h = 4,82	10	
1.4		Stütze 30/60 eingespannt 1,00 m h = 4,32	6	

2. Träger

Pos.	Skizze	Bezeichnung	Progymn. Stück	Volkssch Stück
2.1a 2.1b 2.1c		Träger 30/50 1 Auflager für Konsole l = 7,50 l = 3,35 Träger 30/50 2 Auflager für Konsole l = 3,05	73 5 12	44
2.2a 2.2b 2.2c 2.2d		Träger 30/50 l = 7,65 l = 3,35 l = 3,50 l = 7,80	6 6	15 2 2
3.3		Träger 30/1,30 l = 10,85	3	
3.4		Treppenträger 30/50 l = 6,40 h = 2,23	16	

3. Nichttragende Teile aussen

Pos.	Skizze	Bezeichnung	Progymn. Stück	Volkssch. Stück
3.1a 3.1b		Attika h = 1,27 l = 3,35 l = 2,50	80 24	94 54
3.2		Attika-Eckstück h = 1,27	20	32
3.3		Brüstung h = 1,67 l = 3,35		65
3.4a 3.4b		Verkürzte Brüstung h = 0,85 l = 3,35 l = 2,50	5 27	12
3.5a 3.5b		Giebelwand h = 3,32 l = 3,35 l = 2,50	4 27	24
3.6a 3.6b		Aussenwand h = 3,75 l = 3,35 l = 2,17		4 2
3.7		Eckstück h = 3,95	36	20

4. Nichttragende Teile innen

Pos.	Skizze	Bezeichnung	Progymn. Stück	Volkssch. Stück
4.1		Flurtrennwand mit Fenster h = 3,82 l = 3,05	23	11
4.2a 4.2b		Flurtrennwand mit Tür 1,01/2,17 h = 3,82 l = 3,05 l = 2,01	4 18	4 7
4.3		Flurtrennwand mit 2 Türen 1,01/2,17 h = 3,82 l = 3,05	2	
4.4		Klassentrennwand h = 3,32 l = 2,40	60	27
4.5		Klassentrennwand mit Tür 1,01/2,17 h = 3,32 l = 2,40	6	6
4.6		Installationselement h = 3,82 b = 0,65 l = 1,03	20	11

A 67

complicated, and the project was quickly rejected by the residents. The meta-city was demolished 13 years later due, at least in part, to serious constructional deficiencies. At that time the project was considered to be a "symbol of the misguided development of industrialised building, specifically system building" [21]. It was surely also a symbol of housing structures that were too large and too densely built.

Industrial fabrication – "Synonym for Progress"

The industrialisation of the building industry was the result of a number of factors; society's enormous demand for dwellings and the pressure to build as quickly and as economically as possible, to name but a few. Particularly America, with its highrise buildings and aerospace industry, nourished the enthusiasm for technology. The conventional construction company had to give way to rational production and construction methods. Industrial prefabrication and standardisation of building processes were intended to enable faster, cheaper, and also more contemporary building. The demands and desires proclaimed in the 1920's now became reality; they could even be improved upon and surpassed, thanks to the technical advances that had been made in the intervening period. Gradually the hand-made parts of a building were being replaced by industrially prefabricated elements that could be quickly and efficiently assembled on site. System building did, however, have implications for the external appearance of the buildings. Industrial fabrication methods demanded uncomplicated, serially-produced building elements, modular floor

33

a

b

c

B 9

timbered buildings, are described as building systems, whose elements, however, are prefabricated by hand. Modern building methods, e.g. steel frame construction or systems using large panels, on the other hand, are based upon construction with prefabricated building elements. With their strict regularity these, in turn, determine the form of such a building.

When designing with prefabricated building elements, the classification principles of the individual elements are the deciding factors. Buildings can be created out of linear, planar or spatial elements. These determine the construction principles characteristic of system building: the frame, the panel and the room module (fig. B 9). These three building methods are frequently combined in the building industry and rarely appear in isolation. Frame structures are often combined in a system with panels or room-modules. As regards the level of flexibility of these three building methods the frame is the most flexible, followed by panel systems and then modular building methods, while the level of prefabrication follows the reverse order – modular units are the most highly prefabricated [3].

Elements

Principles specific to each particular system enable individual elements to be combined within a construction system to produce a building. Depending upon the system used, the element can be the brick in a masonry construction, a wall panel in a panel construction or a room unit in a modular construction. For the successful completion of a project, it is of paramount importance to correctly coor-

dinate and harmonise the individual elements, for example by deciding upon a uniform technique for making connections. In the case of more complex buildings the individual elements are organised according to their function i.e. load bearing or non-load bearing, and categorised into hierarchies – primary elements for the load bearing structure and secondary elements for the building envelope, the interior fit-out and technical services [4].

Type standardisation

Building elements can be industrially prefabricated in series in specialised works. In this case their form and function must be determined in the design phase, for example reinforced concrete columns with bearing brackets. In the building industry this process is generally termed type standardisation. The use of these standardised elements in construction work is defined as unitised building. Even entire buildings can be standardised for specific purposes. Generally, however, type standardisation refers to the characteristics of a specific building element [5].

System – building system

Systems define the relationships between the individual elements within a geometrical organisational principle. In a building system, the sum of the elements and the way they are combined is determined in the design. The building elements and way they fit together must be systematically coordinated during the design phase. To achieve this type standardisation and dimensional coordination must be considered in advance (fig. B 10).

When developing a building system it is of decisive importance whether it consists of individual part systems for the shell, the interior fit-out and the building envelope or whether it integrates all part systems. Modern building systems can be designed as either open or closed systems. They consist of elements that include the load-bearing structure in addition to the building envelope, internal fit-out and technical services [6].

Closed systems

In closed systems all elements are fabricated by a single manufacturer. In the building industry, closed systems can be developed for either entire buildings or, as partial systems, for load-bearing structures, for facades or for internal fit-out. All individual elements are coordinated and harmonised with one another and cannot simply be exchanged, altered or extended as desired. Their relationship to one another is comparable with the building instructions of a model kit. The elements of a closed system can only be used within that particular system. Most industrial, serially manufactured products, for example motorised vehicles, are based upon the principle of a closed system. The range of design options is quite limited due to the rigidly determined function of the building parts. The appli-

B 9 Systematic presentation of modular building unitisation principles,
   a frame construction
   b panel construction
   c modular unit construction
B 10 Characteristics of a building system
B 11 Combination options in a modular building system, LBS-system house
B 12 Application of a modular building system, extension to a regional school in Solothurn (CH) 1997, Fritz Haller

a

b   B 22

B 23

value of a building element and the costs of transporting it determine the economical transport radius (fig. B 21).

The order of loading the elements onto the vehicles is dictated by the assembly sequence on the building site, in order to maximise the efficiency between transport and assembly sequences. Optimal assembly processes can be achieved if building elements can be unloaded directly from the transport vehicles by hoisting cranes and immediately placed and fixed in position on the site [12].

Assembly

To erect a building based on prefabricated elements all that needs to be carried out on the building site is assembling and fitting. This includes hoisting, positioning, adjusting, connecting and waterproofing. Building work thus becomes an assembly process. In comparison to construction work in earlier times the manufacture and processing of building elements on site is no longer required. For buildings made up of prefabricated elements the development of a jointing and connecting technique that guarantees fast and simple assembly is of paramount importance, as is exact time coordination. It is, of course, possible to prefabricate and assemble parallel, so as to further reduce the construction period.

The erection of a prefabricated building is a horizontal process and is organised storey by storey; the position of the individual building elements must be determined during the design process. The position, size and weight of the building elements are decisive in selecting the hoisting equipment (fig. B 19). Larger elements may even necessitate the use of transport frames, transport spreader

beams or rope systems for securing hoisting equipment. Precast reinforced concrete elements, for example, are manufactured complete with lifting lugs or anchors for transportation and assembly, which are placed in the formwork during the manufacturing process (fig. B 22a).

In order to simplify positioning and to avoid later adjustment on site, the building elements have reference and fitting surfaces. Additional equipment such as assembly and fitting guides are often helpful. Columns and walls that stand alone are strutted during the assembly process by means of inclined or adjustable auxiliary supports, until they are fully stable (fig. B 22b) [13].

Jointing

Joints occur at the points where building elements meet and exert a great influence on the appearance of a facade (fig. B 23). The grid of the joints is determined by the dimensions of the elements which, in turn, are fixed by production, design and transport conditions.

In order to avoid damage during assembly, joints must be made with great care. The joints serve to take up dimensional discrepancies in building components and must fulfil all the requirements of moisture, thermal and acoustic protection.

Joints can be protected against moisture either by constructional solutions, or in combination with sealants. Constructional jointing must be taken into account during the detail design process. The total number of joints, which is a function of the number of prefabricated elements, can be reduced by selecting elements with a high level of prefabrication, that is to say with the largest possible dimensions.

Tolerances

Tolerances describe possible differences between the nominal and the actual dimension of a building element, and must therefore be taken into account during the planning process. The nominal dimension decided upon during the design process is seldom achieved on site due to dimensional deviations. Deviations in dimensions can also occur during the manufacture of a building element. On this account the connection and jointing system must be designed in such a way that it can tolerate these deviations up to a permissible level, for example by means of elastic joints and bearers, and oblong holes for screw fixings. The tolerances set down in the German DIN standards must be taken into account when designing constructional details.

Tolerances are of particular importance in building methods based on industrially prefabricated elements as, due to the limited range of element dimensions there are more assembly joints than when using conventional construction methods [14].

Notes:
[1] Bock, Thomas: Lightweight constructions and systems. In: Detail 07/08 2006, p. 759
[2] Prochiner, Frank et al.: Automatisierungssysteme im Wohnungsbau. Stuttgart 1999, p. 155
[3] Cheret, Peter et al.: Informationsdienst Holz, Holzbausysteme, Holzbauhandbuch Issue 1, part 1, series 4. Düsseldorf/Bonn 2000, p. 5
[4] ibid. [3]
[5] Koncz, Tihamér: Bauen industrialisiert. Wiesbaden 1976, p. 28
[6] ibid. [3]
[7] ibid. [3]
[8] Herzog, Thomas et al.: Facade Construction Manual. Munich/Basle 2004, p. 48
[9] ibid. [8], p. 49
[10] ibid. [8], p. 48
[11] ibid. [8], p. 51
[12] Weller, Konrad: Industrielles Bauen 1. Grundlagen und Entwicklung des industriellen, energie- und rohstoffsparenden Bauens. Stuttgart/Berlin/Cologne/Mainz 1986, p. 96
[13] ibid. [12], p. 98
[14] ibid. [5], p. 26

Part C   Structural systems

Materials in system building   **50**
Steel   50
Timber   51
Concrete   51

Frame systems   **54**
Steel frame systems   55
    Construction elements
    Connection techniques and elements
    Bracing elements and systems
    Construction principles
Timber frame systems   61
    Construction materials and
    elements
    Connection techniques and elements
    Bracing elements and systems
    Construction principles
Concrete frame systems   68
    Construction elements
    Connection techniques
    Bracing elements and systems
    Construction principles

Panel systems   **110**
Building with steel panels   111
    Steel panel building methods
    Construction materials and elements
Building with timber panels   114
    Timber panel building methods
    Construction materials and
    elements
Building with concrete panels   119
    Concrete panel building methods
    Construction elements
Building with masonry panels and
brickwork elements   124
    Prefabricated masonry building
    elements
    Hollow clay brick elements

Room module systems   **160**
Steel room module systems   160
Timber room module systems   162
Concrete room module systems   163

figure C

Materials in system building

Contemporary architects have at their disposal an enormous variety of building materials for the erection of buildings – ranging from the conventional to the prefabricated. Industrially manufactured products, for example precast concrete elements, wood-based boards products and profiled steel sheeting, are becoming increasingly popular because of their consistently high quality and economy of production. The material properties and the structural behaviour of building elements decide where they are used, whether for the building shell, internal fitout or facades.

In system building, glass, plastic and aluminium are generally used for building envelopes and are less suitable as structural elements.

In addition to float glass, profiled glass and glass blocks can also be used for facade systems. Plastic building elements are usually available as panels, shells and pneumatic cushions.

Metals such as lead, bronze and copper can be processed with great precision and a high level of prefabrication today. Sheets of semi-precious metals are also suitable for prefabricated panels used in facade construction.

In addition to profiled steel building sections, aluminium profiles are also employed as construction elements in erecting load-bearing structures. Compared with steel elements of equivalent weight, aluminium is one-and-a-half times stronger, but is also more brittle and generally more expensive to fabricate.

In element-based building systems prefabricated products used for load-bearing constructions are generally of steel, timber or concrete. They will be discussed in greater detail below [1].

Steel

"…the time is probably drawing near when a new system of architectural principles will be developed, completely adapted to building with iron."
John Ruskin, (1819–1900) [2]

Since the beginning of the 19th century, when steel could be manufactured in huge quantities, building with this material has been greatly influenced by prefabrication. No other building material has affected the possible methods of construction and the appearance of buildings as radically as steel; market halls, railway stations and warehouses are typical examples. The concept of serial production was later taken up and further developed particularly by the architects of modernism.

Steel is an elastic material with great tensile and compressive strength. Building elements made of this material can be loaded up to what is called the yield point. When this point is exceeded, the material behaves in a plastic manner; i.e. it is only from this point that deformations in the material are no longer reversible. Structural steel has a consistent material quality, an advantage in the structural dimensioning of constructions. Due to its excellent structural behaviour, steel allows constructions with large spans to be built.

Due to their dimensional accuracy, steel building elements are particularly suitable for use in modular building systems. Steel constructions are generally put together by way of screw connections which in the case of temporary buildings, for example, allows them to be easily dismantled. An important aspect is the development of a uniform connection

C   Facade of prefabricated concrete panels,
     production and administration building
     in Freiburg (D) 2006, Barkow Leibinger
     Architect
C 1.1 Building assembled with steel construction
     panels, Centre le Corbusier, Zurich (CH)
     1967, Le Corbusier, Jean Prouvé
C 1.2 Forest pavilion Gulpwald, Willisau (CH) 2003,
     CAS Chappuis Aregger Sloèr
C 1.3 Lattice Facade made of a lattice of prefabri-
     cated concrete-elements, Laboratory,
     Wageningen (NL) 2006, Rafael Vinoly
C 1.4 Dispatch storehouse, Chippenham (GB) 1982,
     Nicholas Grimshaw and Partners

C 1.2

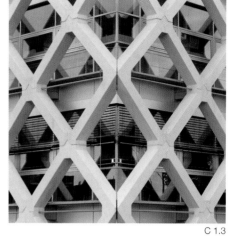

C 1.3

technique within systems which aids speedy assembly.

However, prefabricated steel building elements are not only suitable for structural systems, in the form of steel sheeting they can also be used, for elements that enclose space and for facades. Through the folding and curving steel sheeting, walls used in interior fit-outs can be given a stability otherwise possible only with bracing ribs.

In addition to steel constructions, which are generally based on conventional regular grids, today, with the help of the most modern computer technology, steel building systems can be designed that allow constructions with complex geometries to be built.

The possibilities of the material steel in terms of innovation and economy have by no means yet been exhausted. Structural steel can be worked easily and in a variety of different ways and it is an important component of industrial construction today, with great economic and ecological advantages. Although the manufacture of steel requires a great deal of energy, the material can be 100% recycled. The recycling process for the production of raw steel utilises 100 million tonnes of steel scrap, originating from cars, buildings and bridges, worldwide.

Timber

"Wood is just a one-syllable word, but behind it a world of beauty and wonder is concealed."
Theodor Heuss, (1884–1963) [3]

Building with timber has become increasingly popular over the past few years.

After steel and concrete, timber is the third most widely used material group in the building industry.

It was not only the ecological aspects, but also an awareness of the qualities of this natural and locally available building material that led to a boom in the timber industry. In addition to the traditional uses of timber, industry is continuously developing new systems, and in collaboration with universities research is being carried out into the improvement and optimisation of timber-based construction materials.

In comparison to steel, timber is distinguished by great strenght with a low weight, and a high resistance to thermal transmission; it can be employed for structural systems, internal fit-out and facades. In addition to solid timber, industrial lamination and pressure techniques enable numerous building materials to be made from timber fibres and chips. These can also be produced by simple recycling processes using timber waste products. Semi-finished elements, in the form of glued laminated timber panels, plywood or fibreboard, are easy to work and therefore offer great freedom of design.

In the timber construction systems currently available on the market we can discover a certain analogy to traditional timber techniques such as half-timbering and solid timber log constructions. At the beginning of the 19th century the balloon frame building system was developed in America; this was a forerunner of the timber frame construction systems commonly used today. At the beginning of the 20th century the first attempts at timber log construction were made in Europe, due to the non-standardised building elements the balloon frame system could not establish itself. It was

only with the development of environmental consciousness towards the end of the 1970s that this method reached Europe.

Both modern and traditional timber construction techniques can be divided into frame constructions and solid constructions. Modern timber construction also use the principles of frame systems, panel systems and room module systems. Timber frame elements and solid wall panels make up the largest sector of the timber construction market today. These structural, planar timber elements can be used in a variety of ways in building floor slabs, walls and roofs. They are available at a high level of quality, almost on demand and meet all the demands of building physics. Solid timber wall elements are fabricated automatically and, in the form of large panels and room modules, can be swiftly assembled on site.

Concrete

"It is not easy to see in this conglomerate a high aesthetic property, because, in itself it is amalgam, aggregate, compound... The net result is, usually, an artificial stone at best, or a petrified sand heap at worst...
Surely, here, to the creative mind, is temptation. Temptation to rescue so honest a material from degradation. Because here in a conglomerate named 'concrete' we find a plastic material, that as yet has found no medium of expression that will allow it to take plastic form."
Frank Lloyd Wright (1867–1959) [4]

In comparison to stone, steel and timber, concrete is not a homogeneous material, but a heterogeneous mixture of cement, water, aggregate, additives and agents. Variations in type and quantity of these constituents determine the properties of this material. Concrete is widely used in the building industry on account of its great load-bearing capacity and the variety of ways in which it can be formed. Particularly in conjunction with steel all construction principles – from frame, through panel and on to modular – are possible. These building methods are usually combined, for example the structural system of a building might be made as a concrete frame that is subsequently infilled with prefabricated timber panel elements. Thanks to the availability of both concrete and steel, reinforced concrete is an economical building material that can be produced with simple production techniques; because of this, reinforced concrete is particularly suitable for the serial production of prefabricated elements.

Prefabricated concrete elements, in contrast to in-situ concrete elements, are not made on the building site but in separate production facilities. The advantages are that elaborate formwork is not necessary on site and production is independent of weather conditions. Prefabricated concrete elements are manufactured in either flat or upright forms constructed of either steel or plastic, whereby surfaces of fair-faced concrete quality can be achieved. In flat formwork the concrete is poured into the form and the upper surface manually smoothed.
By using textured materials in the formwork, in addition to special mechanical or chemical surface treatments, the final appearance of the prefabricated concrete elements can be determined during the production process.

Prefabricated concrete building elements can be used at all stages of construction, from the building shell to the facade cladding. In facade construction the options can be divided into single-layer or double-layer curtain wall panels and sandwich elements.
Serial fabrication makes it possible to produce specialised elements, for example stairs, economically. Thanks to the most modern production techniques precise concrete elements can be produced for a large range of vastly different building projects. The size of elements, however, is defined by the limitations in production techniques and the difficulty of transporting large elements.

Notes:
[1] Herzog, Thomas et al.: Facade Manual. Munich/ Basle 2004, p. 183
[2] Ruskin, John: Seven lamps of Architecture. London 1849
[3] Spring, Anselm et al.: Holz. Das fünfte Element. Munich 1999, p. 14
[4] Kind-Barkauskas, Friedbert et al.: Concrete Construction Manual. Munich/Cologne/Dusseldorf 1995, p. 27

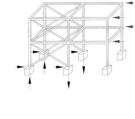

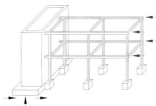

C 2.1

Frame systems

Frame systems are composed of linear building elements such as columns and beams. Combined with bracing elements, they provide an essentially stable construction, which is capable of withstanding both vertical and horizontal loads. In buildings where the load-bearing system is designed as a frame, the load-bearing elements are structurally and functionally clearly separated from the non-load-bearing elements of the external envelope and the internal fit-out.

Generally speaking, when planning frame systems it is important that the load-bearing structure and the junctions be designed in harmony with the fit-out and facade systems as neither the external nor the internal walls are load-bearing. The load-bearing frame can be located either inside or outside the building envelope. As regards thermal insulation, an internal frame is preferable as the external skin of the building can then be thermally insulated without cold bridges. The rooms are enclosed by means of infill wall systems or non-load-bearing room modules.
The beams in frame systems are designed as either simply supported beams spanning between columns which extend the full height of the building, or as continuous beams supported on storey-high columns. The beams are subject to bending stress as they carry the loads of the floor slabs and roof construction. The columns take the vertical loads from the beams and transfer them to the foundations. When designing a frame structure, the layout of the columns should be harmonised with the plan layout. The flexible use of the building is possible within a column grid. Bracing members take, for example the horizontally forces due to wind loads, and stabilise the frame. Brac-

ing can be provided horizontally in the floor slabs, or vertically in the walls, in the form of diagonal ties, frames, rigid corner joints, fixed-end columns or internal cores (fig. C 2.1). It is important that the bracing concept be decided upon early in the design process because the type of bracing has a major influence on the functions of the spaces and the facade design. If stiffening elements are incorporated within the facade plane this allows greater flexibility in the floor plans, whereas rigid corner joints allow continuous facade areas to be created uninterrupted by diagonal bracing or cross-ties in the facade panels.
The types of connection used and the selection of sections are decisive for the appearance of the frame. It is particularly important that the junctions at which all load-bearing and bracing elements are connected be developed with great care and precision during the detailed design phase [1].

C 2.1 Bracing systems in frame construction
 a frame with rigid corner elements
 b diagonal ties
 c wall plates
 d cores
C 2.2 Free-form steel frame, Guggenheim Museum, Bilbao (E) 1997, Frank O. Gehry
 a frame structure
 b building envelope of titanium panels
C 2.3 Combination of bracing and facade elements in steel frame construction, house in Shimgamo, Shimgamo (J) 1994, Waro Kishi and Associates
C 2.4 Exploded isometry, house in Shimgamo

a

C 2.2

C 2.3

Steel frame systems

Steel frames have been used as a constructional principle for a wide variety of building forms ever since the development of modern steel construction. Columns and beams made of steel sections create a frame of linear members with minimal weight that has high load-bearing capacity and allows large spans between the columns. This means that very long spans are possible with few constructional elements, but the most economical spans are between 6 and 18 m [2].
The international standard unit for dimensioning steel construction elements is the millimetre.
During the design work the spacing between columns and beams is determined by means a structural grid. The widespread use of computers today enables designers to abandon orthogonal grids and allows frames of almost any conceivable form to be created (fig. C 2.2).
In frame building systems, loads are transferred to the foundations via beams and columns. Bracing elements ensure the stability of the construction horizontally and vertically. The elements that make up the structural system can be rolled steel sections, hollow steel sections or composite elements. Horizontal bracing is provided by the floor slabs or horizontal girders, and the steel structure can be braced vertically by rigid corner joints, girders or solid wall plates (figs. C 2.3 and 2.4).
In a frame construction system all load-bearing elements are prefabricated and then transported to the construction site. Using the appropriate plant the building elements can be lifted directly from the transport vehicle to the point in the building where they are required. To ensure simple and efficient assembly and dis-

mantling, the choice of the correct connection technique is important.

Construction elements
The process for manufacturing semi-finished building elements out of steel combines the processes of manufacturing primary forms with hot- or cold-forming techniques. The primary shaping process is either one of ingot or continuous casting to achieve the primary form, which is

then refined by hot- or cold-rolling techniques to create various semi-finished elements. Semi-finished elements of cast iron and cast steel are manufactured in a single production step in which the molten raw material is cast into moulds (fig. C 2.6, p. 56).

Steel sections
Sectional steel elements are semi-finished elements used as columns and beams in steel construction.

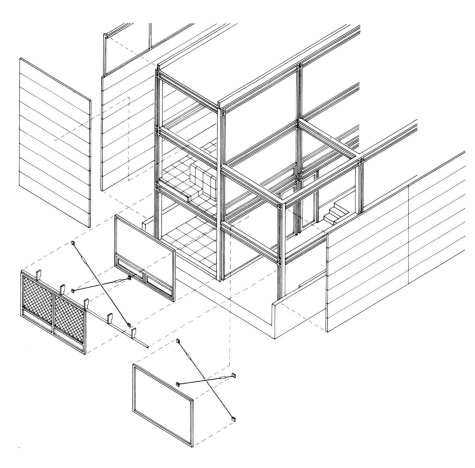

C 2.4

C 2.5

C 2.5 Chromed steel column, Tugendhat House, Brno (CZ)1930, Ludwig Mies van der Rohe
C 2.6 Production process: prefabricated and semi-finished steel building elements
    a Production process: semi-finished building elements
    b Production process: prefabricated building elements
C 2.7 Trusses
    a Heavy-weight truss, struts connected to the chord with two gusset plates
    b Light-weight truss, struts connected to the chord with one gusset plate
    c Truss made of steel sections
    d Tubular steel truss
C 2.8 Castellated beams
C 2.9 Types of sections
    a Angles and small sections
    b Wide flange sections
    c Standard sections
    d Parallel flange sections
    e Hollow sections
    f Round and square sections
C 2.10 Dimensions and weight of steel sections

Structural steel is manufactured in Germany in the qualities S 235 to S 355 (DIN EN 10 027) in addition to the high-strength steels StE 460 and StE 690. Steel bars, steel sections and hollow sections are used for steel frame structures; they are available in a variety of cross-sections and dimensions. For columns wide flange sections, rectangular hollow sections or round hollow sections are generally used, whereas for beams heavy rolled sections or combinations of various sections are chosen [3] (fig. C 2.9).

Standard sections INP and UNP
Standard sections are particularly suitable for welded connections due to their tapered flanges, they are less suitable for screwed connections.

Wide flange sections HEA, HEB, HEM
Wide flange sections can take greater loads and torsion forces due to their larger flange width; they can be used for both columns and beams.

Parallel flange sections IPE, UPE
Due to there duced flange width IPE sections are less suitable to take compression forces and are therefore mostly used as girders subject to bending.
UPE sections or channels, which are C-shaped in cross-section, are very suitable as edge beams for floor constructions. They can also be fixed in pairs to columns, creating a collar-type arrangement.

Hollow sections
Hollow sections can be square, rectangular or round in cross-section. They are usually used as columns or beams in framework and are ideal for central loads. We distinguish between cold-rolled hollow sections, which are lighter and more economical than hot-rolled sections; the latter offer greater resistance to buckling.

Round and square bars RND, VKT
Round and square bars are particularly suitable for taking tensile forces. Larger cross-sections can also be used for compression members in composite concrete columns.

semi-finished project neutral	mechanical refinement	coating	jointing	building element/group project specific
sections	drilling	galvanising	screwing	**wall elements** wall frames/elements sandwich elements
			pinning	
	sawing	plastic coating	clamping	**slab elements** slab/roof elements
tubes			rivetting	
	cutting	membrane coating		**frame elements** columns and beams sections, trusses, frames and castellated beams
			welding	
sheets	stamping	painting	adhesive fixing	

a

prototype (rough form)	hot processed	cold processed	product
	continuous hot-rolling		**sections, tubes, sheets** rough surface low dimensional precision
non-continuous block casting		continuous cold-rolling	**sections, tubes, sheets** smooth surface high dimensional precision
continuous extruding	continuous hot-rolling	continuous rolling	**sections, tubes, sheets** smooth surface medium dimensional precision
		non-continuous edging deep drawing	**formed sheets, sections** smooth surface medium dimensional precision
	non-continuous extruding		**sections, tubes** smooth surface high dimensional precision
continuous casting			**cast elements** cast steel, cast iron medium dimensional precision

b

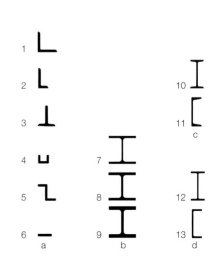

a   b   d

C 2.6

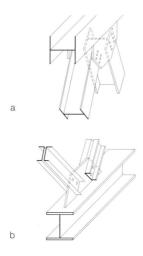

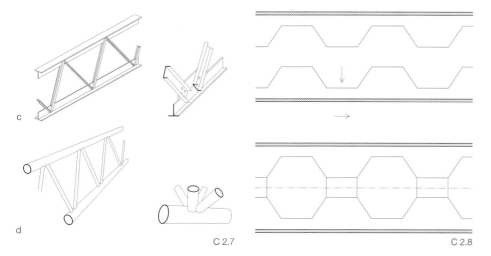

C 2.7   C 2.8

Angles and small sections
Angles and small sections are used for metal work, balustrades, window and door frames. They can take on load-bearing functions as tension members in trusses [4] (fig. C 2.10).

Steel sectional building elements
Prefabricated building elements are manufactured from project-neutral semi-finished units i.e. steel sections, by mechanical refinement, joining and coating. In steel construction they can be trusses, castellated beams or frames. The fabrication of the building elements is carried out by drilling, sawing, cutting or stamping the semi-finished elements prior to screwing, welding or piecing them together. Corrosion protection is provided by coatings of zinc, plastic or paint.

Trusses consist of top chord, bottom chord and diagonal connection struts. When under load, the struts are either entirely subject to compression or to tension forces. Because there are no bending moments to be considered, the

dimensioning of the truss can be optimised. Thus it is possible to span large distances with minimal use of material. The connections between top chord, bottom chord and intermediate members are hinged. For particularly heavy-weight trusses of steel sections, the chords and struts are each connected by means of two junction plates that are welded at right angles to the plane of the chord. The flanges of the struts can later be welded or screwed to the junction plates. Light-weight trusses require only one junction plate for the connection. For trusses of hollow steel sections connections are made by means of butt welded junctions. These types of beam allow services to be laid in the plane of the beams without any obstacles (fig. C 2.7).

Castellated beams
Castellated beams are manufactured from IPE, HEA or HEB sections. The web of a standard solid beam – with the relevant structural calculations – is separated by making two wave-like or one single straight cut, the two pieces thus created

are off-set from one another and welded together again. This increases the structural depth while retaining the same amount of material and the same weight. Castellated beams are particularly suitable for large spans and for the transfer of bending moments.

The openings made in the web as a result of this process, whose diameter should not exceed 70 % of the beam height, can also be used to run services through (fig. C 2.8).

Connection techniques and elements
The type of connection and the material required depends upon the use of the building element and its function within the building system. In steel construction one distinguishes between fixed and demountable connections.

		a	1 steel angle – round-edged, equal legs
14			2 steel angle – round-edged, unequal legs
15			3 T-section – round-edged, deep-webbed
			4 U-channel
			5 Z-section – standard
16			6 flat steel
		b	7 HEA – wide flange I-beam, light
			8 HEB – wide flange I-beam, standard
			9 HEM – wide flange I-beam, heavy
		c	10 IPN – standard flange I-beam
			11 UPN – standard channel
17		d	12 IPE – parallel flange I-beam
			13 UAP – parallel flange channel
		e	14 square hollow section
18			15 rectangular hollow section
			16 round hollow section
		f	17 RND – round bar
			18 VKT – square bar

C 2.9

description	smallest dimension (h x w)			largest dimension (h x w)		
wide flange beams						
HEA light	HEA 100	(96 × 100 mm)	16,7 kg/m	HEA 1000	(990 × 300 mm)	272,0 kg/m
HEB standard	HEB 100	(100 × 100 mm)	20,4 kg/m	HEB 1000	(1000 × 300 mm)	314,0 kg/m
HEM heavy	HEM 100	(120 × 106 mm)	41,8 kg/m	HEM 1000	(1008 × 302 mm)	349,0 kg/m
standard sections						
INP	INP 80	(80 × 42 mm)	5,9 kg/m	INP 550	(550 × 200 mm)	166,0 kg/m
UNP	UNP 65	(65 × 42 mm)	7,1 kg/m	UNP 400	(400 × 110 mm)	71,8 kg/m
parallel flange sections						
IPE	IPE 80	(80 × 46 mm)	6,0 kg/m	IPE 600	(600 × 220 mm)	122,0 kg/m
IPET	IPET 80	(40 × 46 mm)	3,0 kg/m	IPET 600	(300 × 220 mm)	61,2 kg/m
UPE	UPE 80	(80 × 50 mm)	37,9 kg/m	UPE 400	(400 × 115 mm)	72,2 kg/m
hollow sections						
cold/hot square	RRW 40 × 40	(40 × 40 mm)	3,4 kg/m	RRW 400 × 400	(400 × 400 mm)	191,0 kg/m
cold/hot rectangular	RRW 50 × 30	(50 × 30 mm)	3,6 kg/m	RRW 400 × 4200	(400 × 200 mm)	141,0 kg/m
cold/hot round	ROR 21,3	(Ø 21,3 mm)	0,9 kg/m	ROR 813	(Ø 813 mm)	159,0 kg/m
bars						
round	RND 10	(Ø 10 mm)	0,6 kg/m	RND 500	(Ø 500 mm)	1540,0 kg/m
square	VKT 10	(6 × 6 mm)	0,3 kg/m	RKT 200	(200 × 200 mm)	314,0 kg/m

C 2.10

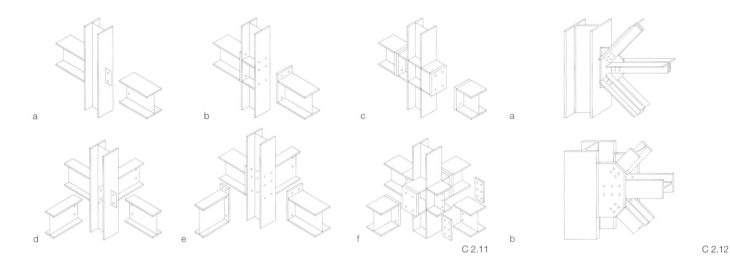

C 2.11

C 2.12

Fixed connections
Rivets

In spite of the high aesthetic quality of this method of making connections, rivet connections are almost exclusively used in the area of listed or protected buildings or for repair work to riveted historical constructions. This method is both labour intensive and uneconomical.

In the classic riveting method the white-hot glowing rivet is taken out of the riveting oven, descaled with a wire brush and placed in the rivet hole. The required pressure is provided by the rivet hammer, rivet gun or automatic rivet tool.

Welding

Steel building elements, for example the individual elements of a truss, can be connected by electric arc-welding or gas-welding. Welding techniques can be divided into hand welding or automatic welding. Building elements must be adjusted prior to welding.

Demountable connections
Bolts

Bolted connections are one of the most important demountable connections in the building industry; they allow building elements to be exchanged and the construction to be dismantled at a later date. They allow frame constructions to be erected in short periods of time. Bolts can take tension and shear stresses, and allow the structural connection of building elements, for example beam to column connections (fig. C 2.11).
When a frame structure remains exposed, the bolts determine the outward appearance of the junctions and must therefore be carefully considered during the design process (fig. C 2.13).

Bracing elements and systems
Frame corners
Rigid frame corners in steel construction can be either welded or screw-fixed. End plates are welded to the ends of beams and columns; depending on the type of construction the end plate is fixed to the

flange of either the column or the beam. In the area of load transmission the beams and columns are additionally strengthened in the flange plane with ribs. Screw-fixed frame corners follow the same principle as welded connections; these highly rigid screw connections take both bending moments and shearing forces (fig. C 2.14).

Diagonal connections
Frame structures that have jointed connections at the junctions between columns and beams can be braced with a system of diagonal members. The design of the junction is determined by the weight of these members.
Light-weight diagonal members are usually steel angles that are either welded or screwed to a junction plate, which is in turn fixed to the junction between column and beam. Heavier connection diagonal members for example T-sections, require two junction plates that are mounted parallel to each other at the junction between column and beam, at the edge of the flange. The flanges of the diagonal members are screwed or welded to the junction plates (fig. C 2.12) [5].

Shear walls
Shear walls of steel sheeting are used to transfer large horizontal loads; they act as infill elements that fill the bays between columns and beams. The panels are fixed to the sections by means of force-locked, welded or screwed connections along all edges. Where horizontal forces are minimal, steel frame structures can be braced just by masonry or concrete walls.
With prefabricated concrete panels, steel junction plates are concreted into the corners of the panels and anchored with steel rods or shear studs. The concrete wall is screwed to the steel structure and

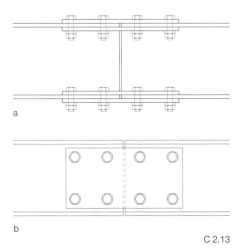

C 2.13

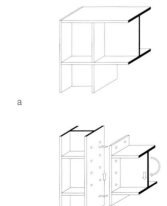

C 2.14

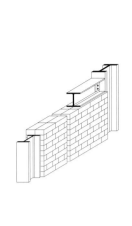
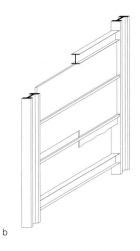

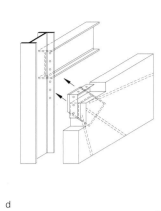

a   b   c   d

C 2.15

the joint between end plate and wall, necessary for assembly, is subsequently filled with mortar (fig. C 2.15).

Intermediate floor slabs

In steel frame structures the intermediate floor slabs are either prefabricated concrete slabs or profiled steel sheets that rest on solid web beams, castellated beams or trusses. The structural connections between the intermediate floor slab and the beam increase the load-bearing capacity of the floor construction and thus reduce deflection.

A particularly economical system for intermediate floors in steel frame construction is the so-called Slimfloorslab (fig. C 2.16). The specially designed beams carry the prefabricated hollow floor elements which means that the floor beams and slab lie in one plane. By filling the joints between the individual floor elements with concrete a composite structural element is created. The structural properties of this slab are equivalent to those of a conventional downstand beam floor slab with composite construction.

Cores

When the stiffening element of a steel frame is provided by a concrete core, the steel beams and floor slabs must be fixed to the walls of the core. There are three ways of doing this:

· Steel connection plates are concreted into the walls of the concrete core. The webs of the steel beams are subsequently screwed to these plates.
· A steel connection plate is set flush in the concrete wall and anchored. Connecting elements can then be welded to this connection plate.
· The concrete wall is cast with recesses in which steel bearing plates can be inserted and anchored to the concrete.

The steel beams are then set into the recesses and fixed to the wall by screwing the flange of the steel beam to the steel bearing plate (fig. C 2.17).

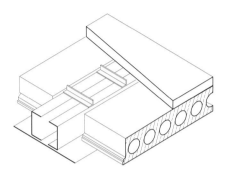

C 2.16

C 2.11   Bolted connections between columns and beams
      a Hinged connection with welded web plate
      b Rigid connection with welded stiffeners and projecting end plate
      c Rigid connection with welded stiffeners and flush end plate
      d Hinged three-dimensional connection
      e Rigid three-dimensional connection
      f Prefabricated rigid three-dimensional connection
C 2.12   Connection of lightweight and heavyweight diagonal bracing in frame structures
      a with a single gusset plate
      b with two gusset plates
C 2.13   Screwed connection of steel sections
      a Connection using steel plates fixed ton flange
      b Connection using steel plates fixed to web
C 2.14   Frame corner connections
      a Welded
      b Screwed
C 2.15   Shear walls
      a Masonry panels for low horizontal loads
      b Sheet metal walls braced to prevent buckling
      c Precast concrete panel
      d Precast concrete panel with gusset plate
C 2.16   Slender floor slab system (Slim-Floor-Slab)
C 2.17   Cores
      a Positioning of one bracing core lin a building
      b Positioning of two bracing cores in a building
      c Steel connecting element concreted into core
      d Steel plate set flush in core
      e Core wall cast with recess for to take steel beam connection

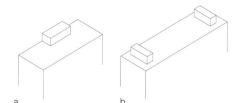

a   b

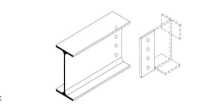

c

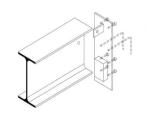

d

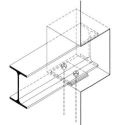

e

C 2.17

C 2.18 Frames with continuous beams
C 2.19 Frames with continuous columns
C 2.20 Non-directional frame
C 2.21 Dywidag Program System
      a Three-dimensional junction
      b Exploded isometric
C 2.22 Space frames
      a Isometric showing principles
      b Elevation
      c Elevation of node
      d Section through node

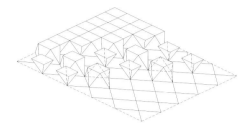

a

C 2.18

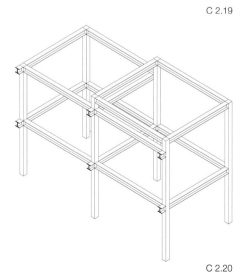

C 2.19

C 2.20

Construction principles

Frames with continuous beams
This structural system is formed by frames that are erected at clearly defined distances to one another.

The continuous beams, which rest on the columns, must be reinforced with additional ribs at the zones where loads are transferred to the columns. The frames are stable due to the rigid connections between beams and columns. To transfer of horizontal forces either diagonal members or the vertical panels brace the structure in the longitudinal direction (fig. C 2.18).

Frames with continuous columns
These frames are positioned according to the same principles as frames with continuous beams. Because the beams are fixed between the columns, they act as simple beams and must therefore have a greater structural depth. The structural depth of the intermediate floor or roof construction can be reduced by placing the floor slab construction in the same plane as the beams (fig. C 2.19).

Non-directional frames
This form of structural system relies on continuous columns that are positioned at the intersection points of a regular square grid. The columns are rolled hollow sections that offer the beams (HEA sections) the same way of making connections on all sides. In order to distribute the loads evenly, the direction of span in the floor elements alternates from field to field. Beams and floor elements are located in the same plane [6] (fig. C 2.20).

▶ DYWIDAG Program System
  (Dyckerhoff & Widmann AG)
In this system the elements are put together to form open frame structures; various possible combinations offer great freedom of design and different methods of fit-out and finishing. The infill facade elements consist of prefabricated timber-framed elements or sandwich panels. Precast concrete panels are inserted into the construction as intermediate floor elements. The construction grid is based on the dimensions $2.75 \times 5.50 \times 2.75$ m (w × d × h) (fig. C 2.21).
- area of application:
  walls, floors, roofs
- used in:
  single-family houses and apartment buildings

a

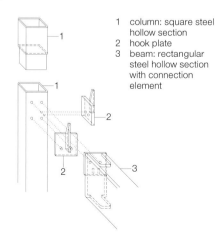

1 column: square steel hollow section
2 hook plate
3 beam: rectangular steel hollow section with connection element

b

C 2.21

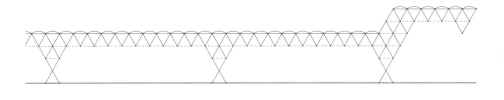

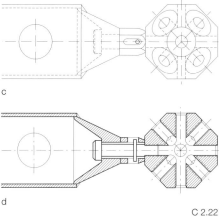

b

c

d

C 2.22

Space frames

Space frames are constructed of two basic elements: hollow tubes and spherical nodes, with up to 18 connection options, are connected to form a three-dimensional structural system. The tubes are of different lengths and different diameters with conical end pieces that take the form of threaded bolts allowing them to be screwed together with the threaded openings in the nodes. The space-frame structure consists of top and bottom chord planes that are connected by a three dimensional diagonal framing; the assembly of these elements is relatively simple.

Max Mengeringhausen invented the MERO space frame node in 1942; a node element for screw connections that is still used for space frame constructions today. The high load-bearing capacity combined with minimal weight allows wide-span roof or space frame structures to be constructed, without the need for intermediate columns. This system offers architects and planners a maximum of freedom when designing and planning (fig. C 2.22).

Timber frame systems

Timber frame building systems are a further development of traditional frame constructions. Analogous to steel frames, timber frames are made up of columns and beams. Stiffening is provided by diagonal tension or compression members, wall panels connected to the frame or solid cores extending the full height of the buildng. The difference between timber frame structures and other timber building systems is that the load-bearing structure is independent of the elements that enclose space.
The elements used for modern timber

frame building methods are usually solid timber or high-quality glued laminated timber members, generally termed structural timber. This timber is divided into three different classes according to its load-bearing capacity, natural defects and the width of annual growth rings. These classifications are defined in industrial standards, for Germany standard no. DIN 4074. The planner decides which quality of timber should be used for a construction. The cross-section of the timber members used depends upon the load-bearing performance and the fire protection regulations. The cross-sectional dimensions can be optimised according to the loads and desired spans.
Hand crafted timber connections are being increasingly replaced by engineering methods of making connections. Connections are usually made with gusset and let-in plates or steel dowel fixings. Timber frame systems are suitable for a large variety of building types; from large halls to low-rise single-storey buildings.
There are very many construction methods available, they differ in the way the columns and beams are made as well as in the kind of connections used.

Construction materials and elements
Solid timber
According to DIN 1052-1 solid timber is both hardwood and softwood, sawn in the sawmill from a single log and shaped to scantlings, planks, boards and battens. Regular conifers are debarked to produce round structural timber poles. in Germany timber members of solid wood are graded into quality classes; S 7, S 10 and S 13, for the purposes of structural dimensioning. These classes are the equivalent of the previous classes

I, II and III. Solid timber of class S 10 is termed solid structural timber.
Solid timber members can be employed for all methods of timber construction, although changes in dimensions due to swelling and shrinking of the material must be taken into account.

Glued laminated timber (gluelam)
According to DIN 1052-1/A1 glued laminated timber consists of at least three layers of boarding in which the fibres are parallel that laminated together under pressure to produce stable building elements. Glued laminated timber members – are stronger than solid timber members, due to the fact that only timber entirely free from defects, that is without knotholes or shrinkage cracks – is used. Glued laminated timber members can span greater distances than solid timber members of the same cross-sectional size.

Composite wood-based beams
These beams consist of upper chord, lower chord and web. Their use is limited to building elements subject to under bending forces, where the compression and tension forces are carried by the upper and lower chords. Although these composite beams have greater structural depth, they have better strength to weight ratios.
Manufacturers offer composite beams made of various timbers and different constructions for building systems [7]. Two examples of web beams are described below, which are made up of differen wood-based materials, are described here:

61

C 2.23 Column-beam connection; vertical plate and
annular ringed shank nails
a Section secondary beam
b Section primary beam
C 2.24 Agepan structural beam system
a Agepan beams with solid timber flanges
and timber fibreboard webs
b Floor construction with Agepan beams
and service runs
C 2.25 TJI-beams
a TJI-beam; semi-finished element for
further processing
b Making a frame structure of TJI-beams

1 column
2 secondary beam
3 primary beam
4 plate with annular ringed shank nails

a

b

C 2.23

▶ AGEPAN structural beam system
(Glunz AG)

The AGEPAN beam is a combination of
upper and lower chords made of solid
timber with a fibreboard web 8 mm thick.
The depth of the beam varies between
160 and 500 mm.

When the web is of made of OSB it is
12 mm thick, or for beams subject to
heavy loads 15 mm. Beams with 12 mm
thick webs have depths of 200 to
400 mm, and beams with 15 mm thick
webs have depths of 240 and 320 mm
(fig. C 2.24).

• application:
walls, slabs, roofs
• used in:
single-family houses and apartment
buildings, office and administration
buildings, schools and kindergartens

▶ TJI beams
(Trus Joist sprl)

TJI beams are I-beams with chords of
veneered laminated timber and an OSB
web. The structural depths are between
200 and 600 mm. Distances of up to 20 m
can be spanned with this type of beam.
Openings for service runs can be made
in the web (fig. C 2.25).

• application:
walls, slabs, roofs
• used in:
single-family houses and apartment
buildings, industrial and administration
buildings, schools and kindergartens

Connection techniques and elements

Traditional timber connections such as
shiplap or dowel joints are rarely used in
system building. These connections
demand the use of highly developed

manual skills by experienced carpenters,
the labour input is considerable and for
serial production uneconomical. Modern
joining and turning machines, however,
enable the computer operated production
of these traditional connection techniques.
Engineered elements of steel or cast iron
are the most widely used means of
making connections as they are simple
and efficient to manufacture and their
strengths can be easily calculated.
Timber members are butt-jointed and
fixed using steel plates, bolts or screws,
or dowels (fig. C 2.23). In most cases the
steel angles or brackets used in fitting are
left exposed.

Where wood-based panels sit in a frame,
nail and screw connections are usually
sufficient.

To connect rod-shaped elements special
connecting pieces are needed, which
can be individually manufactured to meet
specific structural and design requirements.

Another method of connecting timber
elements is the use of plywood plates.
They are often used in pairs, for example
at the corner connections of columns and
beams. They are fixed to the sides of the
building elements and connected with
dowels. When column/beam intersections are particularly challenging, either
structurally or creatively, they can be
fixed by means of special steel junction
plates.

Columns are connected to foundations by
way of plates or angles. To avoid splash-
ing water damaging columns, they are
mounted on support bases to ensure an
intermediate space between them and
the floor level of the building.

Joints must be elastic due to the possible
shrinkage of building elements at the connection points between columns and wall
elements.

a

b

C 2.24

a

C 2.25

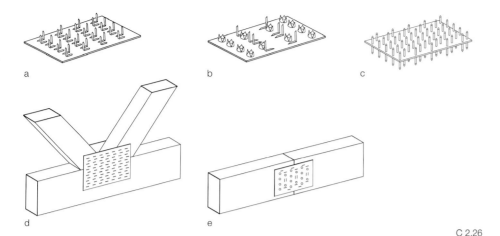

a b c

d e

C 2.26 Nail plates
       a Gang nail
       b Twinaplatte
       c Double nail plate, with multiple cross-
          sections
       d Application of a gang nail
       e Application of a Twinaplatte
C 2.27 Angle connections
C 2.28 Column support bases
C 2.29 Janebo "hook plate": system for connecting
       four beams to a column

C 2.26

Steel dowels
Solid steel dowels of circular in cross-section, are connecting elements that are driven under pressure into pre-drilled holes. They are manufactured in lengths from 60 to 160 mm and with possible diameters of 8 to 16 mm.

Bolts
Bolts are connection pieces made from steel rods with head, thread and a matching nut counterpart. Similar to dowels, bolts penetrate the timber members to be connected at right angle to their length. Bolts are manufactured in lengths from 16 to 200 mm and usually have thread diameter of M8 to M24 [8].

Nail plates
Nail plates are either steel plates with nails welded vertically to them, or plates in which teeth punched out of the plate are bent at right angles on one or both sides of the plate (fig. C 2.26).

Angle connections
Anglebrackets made of perforated steel sheets are used for the corner connections of timber frame elements. To connect beams or joists in one plane angle brackets are made in the form of joist hangers. These can be used for timber members of widths between 38 and 200 mm (fig. C 2.27).

Column feets
Column feets are used to connect columns to foundations or slabs. They consist of a base plate, a steel tube and a connecting element. This can either be bent, U-shaped flat-steel, a steel angle or a threaded screw. The columns are fixed to the foot with either wood screws or steel dowels [9] (fig. C 2.28).

▶ Janebo hookplate/Bulldog timber connector/Bozett steel SK (SIMPSON STRONG-TIE GmbH)
The most widely employed product from this manufacturer is the Janebo "hook plate" used to connect columns to joists or beams. The hook plate consists of a number of parts that are each inserted centrally into the building elements to be connected. When connected the hook plate parts in the column lock with those in the beam. All that remains visible externally are the steel dowels that fix the hook plate to the timber members. This system allows four-way connections to be made between columns and beams in one plane (fig. C 2.29). Other products offered by this company are the Bulldog timber connector, the Bozett steel angle connector and the Jane-TU drop-in beam.

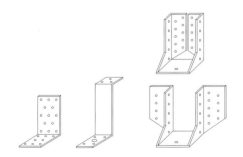

C 2.27

C 2.28

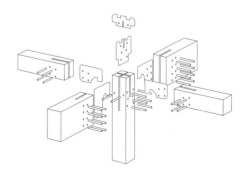

C 2.29

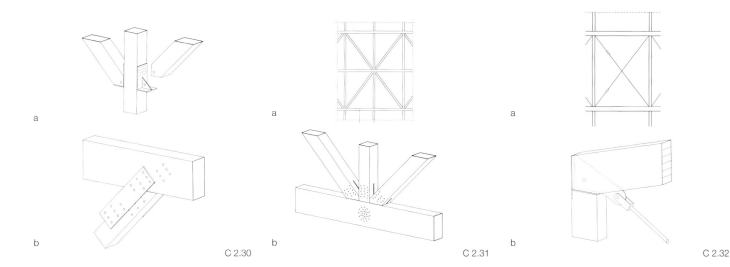

a

b

C 2.30

a

b

C 2.31

a

b

C 2.32

▶ Merk MKD Multi-claw dowel
(Merk Holzbau GmbH & Co)
The Merk multi-claw dowel consists of
a steel base plate with 50-mm-long
nails welded to it. The dimensions of
the base plate, which is 10 mm thick,
depend on the timber members to be
connected. These claw dowels are
mostly used for timber frame construction
(fig. C 2.33).

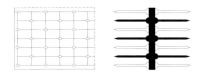

C 2.33

▶ MiTek connector plate
(MiTek Industries GmbH)
MiTek nail plates are manufactured of
hot-dip galvanised steel and have nails
punched out on one side. Available as
either plates or angles, they are pressed
into the sides of the butt-jointed timber
members (fig. C 2.34).

Bracing elements and systems
Panels
Timber frames can be stiffened and stabilised with timber or metal panels, as well
as walls of concrete or masonry that act
structurally as panels. Due to their biaxial
span and the ease of fixing OSB, MDF or
plywood panels are particularly suitable
required for planking and bracing timber-
frame buildings. The structural connections to the frame structure are achieved
with screw and nail fixings.

Bracing struts
Struts are diagonally attached boards or
squared members. They brace the corners of the frame and can simultaneously
provide stiffening against buckling for the
columns. Scantlings are fixed to the construction by means of gussets, steel
angles inserted in slits, steel hangers or
connected to the construction by means
of a notch Boards can be screwed or
nailed to both sides of the frame corners
(fig. C 2.30).

Diagonal bracing elements
Timber frame structures can be braced,
both horizontally and vertically, by diagonally placed struts in the form of squared
members or boards. They are connected
to opposite corners of the frame by notch-
ing or the use of connecting elements,
such as steel plates placed in incisions,
or steel hangers. Timber struts also provide the sub-structure for wall construction. The boards are connected by nails
or screw-fixings (fig. C 2.31).
In both rafter and timber post construction systems, longitudinal bracing in the
form of steel bands or timber battens is
nailed to the structure.

Cross-bracing
Steel cables, steel rods or steel flats that
cross each other can act as bracing
members for a timber frame – however,
they can only take tension forces.
To connect the cross-bracing with the
timber elements in the corners of the
frame, steel plates inserted in slits or steel
gussets are required. Steel cable or rod
cross-bracing should be additionally sta-

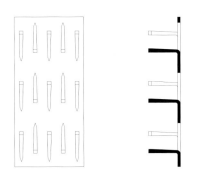

C 2.30 Bracing struts
  a Column with inset angle
  b Beam with plate
C 2.31 Diagonal bracing elements
  a Diagonal bracing for framework
  b Diagonal bracing in framework with inset
    steel plates and nailed connections
C 2.32 Cross-bracing
  a Positioning of turnbuckles in steel tension
    rods for cross-bracing steel structures
  b Connection of cross-bracing at frame cor-
    ner using fabricated steel angle
C 2.33 Merk MKD multi-claw-dowel: arrangement
  of the claws (nails) on the steel plate
C 2.34 Elevation and section of a MiTek plate

C 2.35 Construction principles (1 column, 2 beam,
  3 secondary beam): junction points for
  a Column and rail
  b Beam on column
  c Column with double beams
  d Double columns with beam
C 2.36 Secondary/main beam connection with preformed steel angles and steel dowels
C 2.37 Beam on column
  Connection of primary beam to column, connection of secondary beam to primary beam
  with preformed steel angles and steel dowels
C 2.38 Timber space frame, section through node
C 2.39 Timber space frame roof structure

C 2.34

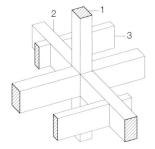
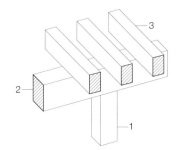
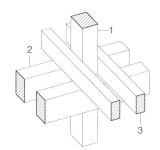
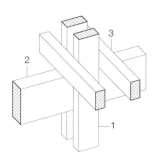

a   b   c   d

C 2.35

bilised by turnbuckles or clamping sleeves [10] (fig. C 2.32).

Construction principles
Timber frame constructions differ according to the layout and form of the columns and beams.

Post and beam
In these frame structures the columns are the entire height of the building, the beams can be fixed to all sides of the columns and are thus simple beams (fig. C 2.35a). Primary and secondary beams lie in one plane. Steel plates, dowel connection systems or hook plates that are manufactured in series for the construction of junctions are all suitable fixing systems (fig. C 2.36).

Beam on column
This construction consists of storey-high columns supporting primary beams, in the form of either simple or continuous beams. The secondary beams for the substructure of the floor slabs can be designed as planks or beams (fig. C 2.35b). At the bearing points the beam is

loaded perpendicular to the fibre direction and the column parallel to the fibre direction. If the bearing pressure on the bearing point exceeds 2.0 N/mm^2 it must be taken by additionally incorporated steel elements; such as angles or beam hangers (fig. C 2.37).

Column and double beam – double column and beam
In this case the beam consists of two members that are fixed to either side of the column. The beams are connected to the column with bolts, dowels or steel profiles. The secondary beams can, analogous to the column-beam system, either be made as planks or beams. The twin ends of the beams, that are generally externally visible which help determine the appearance of the facade are characteristic of this method of construction (fig. C 2.35c). The system can also be designed the other way around; that is, in the form of double columns and single beams. In this case a solid timber filling piece is required between the two columns as support for the primary beam [11] (fig. C 2.35d).

MERO timber space frame
Timber space frames have developed from their steel counterparts, and are a composite construction of rod-like glued laminated timber members (see p. 61) and spherical steel nodes with 18 possible connections. Steel tubes are set into the timber rods and are connected to the nodes by means of dowels to create a structural frame. Thanks to the screw connections, this type of construction can be easily dismantled (figs. C 2.38 and C 2.39) [12].

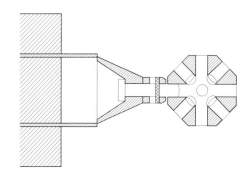

C 2.38

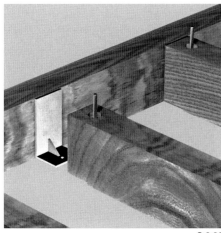

C 2.36

C 2.37

C 2.39

65

C 2.40   Induo timber frame system
         a Beam to column connection
         b Exploded isometry of a junction
C 2.41   HD-House timber frame system
         a Beam to column connection
         b Isometry, Beam to beam connection
C 2.42   Section through facade of a modern frame
         construction

C 2.43   Frame connection
         1 column
         2 beam
C 2.44   Platform construction
C 2.45   Balloon-frame construction
C 2.46   FrameWorks construction system
         a Vertical section: slab to wall connection
         b Assembly of a timber framed building

▶ Induo
(induo-Systemholztechnik)
Induo is an industrially prefabricated frame construction system of columns and beams. The connection elements are cast iron anchors with internal threads, which are set lengthwise in the beam and screwed together with a steel element set into the column. To stiffening the frame cross-bracing can be made with steel rods or steel cables (fig. C 2.40). This system is independent of module or grid restrictions [13].
· application:
  walls, slabs, roofs
· used in:
  single-family houses and apartment buildings, industrial and administration buildings, extra storeys, conservatories, balconies, space frames, single-storey sheds

▶ HD-House
(Hansen & Detlefsen GmbH)
The HD house is a frame system made up of glued laminated timber members which is fully prefabricated including all connecting elements. Timber joist floors using solid or glued laminated timber members or solid and hollow-box units can be used for the intermediate floors (fig. C 2.41).
The wall posts, floor beams and rafters are placed at standard 1.25 m centres, which allows timber-based panels to be used without any need for cutting. The simplicity of this system means that it can be erected by self-builders [14].
· application:
  walls, slabs, roofs
· used in:
  single-family houses and apartment buildings

Timber frame construction
The traditional half-timber construction included some of the first attempts of pre-fabrication – the individual elements which were fabricated in the carpentry workshop and dimensionally coordinated with each other. The structure of this type of construction consists of base plates, posts, rails, purlins and diagonal bracing struts, all of which are connected to each other by tenons, mortises and half-lap jointing. The classic type of half-timber construction where the construction elements are visible in the facade is seldom seen nowadays. Modern frame constructions are usually externally clad with timber-based panels, internally with plasterboard panels and the cavity between filled with insulation material. In these structures the loads are still transferred according to traditional principles (fig. C 2.42).

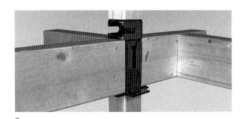

a

a

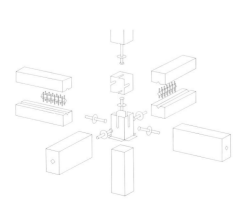

b

C 2.40

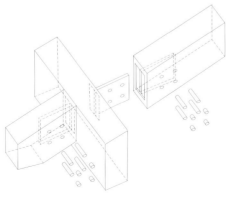

b

C 2.41

5
4

3   7

2   6

1 bottom plate
2 rail
3 lining
4 battens, insulation
5 frame wall, with in-
   fill (structural)
6 beams (floor
   structure)
7 structural sheating

1

C 2.42

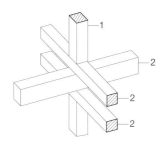

C 2.43

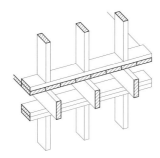

C 2.44

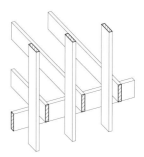

C 2.45

The sill plate forms the base of the system and is the connecting element between floor and wall. It rests on a concrete or masonry base and takes the compression loads from by the posts or studs, at right angles to the direction of the fibres. The studs in a timber frame-wall transfer the vertical loads from the floor and roof structures and must resist both buckling and bending forces. The centres at which the studs are placed depends on the placing of windows and doors. The horizontal rails function as sub-structure for wall cladding and can also act as lintel and sill elements for windows and doors. The top plates form the top edge of the wall; they provide the support the ceiling joists or beams and transfer their loads to the studs. The frame is braced by diagonal struts; they are always placed in pairs running in opposite directions to each other, and transfer the horizontal loads from the posts and sill plate (fig. C 2.43).

All loads are transferred via direct contact between the timber members. The members are connected by means of engineered fixing elements such as hook plates or angle sections. They are simple to use and the dimensions required can be easily calculated.

In timber frame construction very many of the elements are horizontal e.g. rails, top and sill plates, therefore when designing the dimensions after shrinkage must be taken into account.

Timber stud construction
This form of construction was developed in America in the mid 19th century, as a response to the increased need for housing that accompanied industrialisation. The new possibility to mass produce

nails helped establish this type of construction. A large proportion of the housing built in America today still utilises this system.

The timber stud frame is a frame made of studs (uprights) connected with nails that can be quickly erected. The studs provide the structure of both the floors and walls. These structures consist of standardised dimensional studs positioned close to one another, that are then braced with cladding of horizontal boards (siding) or wood-based panels. The timber members can be directly nailed to one another without the need for additional fixing elements. Timber stud frame constructions are subdivided into platform and balloon frame constructions.

In platform frames, the structure of the floor rests on top of storey-high studs (fig. C 2.44). The building is erected storey by storey; that is, the walls of the next storey are erected on top of the floor structure of the storey below.

The first timber stud structures in Europe were built at the beginning of the 20th century, influenced by platform construction techniques. The further development of the platform frame led to frame constructions which, in terms of the construction principles involved, should be considered as timber panel construction (see system example p. 117).

In balloon frame construction the vertical timber members of the external walls continue through several storeys. The intermediate floors are either directly fixed to the walls by means of attached brackets, or the floor joists or beams rest on transverse members connected at the level of each story to the vertical members (fig. C 2.45).

▶ FrameWorks building system
(Trus Joist sprl)
The FrameWorks building system is based on the balloon frame. In this system beams and columns are made from Paralam (laminated veneer strips), beams and edge beams of TimberStrand (laminated strand lumber) and TJI web beams (see p. 62). The flanges of the TJI beams are made of veneered plywood and the webs of OSB. They can be used as columns in timber frame construction, and as floor joists and roof beams (fig. C 2.46). This system is not restricted to a grid. [15]
• application:
  walls, floors, roofs
• used in:
  single-family houses and apartment buildings, industrial and administration buildings, schools and kindergartens

a

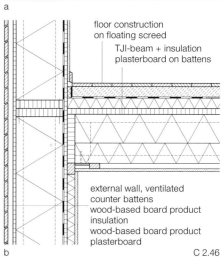

floor construction
on floating screed
TJI-beam + insulation
plasterboard on battens

external wall, ventilated
counter battens
wood-based board product
insulation
wood-based board product
plasterboard

b

C 2.46

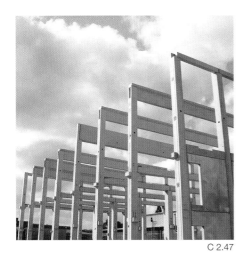

C 2.47

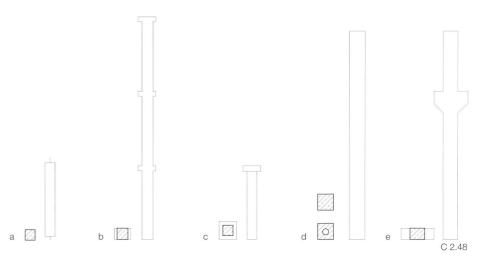

a   b   c   d   e

C 2.48

Concrete frame systems

Frames manufactured of prefabricated reinforced concrete elements are, due to their greater dead loads, only suitable for buildings with a limited numbers of storeys. The construction elements used are columns, beams, walls and intermediate floor slabs. In these systems the loads are transferred through the columns, beams and floor slabs. The columns transfer the vertical loads from the beams, floor slabs and roof to the foundations. Vertical bracing is provided by the walls, cores, or fixed-end columns (fig. C 2.47).

Construction elements
Columns
Prefabricated reinforced concrete columns can be produced in a great variety of cross-sections. For example, in single-storey shed structures with a height of up to 10 m columns with a rectangular cross-section are used. To take larger loads in higher sheds, columns and beams with a rigid connection can act as a a portal frame or the column can be constructed like an I-beam (fig. C 2.48). columns with a circular cross-section are also pro-

duced, often for architechtural reasons. Columns with a square cross-section are preferrable for multi-storey buildings because, compared to columns with a rectangular cross-section they have the same buckling resistance about both axes.

The prefabricated columns can either be erected on site in individual pocket foundations or rigidly fixed to the foundation in the factory and subsequently transported to site as a complete unit (fig. C 2.53). If the column is fixed to the foundation with a hinged connection, it acts structurally as a pinned-end column; in this case the bracing to the building must be provided by vertical cores or wall plates.

Corbels are the most widely used method of providing bearings for beams and floor slabs; they are usually formed on both sides of the columns. Columns with corbels on three or even four sides are extremely expensive to construct and are, therefore, only manufactured in exceptional situations.

In order to compensate for deformation of elements due to bending moments and to transfer the loads as designed, make-up layers, for example elastomers, are often

inserted between the corbels and the beam or floor slab that rests upon them. In order to ensure a sufficient bearing area, the corbels should be at least 20 cm long. The depth of the corbels is determined by the structural requirements.

Beams
Reinforced concrete beams are constructed as T-sections, I-beams and rectangular or angle sections (fig. C 2.49). For reasons to do with formwork, such beams usually have a slightly trapezoidal cross-section (fig. C 2.50). Beams serve as supporting elements for floor and roof elements. If it is necessary for the floor slabs and beams to lie in the same plane, the beams are produced with a continuous nib on either side at the bottom of the beam. These nibs should be at least 20 × 20 cm so as to take the loads applied by the slabs and to provide sufficient bearing depth (fig. C 2.51).

The most economical solutions for short-span constructions with beams at centres of about 4 m are beams with a rectangular cross-section and solid concrete slabs, as here the relationship between

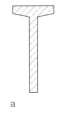
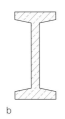

a   b   c

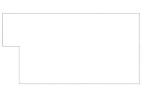

a

a   b

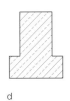
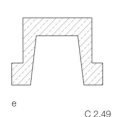

d   e

C 2.49

b

C 2.50

c   d

C 2.51

68

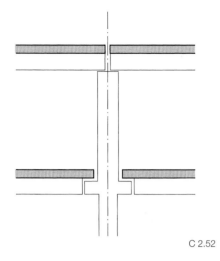

C 2.52

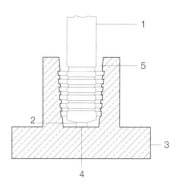

C 2.53

the amount of concrete used and the structural depth is optimised. With this system, beams and slabs form one structural entity, allowing greater loads to be carried. For longer spans, beams with I-section and slabs with hollow or double-T-sections are the most appropriate. Openings can be made in the webs of such beams to accommodate service runs.

In order to limit the depth of the floor construction, the webs of double-T-slabs are cut back in the plane of the bearing corbel (fig. C 2.52).

Connection techniques

In concrete frame construction junctions must be designed for the connections of columns and beams, or beams and floor slabs. Not only must structural and architectural considerations be taken into account, but also the planning of service runs.

The connections between columns and beams can be either hinged or rigid. With hinged connections, the column is restrained in order to brace the structure. The beam rests either directly on the column or on corbels formed on the sides

of the column. In order that the corbel and the beam are in the same plane, it may be necessary to notch out the beam at the bearing point (figs. C 2.54–C 2.56). Rigid connections between columns and beams are analogous to the connection techniques used in steel frame constructions. Bolted connections are particularly appropriate for simple and rapid erection of concrete frame structures. The columns are cast with integral threaded bars and the beams cast with steel hangers, the bolts and hanger are then bolted together on site and secured with nuts (fig. C 2.57, p. 70). After connection the joint is completed with low-shrinkage, high-strength grout.

Bolted connections of this type are also suitable for column-foundation junctions and structural splices between two butt-jointed beams. Such bolted connections allow the transfer of both shear forces and bending moments in concrete frame construction.

Connections between floor slabs and walls are divided into internal and external wall connections. In the case of the external wall, usually a triple-layer sandwich panel, the floor slab rests on the

C 2.47 Structure of a concrete frame construction
C 2.48 Prefabricated concrete columns
    a Hinged column
    b Column extending through several
      storeys, with corbels
    c Column with corbel on all sides
    d Square section or hollow section
      column
    e Column with beam corbels
C 2.49 Beam cross-section
    a T-beam
    b I beam
    c Rectangular section beam
    d T-beam with corbel
    e Inverted trough beam
C 2.50 Reinforced concrete beam, in section and
    elevation
    a Trapezoidal beam
    b T-beam with trapezoidal web
C 2.51 Beam sections
    a Rectangular beam
    b Beam with nibs on both sides
    c Beam with nibs on one side
    d Isometric view of double T-slab supported
      on continious beam nib
C 2.52 Beam-column junctions, multi-storey
    columns
C 2.53 Precast reinforced concrete column in
    a pocket: (1) precast reinforced concrete
    column (2) with pin alignment plate (3) in a
    pocket base (4) with hole alignment plate (5)
    and final grout fill
C 2.54 Connection of beam with bearing nib to col-
    umn with corbel
    a without notching
    b with notching
C 2.55 Connection of rectangular beam to column
    with bearing corbel
    a without notching
    b with notching
C 2.56 Connection of T-section beam to column

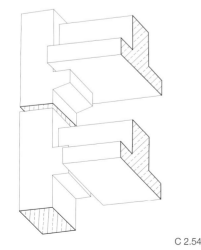

C 2.54

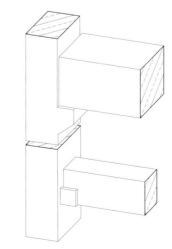

C 2.55

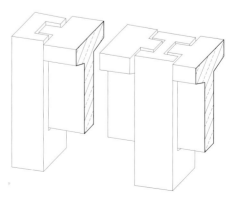

C 2.56

C 2.57 Screwed connections in reinforced concrete
frame construction
a, b column-beam connection
c column-foundation connection
d beam splice
C 2.58 Concrete frame constructions
a with continuous columns
b with continuous beams
C 2.59 Bracing reinforced concrete frame
constructions
a with plates
b with core

internal loadbearing leaf of the panel.
The joint between the slab and the wall
panel is filled with grout. With internal
partitions, the floor slabs generally meet
as butt joints above the storey-high internal walls.

Bracing elements and systems
Columns
Due to the high bending loads columns
provide suitable bracing only for single-
or two-storey buildings. They are generally one storey high and are rigidly
restrained at the foundations.

Walls
Concrete wall plates are the bracing elements most commonly used to stabilise a
reinforced concrete construction against
displacement and torsion. At least three
plates must be employed, and located in
such a way that their axes intersect at two
points.

Floor plates
Floor slabs transfer imposed loads and
horizontal wind loads to the columns,
walls and cores. Because shrinkage and
variations in temperature can lead to
stresses in the building elements, expansion joints are incorporated into the slabs
to counteract cracking. These expansion
joints divide the slabs into independent
units, each of which must be individually
and sufficiently braced.

Cores
Torsion-resistant cores made of concrete
walls commonly provide bracing for reinforced concrete frame structures. It is
advantageous when the core is centrally
located or, where there are several cores,
that the cores be so located that the end
points of the cantilevered beams are equidistant from the core [16] (fig. C 2.59).

Construction principles
The various principles of concrete frame
construction can be subdivided according to the column and beam types, i.e.
whether the columns or the beams are
continuous. The technology of the construction process and transport restrictions mean, however, that the length of
both types of elements is limited.
Where the columns are continuous, in
buildings with a height of more than five
storeys they must have joints in the vertical direction. In order to guarantee structural connections, the columns should be
designed with lapped joints, similar to
timber construction. With this system the
beams are designed as simply supported
beams with hinged connections to the
column corbels. In order to reduce the
depth of the floor construction, if the
loads are not excessive the beams can
be notched at the level of the corbels at
the bearing point.

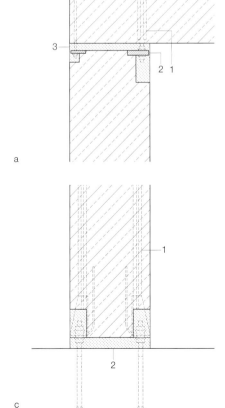

a

c

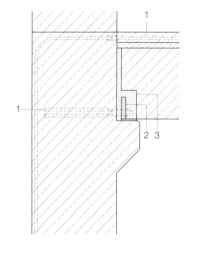

b

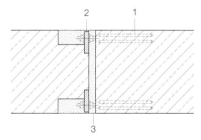

d

1 anchor bolt
2 steel connector
3 grout

C 2.57

Where the beams are continuous, they rest on top of storey-high columns; this is repeated storey by storey for high-rise buildings. The structural depth of the continuous beam is determined by the applied loads, the span between the columns as well as the number of supports. Continuous beams can be extended to greater lengths by rigid splices located either directly above the supports, i.e. the columns, or at the centre of the span.

Notes:
[1] Neumann, Dietrich et al.: Frick/Knöll. Baukon-
     struktionslehre 1. 133rd ed., Stuttgart 2002,
     p. 223 ff.
[2] Stahlbau Zentrum Schweiz: Steeldoc 01/06
     Bauen in Stahl. Konstruktives Entwerfen. Grund-
     lagen und Praxis. Zurich 2006, p. 12 ff.
[3] ibid. [1], p. 236
[4] ibid. [2], p. 12 ff.
[5] Stahl-Informations-Zentrum: Merkblatt 115.
     Stahlgeschoßssauten Grundlagen für Entwurf
     und Konstruktion. Dusseldorf 1989, p. 12 ff.
[6] ibid. [2], p. 27 ff.
[7] Hugues, Theodor et al.: Detail Practice.
     Timber construction. Munich 2002, p. 34 ff.
[8] ibid. [7], p. 71
[9] ibid. [7], p. 73 ff.
[10] Natterer, Julius et al.: Holzbau Atlas Zwei.
     Dusseldorf 1991, p. 125 ff.
[11] Kolb, Josef: Holzbau mit System. Basle 2007,
     p. 94 ff.
[12] Landsberg, Heike et al.: Holzsysteme für den
     Hochbau. Grundlagen, Systeme. Beispiele.
     Stuttgart/Berlin/Cologne 1999, p. 104
[13] Cheret, Peter et al.: Informationsdienst Holz.
     Holzbausysteme. Holzbauhandbuch Reihe 1,
     Teil 1, Folge 4. Dusseldorf/Bonn 2000, p. 20
[14] ibid. [12], p. 110
[15] ibid. [13], p. 18 ff.
[16] Fachvereinigung Deutscher Betonfertigteilbau
     e.V.: Wissensdatenbank. Horizontale Lastab-
     tragung

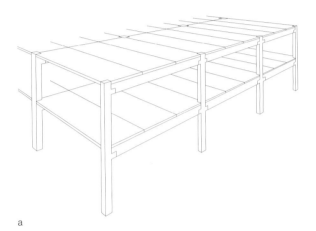

a

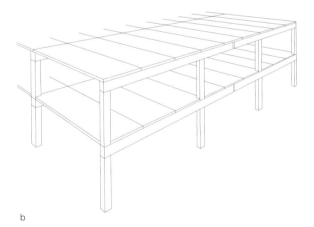

b

C 2.58

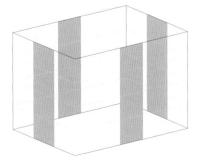

a

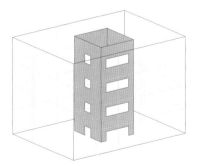

b

C 2.59

71

Temporary House in Paris

This house – a prototype which was displayed at an exhibition at the Parc de la Vilette in Paris – is the result of a competition that looked for modern forms of living. With the support of France's Ministry of Culture and a number of sponsors from the business sector, the "Maison en Bois" (wood house) and the "Maison en Métal" (metal house) were constructed for the duration of the exhibition.

The steel house, at a cost of 1600 Euros per square metre, has yet to be constructed at another location as a permanent residence.

This "metal house" is innovative, not only in regard to its internal organisation, but also in terms of its construction: the load-bearing structure consists of light-gauge steel sections, partially prefabricated as elements under factory conditions, that can be erected or dismantled quickly and easily. On the upper level the steel structure is enveloped in a severe, perfectly smooth, closed metal facade, in marked contrast to the ground floor where glass and highly polished stainless-steel surfaces dominate. At ground floor level the house opens out to the garden, which is bordered by a kind of steel trellis. The planted trellis ensures privacy, yet simultaneously allows dappled sunlight to penetrate through the vegetation deep into the internal spaces.

The organisation of the upper level is an inversion of the ground floor: the rooms are oriented inward, to an internal roof garden, which is surrounded by protecting walls. The roof garden is dominated by artificial grass mounds that cover multiple layers of rigid polystyrene insulation panels. The children's bedroom is on the upper floor, whereas the parents' bedroom adjoins the living room on the ground floor. The character of this living area is shaped by photo wallpaper with a woodland motif and generously sized sliding glass doors, which allow the internal spaces to flow into the garden and the internal courtyard, allowing architecture and landscape to merge.

project team • building details

architects:	Hamonic + Masson, Paris Gaëlle Hamonic, Jean-Christophe Masson
with:	Julien Gouiric
landscape architects:	Daphné Mandel-Buvard + Claire Gilot, Paris
function:	single-family house
construction:	steel
system:	frame construction
internal ceiling height:	2.26–2.7 m
site area:	450 m²
gross floor area:	180 m²
total internal volume:	493 m³
total construction cost:	€ 288,000 (gross)
date of construction:	2003
period of construction:	5 months

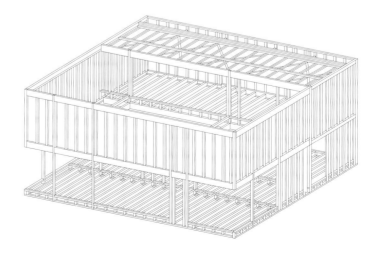

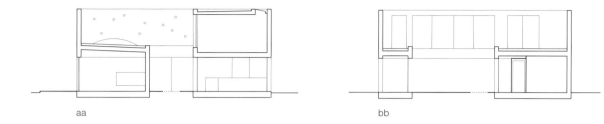

aa   bb

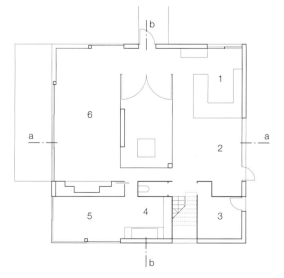

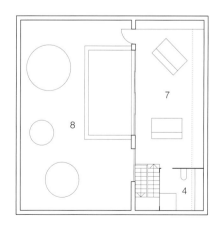

axonometric of
steel frame
sections · floor plans
scale 1:250

1   kitchen
2   dining
3   guest room
4   bathroom
5   bedroom
6   living room
7   nursery
8   roof garden

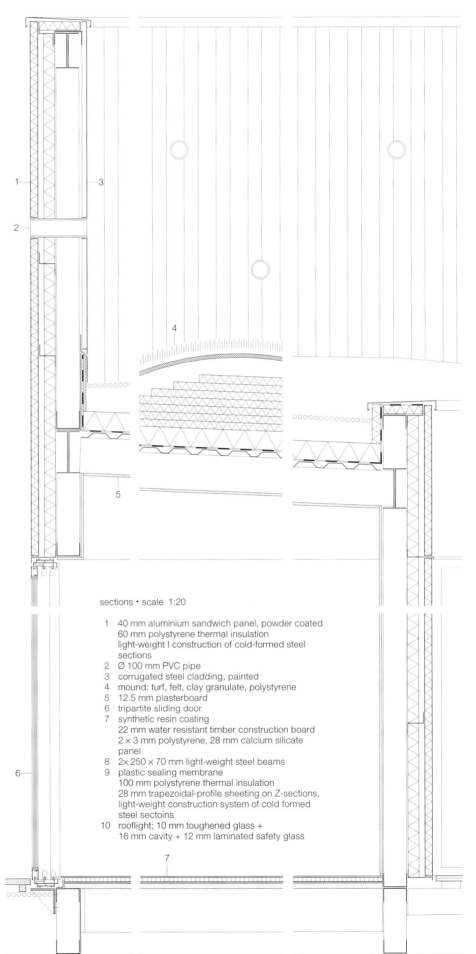

sections · scale 1:20

1 40 mm aluminium sandwich panel, powder coated
   60 mm polystyrene thermal insulation
   light-weight I construction of cold-formed steel
   sections
2 Ø 100 mm PVC pipe
3 corrugated steel cladding, painted
4 mound: turf, felt, clay granulate, polystyrene
5 12.5 mm plasterboard
6 tripartite sliding door
7 synthetic resin coating
   22 mm water resistant timber construction board
   2 × 3 mm polystyrene, 28 mm calcium silicate
   panel
8 2× 250 × 70 mm light-weight steel beams
9 plastic sealing membrane
   100 mm polystyrene thermal insulation
   28 mm trapezoidal-profile sheeting on Z-sections,
   light-weight construction system of cold formed
   steel sectoins
10 rooflight; 10 mm toughened glass +
   16 mm cavity + 12 mm laminated safety glass

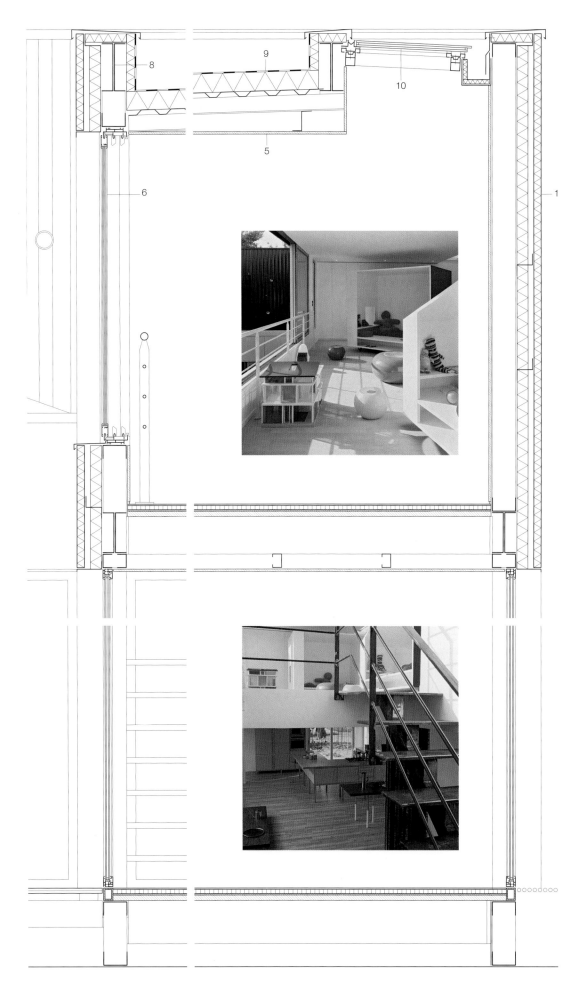

House in Rothenburg / Wümme

The design of this house was based on the theme "living with nature" and built on a site in a forest clearing. In contrast to the usual detached family homes in this development, which require artificial lighting even during the daytime due to the overshadowing trees, the transparency of this building allows the changing seasons and times of day to be experienced internally. The modular layout meant that it was not necessary to fell any trees worth preserving.

The construction consists of two parts, shifted in relation to each other with their rooms arranged along a central corridor. The single-pitch glass roof over the corridor ensures that sufficient light penetrates the centre of the house. The solar heat gain through this glass construction contributes to the heating of the house on sunny winter days.

The non-glazed sections of the facade employ a sandwich construction consisting of plasterboard internally and a ventilated, weatherproof skin of coated corrugated aluminium panels.

The load-bearing frame is constructed of rectangular hollow sections on a basic grid of 1.8 × 1.8 m. Trussed beams span the individual rooms. The soffit of the roof consists of trapezoidal profile sheeting laid directly onto the beams. Internal steel components are finished with an anti-corrosion coating, while the external parts are hot-dip galvanized.

floor plan   scale 1:500
isometry
vertical section   scale 1:20

1   18 × 76 mm corrugated aluminium panels
     45 mm battens with ventilation cavity
     wind/rain-proof membrane
     19 mm particleboard
     50 mm mineral-fibre insulation,
     between battens
     70 mm mineral-fibre insulation
     vapour barrier
     2× 12.5 mm plasterboard
2   welded elastomer bitumen sheeting
     80 mm rolled insulation with
     vapour pressure equalisation
     80 mm min. insulation wedge (to provide fall)
     vapour barrier, E40 steel profile sheeting
3   top chord: 80 × 80 × 9 mm T-section
4   18 mm Ø tie
5   2× steel channels 40 × 20 mm
6   9 mm gusset plate
7   columns, 80 × 80 mm glulam (plywood) columns

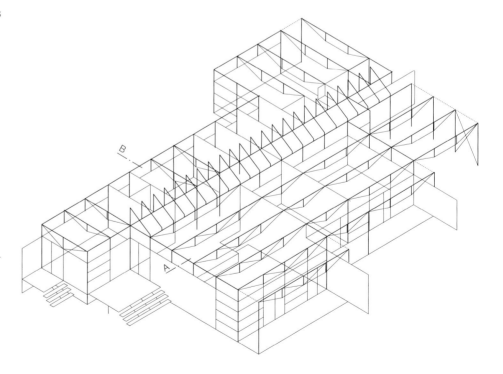

project team • building details

architects:	Schulitz + Partner, Braunschweig
with:	H. C. Schulitz, M. Rätzel, J. König
structural engineers:	Michael Sprysch, Vechelde
client:	Family Günther
function:	single-family house
construction:	steel
system:	frame construction
internal ceiling height:	2.85 m living room 3.55 m
site area:	3830 m²
gross floor area:	250 m²
total internal volume:	740 m³
total construction cost:	€ 296,000 (gross)
date of construction:	1996
period of construction:	approx. 10 months

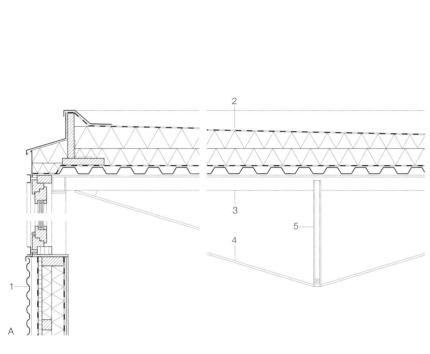

A

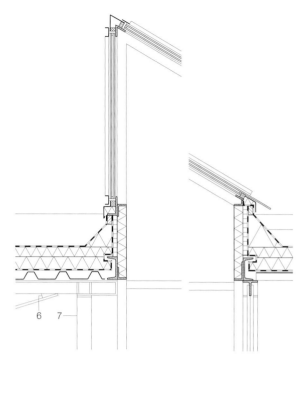

B

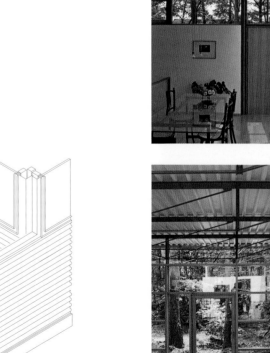

House in Phoenix

The Xeros project is located where the outskirts of Phoenix give way to the organic landforms of the North Mountain nature protection area. Located on a sloping site, at the end of two cul-de-sacs, the narrow building is orientated towards the mountain reserve to the north and the city centre to the south. A short flight of steps brings you down to a courtyard enclosed by metal mesh which leads to the double-height studio on the lower ground floor. To reach the living area at first floor level you climb an external steel staircase that starts at ground level. It brings you onto a balcony that provides access to the living and dining areas. The sleeping area, which is at the end of a central corridor, cantilevers out on one side. While this part of the dwelling with its full height glazing opens up a view of the mountains, the balcony facing back towards the city is concealed behind an external layer of metal mesh. The structural system consists of a steel frame combined with prefabricated engineered timber floor joists. The building envelope is constructed of corrugated steel cladding and wire-mesh shade screens.

project team • building details

architects:	blank studio, Phoenix
	Matthew G. Trzebiatowski
structural engineers:	The BDA Group, Greg
	Brickey, Scottsdale, Arizona
client:	Matthew and Lisa
	Trzebiatowski, Arizona
function:	single-family house
construction:	steel
system:	frame construction
internal ceiling height:	2.44–6.20 m
site area:	1,241 m²
gross floor area:	209 m²
total internal volume:	487 m³
total construction cost:	€ 379,750 mill. (gross)
date of construction:	2006
period of construction:	13 months

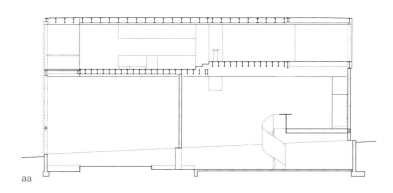

aa

floor plans
section
scale 1:250

1 studio entrance	6 library
2 reflecting pool	7 bathroom
3 external courtyard	8 terrace
4 studio	9 living
5 residence entrance	10 kitchen/dining
	11 gallery
	12 dressing room
	13 bedroom
	14 media room

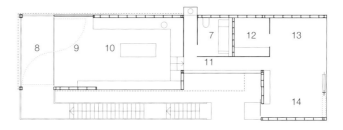

first floor

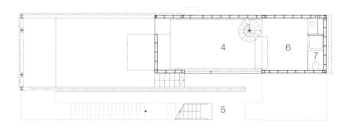

ground floor

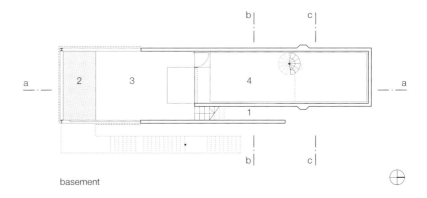

basement

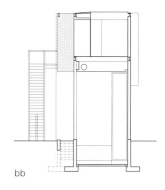

bb

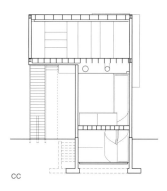

cc

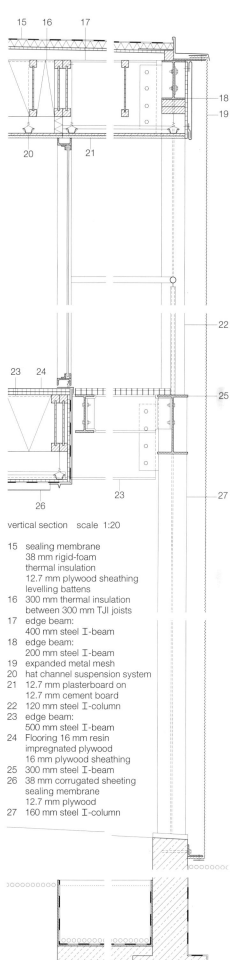

vertical section   scale 1:20

15 sealing membrane
    38 mm rigid-foam
    thermal insulation
    12.7 mm plywood sheathing
    levelling battens
16 300 mm thermal insulation
    between 300 mm TJI joists
17 edge beam:
    400 mm steel I-beam
18 edge beam:
    200 mm steel I-beam
19 expanded metal mesh
20 hat channel suspension system
21 12.7 mm plasterboard on
    12.7 mm cement board
22 120 mm steel I-column
23 edge beam:
    500 mm steel I-beam
24 Flooring 16 mm resin
    impregnated plywood
    16 mm plywood sheathing
25 300 mm steel I-beam
26 38 mm corrugated sheeting
    sealing membrane
    12.7 mm plywood
27 160 mm steel I-column

79

vertical sections · horizontal section
scale 1:20

1　roof construction:
　　sealing membrane
　　38 mm rigid-foam thermal insulation
　　12.7 mm plywood sheathing
　　levelling battens
　　300 mm thermal insulation
　　between 300 mm TJI joists
　　aluminium hat channel suspension system
　　12.7 mm cement board
　　12.7 mm plasterboard
2　blocking
3　5 mm steel sheeting
4　edge beam: 200 mm steel I-beam
5　120 mm steel I-column
6　wall construction:
　　38 mm corrugated metal cladding
　　waterproof membrane
　　12.7 mm exterior plywood
　　150 mm thermal insulation
　　between metal channel sections
　　15.8 mm gypsum fibreboard
　　12.7 mm wax-coated gypsum plaster
7　floor construction media room:
　　16 mm resin impregnated
　　plywood
　　16 mm plywood sheathing
　　300 mm thermal insulation
　　between 300 mm TJI joists
　　aluminium hat channel suspension system
　　12.7 mm exterior plywood
　　waterproof membrane
　　38 mm corrugated metal cladding
8　ventilation cavity
9　RHS 200 × 150 mm steel column
10　floor construction library:
　　19 mm oriented strand board
　　12.7 mm plywood sheathing
　　200 mm acoustic insulation
　　between 240 mm TJI joists
　　12.7 mm oriented strand board
11　200 mm reinforced concrete plinth
12　100 × 100 × 18 mm steel angles
13　13 mm clear toughened glass
14　square section steel bar 13/13 mm
15　sliding door 13 mm
　　laminated glass with polished edges
16　glazing 13 mm coloured laminated glass
　　with polished edges
17　50 mm grating
18　140 mm steel I-beam
19　400 mm steel I-beam
20　160 mm steel I-column
21　12.5 mm steel plate

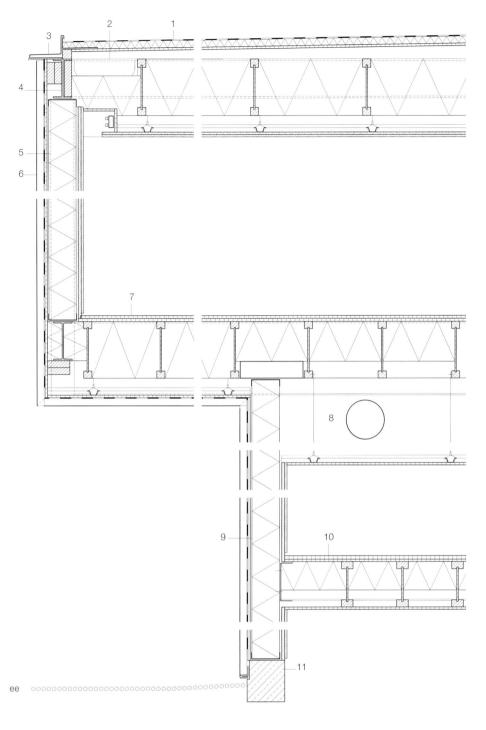

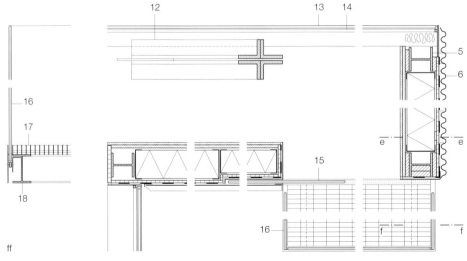

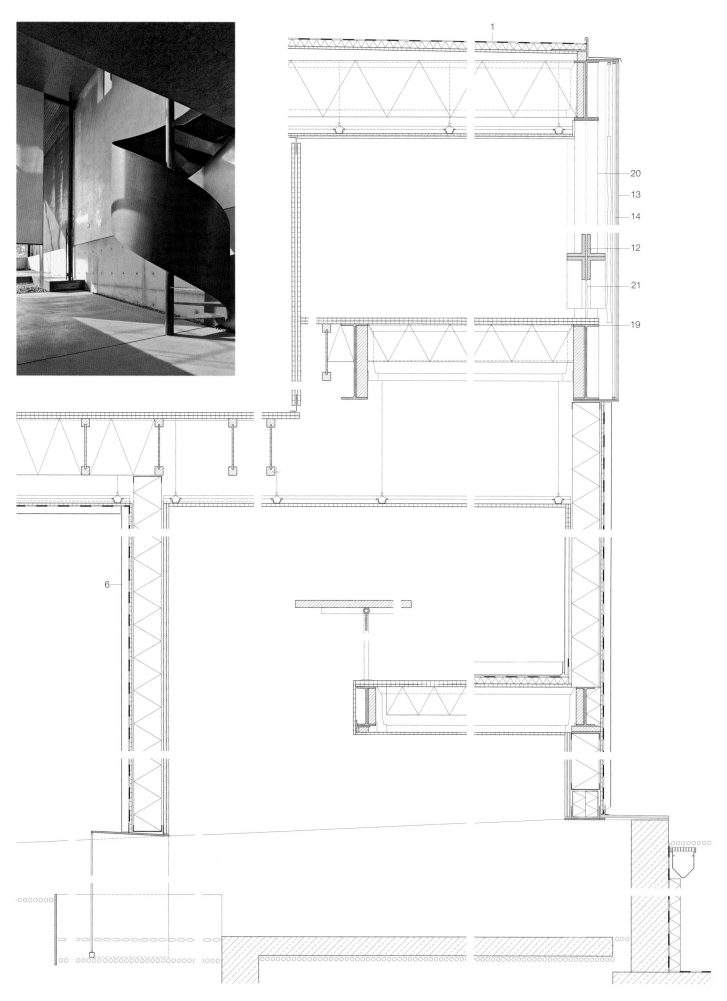

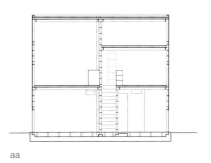

aa

Model House in Tosu City

Japan has a long and flourishing tradition of modular construction systems. To the present-day, rush-covered tatami mats serve as the most important unit for dimensioning apartments and rooms, and form the basic module for traditional floor plan design.

Riken Yamamoto's work brings classic modular construction into the present day, in the form of a prototype for an industrial lightweight construction system, for a firm which specialises in metal sections and modular aluminium furniture. It is intended to optimise the characteristics specific to aluminium, and to express an aesthetic identity that would not be possible with more conventional, standard construction materials, including steel.

The Ecoms House is located next to the factory (constructed using the same system) in the Saga prefecture, and demonstrates the flexibility of this modular, configurable lightweight system. With this prototype Yamamoto searches for an architectonic solution to the changing patterns of urban living – in addition to using a building method that is both structurally and visually innovative. Living and working can be combined here in a flexible

way. The ground floor accommodates two bedrooms, the bathroom and storage area; located on the upper floor are the kitchen, living, dining, and work areas. Thanks to the modular construction method this layout can be varied, totally reversed or only partially altered. For example, the living and office functions could be separated vertically, with the office (or, alternatively a shop) on the ground floor and living spaces above.

Extruded aluminium sections can be manufactured with extreme precision, in practically any shape. Compared with steel, its melting point is lower and – for the same unit weight, its strength is one-and-a-half times that of steel. Recycled material can be used in the manufacturing process, to a certain degree. If the number of standardised components is kept to a practical minimum, this results in an extremely economical and easily calculable form of construction.

The optimisation of prefabricated, pre-assembled, quality-controlled elements reduces construction time and, consequently, costs.

Each basic module measures 1200 × 1200 mm. The diagonal lattice is made

up cross-shaped sections that are rigidly connected by means of interlocking ends. With this potential for almost unlimited additions, the modules can be configured at the factory into varying sizes and subsequently flexibly arranged to any required spatial configuration.

On site, the individual modules are simply bolted together with cross-shaped coupling pieces. Facade, door and window elements, tailored to the grid dimensions, constitute the exterior skin. Due to the high degree of precision in manufacturing, the tolerances are minimal and can be adjusted at the bolt connections.

Since the floor elements also use a modular aluminium system the structure can readily be adapted to different ceiling heights or be expanded by adding intermediate mezzanine floors and gallery levels. Thus far, in addition to the factory and the Ecoms House, two smaller buildings have been completed. For future projects, Riken Yamamoto is considering leasing out of complete or partial systems. The buildings can be altered or expanded – horizontally and vertically – with minimal effort, at any point in time, to accommodate a variety of changing requirements. Dismantling a structure that has been in use as a temporary pavilion, for example, is also fast and uncomplicated. Because the components are lightweight, transport costs are also economical. One aspect of the commission was also the development of an associated line of furniture, which is based on the same serial principle, and can be successfully combined with it, both aesthetically and functionally. Both the furniture and the construction system have been structurally optimised in a series of tests, fully developed for mass production and patented. Further development of both lines is already at the planning stage.

Jan Dominik Geipel

project team • building details

architects:	Riken Yamamoto & Field Shop, Yokohama
with:	Naoko Kawaguchi, Koji Toki
structural engineers:	Iijima Structural Design Office, Nagoya
client:	SUS Corporation, Shizuoka
function:	demonstration house
construction:	aluminium
system:	frame construction
module:	1.2 × 1.2 m

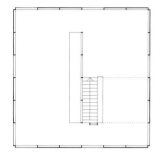

section · floor plans
scale 1:200

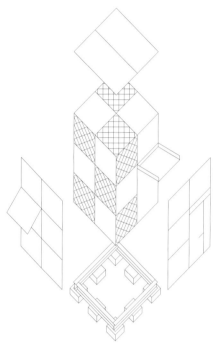

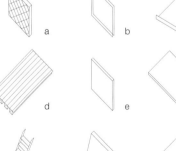

a   b   c

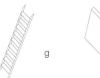

d   e   f

g   h   i

schematic exploded   d   floor unit
diagram   e   aluminium panel
                            f   roof panel
a   lattice panel   g   ladder
b   double glazing   h   window
c   eaves   l   door

1

2

3

4

5

6

7

8

9

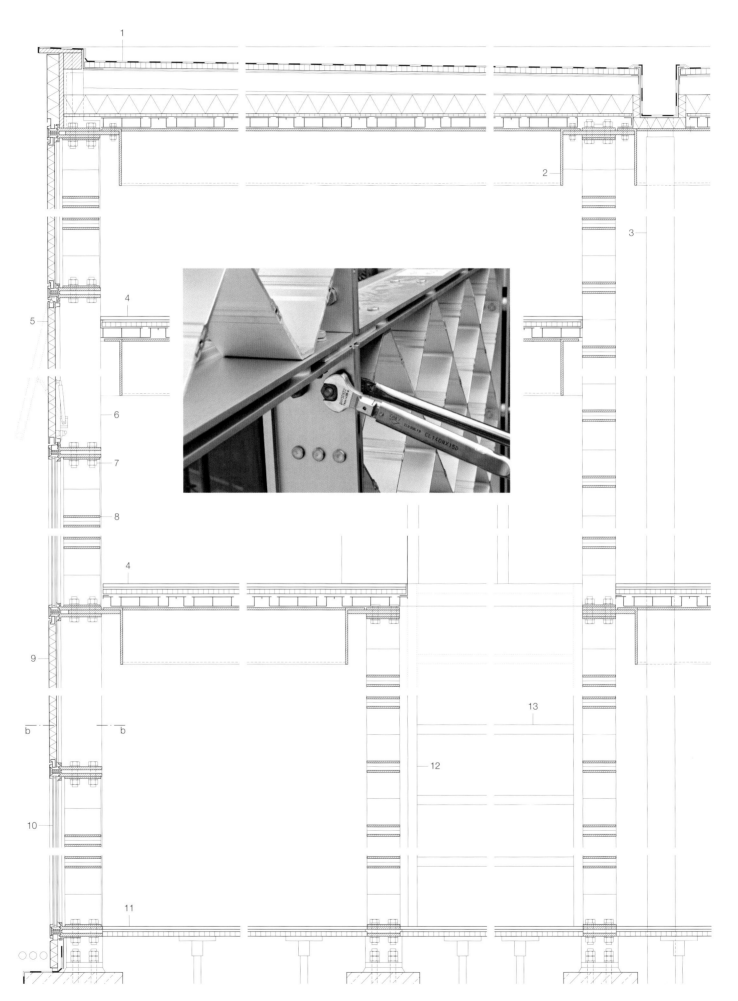

4

13

12

b───── ──b

10

11

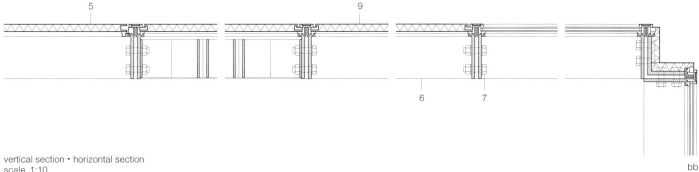

vertical section · horizontal section
scale 1:10

detail
scale 1:5

bb

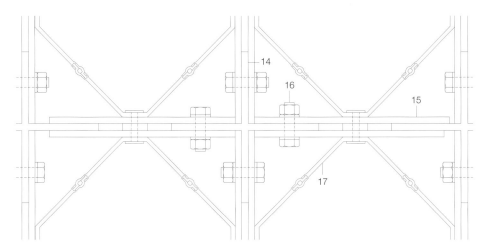

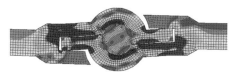

thermal image of connection, at early stage

connection as executed, thermally improved

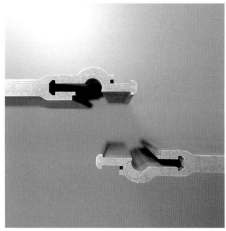

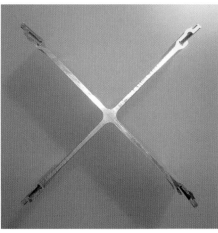

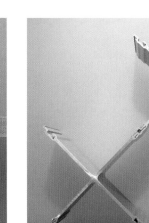

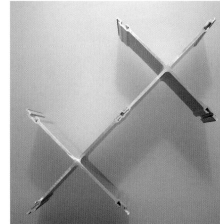

1 roof construction:
   synthetic sealing membrane
   15 mm wood fibreboard
   50 × 50 × 3 mm aluminium angle
   50 mm polystyrene,
   10 mm plywood
   prefabricated
   ceiling elements 1200 × 3600 mm of
   20 × 200 mm
   on 150 × 200 mm extruded
   aluminium sections
2 50 × 150 mm aluminium angle
3 drainage
4 floor construction:
   9 mm carpet tiles, 6 mm felt
   12 mm plywood
   1200 × 3600 mm prefabricated
   ceiling element of 20 × 200 mm
   on 150 × 200 mm extruded aluminium-sections
5 opening panel 20 mm brushed aluminium
6 1200 × 1200 mm aluminium frame of
   8 × 120 × 1200 mm RHS
7 M12 bolt
8 5 mm extruded section lattice,
   205 mm mesh size
9 20 mm brushed aluminium insulated panel
10 double glazing: 3 mm float glass +
   6 mm cavity + 3 mm float glass
11 floor construction:
   9 mm carpet tiles, 6 mm felt
   12 mm plywood,
   raised floor system
   250 mm reinforced concrete
   separation layer
   50 mm rigid foam insulation
   50 mm sub-base, 60 mm gravel
12 130 × 25 mm stringer of extruded
   aluminium sections
13 240 × 25 mm aluminium runner
14 10 mm aluminium cross connection
15 1200 × 1200 mm frame of
   8 × 120 mm aluminium sections
16 M12 bolt
17 5 mm extruded aluminium section

axonometric

1 146 × 70 × 8 mm aluminium T-sections
2 146 × 70 × 6 mm aluminium I-sections
3 70 × 70 × 2 mm aluminium SHS
4 4 mm aluminium sheeting

floor plans
section
scale 1:200

5 tatami room
6 living room
7 kitchen
8 bedroom
9 void
10 guest room
11 terrace

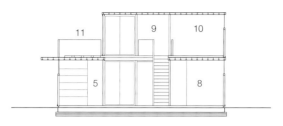

aa

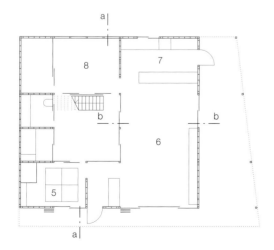

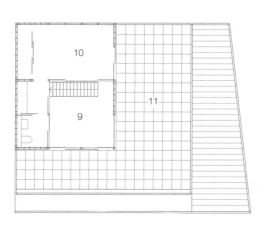

Extra storeys in Preding

This farmhouse near Graz was built in the 19th century. After part of the roof structure was destroyed by fire in 1997, the owner decided to add two new storeys in light-weight construction which contain three dwellings. The existing conventional brick structure functions as a plinth for the additional storeys. Although the lower of the two new floors is set flush with the original brick walls, the upper level is set back, creating two roof terraces. The apartments are accessed by an external single-flight steel staircase, its coarse oxidised surface presenting a marked contrast to the otherwise clean-cut built form. The loadbearing steel columns in this hybrid steel and timber construction are positioned at 2.5 m centres, supported on the brick structure below. Because the new floors and roofs are constructed of prefabricated timber elements which easily span the 8 m width of the building, the new apartments benefit from clear, uninterrupted spaces. The closed elements of the facade are also prefabricated and clad with aluminium panels. A major part of the facade is glazed, allowing generous views of the surrounding countryside and simultaneously emphasising the lightness of the new structure.

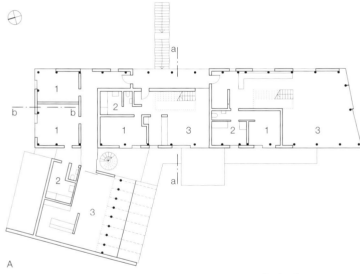

B

A

A   first floor
B   second floor

1   bedroom
2   bathroom
3   living/dining room
4   gallery
5   terrace

project team • building details

architects:	Gangoly & Kristiner Architects, Graz
project leader:	Irene Kristiner
with:	Raimund Kuschnig
structural engineers:	Johann Birner, Graz
client:	Jörg Holler, Predin
usage:	apartments
construction:	steel and timber
system:	frame construction with prefabricated timber elements
internal ceiling height:	2.56 and 2.40 m
gross floor area:	400 m²
total internal volume:	1450 m³
date of construction:	1997–1998
period of construction:	13 months

axonometric

1   146 × 70 × 8 mm aluminium T-sections
2   146 × 70 × 6 mm aluminium I-sections
3   70 × 70 × 2 mm aluminium SHS
4   4 mm aluminium sheeting

floor plans
section
scale 1:200

5   tatami room
6   living room
7   kitchen
8   bedroom
9   void
10 guest room
11 terrace

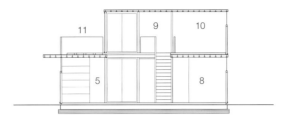

aa

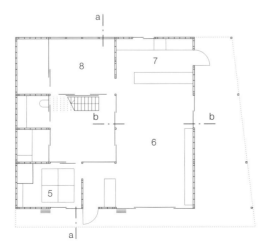

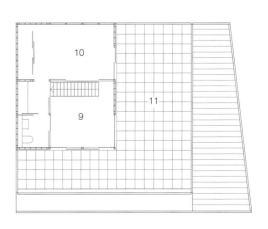

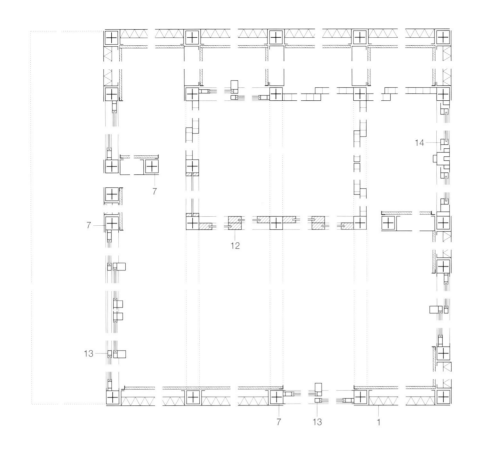

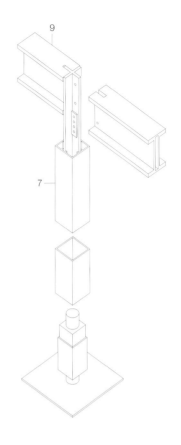

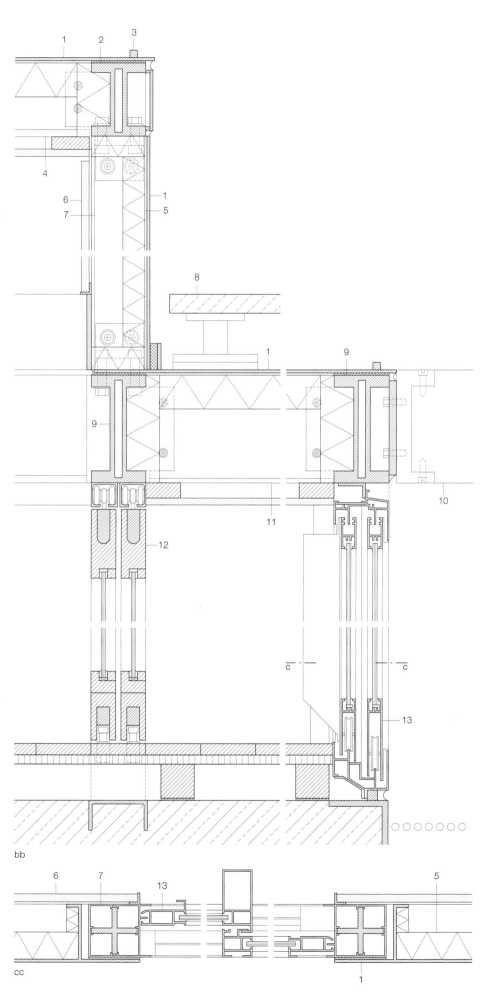

horizontal section
scale 1:20
axonometric
vertical section · horizontal section
scale 1:5

1 4 mm aluminium sheeting on rubber layer
2 96 × 70 × 6 mm aluminium I-section
3 10 × 10 mm aluminium section
4 96 × 70 × 8 mm aluminium T-section
5 30 mm thermal insulation
6 10 mm plasterboard
7 70 × 70 × 2 mm aluminium SHS
8 30 mm concrete slab
9 146 × 70 × 6 mm aluminium I-beam
10 150 × 15 mm aluminium sheeting
11 146 × 70 × 8 mm aluminium T-section
12 32 mm timber sliding door with
    6 mm toughened glass
13 20 mm aluminium sliding door with
    6 mm toughened glass
14 20 mm aluminium sliding door with
    6 mm toughened glass

89

Extra storeys in Preding

This farmhouse near Graz was built in the 19th century. After part of the roof structure was destroyed by fire in 1997, the owner decided to add two new storeys in light-weight construction which contain three dwellings. The existing conventional brick structure functions as a plinth for the additional storeys. Although the lower of the two new floors is set flush with the original brick walls, the upper level is set back, creating two roof terraces. The apartments are accessed by an external single-flight steel staircase, its coarse oxidised surface presenting a marked contrast to the otherwise clean-cut built form. The loadbearing steel columns in this hybrid steel and timber construction are positioned at 2.5 m centres, supported on the brick structure below. Because the new floors and roofs are constructed of prefabricated timber elements which easily span the 8 m width of the building, the new apartments benefit from clear, uninterrupted spaces. The closed elements of the facade are also prefabricated and clad with aluminium panels. A major part of the facade is glazed, allowing generous views of the surrounding countryside and simultaneously emphasising the lightness of the new structure.

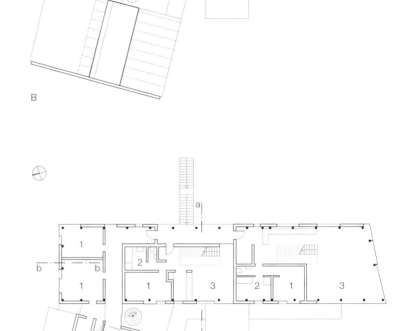

B

A first floor
B second floor

1 bedroom
2 bathroom
3 living/dining room
4 gallery
5 terrace

project team • building details

architects:	Gangoly & Kristiner Architects, Graz
project leader:	Irene Kristiner
with:	Raimund Kuschnig
structural engineers:	Johann Birner, Graz
client:	Jörg Holler, Predin
usage:	apartments
construction:	steel and timber
system:	frame construction with prefabricated timber elements
internal ceiling height:	2.56 and 2.40 m
gross floor area:	400 m²
total internal volume:	1450 m³
date of construction:	1997–1998
period of construction:	13 months

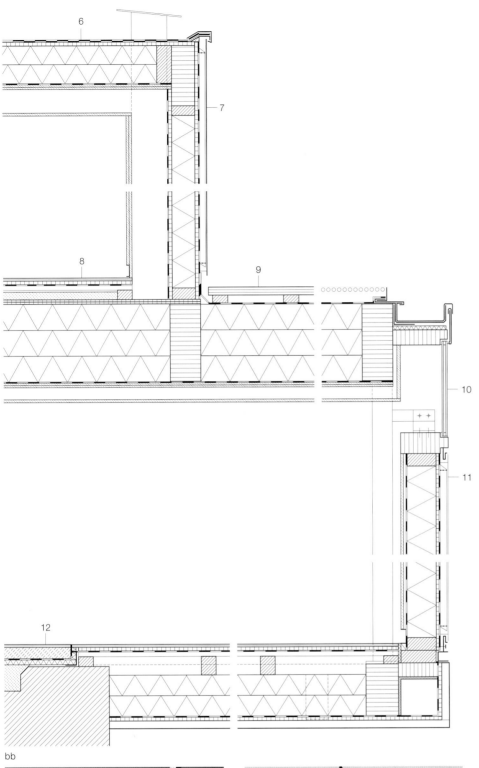

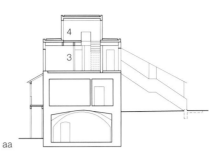

aa

vertical section   scale 1:20

6   roof construction:
     50 mm gravel, protective membrane
     waterproof sheeting, single layer laid loose
     separating layer, levelling fleece
     28 mm particleboard
     insulation between 80 × 200–240 mm rafters
     vapour barrier, 2× 12.5 mm gypsum fibreboard
     40 mm ventilation cavity
     15 mm suspended plasterboard ceiling
7   wall construction:
     facade panel, ventilation cavity
     2 mm aluminium sheeting, with folded edges
     30 × 50 mm counter battens
     diffusion-permeable membrane, 19 mm
     particleboard
     insulation between 120 mm timber framing
     19 mm particleboard, vapour barrier
     200 mm services cavity
     2 × 15 mm gypsum fibreboard
8   floor construction:
     15 mm wood-block flooring, 19 mm particleboard
     24 mm battens, 50 × 80 mm timber blocks
     40 mm loose fill as levelling layer
     28 mm particleboard
     insulation between 120 × 340–420 mm joists
     vapour barrier, 2× 12.5 mm gypsum fibreboard
     40 mm cavity
     15 mm suspended plasterboard ceiling
9   timber grid
10   fixed glazing
11   facade element:
     facade panel, ventilation cavity
     2 mm aluminium sheeting, with folded edges
     30 × 50 mm counter battens
     diffusion-permeable membrane, 19 mm
     particleboard
     insulation between 160 mm timber framing
     vapour barrier, 12.5 mm gypsum fibreboard
     15 mm plasterboard
12   floor construction on existing construction:
     15 mm parquet
     60 mm screed, membrane
     25 mm impact-sound insulation panels
     140 mm loose fill

bb

House in Andelsbuch

Located in the Bregenz Forest, this two-family house is set on a raised site, open to the elements. The fully enclosed stairwell is articulated as a separate volume and provides access to both dwellings. Parking spaces and house services are located in the basement level. The house is a pilot project for a construction system, based on a simple 5 × 5 m timber frame module. The modules can be connected horizontally or stacked vertically as desired, thus permitting flexible layout and dimensioning of the individual spaces.

The structural frame is filled with prefabricated wall and floor elements. The wall units include both external and internal cladding, insulation, windows and glazing, sunscreens and service runs. All elements were designed with identical abutment details. Although the bathroom and kitchen are – in this prototype – centrally installed as complete units, they benefit from natural light through the partially glazed walls. Site assembly for construction, facade and floor elements, and bath and kitchen units took just two days and only the service connections and floor finishes had to be carried out on site.

project team • building details

architects:	Oskar Leo Kaufmann and Johannes Kaufmann, Dornbirn
structural engineers:	Oskar Leo Kaufmann and Johannes Kaufmann
with:	Markus Flatz, Bregenz
client:	private
function:	house
construction:	timber
system:	frame/panel construction
internal ceiling height:	3.1 m
site area:	1,500 m²
gross floor area:	200 m²
total internal volume:	650 m³
total construction cost:	€ 450,000 (gross)
date of construction:	1997

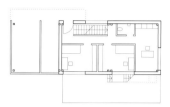

A

B

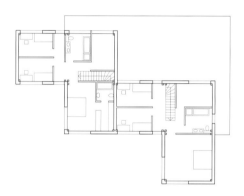

A

B

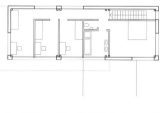

A

B

alternative system layouts
with 5 × 5 m basic module

A upper floor plan
B ground floor plan
scale 1:400

92

layout of floor elements
ground floor
scale 1:200

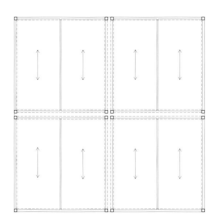

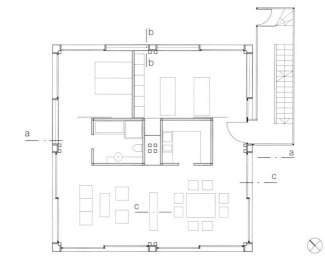

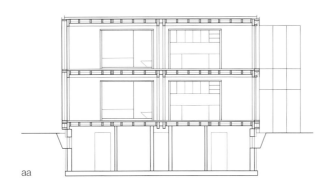

aa

section
scale 1:200

horizontal sections
vertical sections
bearing point of central columns
scale 1:20

1 roof construction:
   layer of gravel
   plastic waterproof membrane
   60–100 mm insulation to falls
   20 mm sandwich sheet
   2× 100 mm thermal insulation between
   60 × 200 mm timber framing
   vapour barrier
   20 mm sandwich sheet
   9 mm veneered plywood
2 150 × 370 mm laminated timber edge beam
3 150 × 150 mm laminated timber column
4 floor construction:
   9 mm veneered plywood
   25 mm sandwich sheet
   20 + 30 mm impact sound insulation
   20 mm sandwich sheet
   100 mm thermal insulation and
   100 mm crushed limestone between
   60 × 200 mm timber framing
   20 mm sandwich sheet
   9 mm veneered plywood
5 wall construction:
   20 mm tongue-and-groove boarding
   30 mm battens, ventilation cavity
   15 mm pressed chipboard
   2× 120 mm thermal insulation between
   60 × 235 mm timber framing
   vapour barrier
   20 mm tongue-and-groove boarding
6 service cavity
7 8 mm sheet steel fixing element
   for central columns
8 150 × 300 mm timber packing piece
   between timber columns
9 15 × 25 × 2 mm aluminium track
   for roller-shutter

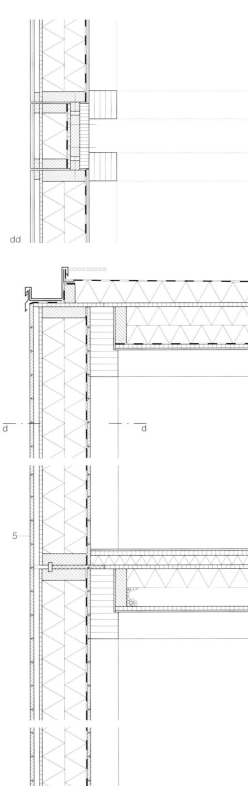

dd

d

d

5

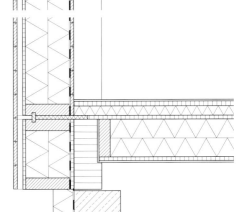

bb

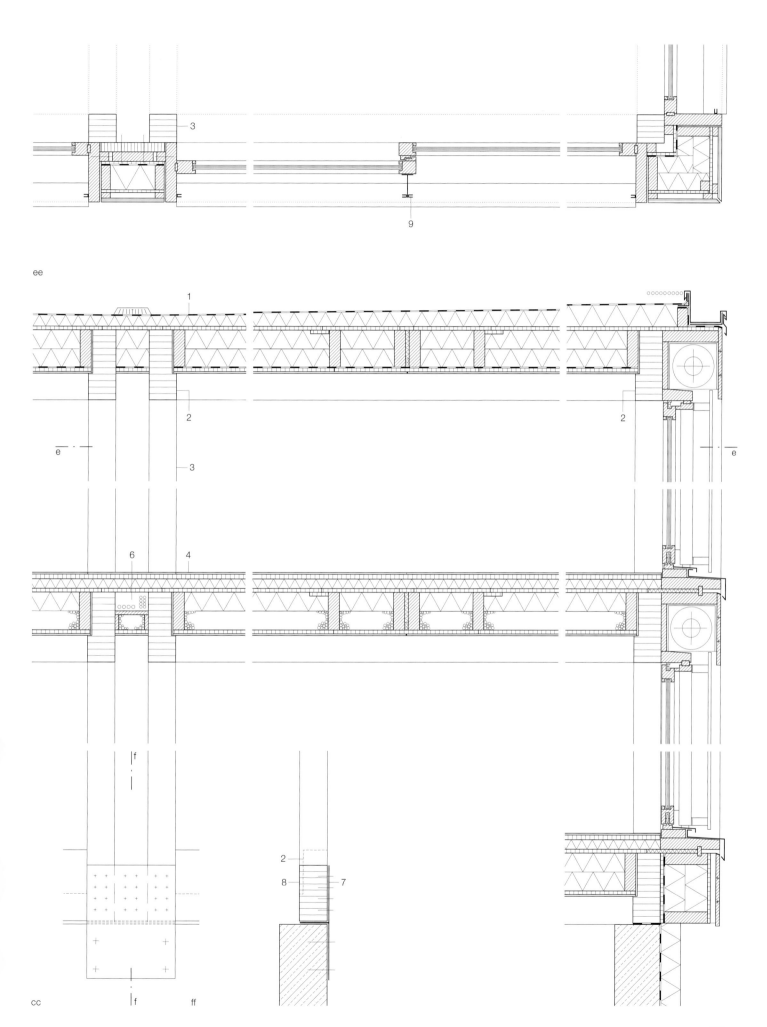

ee

e

e

6   4

f

f   ff

cc

95

isometry of structure:
standardised system of
precast concrete elements
on in-situ concrete base

section • floor plans
scale 1:200

1   guest room
2   living room
3   conservatory
4   library
5   bedroom

House in Gams

This clear-cut house is situated on the outskirts of a residential area comprised of single-family dwellings, in the Rhine valley near Chur. The simple cubic building is screened from the adjacent road by a low, elongated garage.

The ground floor, which is set down from the entrance level by two steps, is conceived as an open plan layout around the sanitary and circulation core. A discrete zone that is oriented towards the garden, fully glazed and uninsulated, functions as an integrated conservatory. The upper level – in contrast to the ground floor – is divided into four individual rooms, all accessed from the long central corridor.

The construction of the building is a combination of standardised building units and customised, prefabricated elements. The clients specified an economical timber building with a durable load-bearing structure. Thus a precast concrete, load-bearing frame consisting of readily available construction elements was erected above an in-situ concrete basement. Two-storey columns, with integral bearing brackets, together with beams spanning the longitudinal

direction form two rigid frames that are horizontally braced by cross-beams at roof level. The precast concrete elements were cast in metal forms under closely controlled conditions and therefore have particularly smooth surfaces and sharp arrises. The upper floor slab consists of standard, hollow-section modular timber elements – also widely available products – supported by bearers, which in turn are fixed to the longitudinal beams, and spans across the width of the building. Building regulations stipulated a pitched roof, but its minimal required slope is concealed by the broadly eaves.

Prefabricated timber facade panels were set in the concrete frame. The external surfaces of the infill elements, untreated plywood sheets in massive timber surrounds, project slightly beyond the plane of the structure, emphasising the concept of frame and infill. Internally, an eight-centimetre-thick plasterboard lining gives the walls a weight and solidity that is advantageous in both climatic and acoustic terms.

project team • building details

architects:	Christian Wagner, Trübbach
	Jürg Graser, Zurich
with:	Jörg Koch
structural engineers:	Egeter and Tinner, Lienz
	(basement and slabs)
client:	Josef and Claudia Lenherr,
	Gams
function:	single-family house
construction:	concrete
system:	frame construction
internal ceiling height:	2,09–2,31 m (basement)
	2,86 m (ground floor),
	2,40 m (first floor)
site area:	773 m²
gross floor area:	320 m²
total internal volume:	890 m³
total construction cost:	€ 534,000 (gross)
date of construction:	1995
period of construction:	8 months

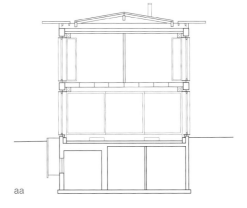

aa

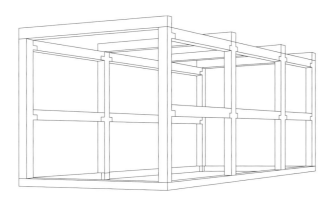

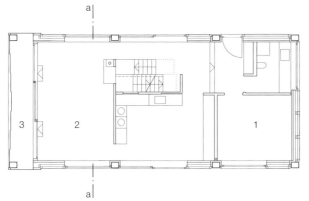

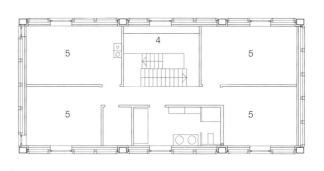

longitudinal vertical section
longitudinal horizontal section
transverse vertical section with conservatory
scale 1:20

1 ventilated roof with zinc standing-seam sheeting
2 80 mm solid softwood soffit
3 400 × 300 mm precast concrete roof beam
4 300 × 400 mm precast concrete beam

5 double glazing in softwood frame
6 floor construction: 8 mm beech parquet
   60 mm heating screed on separating layer
   40 mm impact-sound insulation
   on plastic membrane
   240 mm softwood hollow floor elements
7 40 × 60 mm timber bearer for floor elements
8 300 × 400 mm precast concrete column
   with integral brackets
9 in-situ concrete basement construction

10 toughened glass sliding element to conservatory
11 aluminium sheeting bent to shape, foam filled
12 60 mm insulation and plasterboard to column
13 Douglas fir frame
14 wall element:
   21 mm Douglas fir plywood
   19 mm timber-fibre board
   160 mm cellulose-fibre insulation
   80 mm plasterboard, filled and painted
15 sheet zinc drip

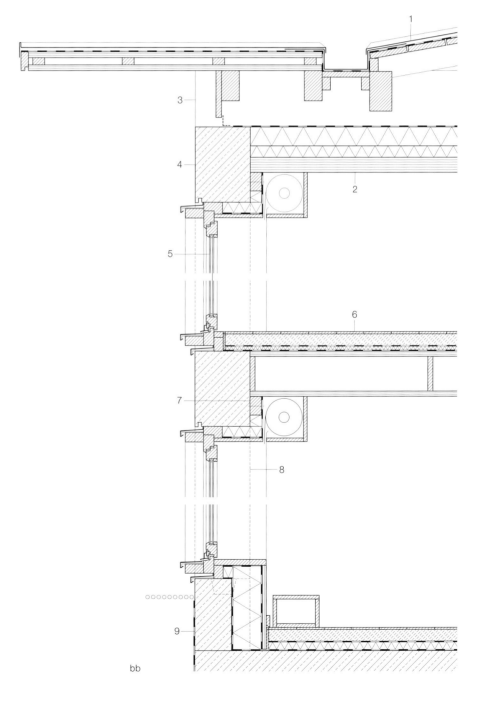

bb

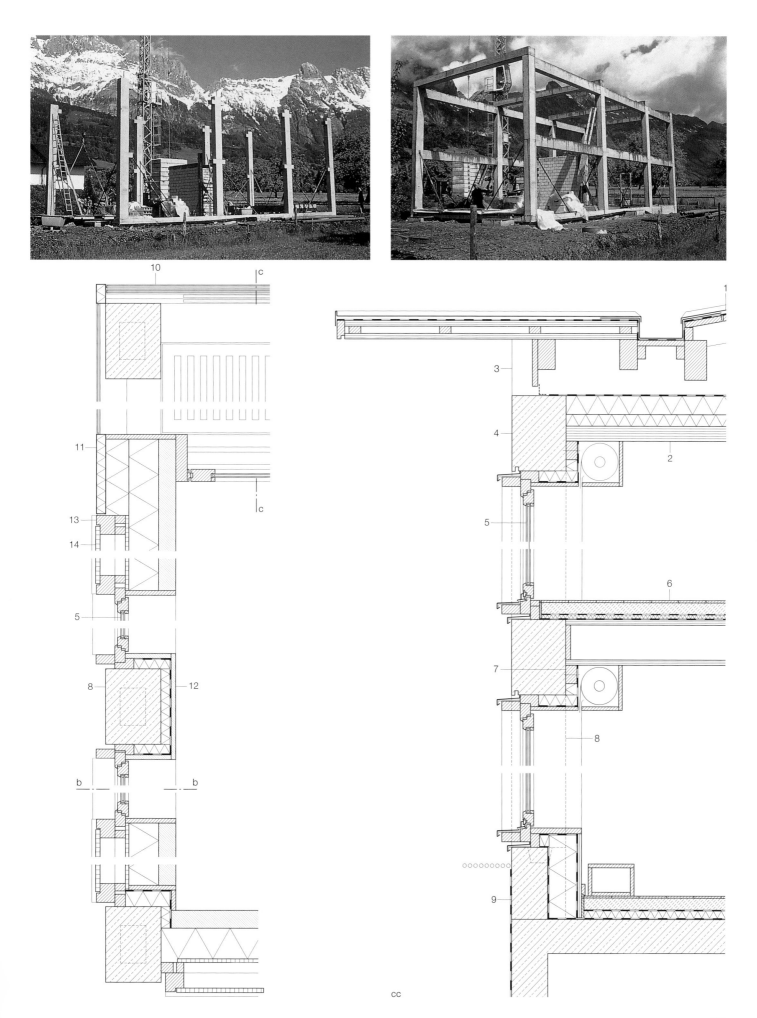

A   assembly of prefabricated elements, connection
    with vertical tension rods in the columns
B   temporary fixing of precast concrete units with
    steel angles

Fashion Centre in Fukuoka

Originally, this fashion school was to have
been executed as a timber frame structure, in accordance with Japanese craft
traditions. As a result of fire regulations
and time and cost constraints, however,
concrete ultimately proved to be a more
suitable material. In contrast to projects
from the 1960s, in which the principles of
timber construction were simply applied
to concrete, the elements of the present
building were not cast in-situ, but manufactured as precast pre-stressed reinforced concrete elements. The cables
that provide stability and precise form
were tensioned after connecting the columns, beams and floor slabs. For this
system of construction, the architects
were able to draw on the services of well-
trained skilled workers who were familiar
with similar techniques used for timber
temples and shrines. As a result, the
building is wholly Japanese in spirit. The
courtyard provides sufficient space and
expanse in a very densely developed setting. Similar to the traditional translucent
Shoji paper screens, the profiled glass
facade produces diffuse light internally,
from which the fashion school derives its
name: "Luminare".

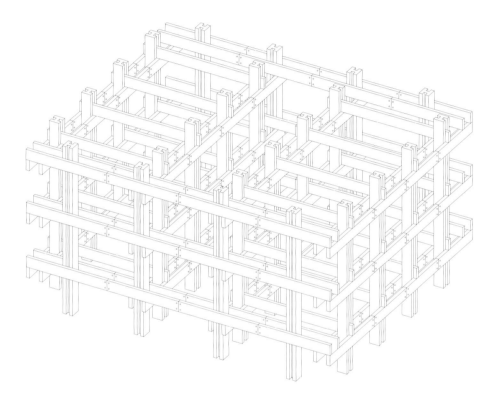

project team • building details

architects:	Takamatsu Architects and Associates, Kyoto
with:	Kim Kihong
structural engineers:	SD ROOM, Osaka
client:	Omula Bunka Gakuen, Fukuoka
function:	education
construction:	reinforced concrete
system:	frame construction
internal ceiling height:	2.5–2.6 m
site area:	478 m²
gross floor area:	1,308 m²
total internal volume:	3,400 m³
total construction cost:	€ 2.3 mill. (gross)
date of construction:	2002
period of construction:	10 months

A   B

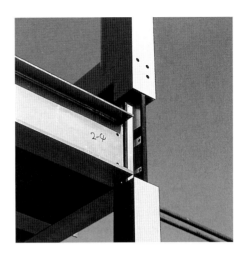

House in Sakurajosui

This single-family house in Sakurajosui stands directly beside another house Toyo Ito built for the same client in 1975. Located in a densely developed residential district of Tokyo, the new building covers almost the entire site area. In spite of the high-density development, the facade of this house is not completely closed; room-height glass sliding elements allow views of the immediate surroundings. Instead of the traditional courtyard garden, the house has a two-storey "sun space" at its centre, which allows additional daylight to penetrate to the living areas. A steel staircase leads up to the guest room and a broad terrace that takes up almost two thirds of the area of the upper floor.

The slender aluminium structural members and the glazed sliding elements lend the interior a quality of spaciousness. The generous glazing on the upper floor also allows the occupants to experience

changes in the weather – sunshine and clouds, wind and rain – a theme that Ito also explored in a number of his early housing schemes.

The house was originally planned with a reinforced concrete structure. As a result of his participation in a research project for model houses in aluminium, however, Ito modified the construction and erected the building with an aluminium frame. One condition for this change was that the budget should not exceed that previously agreed upon with the clients.

The research group working on the model houses realized the first project of this kind in 1999 in the form of an "eco-material house".

The system for the present structure is based on a 3.60 × 3.60 m column grid (1.80 m in peripheral areas). The square columns have an exceptionally small cross-section – only 70 × 70 mm – which results in a very slender load-bearing

structure. These minimised dimensions were achieved by inserting a cruciform core into the hollow columns to ensure greater stability. A grid of primary extruded I-beams and transverse secondary I-beams at very close centres of only 300 mm was placed on top of the columns. The structural grid, together with rigid column connections, provides the necessary horizontal bracing. Externally, the house is clad with uniform rectangular storey-height sheet-aluminium elements. In contrast, the interior is dominated by the warmer wood tones of the furnishings, doors and floor.

The clarity of the architecture, the relationships established with the surroundings, and the links between the internal spaces reflect Ito's own formal language. What is unusual for him, however, is the application of these principles to standardised system building units.

project team • building details

architects:	Toyo Ito & Associates, Tokyo
structural engineers:	Oak Structural Design Office, Tokyo
function:	single-family house
construction:	aluminium
system:	frame construction
internal ceiling height:	2.2 – 5.0 m
site area:	184 m²
gross floor area:	86.5 m²
total internal volume:	295 m³
date of construction:	2000
period of construction:	4 months

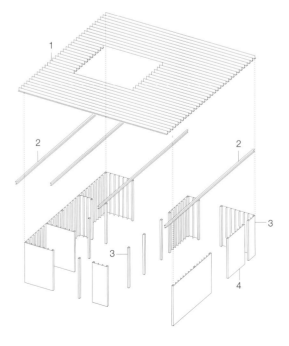

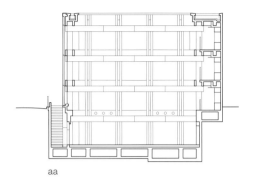

aa

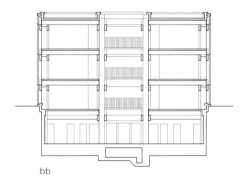

bb

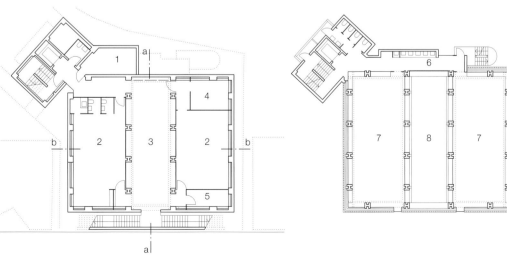

axonometric of structural
arrangement
sections · floor plans
scale 1:400

1   water tank
2   office
3   courtyard
4   services
5   changing room/lockers
6   sanitary rooms
7   classrooms
8   void

University Institute in Grenoble

The project sprang from an architectural competition and has become a fundamental element of the "University 2000" on the Grenoble campus. Inserted into the existing linear development of the university, this complex was realized in two stages. Initially, the western section functioned as an independent entity. Five years after its erection, a similar but somewhat smaller structure was added at a distance of 13 m.

Narrow conservatory spaces constructed along the north and south facades on the upper floors unify the elements into a single volume. Three enclosed bridges also link the two tracts across the intermediate courtyard. The transparent facades open the building to the campus and the surroundings beyond; teaching takes place against a background of the mountains that encircle Grenoble. The views in and out are filtered by the plants in the conservatories – bougainvillea on the south side and various types of bamboo

along the north face. Management of the conservatories is surprisingly simple – the watering of the plants, heating and ventilation are automatically regulated as in commercial plant nurseries.

The internal life of the building is pervaded by simplicity and reduced to the bare essentials. Only necessary, useful and important elements were incorporated; elaborate details were rejected in favour of spatial quality and good, atmospheric lighting. The load-bearing system of the building is a simple precast reinforced concrete structure.

Planning economies made it possible to create additional teaching areas, a larger hall and more generous internal corridors, with integrated recreational zones, without reducing the quality of the fit-out.

The conservatories, enhanced by the colours of the plants, create a surprisingly poetical element within the restrained atmosphere and severity of this otherwise austere construction.

aa

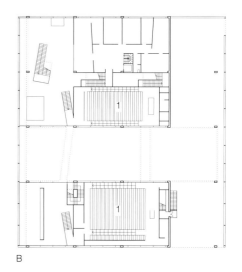

B

project team • building details

architects:	Anne Lacaton & Jean Philippe Vassal, Bordeaux
with:	Sylvain Menaud, Emmanuelle Delage, Mathieu Laporte, Pierre Yves Portier
structural engineers:	Ingérop Sud Ouest, Merignac
client:	University Pierre Mendès, Grenoble
function:	institute
construction:	concrete
system:	frame construction
internal ceiling height:	4.0 m (ground floor), 2.7 m (upper floors)
site area:	2,250 m²
gross floor area:	5,062 m²
total construction cost:	€ 3.078 mill. (gross)
date of construction:	1st building stage 1995 2nd building stage 2001
period of construction:	1st building stage 11 months 2nd building stage June 11 months

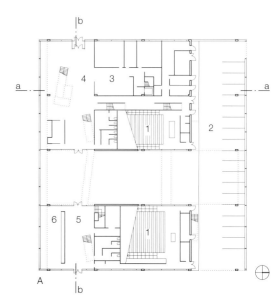

A

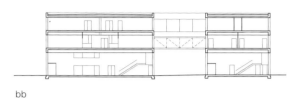

bb

floor plans
sections
scale 1:800

A   ground floor
B   mezzanine
C   first floor
D   second floor

1   lecture hall
2   parking area
3   administration
4   foyer (1st phase)
5   foyer (2nd phase)
6   EDP room
7   library
8   departmental rooms
9   seminar rooms

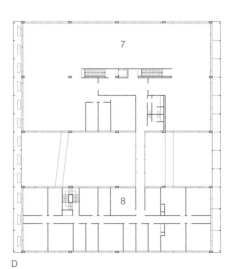

D

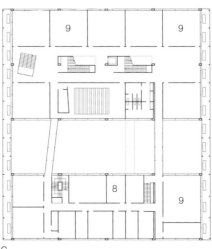

C

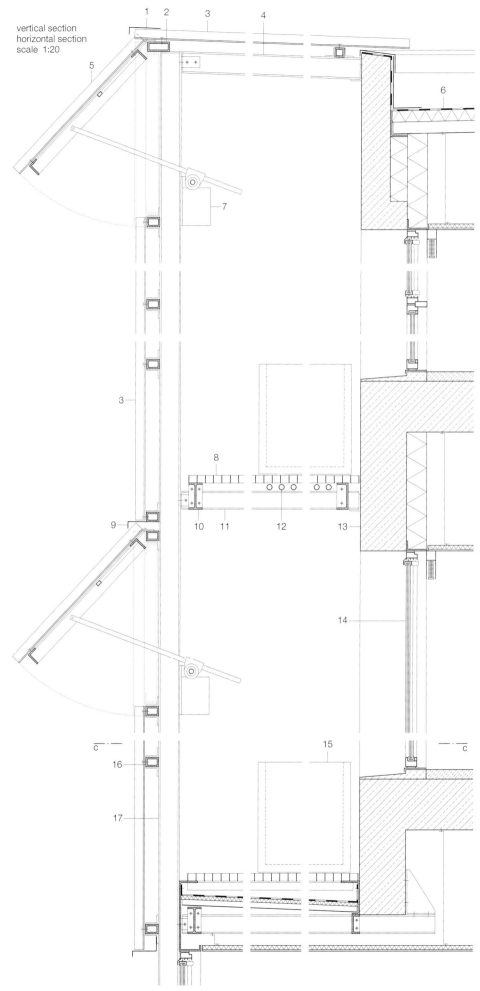

vertical section
horizontal section
scale 1:20

1   heat-formed transparent polycarbonate
    edge-section with UV-protection layer
2   100 × 50 mm galvanized steel RHS
3   177 × 51 × 3 mm corrugated transparent
    polycarbonate sheeting with UV-protection layer
4   120 mm galvanized steel I-column
5   ventilation flap: corrugated polycarbonate
    sheeting
    50 × 50 × 5 mm steel angle frame with
    20 × 20 × 2.3 mm steel SHS bracing
6   roof sealing membrane
    80 mm rigid-foam thermal insulation
    vapour barrier
    70 mm ribbed metal sheeting
7   electric motor for opening flap
8   40 mm pressed steel grating
9   galvanized sheet steel bent to shape
10 140 mm galvanized steel I-beam
11 120 mm galvanized steel I-beam
12 heating pipes
13 reinforced concrete frame
14 aluminium sliding window
    with insulating double glazing
15 planting tub
16 70 × 50 × 4 mm galvanized steel
    RHS sub-structure
17 100 mm galvanized steel I-column

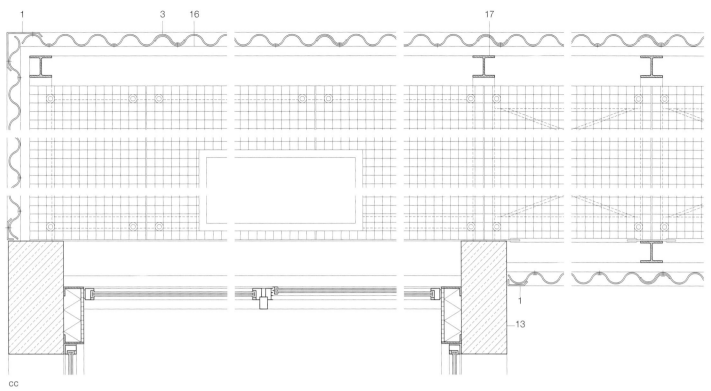

cc

Residential and Office Building in Kassel

The modular principle on which this urban residential and office block is based was developed in response to the competition brief, which required a building type suitable for eight differently shaped sites within a residential development on the outskirts of Kassel. The architects designed a flexible load-bearing structure that can be extended in all directions and allows functionally neutral spaces to be created.

Based on a column grid of 3.0 by 3.3 m, this building can be extended or altered according to function. The prototype constructed here is strictly cuboid with external dimensions of 13.52 × 12.30 × 15.40 metres. The seven companion buildings were constructed by other competition prizewinners.

Set idyllically in a park in close proximity to the River Fulda, with its nearby quay and historical cable suspension bridge, the building has a southern flair, which is accentuated by the combination of untreated, larch infill panels and storey-height glazing to the living rooms that allow parkland views.

In order to ensure an even weathering process the external timber was left untreated. The folding-sliding shutters of varying heights can be opened to any position thereby animating the facade.

In order to achieve the desired diversity of facade treatments and the necessary structural stability, the building was organised in a number of different systems.

The load-bearing structure was designed as a concrete frame, with columns, filigree floor slabs and bracing filigree walls, which are grouped together to provide service and access cores. The timber-framed elements which were mounted to this basic structure include fully closed elements and elements with large or small bands of windows. These panels were constructed in small series in a local carpentry works. Ship-lap boarding and window shutters were assembled at a later date in order to achieve the desired flush junctions with the precast concrete facade elements. The uniform dimensions of both the load-bearing and infill elements made it possible to limit the project to serial fabrication with all its associated benefits; precise dimensions, independence of weather and economy of time and money. In order to achieve slender dimensions, the reinforced concrete frame and the solid external elements were clad with prefabricated panels of glass-fibre concrete, whereby the various functions of the internal spaces – garage, bathrooms and storage spaces – remain highly legible externally. The storage spaces that replace a basement were moved outside on the northern side of the building and wholly clad with glass-fibre concrete; a fine concrete with an additive of alkaline-resistant glass fibres. Since these fibres are non-corrosive, there are no minimum material cover requirements.

To bring out the character of a free-standing villa, the architects avoided all ancillary structures, incorporating eight of the required nine parking spaces, for example, within the volume of the building in a combined lift and parking system. The plinth level and ground floor contain a 120 m² maisonette, which can be used as either office or dwelling. The upper floors can be divided into two or three-room dwellings, while the maisonettes on the top floors have large roof terraces with views towards the water.

project team • building details

architects:	Alexander Reichel, Kassel/Munich
with:	Johanna Reichel-Vossen, Stefan Seibert, Caroline Ossenberg-Engels, Elke Radloff
structural engineers:	Hobein, Kleinhans, Marx, Hochtief AG, Kassel

function:	housing and offices
construction:	concrete
system:	frame construction
internal ceiling height:	2.5 m
site area:	552 m²
total internal volume:	3,079 m³
total construction cost:	€ 1,9 mill. (gross)
date of construction:	1999
period of construction:	14 months

isometric
floor plans • section
scale 1:500

A   basement
B   ground floor
C   1st and 2nd floor
D   3rd floor
E   4th floor

1   entrance
2   bicycle storeroom
3   garage
4   office
5   store
6   two-bedroom dwelling
7   maisonette dwelling
8   roof terrace

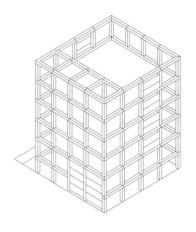

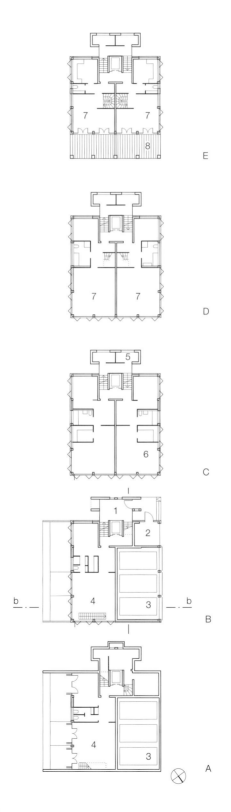

E

D

C

B

A

b —·— —·— b

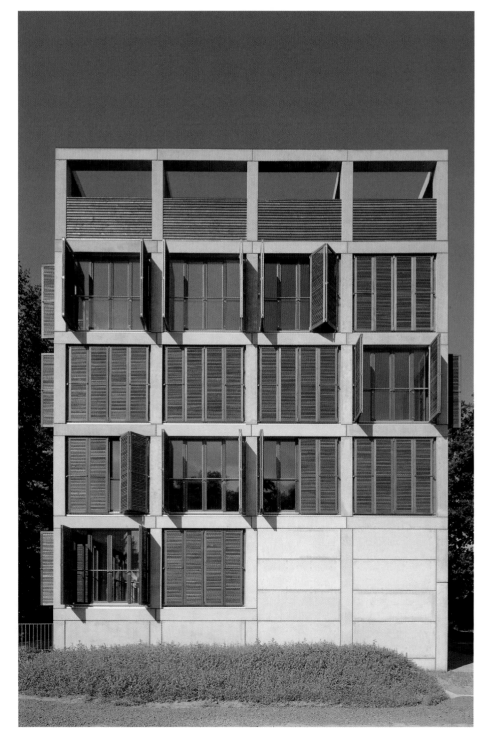

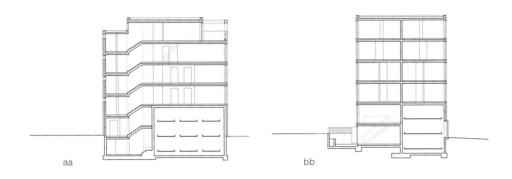

aa

bb

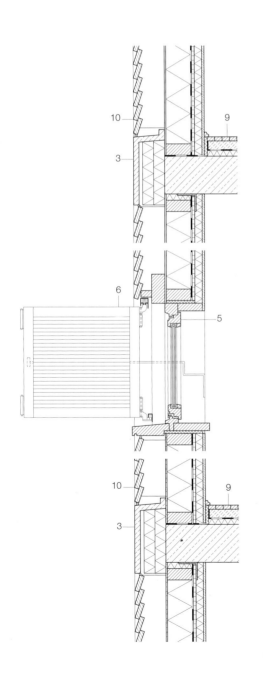

10

9

3

6

5

10

9

3

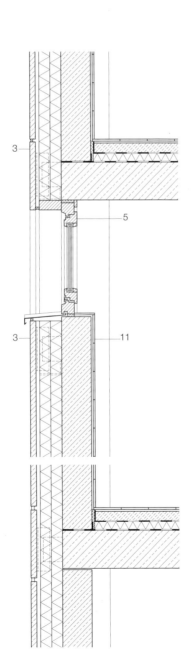

3

5

3

11

a   b   c

Panel systems

In panel constructions the structural systems consist of planar wall and slab elements, which simultaneously form an enclosed space. The panels can be constructed of steel, timber construction materials, concrete or masonry. Both small, narrow panels and large, room-sized panels are self-supporting elements.
Panel construction methods are differentiated according to three construction principles:

Small panel construction
Today, small panel construction is only used in low-level, multi-storey buildings. In this system, the walls are constructed of narrow, storey-high panels, between which slender slab elements are spanned. The wall and slab elements are constructed in widths of 60 to 120 cm. Small-format panels allow more individual design processes than the larger-format panels; however, the number of joints is considerably greater and should be considered when planning. Although small elements are more easily assembled using simpler hoisting equipment, they require more time for assembly.

Large-panel construction
The structural system of large-panel construction consists of floor slabs supported on four edges by the longitudinal and transverse walls below. If the slab span is limited to 6 m, it is possible to support it on only two axes; that is, in either the longitudinal or transverse direction. Should the slab be supported in the transverse direction by the longitudinal walls, the non-load-bearing transverse walls only act as bracing and partitioning elements.

Crosswall construction
The structural system for crosswall constructions consists of transverse walls as arranged parallel to act as supports for the floor slabs above. As the direction of span of the slabs is longitudinal, the slab can be constructed continuously across a number of fields. The economical moment situation allows a slab construction of minimal static depth, which leads to a saving of construction materials. Bracing is provided by longitudinal walls or stairwells. As the facades on the shorter ends of the compartments do not carry any loads, they can be enclosed with lightweight partitioning elements (fig. C 3.1).

Generally, external wall elements must fulfil all the necessary requirements of building physics and, subsequent to assembly, be absolutely tight at all junctions. They must be light enough to ensure ease of transport and assembly, even when thermally and acoustically insulated to the required levels.

The dimensions of the panels are dependent upon material selection, transport conditions and constructional grid dimensions; panel height is equivalent to storey height. The panels are connected using standard methods; the choice of technique is influenced by both the wall panel material and overall construction system.
The supporting consoles are the load-transferring construction elements; the connections must transfer all forces of compression, tension and shear from the load-bearing members.

C 3.2

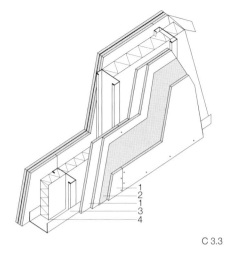

C 3.3

C 3.1 Construction principles of panel systems
    a Small-panel construction
    b Large-panel construction
    c Crosswall construction
C 3.2 Manufacture of a steel frame construction
    in a factory
C 3.3 Steel frame wall construction
    1 12.5 mm plasterboard cladding
    2 0.38 mm metal panel
    3 C-section (416 mm centre distance)
    4 insulating fibreboard
C 3.4 Isometric representation of steel-frame con-
    struction; intermediate floor connection and
    footing connection
C 3.5 Construction principles of steel-frame con-
    struction
    a Platform building method
    b Balloon frame building method

Building with steel panels

Steel panel building methods

Framework construction is the basic principle employed when building with steel
panels. The differences, however, are that
the loads are transferred via the columns
in the skeleton in timber framework construction, whereas, in conjunction with the
cladding, the steel frame acts as a plate.
The steel frames and cross ribs are manufactured in the factory and the panels
are delivered to the site either as framework or complete with cladding, depending on the level of prefabrication.

Steel framework construction
In this form of construction, the load-
bearing panel elements are constructed
out of cold rolled-steel sections as rough
building elements for walls, slabs and
roofs (fig. C 3.2). The advantages of this
building method are the low weight and
high load-bearing capacity of the construction elements. The metal frames are
constructed of vertical standing sections
(studs), arranged at intervals of 40 to
80 cm, which are connected at the top
and bottom by U-profile channel sections.
The connections are either welded or
screwed. The construction owes its stability to the double-sided cladding of various materials. A wall is produced that
acts either as a panel or slab and transfers all applied loads to the adjacent
building elements. The cavities between
the studs are insulated according to thermal and acoustic requirements (figs. C
3.3 and C 3.4). In order to minimise the

thermal bridging effects of the metal
studs, the elements can be equipped with
an additional insulation layer. It is possible to produce the finished elements
complete with installations and finished
surfaces. Site assembly connection of the
prefabricated panels is carried out by
screwed and bolted fixings using simple
hand or electric tools. Planning and construction grids are based on the axial grid
principle. Analogous to timber framework
construction, there are two different
approaches to the assembly:

Platform construction systems
Buildings constructed using platform
building methods are erected storey by
storey. The floor slabs rest on the storey-
high wall units (fig. C 3.5a).

Balloon frame construction systems
In balloon frame construction systems,
the external walls stretch over the full
height of the buildings. The floor slabs are
not connected to the wall construction,
but to console elements that are welded
to the stud sections (fig. C 3.5b, p. 111).

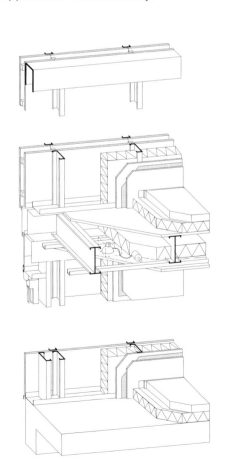

C 3.4

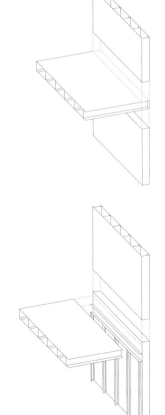

a

b

C 3.5

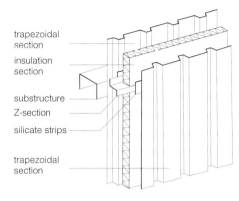

trapezoidal
section

insulation
section

substructure

Z-section

silicate strips

trapezoidal
section

C 3.6

The weight savings of steel, compared with timber, framework constructions is approximately 30% and about 66% compared with solid wall constructions.
This building method is widely used for prefabricated homes in Japan, but has also broken into the housing markets in the USA, Canada and Australia. In Germany, however, this "new" building method has not gained acceptance and only about 1% of housing construction is carried out using these techniques. Here, they are predominantly used in industrial construction for halls and warehouses.
Both large and small panels can be used in steel framework construction systems. Small-size wall panels have the advantage that they are adaptable to a great variety of different building forms. Large panels are manufactured as wall units with widths of up to 12.5 m and slab elements with span dimensions of up to 14 m.

▶ Cocoon Transformer
  (Cocoon Systemleichtbau AG)
This steel frame construction is most suitable for new buildings, extensions and the addition of one or more storeys. The wall units are manufactured, fully finished, in the plant and are ready for assembly on site (fig. C 3.8). The cladding and insulation are coordinated with the individual wishes of the client. These system elements are particularly appropriate for wide spanning wall and slab constructions. They can be extended and added to in both vertical and horizontal directions as desired.
For example, with this system, the load-bearing structure of a single-family house can be erected within three to four days (fig. C 3.7).
• application:
  external and internal walls, intermediate floor slabs, fire-proof walls
• usage:
  office and administration buildings, housing, social facilities, small industrial facilities

Construction materials and elements
Sectional sheet panels
Wall panels of sectional sheeting are prefabricated, non-load-bearing elements and are solely suitable for partitioning and enclosure (fig. C 3.9). They can be manufactured as single or double-layered elements, with or without insulation (fig. C 3.6). Coated sectional sheets are mounted to substructures in production plants to produce wall elements; the cavities between can be filled with thermal insulation on site, as desired. They are very economical building materials due to the minimal assembly required and can be easily reused when building alterations are carried out. Due to their low thermal storage capacity, these panels do not satisfy the requirements of structural physics for housing construction and are, therefore, mostly used for industrial applications.
In the housing industry, double-layered, thermally insulated, trapezoidal or corrugated metal wall panels are well established. The highly processed external layer and the internal layer are connected by spacers, although still thermally separated. The humidity that penetrates the

C 3.7

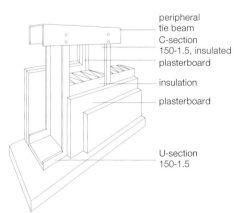

peripheral
tie beam
C-section
150-1.5, insulated
plasterboard

insulation

plasterboard

U-section
150-1.5

C 3.8

C 3.9

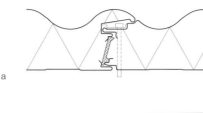
a

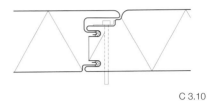
b

C 3.10

U-section	C-section	Z-section	S-sectionl	Hat-section	I-section (double C-section)
slabs floors	studs floor beams	purlins	purlins joists	purlins	joists

C 3.11

panels from the inside of the building is transferred to the outside via the air layer behind the outer surface. The cavities between the spacers are filled with mineral fibre thermal insulation. Fixing the sheeting to the substructure, and the wall panels to each other, are both executed with screws and keyed joints.

Sandwich elements
Sandwich elements are self-supporting composite building units that can be used for both facade and roof cladding. They consist of two thin metal layers fixed together in a shear-resistant manner with an internal insulating core; they are resistant to bending moments and can easily absorb out-of-phase forces, such as wind, in spite of their minimal thickness and weight. The stability of the metal layers of the sandwich elements is enhanced by additional preliminary rolling and folding processes; suitable materials are aluminium, steel and stainless steel. The insulating core is usually manufactured of rigid polystyrene foam panels. The production of sandwich panels takes place in specially equipped fabrication plants that

produce continuous lengths. Sandwich roof panels are usually 1000 mm wide and measure between 70 and 110 mm in depth. Facade elements are produced in standard construction dimensions of 600 to 1200 mm with depths of 40 to 200 mm. Both panels can be delivered in lengths of up to 20 m.
System-specific connections and intersections have been developed for sandwich element based building systems (fig. C 3.10). In addition to the standard screw fixings, non-visible connections such as concealed screw fixings and pin connections are available for more highly developed facades. Surface structure, colour selection, joint arrangement and manner of fixing are critical for the final appearance of sandwich panel facades [1].

Lightweight steel sections
Lightweight steel sections are formed of hot-dipped galvanised steel sheeting with thicknesses of 1 to 2.5 mm. The most common sections are C, U and Z-sections that are available in lengths of up to 12 m (fig. C 3.11).

Steel sheeting
Steel sheeting is rolled in fabrication plants in widths of 2000 mm. Cold-rolled sheeting can be up to 100 mm thick, and hot-rolled sheeting up to 3 mm thick, prior to being further processed as trapezoidal or corrugated sectional sheeting. The stability of non-sectional sheeting can be enhanced by further processing, such as the forming of ridges or ribbing (fig. C 3.12).

C 3.6   Trapezoidal sheet steel wall
C 3.7   House, steel frame construction (Cocoon Transformer), Zagreb (HR) 2006
C 3.8   Construction of a cocoon wall
C 3.9   Manufacture of trapezoidal steel sheeting
C 3.10 Concealed jointing for sandwich elements
        a Sandwich element with corrugated cover plate
        b Sandwich element with flat cover plate
C 3.11 Lightweight cold-rolled steel sections
C 3.12 Steel sheet sections
        a Trapezoidal sheeting
        b Asymmetric corrugated sheeting
C 3.13 Sandwich element facade, administration building telecommunication concern, Oporto (P) 1997, Joao Alvaro Rocha and José Manuel Gigante

a

b
C 3.12

C 3.13

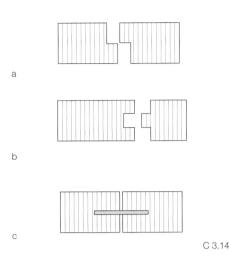

a

b

c

C 3.14

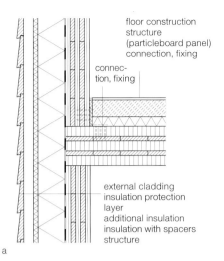

floor construction
structure
(particleboard panel)
connection, fixing

connec-
tion, fixing

external cladding
insulation protection
layer
additional insulation
insulation with spacers
structure

a

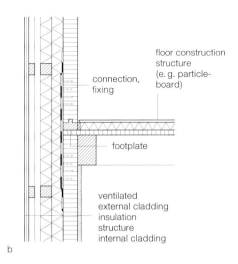

floor construction
structure
(e. g. particle-
board)

connection,
fixing

footplate

ventilated
external cladding
insulation
structure
internal cladding

b

Building with timber panels

Timber panel construction systems are subdivided into panel construction, framework construction, block construction and building with timber modules. The elements used in timber panel construction are usually made of solid timber or processed timber construction materials with stiffening cross ribs, whereas clad timber frames are used in framework construction.

Timber panel building methods
The different building methods are described below:

Timber panel construction
The load-bearing elements in timber panel construction can be both small or large panels of timber building materials. They fulfil both structural and partitioning functions (fig. C 3.15). The loads are transferred to the foundations via the panels; in timber building methods, the foundations are concrete floor slabs. The junctions between the timber panels are fabricated as butt connections gener-

ally fixed with either tongue-and-groove joints, with rebated joints, pinned with either hardwood or steel dowels, or nailed with perforated steel plates (fig. C 3.14). Corner junctions are secured by either screws or bolts. Sealing profiles or sealing strips are necessary to protect the joints against moisture penetration.
The selection of transport vehicles and hoisting equipment is dependent upon the dimensions of the elements and their resultant weight.
Large panels are often used in housing construction where they are employed in room-high or building-high sizes. Timber panels for external walls can measure up to 14.5 m in length. Slab elements can be up to 2.5 m wide and span up to 10 m. Small panels are also room-high but with widths of 60 to 125 cm. The dimensions of the slab elements correlate with the large panels. Due to the minimal weight of these elements, simple lifting equipment can be used. Both small and large panels are between 60 and 120 mm thick. Timber panel building is divided into construction with timber block panels and solid timber building units.

Timber block panels
Timber block panels are manufactured of processed timber construction materials and stabilised against bending with cross ribs making them exceptionally stiff and dimensionally stable building elements. The fields between the ribs are either filled with thermal insulation or used for installation lines (fig. C 3.17).

Solid timber panels
Solid timber panels are produced by laminating solid timber, processed timber construction materials or timber shavings under pressure (fig. C 3.18). Compared with timber block panels, they can carry loads in two directions. The panels are fully prefabricated in the factory, openings for door and windows as well as cavities for installation lines, are accurately pre-cut (fig. C 3.16). All necessary insulation materials are mounted to the exterior of the structural system; the thickness of the insulation varies according to the individual requirements (fig. C 3.19) [2].

C 3.15

C 3.16

C 3.17

C 3.18

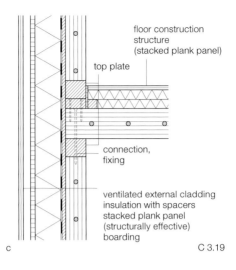

floor construction structure (stacked plank panel)

top plate

connection, fixing

ventilated external cladding
insulation with spacers
stacked plank panel (structurally effective)
boarding

c   C 3.19

C 3.14   Connection of solid timber panel
          elements
          a rebated connection
          b tongue-and-groove connection
          c pin/dowel connection
C 3.15   Assembly of timber panels
C 3.16   Shell construction of a solid timber panel
          building, Atelier, Hellerau (D) 2004,
          Deutsche Werkstätten Hellerau,
          Albrecht Quinke
C 3.17   Timber block panels
C 3.18   Solid timber panels
C 3.19   Slab to wall connection with load-bearing
          laminated timber panels

          a Plywood panel construction
          b Particleboard panel construction
          c Stacked plank construction
C 3.20   Haas System
          a Double tongue-and-groove connection
            between stacked plank elements
          b Vertical section; wall-slab connection
C 3.21   LIGNOTREND planar element
          a Timber block panel elements
          b Vertical section; wall-slab connection
C 3.22   Lignatur planar element
          a Box, shell and planar elements
          b Vertical section; wall-slab connection in
            timber frame construction

▶ System Haas
  (Haas Fertigbau GmbH)

In this case, the solid timber units are
stacked-plank-panels that measure up to
600 mm in width with thicknesses of 80 to
240 mm. Single span beams can span
widths of 6 m, and continuous beams up
to 7.5 m. The elements are jointed with
tongue-and-groove connections, splices
or timber construction strips. The great
advantage of this system is that the
panels can be finished with CNC controlled machines (fig. C 3.20).
• application:
  walls, slabs, roofs
• usage:
  single and multi-family housing, industrial and administration buildings,
  schools and kindergartens, sports halls
  and agricultural constructions

▶ LIGNOTREND planar elements
  (LIGNOTREND AG)

The timber block panels of this system
can measure up to 18 m in length and are
600 mm wide with a thickness of 282 mm.
These panels are exceptionally stable
due to their multi-layered construction
and also offer high quality sound protection. The cavities between the cross-
bracing can be filled with insulation (fig.
C 3.21).
• application:
  walls, slabs, roofs
• usage:
  single and multi-family housing, industrial and administration buildings,
  schools and kindergartens

▶ Lignatur
  (Lignatur AG)

The timber block panels are available as
load-bearing box, planar or shell elements. They are connected by tongue-
and-groove or steel pin fixings. The elements are available in thicknesses of 120
to 320 mm, the box elements are 195 mm
wide and the planar and shell elements
514 mm and 1000 mm wide. All units
comply with thermal and sound protection
requirements, the box elements are additionally filled with insulation. The panels
can be processed by CNC controlled
machines (fig. C 3.22).
• application:
  walls, slabs, roofs
• usage:
  single and multi-family housing, industrial and administration buildings,
  schools and kindergartens

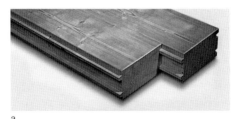

a

a

a

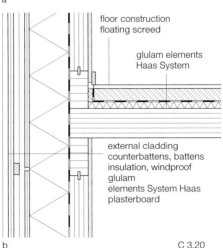

floor construction
floating screed

glulam elements
Haas System

external cladding
counterbattens, battens
insulation, windproof
glulam
elements System Haas
plasterboard

b   C 3.20

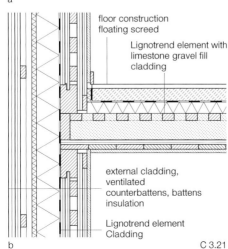

floor construction
floating screed

Lignotrend element with
limestone gravel fill
cladding

external cladding,
ventilated
counterbattens, battens
insulation

Lignotrend element
Cladding

b   C 3.21

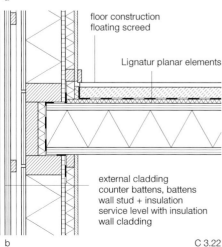

floor construction
floating screed

Lignatur planar elements

external cladding
counter battens, battens
wall stud + insulation
service level with insulation
wall cladding

b   C 3.22

C 3.23

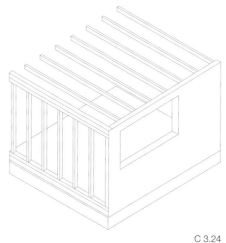
C 3.24

Timber framework construction
This technique is a further development of the traditional timber frame and lightweight stud construction techniques. The most important difference between these methods is the bracing principle. Traditional timber framed buildings are braced by struts or stays, while timber studwork structures are stabilised by being clad with processed timber construction panels. This modern system, however, combines these two techniques (fig. 3.24). Although timber frame elements act as non-load-bearing infill members in frame construction, they function as load-bearing walls in panel constructions.

In order to ensure the condition of the timber, the framework elements are manufactured in climatically controlled production plants. The first step is the cladding of the load-bearing substructure on at least one side with the panels of processed timber construction material and pre-assembly. Subsequently, openings are cut. The building unit is then insulated and clad on the second side (fig. C 3.25). The elements are available with varying

levels of prefabrication depending on the required functions and standards of building physics. A high level of prefabrication is achieved when the panels are produced with complete facade treatment, internal wall cladding surfaces and installation ducts for technical services. The load-bearing structure consists of frames of strut-like scantlings, which are clad with planar processed timber construction materials, thereby ensuring plate-like static performance. The vertical scantlings transfer the vertical loads from the roof and ceiling slabs, while the timber panels absorb the horizontal loads. The use of laminated spruce and fir timbers assists in the dimensional stability of the panels.
The cross-sectional dimensions of the scantlings are determined after calculations on the static situation have been made. Generally, the cross-sections are between 60 × 120 and 80 × 160 mm. The fields between the timbers provide space for thermal insulation panels (fig. C 3.26). In order to prevent thermal bridging, the external walls can be additionally clad with conventional materials. This makes it possible for the building to

achieve low-energy or even passive-building standards.
On site, the framework elements are placed with the help of hoisting equipment, anchored on the foundation or slab and, in this way, assembled storey-wise to produce a building.
The force-locked connections between the individual members are provided by steel elements which can be screwed to the wall panels (fig. C 3.23).
Although the maximum unit sizes are subject to transportation limitations, the dimensions of the rooms are determined by the allowable spans of the floor and ceiling slabs.
Processed timber construction panels, shingles and solid timber panels are often used as extra external facade cladding. The internal cladding also provides air and moisture sealing barriers.
When planning timber frame constructions, setting and shrinkage of the structure, which can be as much as 240 to 500 mm per storey, must be taken into account. [3].

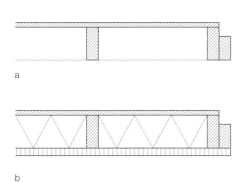
a

b

C 3.25

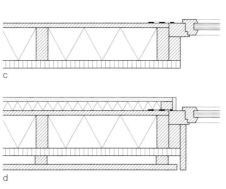
c

d

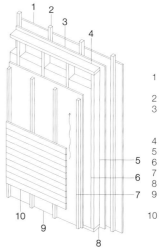

1 internal cladding
2 vertical battens
3 processed timber panel (impermeable)
4 frame top
5 side frame
6 insulation
7 battens
8 frame bottom
9 fibreboard, bituminised
10 horizontal boarding

C 3.26

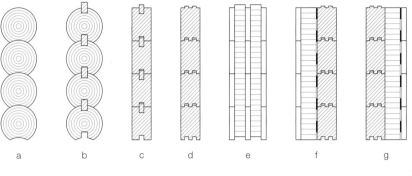

a   b   c   d   e   f   g

C 3.28   C 3.29

▶ AGEPAN building system
(Glunz AG)

The panel elements of the Agepan building system are frame constructions constructed of OSB panels and web beams. The system is not confined to a particular grid and the elements are specialised for each building project. The moisture-permeable roof elements are completed with cellulose insulation and the walls comply with the low-energy requirements for external walls (NEW-F30-B) (fig. C 3.27).

· application:
  walls, slabs, roofs
· usage:
  single and multi-family housing, industrial and administration buildings, schools and kindergartens, specialised facilities

Timber block construction

Timber block construction has a long tradition and can be considered as being the forerunner of modern-day timber panel construction techniques using solid timber panels (figs. C 3.28 and C 3.29). The walls are constructed of horizontal beams that are fixed at the corners. Thus, the beams fulfil the functions of partitioning and load-bearing. Bracing occurs through the plate effect of the solid timber walls and the corner detailing which is based on cog junctions at the intersection of the wall panels and resistant to bending. It is important to take into account that the contraction of the solid timber elements can reach 25 mm per storey after assembly. However, the insulation level of traditional block construction no longer complies with modern requirements. In order to retain the traditional character of solid timber walling in spite of the additional insulation level, double-leaf walls are constructed, with insulation in the cavity. A variety of different systems have been developed with thermal insulation, installation cavities and cladding already provided (fig. C 3.30).

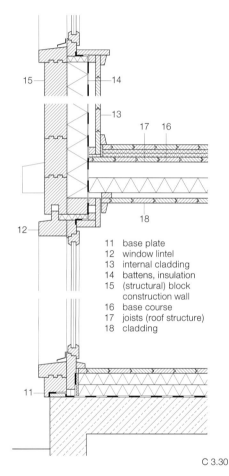

11   base plate
12   window lintel
13   internal cladding
14   battens, insulation
15   (structural) block
      construction wall
16   base course
17   joists (roof structure)
18   cladding

C 3.30

a

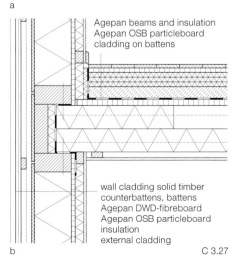

Agepan beams and insulation
Agepan OSB particleboard
cladding on battens

wall cladding solid timber
counterbattens, battens
Agepan DWD-fibreboard
Agepan OSB particleboard
insulation
external cladding

b   C 3.27

C 3.23   Shell, timber frame construction
C 3.24   Isometric diagram of timber frame structural system
C 3.25   Process of wall construction in timber frame construction
        a single-sided cladding of a timber frame element
        b double-sided cladding of a timber frame element with thermal insulation infill
        c element, including built-in units; (windows and doors)
        d element, including external and internal cladding
C 3.26   Isometric diagram of the layers of a timber frame wall
C 3.27   Agepan building system
        a Agepan beam

        b vertical section, wall-slab connection
C 3.28   Development of the external wall from traditional to modern block construction
        a round timbers
        b notched round timbers
        c notched scantlings
        d tongue-and grooved scantlings
        e prefabricated sandwich elements
        f block-construction wall with external insulation
        g block-construction wall with internal insulation
C 3.29   Application of modern block construction in Switzerland, house, Blatten, Wallis (CH) 2001, Gion A. Caminada, Vrin Cons
C 3.30   Section through a house facade built in modern block technique

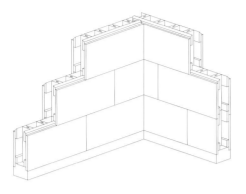

a   b   C 3.31

Building with timber modules
Industrially fabricated timber modules based on the cross-wise lamination of solid timber slats is a new development in solid timber construction (fig. C 3.32a). Similar to masonry blocks, these practical modules can be assembled to form load-bearing walls in a specialised, interlinked course (fig. C 3.31a). The structural system appears planar and can absorb both vertical and horizontal loads. Continuous hollow cavities through the elements provide access for the installation of technical services or insulation. The small size of these construction elements makes a great variety of different building forms possible.

The coordination of the modules and special building units, such as window sills and lintels, enables the creation of a closed building system combining the constructional advantages of masonry work with the positive characteristics of the natural building material, wood [4].

▶ Steko timber module connector system (Steko Holz-Bausysteme AG)
These modules are small box elements; the interlinked courses allow the assembly of walls (fig. C 3.31b). The modules are available in the standard width of 160 mm with lengths of 160, 320, 480 and 640 mm, and heights of 240 and 320 mm. The system is modular, creating great scope for design freedom in conjunction with simple assembly techniques. The timber module is constructed of cross-wise laminated solid timber panels and thus offers great stability and durability (fig. C 3.32b).
• application:
 walls
• usage:
 single and multi-family housing, industrial and administration buildings, schools and kindergartens, infill elements for frame constructions

Construction materials and elements
In timber panel construction, simple panels can be regarded as elements and, if they are sufficiently thick, can then be considered to behave as solid panels.

Wood fibreboard
Wood fibreboard panels are produced by compacting and pressing fibrous timber particles. Their homogeneous panel structure allows spanning in both axes. In unitised construction, wood fibreboard panels are used for cladding and bracing timber framed elements.

Particleboard
Particleboard panels are produced of sawdust mixed with an adhesive agent and pressed flat. In unitised construction, they are most widely used as load-bearing and bracing elements for cladding walls, ceilings and roofs.

OSB panels
OSB panels (Oriented Strand Board) are produced of large chips of wood, glued under heat and pressure with their strands at 90° to each other. Due to the alternation of the strand directions, these boards can be loaded in both the longitudinal and transverse direction. Typical areas of application are the cladding of load-bearing and bracing walls in timber frame construction.

Cement-bonded particleboard
The standard dimensions of cement-bonded particleboard (produced with timber fibres, Portland cement and water) are 3100 × 1250 mm. The panel thicknesses vary between 12 and 18 mm. They are particularly suitable as facade elements due to the specific material characteristics of frost resistance, mois-

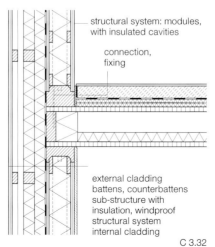

structural system: modules, with insulated cavities

connection, fixing

external cladding
battens, counterbattens
sub-structure with
insulation, windproof
structural system
internal cladding

a   b   C 3.32

C 3.35

C 3.33

C 3.34

C 3.31 Steko timber module connector system
     a Corner connection
     b Construction process
C 3.32 Steko timber module
     a Front view of module
     b Vertical section; wall-slab connection
C 3.34 Heavy-gauge laminated timber panel
C 3.35 Stacked-plank timber element
C 3.36 Shell of a multi-storey housing block in large-
     panel construction

ture resistance and minimal moisture expansion.

Glue-laminated timber panels (glulam)
Glue-laminated timber panels are manufactured of three or five glued timber layers orientated according to alternating direction of fibre to produce a building material suitable for the planar transfer of loads. They absorb loads in both vertical and horizontal directions and are dimensionally very stable. Glue-laminated timber panels are used for load-bearing timber construction and bracing cladding for walls, slabs and roofs in unitised constructions.

Laminated veneer timber panels
Laminated veneer timber panels are constructed of multiple layers of timber veneer which, in contrast to glue-laminated timber panels, are laminated parallel to the direction of the fibres. The veneers are pressed with a water-proof binding agent with the edges off-set. Laminated veneer timber panels can be considered as acting like glulam panels.

Heavy gauge laminated timber elements
Laminated timber elements of pressed timber shavings or multiple layers of laminated timber construction panels can also be produced with thicknesses of 60 to 100 mm. Wall elements constructed of these industrially manufactured heavy gauge panels can act as load-bearing elements. The panels can be produced in any desired dimension and standard elements such as door and windows can easily be inserted in the factory (fig. C 3.33).

Stacked-plank panels
Stacked-plank panels are solid timber elements with a high load-bearing capacity. They are constructed of planks or boards that are stacked parallel to each other and connected with special nails or hardwood dowels. Stacked-plank panels usually have a thickness of 80 to 240 mm and their maximum length is 12 m. Openings for doors, windows and other slab penetrations can be allowed for during production [5] (fig. C 3.34).

Building with concrete panels

Concrete panel building methods
The most frequently used form of panel construction system is prefabricated reinforced concrete panels (fig. C 3.35). Although multi-storey housing construction makes use of crosswall, small and large panel construction techniques, crosswall construction is the most commonly employed method (fig. C 3.36a, p. 120). The load-bearing walls, which are set transverse to the building length (crosswalls), can act simultaneously as partitioning elements between two dwelling units. A flexible planning layout is possible between the crosswalls. These load-bearing elements are dense enough to also fulfil sound insulation and fire protection requirements. An economical load-bearing system is accomplished when the floor and ceiling slabs are set directly onto the crosswalls as continuous elements.

Small panel construction methods are commonly used techniques for low-rise housing. The small sizes of the building units allow a great variety of design and combination alternatives. Due to their minimal weight, aerated concrete panels are particularly suitable here as they only require small-scale hoisting equipment on site.

In large panel construction, the elements for walls and floors are reinforced concrete slabs, which are prefabricated as either normal or lightweight concrete according to the specific requirements. Wall panels can be prefabricated in the factory room-high and up to 6 m long, with windows, doors and service ducts already installed. The assembly on site is carried out storey by storey. Dimensional

119

C 3.36 Structural system of large-panel construction
  a Crosswall construction with load-bearing
     transverse walls and continuous slab
  b Large-panel construction with load-bear-
     ing longitudinal walls and non-load-bear-
     ing transverse walls
  c Large-panel construction with load-bear-
     ing longitudinal and transverse walls
C 3.37 Reinforced concrete sandwich element
C 3.38 Fixing anchor for the connection of layers of
        a sandwich element
  a Fixing anchor
  b Connection of anchor with reinforcement
C 3.39 Joint treatment with tongue-and-groove
C 3.40 Joint treatment of sandwich panels
  a Sealing strip with chamfered bond
  b Sealing with sealing compound
  c Tie-shaped sealing strip with edge
     bonding
  d Horizontal and vertical joints
C 3.41 Filling of cavity with in situ concrete

C 3.37

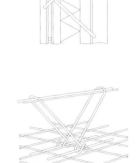

a

b

C 3.38

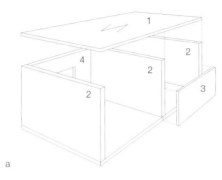

a

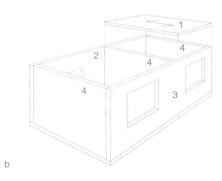

b

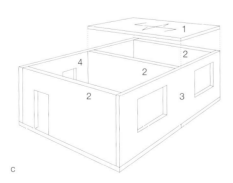

c

1 slab
2 transverse wall
3 facade element
4 longitudinal wall

C 3.36

tolerances are fixed in the German DIN 18 203-1 building standard.

This type of construction technique was decisive for building the mass housing that was necessary after the Second World War. The characteristic appearance of these buildings results from the fact that the internal layout is recognizable from the visible arrangement of the joints on the facades. The subsequent departure from multi-storey housing developments, and the desire for more individualised architectural design solutions, caused large concrete panel construction to be confined to projects where speedy assembly is required and where heavy-duty hoisting equipment can be economically employed (figs. C 3.36b–c).

Construction elements

Reinforced concrete wall elements
Reinforced concrete wall elements are the characteristic features of both large panel and crosswall construction methods; they can be used as either load-bearing or non-load-bearing building elements. The thickness of the load-bearing walls is determined by static calculations and the minimum allowable depth of the floor slab which is between 14 and 20 cm. This is also sufficient to fulfil the necessary sound and fire protection requirements. Non-load-bearing walls are employed as bracing and partition elements.

After setting and adjusting the reinforced concrete wall elements on site, the butt joints are filled with special mortar to ensure a rigid connection.

In contemporary building applications, shell constructions are usually erected with reinforced concrete panel techniques, while individual systems are used for interior fit-out construction and external building envelopes.

Sandwich elements
Sandwich panels are manufactured in plants for use as external walling. They consist of three layers – load-bearing, insulating and facing (fig. C 3.27). High-strength concrete is poured into steel formwork and can harden under optimal conditions, independent of weather. A better surface finish and narrower elements are possible with factory-controlled prefabrication than with in situ production methods. The individual elements are horizontally produced in a number of stages and finally assembled to create the final panel. During production the surface treatment and structure of the external facade is determined; usually by the base of the formwork. The upper surface of the slabs are planed, either manually or mechanically, or later rendered or clad on site. The same applies when exposed concrete is desired for the internal surface. The fixing anchors, which are poured with the slabs, can absorb loads from all directions and are responsible for the connection of the individual layers of the sandwich panels (fig. C 3.38).

The load-bearing layer of the sandwich panels, which supports the floor slab, transfers all vertical and horizontal loads to the foundation. Therefore, it must be statically correct and reinforced; the thickness of this layer is usually between 80 and 150 mm. The thermal insulation between the concrete layers consists of flame retardant, closed-pore rigid foam. The thickness of the insulation is dependent upon thermal protection requirements. The facing concrete layer provides protection from the weather and determines the design of the facade. Due to the required steel reinforcement, this layer is at least 70 mm thick.

Should increased levels of moisture make a ventilation layer necessary, this must

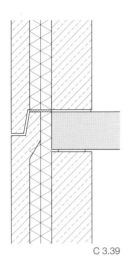
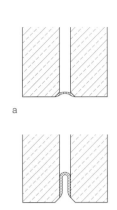
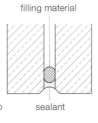
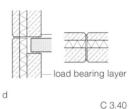

C 3.39

filling material

a

b   sealant

c

d   load bearing layer

C 3.40

C 3.41

measure at least 40 mm and be coordinated into the sandwich panel between the insulation and facing layers. Additionally, during assembly, protective plastic stippled membranes or removable polystyrene blocks are set between the layers.

The dimensions of the sandwich panels are determined by production, transport and assembly possibilities. The standard lengths are between 4 and 10 m. Larger panels are usually considered more economical due to the reduced assembly time on site. The maximum size of the facing concrete layers is usually restricted to 15 m² which is smaller than the dimensional restrictions of the load-bearing layer. This is so because the external facing layer is exposed to the elements and temperature-dependent expansion can occur. The small-scale joint arrangement of the facade must be taken into account by the designers during planning.

The corners are usually formed using special moulds [6].

Joint treatment

It is of great importance that a suitable detailing of joints be developed during the design of sandwich panels in order to prevent the penetration of water, among other things, into the joints. Structural solutions are, for example, tongue-and-groove joints, where the horizontal connections are rebated (fig. C 3.39). Another possibility is to ensure that the vertical joints are off-set from one another at the joint intersections.

Waterproofing by way of sealant materials is usually carried out using pre-compacted sealing strips or sealing masses. These materials must be capable of fulfilling the requirements of permanent elasticity and weatherproofing over long periods of time. They must not become brittle, in order to avoid the development of cracks. During planning, building joint tolerances must be calculated exactly to prevent overstraining of sealant materials [7] (fig. C 3.40).

Double wall elements

An economical and precise system for the production of load-bearing concrete walls is the semi-prefabrication of double wall elements with in situ concrete completion. Thin concrete walls are fitted together with intermediate steel gratings; all necessary reinforcement is already installed between the walls. These double walls are delivered to the site where they are poured with filling concrete to produce a stable, single-layered wall construction element. (fig. C 3.41).

The external surfaces of the reinforced concrete shells have exposed concrete quality and do not require any further processing after assembly. Openings for windows and doors, as well as installation ducts, can all be incorporated during prefabrication in the factory. Walls are prefabricated with heights and widths of up to 12 m which enables the minimisation of constructional butt joints. Cranes are used to set the double walls onto the prepared reinforcement bars of the floor slabs on site.

The building elements, which are constructed with a double wall system, can transfer loads both vertically and horizontally. Their positive properties, such as sound protection and moisture resistance, enable the application of these elements in housing construction for external, internal and even basement walling. Depending on the requirements, double walls can be constructed to resist fire and thus be used as protection walls [8].

Porous concrete elements

Porous, or aerated, concrete elements belong to the class of lightweight concrete that provide great stability with minimal weight. Porous concrete units are used as wall, slab and roof elements. As load-bearing members, they are produced in heights of up to 350 cm, widths of up to 150 cm and thicknesses of up to 37.5 cm. Slabs and roof panels of porous concrete have maximum dimensions of 800 cm in length and 75 cm in width. If they are to be subjected to bending loads, load-bearing, porous concrete elements are stabilised with additional corrosion-protected reinforcing steel.

Due to their material properties, porous concrete elements have the advantage that, even as single-layer panels, they fulfil the requirements for thermal and sound insulation and fire protection. It is possible to design entire construction systems based on porous concrete wall, slab and roof elements for buildings up to three storeys high. These wall elements are also capable of absorbing soil pressure and, as such, are suitable for use as basement walls. Porous concrete panels can also be prefabricated with ducting for technical installations and openings for windows as desired.

Porous concrete wall panels are set onto foundations or strip footings in a mortar bed (fig. C 3.43, p. 122). The panels can be butted against each other, connected by tongue-and-groove joints or by open hollow joints. When open joints are selected, the hollow cavities require filling with concrete after the panels have been erected. Butt joints and tongue-and-groove joints must also be fixed – however with thin mortar.

The strip-like slab elements are laid on top of the wall panels during assembly. The connections between the slabs and

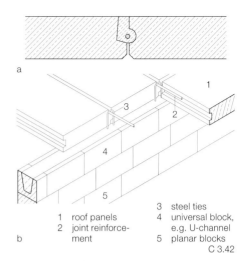

a

b

1 roof panels
2 joint reinforce-
  ment
3 steel ties
4 universal block,
  e.g. U-channel
5 planar blocks

C 3.42

C 3.43

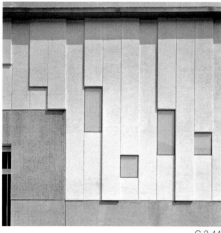

C 3.44

roof elements comply with the principles of wall panel connections. By connecting the slab panels with joint mortar, the slab as a whole behaves as a panel (fig. C 3.42). Due to the minimal weight of porous concrete panel elements, light-weight hoisting equipment is sufficient for assembly on site.

Porous concrete facade elements
Porous concrete elements can be employed both horizontally and vertically as facade elements or as infill panels for frame structures (fig. C 3.44). In addition to the bracing functions which these panels provide, they also perform functions relevant to building physics. Hori-

zontally arranged elements are fixed to the load-bearing substructure by way of splices inserted into the horizontal joint of the concrete wall and fixed with angles or sleeves (fig. C 3.45). Vertical wall panels are fixed by way of reinforcement rods set into the hollow sections of the vertical joints. The reinforcement rods are connected to the substructure with anchoring sleeves. The joints are subsequently filled to ensure force-locked, rigid connections [9] (fig. C 3.46).

Ceiling and floor slabs
Prefabricated concrete slab elements are produced as solid, hollow or web panels. They offer planar structures of reinforced

concrete or pre-stressed concrete which act as the partitioning elements for frame or panel constructions. These elements are predominantly responsible for the absorption of bending moments, and transfer both vertical and horizontal loads – such as wind loads – to the load-bearing structure. The slabs are required to fulfil the requirements of structural stability, thermal and sound insulation and fire protection.

Solid slabs
Solid slabs can rest on wall edges in a linear manner or be point-loaded on columns. They are seldom applied for spans exceeding 6 m as the necessary thick-

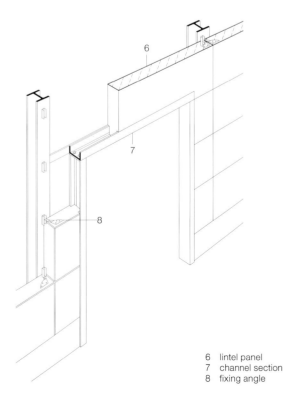

6 lintel panel
7 channel section
8 fixing angle

C 3.45

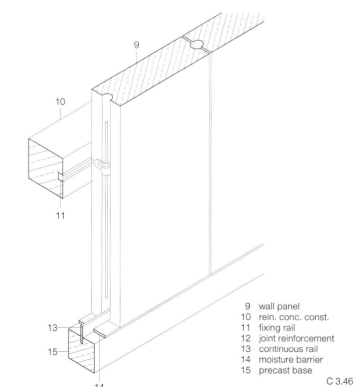

9 wall panel
10 rein. conc. const.
11 fixing rail
12 joint reinforcement
13 continuous rail
14 moisture barrier
15 precast base

C 3.46

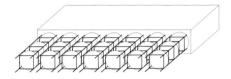

C 3.47   C 3.48   C 3.49

ness of the slab for larger spans would become prohibitively heavy. In practice, solid slabs are used in conjunction with large-panel and crosswall building methods. Individual slab elements are connected on site with mortar fixed butt junctions, whereby rigid connections are achieved.

Unitised slabs
Another widely used slab system is the unitised slab of partially prefabricated slab panels with in situ concrete completion. The elements are manufactured in widths of up to 3 m and consist of a prefabricated slab measuring approximately 5 cm with exposed steel reinforcing anchors. These reinforcements act as the connecting elements between the prefabricated elements and the in situ concrete. Longitudinal and cross-reinforcement is laid on the anchors, whereby biaxial directions of span are achieved (fig. C 3.47).
Joint-free in situ concrete completion enables the unitised slab to behave as a continuous slab [10].

Hollow slabs
Elements constructed of hollow reinforced concrete panels are highly economical for large spans because they make it possible to economize on concrete. Weight reductions of up to 50 % are possible using hollow slabs compared with solid slabs of the same dimensions. Depending upon the production techniques, the cavities are oval, round or rectangular. Displacement forms are inserted in the direction of span of the hollow slabs during production, although here only a single direction of span is possible. The panels have standard dimensions of 60 cm which enable flexible coordination with a large variety of different layouts.

With panels measuring 15 to 40 cm in depth, it is possible to span distances of 6 to16 m. In order to achieve the static action of a diaphragm, it is necessary that the joints be filled with mortar. The mechanical production of these elements in steel formwork ensures high-quality, exposed concrete surfaces.

In order to manufacture hollow slabs with biaxial span directions, plastic spheres are used as displacement forms (fig. C 3.48). They ensure that the concrete is repelled from the areas where it would have the least static influence. Slabs with thicknesses of 23 to 60 cm may include spheres with diameters of 18 to 36 cm. These spherical cavities reduce the self-weight of the slabs by up to 35 % (fig. C 3.49). These systems are available as semi, or fully, fabricated elements. In the semi-fabricated modules, the plastic spheres are fixed to the, statically necessary, reinforcement grids. After assembly on site, the hollow-core slabs are finished with in situ concrete thereby forming a single shell hollow slab.

Web panel slabs
For much greater spans and larger loads TT-panels can be employed; for example, in industrial situations. They are particularly suitable for the installation of services between the webs which are usually spaced at 120 cm. The maximum dimensions measure 250 cm in width, 80 cm height and 160 cm in length. Spans of up to 20 m can be achieved with prestressed elements, but the maximum height of the slab is then extended to 95 cm. TT-panels can also be produced as semi-prefabricated elements and finished with in situ concrete [11].

Special elements
With regard to concrete panel construction methods stairs, lift wells and balcony balustrades are considered to be special elements. Stairs act as linear elements within a structural system, while lift wells are prefabricated room elements and can be used to provide bracing. Balcony balustrades, as non-load-bearing building units, are also prefabricated in factories and can have a huge variety of forms. These components are also used as special prefabricated elements in in situ buildings where they receive supplementary treatment.

C 3.42   Porous concrete slabs
           a Connection of butt-joint between two porous concrete slab elements
           b Location and connection of porous concrete slab onto load-bearing walls
C 3.43   Assembly of a large porous concrete panel
C 3.44   Plastic facade treatment with porous concrete elements, warehouse and sales building in Eichstätt (D) 1995, Hild & Kaltwasser
C 3.45   Assembly of horizontally fixed porous concrete elements
C 3.46   Assembly of vertically fixed porous concrete elements
C 3.47   Assembly of unitised slabs
C 3.48   Hollow slabs with plastic, spherical displacement forms prior to in situ concrete finishing
C 3.49   Schematic diagram of hollow slabs

123

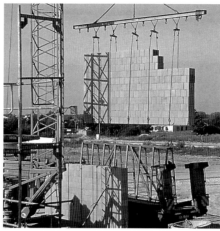

C 3.50 C 3.51 C 3.52

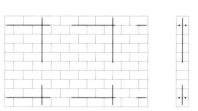

a

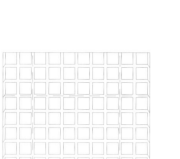

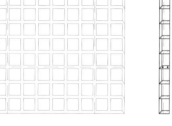

b

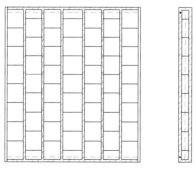

c

C 3.53

Building with masonry panels and brick-work elements

Prefabricated masonry building elements

The industrialised manufacture of prefabricated building units is the natural further development of traditional elements, manually produced on site. The brick manufacturing companies, in particular, have been responsible for the advancement of industrially prefabricated masonry panels in the last few years. This construction technique combines the advantages of traditional building materials with the possibilities of industrial fabrication and permits cost-and time-intensive on-site building procedures to be rationalised.

Prefabricated masonry building elements are high-quality wall, floor and roof elements of various thicknesses that have been produced out of clay bricks, pumice or calcium silicate bricks in factories. It is possible for the panels to be manufactured ready for the installation of services.

Prefabricated masonry elements are essentially suitable for all areas of residential, commercial and industrial building and offer great architectural design freedoms. During the fabrication of masonry panels, looped reinforcing bars are inserted into the bed joints for later assembly; these overlap at the joints between adjacent building units. Storey-high vertical reinforcing bars are inserted into these loops and the panels are subsequently fixed with mortar to provide compression and tension-resistant connections (fig. C 3.50). The assembly of heavy, storey-high masonry panels can only be carried out with the help of heavy-duty lifting equipment (fig. C 3.51). External walls must fulfil all the requirements of thermal and insulation, also moisture control.

Masonry panels are manufactured as hand-laid, cast, or composite panels.

Hand-laid masonry panels
Today, it is possible to produce masonry panels in almost any desired form using the latest production technology. The dimensions and tolerances of prefabricated masonry panels are comparable with those of precast concrete panels. The dimensional accuracy of prefabricated masonry panels is so high that only a thin coat of plaster must be applied with a trowel to finish the interior.

The production of hand-laid panels is completed under factory conditions; the bricks or blocks are laid in the traditional manner with mortar joints to form storey-high panels. Standard clay, calcium silicate or concrete blocks are all suitable for this process. Masonry robots or automatic machinery assist in the production of the vertical panels in manufacturing plants. The standard dimensions of these panels are 6.5 to 7 m in length and 2.65 m in height, although alternative dimensions are possible under factory-controlled conditions. According to the DIN 1053-4, the masonry panels should include vertical ducts for inserting and fixing transport anchors. Prefabricated masonry elements weighing up to 5 t can be positioned with mobile cranes without any problems. The structural and building physics properties of masonry elements are specified in the DIN 105.

Cast masonry panels
In contrast to hand-laid masonry panels, cast panels are produced horizontally in moulds. Perforated or hollow bricks are laid in prepared beds and bonded by special grouting concrete. Due to the higher proportion of concrete used in this technique, an additional layer of insulation should be applied to external wall panels in order to achieve the necessary

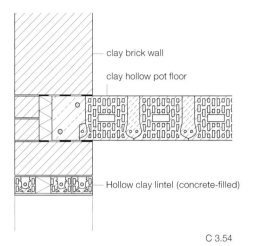

— clay brick wall

— clay hollow pot floor

— Hollow clay lintel (concrete-filled)

C 3.54

C 3.50   Positioning a prefabricated masonry panel
          on a bed of mortar
C 3.51   Erection of prefabricated masonry panels
C 3.52   Erecting a clay hollow pot floor
C 3.53   Drawings of a hand-laid panel, a cast ma-
          sonry panel and a composite masonry panel,
          (elevation, horizontal and vertical sections)
          a hand-laid masonry panel
          b cast masonry panel
          c composite masonry panel
C 3.54   Junction between clay hollow pot floor and
          loadbearing wall
C 3.55   Isometric view of a clay hollow pot floor on
          concrete-filled hollow clay beams
C 3.56   Junction between floor shown in C 3.55 and
          internal wall (floor finishes also shown)

U-value. Individual elements are room-high and up to 10 m long. A high level of prefabrication can be achieved when windows, door frames and service ducts are installed in the production plant.

Composite masonry panels
Composite panels are a special form of cast masonry panels. They are essentially precast reinforced concrete elements that include specially formed perforated bricks 25 to 50 cm long. During production, the bricks are laid in a freshly poured concrete backing 35 mm thick. The spacing between the bricks must be at least 30 mm. Subsequent to the laying of the bricks, another layer of concrete is poured in order to fill the joints between the bricks and cover them with at least 35 mm of concrete. All the work is carried out under factory conditions [12] (fig. C 3.53).

Hollow clay brick elements
Room-high elements
The standard height of hollow clay brick wall panels is 250 to 280 cm with widths ranging from 30 to 60 cm. Such panels can also be used for roofs. Room-high elements are individual units that can be combined as required with special corner, lintel and spandrel units within a system. The basic unit is a perforated brick, which functions as a loadbearing element – fabricated either with or without core insulation – and forms the external surface of the panel without further treatment. Reinforcing bars are integrated into the panels in the factory, or can be inserted into the cavities on site and subsequently fixed with in situ concrete. These reinforcing bars are anchored to the foundations or other building elements with further reinforcing bars.

Clay hollow pot floor elements I
Clay hollow pot floor elements (the pots are also known as hollow blocks or tiles) are industrially prefabricated panel elements (fig. C 3.52). They are manufactured from specially formed hollow clay elements laid next to each other. The joints between the elements are reinforced with steel bars and subsequently filled with grout. When the individual panels are connected together, the suspended floor act is structurally like a plate; the discrete hollow clay elements contribute to this action. With individual element sizes of 1.0 to 2.5 m, distances of up to 6 m can be spanned without support from intermediate walls or columns. The clay hollow pot floor offers a formwork-free and efficient construction technique which requires no additional concrete topping. The finished slabs can be subjected to loads immediately after construction (fig. C 3.54).

Clay hollow pot floor elements II
In this variant of the clay hollow pot floor, the hollow clay elements are supported on concrete-filled hollow clay beams (fig. C 3.55). On site, the beams are laid on load-bearing walls at a spacing equal to the width of the hollow clay elements. Special lifting equipment is used to lay the hollow clay elements between the beams, and the joints between the elements, above the beams, are subsequently filled with mortar. Depending upon the loads to be carried, the structure can be strengthened with in situ concrete and reinforcement. This form of suspended floor requires no formwork and can be quickly assembled [13] (fig. C 3.56).

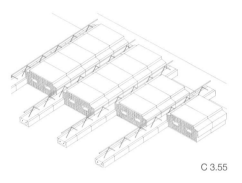

C 3.55

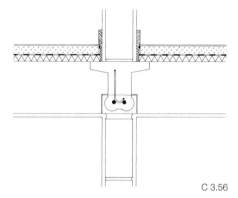

C 3.56

Notes:
[1] Stahl-Informations-Zentrum: Dokumentation 558.
     Bausysteme aus Stahl für Dach und Fassade.
     Düsseldorf 2000, p. 25ff.
[2] Kolb, Josef: Holzbau mit System. Basle 2007,
     pp. 112–115.
[3] ibid. [2], pp. 62–67.
[4] ibid. [2], pp. 1134–1135.
[5] Hugues, Theodor et al.: Detail Practice. Timber
     Construction. Munich 2002, p. 37ff.
[6] Döring, Wolfgang et al.: Fassaden. Architektur
     und Konstruktion mit Betonfertigteilen. Cologne/
     Bonn 2000, p. 56ff.
[7] ibid. [5], pp. 62–63
[8] Syspro-Gruppe Betonbauteile e.V. (ed.):
     Die Technik zu Decke und Wand. Wie wird's
     gemacht?, p. 21ff.
[9] Weber, Helmut et al.: Porenbeton Handbuch.
     Planen und Bauen mit System, (5th ed.),
     Gütersloh 2002, p. 25ff.
[10] Fachvereinigung Deutscher Betonfertigteilbau
     e.V. (FDB). Wissensdatenbank. Elementdecken
     www.fdb-wissensdatenbank.de
[11] ibid. [9], Vertikale Lastabtragung. TT-Platten
[12] Pfeifer, Günter et al.: Masonry Construction
     Manual. Munich/Basle 2001, p. 119ff.
[13] Arbeitsgemeinschaft Ziegeldecke: Extract from
     the brochure "Planen und Bauen mit Ziegel-
     decken", chapters 1.3–4.4.2.

House in Sumvitg

This tower-like, larch-shingle-clad house is located on the outskirts of the Swiss village of Sumvitg. A clean-cut, compact form has been achieved through the conscious reduction of materials and restrained detailing. Floor-to-ceiling glazing on the narrower facade denotes the entrance and then wraps around the building to offer ground floor access to the garden. There are two long rooms on the upper levels which can be utilised and subdivided as desired. Rather than a conventional timber-framed structure, the architects decided to execute this building in a timber panel system of prefabricated elements. The basic elements are 3.5 cm thick three-ply core plywood panels which act as the load-bearing structural components. In order to provide stability against buckling, 20 cm deep laminated horizontal ribs were bonded to the panels and thermal insulation packed between these. Simple boarding completes the sandwich panels and simultaneously acts as a backing for the external cladding. The solid block timber flooring was laid directly on the 3.5 cm three-ply panels making it possible for the structural system and thermal insulation to continue uninterrupted.

floor plans
scale 1:200

1 entrance hall
2 boiler room
3 storage
4 bedroom
5 dining room
6 kitchen
7 living room
8 bathroom

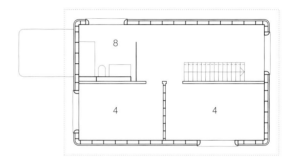

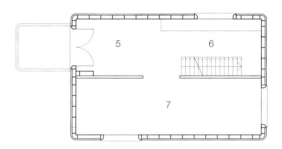

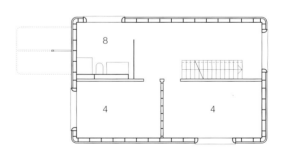

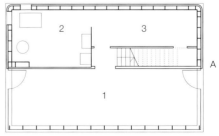

project team • building details

architects:	Bearth & Deplazes Architects, Chur/Zurich Valentin Bearth, Andrea Deplazes
with:	Daniel Ladner, Bettina Werner
structural engineers:	Branger, Conzett + Partner, Chur
client:	Claudia and Armon Bearth-Candinas
usage:	single-family house
construction:	timber
system:	panel construction
internal ceiling height:	2.5 m
site area:	964 m²
gross floor area:	220.2 m²
total construction cost:	€ 515,168 (gross)
date of construction:	1998
period of construction:	7 months

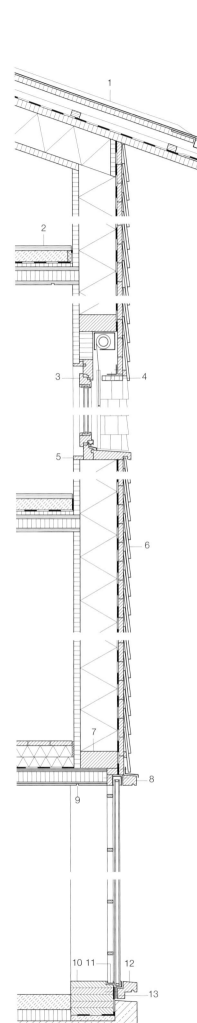

vertical section · horizontal section
scale 1:20

1   roof construction:
    6 mm stainless steel
    standing-seam sheeting
    30 mm boarding
    50 mm battens
    30 × 50 mm counterbattens
    ventilation cavity
    roof membrane
    40 mm fibreboard with
    thermal insulation between
    40 × 180 mm timber rafters
    boarding, 30 mm fibreboard
2   top floor construction:
    25 mm larch floorboards
    60 mm screed, separating layer
    20 mm impact-sound insulation
    90 mm three-ply core plywood,
    underside in facing quality

3   larch window frames
4   20 mm larch lintel, removable
5   20 mm spruce window sill, painted
6   302 mm external wall:
    300 × 40 mm larch shingles
    27 mm rough-sawn horizontal boarding,
    butt jointed, wind-proof paper
    40 × 200 mm timber studs with
    200 mm mineral wool between
    35 mm three-ply core plywood
7   100 × 200 mm window lintel,
    bonded to three-ply core plywood
8   50 × 82 mm larch fascia board
9   slot for curtain rail
10 190 × 213 mm glued laminated timber threshold
11 steel section as rainwater drip
12 larch outer threshold, let into door frame both sides
13 steel section, hot-dip galvanised
14 steel section as rainwater drip
15 larch door frame
16 squared timber, larch 50 × 103 mm

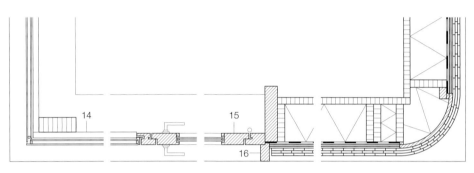

A

House in Dalaas

Situated on a steeply sloping site in Vorarlberg, Austria, this single-family house, with its monolithic volume and uncomplicated formal language, makes reference to the vernacular timber huts of the area. However, the black facade of composite resin sheeting and the absence of any roof projections clearly distinguish the house from the conventional surrounding structures. In keeping with the building traditions of the Vorarlberg region, the entrance is recessed in a loggia. This serves as a vestibule and makes the garage entrance less prominent. A surprising feature of the house, with its seemingly closed outer skin, is the open, flowing quality of the internal spaces. The two-storey-high living room, for example, creates physical links with both the upper level and the garden terrace that is enclosed by an exposed concrete wall and protected by a pergola. The outer walls and floors of the basement are partially buried into the slope of the site and were executed in waterproof concrete. A modular timber construction

system that allows a variety of different layouts was used for the upper storeys. Available in three different storey heights, the 1.2-metre-wide wall elements were stacked onto each other and connected by continuous, solid-timber edge beams. Nailed to the inside faces of these beams, and projecting at the top and bottom, is a strip of oriented-strand-board which acts as a tension anchor against wind suction. This element is glued into grooves in the wall elements above and below with windproof horizontal butt joints. The timber stacked-plank floors are borne by the inner third of the cross-section of the wall. With this constructional system it would have been possible to have built a flat roof. Here, however, the architects opted for a pitched roof with solid timber rafters. The timber structure was erected within two days and only one more week was needed to complete the facades and roof. Depending on the choice of screed, a house built with this system can be completed within two months, including all interior fittings and service installations.

floor plans
sections
scale 1:200

1 void
2 room
3 bathroom
4 terrace with pergola
5 living-dining
6 kitchen
7 storage
8 bedroom
9 dressing room

A ground floor
B first floor

project team • building details

architects:	Gohm & Hiessberger, Feldkirch, Markus Gohm, Ulf Hiessberger
with:	Otto Brugger
structural engineers:	Berlinger Holzbau, Alberschwende
client:	private
usage:	single-family house
construction:	timber
system:	panel construction
internal ceiling height:	2.27–2.45 m
total internal volume:	964 m³
site area:	976 m²
gross floor area:	311 m²
date of construction:	2005
period of construction:	6 months

A

B

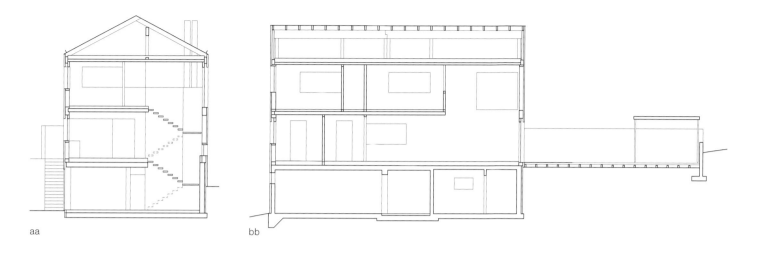

aa   bb

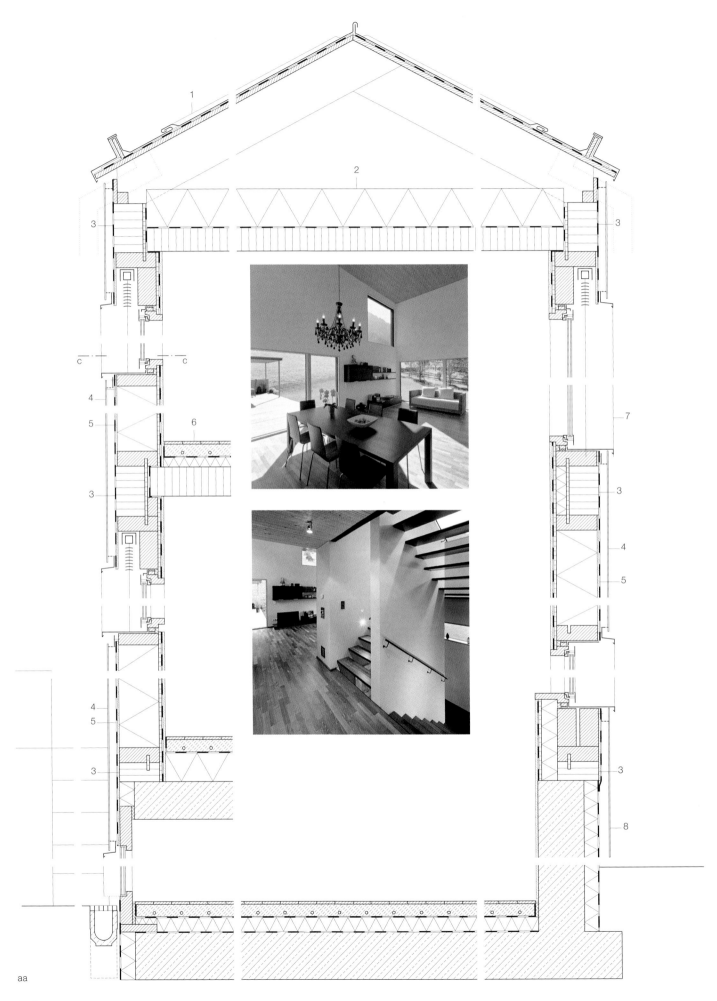

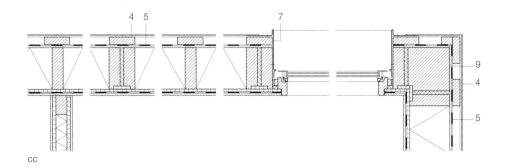

cc

vertical section
horizontal section
scale 1:20

1   0.7 mm grey-black, plastic-coated aluminium
    double welted-seam covering
    windproof building paper
    24 mm softwood boarding
    80 × 240 mm timber joists
2   200 mm insulation, vapour barrier
    115 mm vertically stacked plank floor
3   160 × 260 mm and 80 × 160 mm
    lam. timber edge beams
    15 mm oriented-strand board tie member
4   6 mm matt-black composite resin HPL sheeting
    40 mm ventilation cavity
5   timber wall elements 1.20 × 2.65 m:
    acrylic-coated moisture-diffusing polyester mat
    10 mm gypsum fibreboard,
    mineral-wool insulation
    between 220 mm timber framework
    15 mm oriented-strand board
    vapour barrier, 12.5 mm plasterboard
6   15 mm acacia parquet
    65 mm underfloor heating screed
    polyethylene sheeting
    50 mm polystyrene-concrete insulation
    155 mm vertically stacked plank floor
7   3 mm grey-black plastic-coated aluminium reveal
8   6 mm matt-black composite resin HPL sheeting
    40 mm ventilation cavity
    embossed foil
    80 mm expanded polystyrene insulation
    250 mm waterproof concrete wall
    12.5 mm plasterboard
9   245 × 245 mm lam. timber corner column

Weekend House near Tokyo

Views of the nearby mountains can be enjoyed from the open living space of this weekend house in the Nagano prefecture of Japan. The full-height glazing is uninterrupted by columns and the single-storey layout remains clear of any visible structural elements. The floor to ceiling furniture units – wardrobes, bookcases and kitchen cupboards – function as both space-dividers and structural elements, and give the project its name. This house, the first of a series of three, is called the "furniture house". Prefabrication under factory conditions guarantees higher quality than in-situ construction and the transport of the "building materials" was also unproblematic. The individual elements are only 240 cm high, 90 cm wide and have a depth of 70 cm (45 cm for the bookshelves) and can be assembled by a single person. The elements are first fixed to each other and then to the floor. The roof structure consists of prefabricated beams clad with plywood panels to provide horizontal bracing. This unusual form of construction makes considerable savings in materials, time and costs possible.

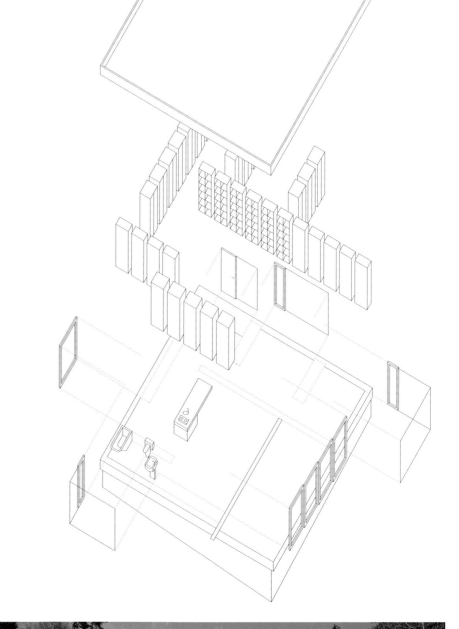

project team • building details

architects:	Shigeru Ban, Tokyo
with:	Yoko Nakagawa
structural engineers:	Gengo Matsul,
	Minoru Tezuka,
	Shuichi Hoshino, Tokyo
client:	private
usage:	single-family house
construction:	timber
system:	panel construction
internal ceiling height:	2.4 m
site area:	562 m²
gross floor area:	111 m²
date of construction:	1995
period of construction:	17 months

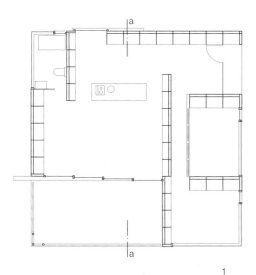

exploded sketch

floor plan
scale 1:200
vertical section
scale 1:20

1 roof construction:
  coloured sheet steel
  bituminous sheeting
  12 mm waterproof-bonded
  plywood,
  laid to falls, adhesive fixed
  12 mm plywood sheet bracing
  100 mm thermal insulation between
  356 mm timber web beams
  plasterboard on supporting
  structure
2 25 mm plywood sheet
3 5.5 mm particleboard
  cupboard door

4 cupboard rear wall:
  12 mm timber boarding
  with coloured varnish
  9 mm plywood sheet
  90 mm thermal insulation
  5.5 mm plywood sheet
5 2× 50 × 100 mm timber rail
  bolt fixed to foundation
6 floor construction:
  synthetic floor covering
  2× 12 mm plywood sheets
  100 mm thermal insulation
  between
  45 × 105 mm timber studs
  waterproof-bonded plywood
  sheet, adhesive fixed
7 sliding elements:
  4 with glass panels
  1 with wire mesh panels
8 19 × 44 mm steel RHS
  balustrade

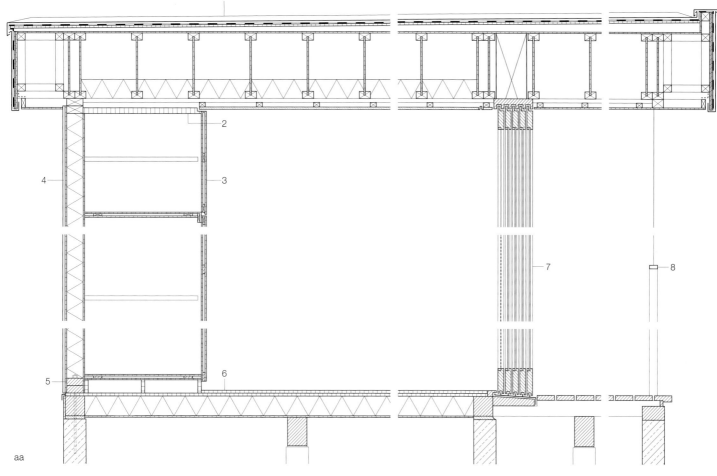

aa

Weekend House in Northport

This weekend house, located on a peninsula in Lake Michigan, was completed in a mere eight weeks. It is a prefabricated prototype house of mixed construction uniting the advantages of lightweight building systems with those of solid construction techniques. Prefabrication and short assembly times are combined with thermal storage mass to create a highly economical product. The solid, reinforced-concrete plinth level of the building is partially set into the slope of the site and accommodates the bedrooms and technical service spaces. The generously glazed lightweight structure above is constructed of timber panels, while a steel framework provides bracing and the necessary stability for relatively large spans and cantilevering elements. Wall elements were initially interconnected and subsequently assembled on the slabs. The roof and stairs were also prefabricated. The clear-cut, highly structured cuboid is organised on a split-level basis, yet exhibits a surprisingly open layout. The double-storey living space on the upper floor benefits from visual interaction with both internal domestic spaces and external views.

project team • building details

architects:	Anderson Anderson Architecture, San Francisco Mark Anderson, Peter Anderson
with:	Brent Sumida, Hannah Brown, Dennis Oshiro, Rito Sio, Carla Dominguez, Lawton Eng
structural engineers:	Terry Nettles, Gig Harbor
client:	Dan and Sue Brondyk
usage:	single-family house
construction:	timber
system:	panel construction
internal ceiling height:	2.47–3.77 m
gross floor area:	137 m²
total construction cost:	€ 298,524 (gross)
date of construction:	2002
period of construction:	8 weeks

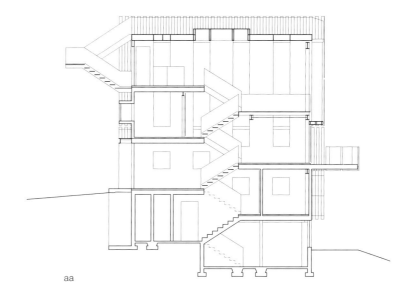

aa

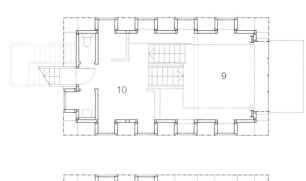

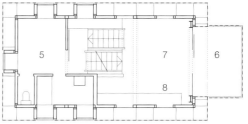

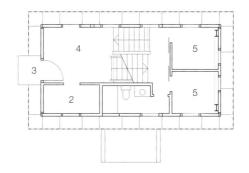

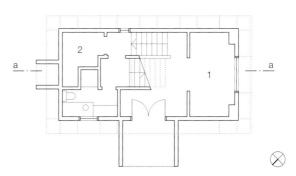

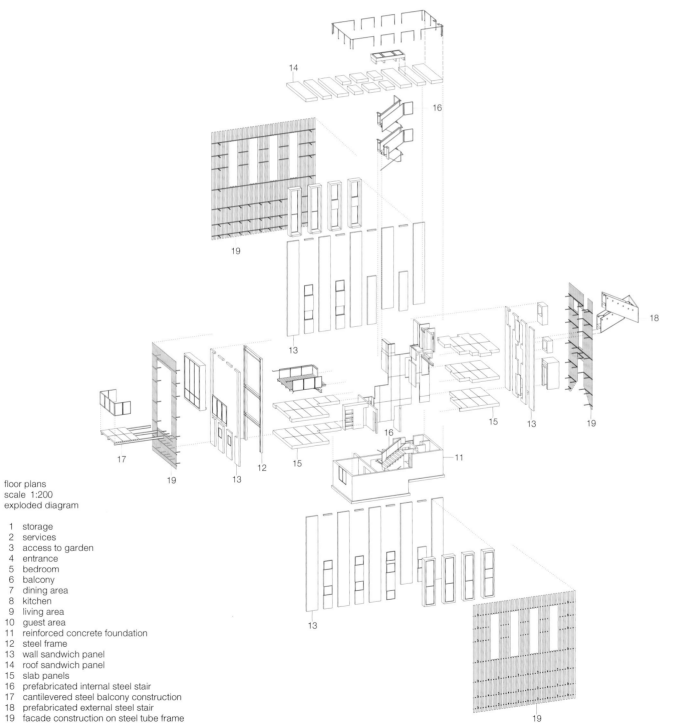

floor plans
scale 1:200
exploded diagram

1 storage
2 services
3 access to garden
4 entrance
5 bedroom
6 balcony
7 dining area
8 kitchen
9 living area
10 guest area
11 reinforced concrete foundation
12 steel frame
13 wall sandwich panel
14 roof sandwich panel
15 slab panels
16 prefabricated internal steel stair
17 cantilevered steel balcony construction
18 prefabricated external steel stair
19 facade construction on steel tube frame

House in Münchenbuchsee

Marine images and nautical architecture played a large role in the design of this unique house which looks somewhat like a black box relocated to this Swiss residential area.

The architects acknowledge the influence of the shipyard buildings and fishermen's huts of the Atlantic coast, recognisable in the porthole windows along the narrow corridor, in the gangway gallery with its rhythmic pattern of metal gratings, and in the exposed steel structure which dominates the interior of this house. In contrast, the walls and soffits are constructed in timber and are largely left in a natural, untreated state. The aging process of the various building materials was taken into account and provided an influential element of the design procedure.

The house has a simple, linear layout. Access is at the upper-floor level via a steel gangway. Almost immediately, one finds oneself in the main living area that extends over the entire length of the building. It is articulated into discrete living areas by the pairs of steel columns and diagonal bracing members. The huge cylindrical water tank dominates the centre of this long, narrow space.

A single small window in the elongated sides is the only source of light. The space is orientated towards the fully glazed facades at the north and south ends. In order to absorb the wind loads affecting the structural system, bracing elements constructed of galvanised steel tubing were applied to the facade. On the lower floor, the rooms are aligned along the length of the corridor. This sequence is only interrupted by the service core in the centre of the house, which is located around the water tank. These rooms are illuminated by a continuous strip of small windows with wooden frames. The outer skin, the partitions and the floors of the building consist of prefabricated timber-frame elements with members of uniform cross-section (80 × 210 mm). Insulated with cellulose, the structure is permeable to the outside, clad externally with okoume plywood and internally with birch plywood sheets. The heating and warm water requirements are met by 23 m² of solar collectors and a 30 kW wood-fired boiler. The warm water is stored in a 7500 litre tank and distributed throughout the house by a floor register system.

project team • building details

architects:	Arn + Partner, München-buchsee
structural engineers:	Berger + Wenger, Zollikofen Mosimann Holzbau, Köniz Michael Arn, München-buchsee
client:	Sandra Wilhem Arn, Michael Arn, Münchenbuchsee
usage:	single-family house
construction:	timber
system:	panel construction
internal ceiling height:	2.45/5.3 m
site area:	418 m²
gross floor area:	328 m²
total internal volume:	1410 m³
total construction cost:	€ 576,514 (gross)
date of construction:	1997
period of construction:	8 months

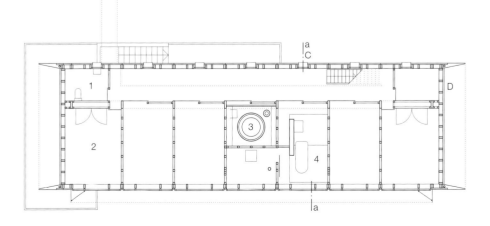

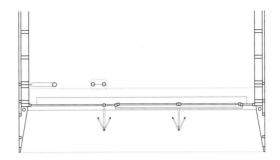

bb

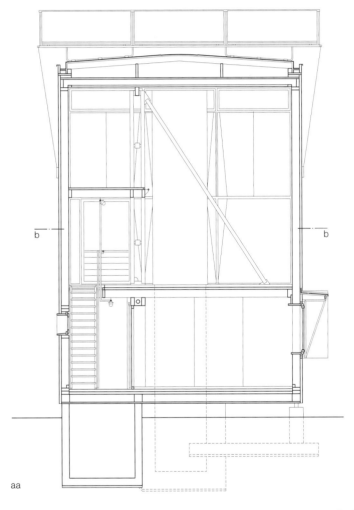

b ————   ———— b

aa

horizontal section · vertical section
scale 1:100
floor plans ground floor and upper floor
scale 1:200

1   WC
2   bedroom
3   (rain)water tank
4   bathroom
5   access bridge
6   living/dining area
7   gallery
8   cooking area
9   library

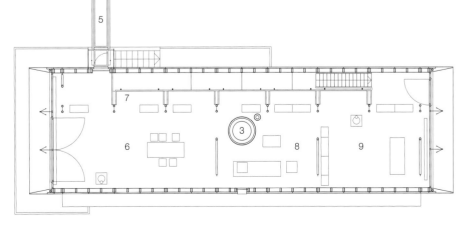

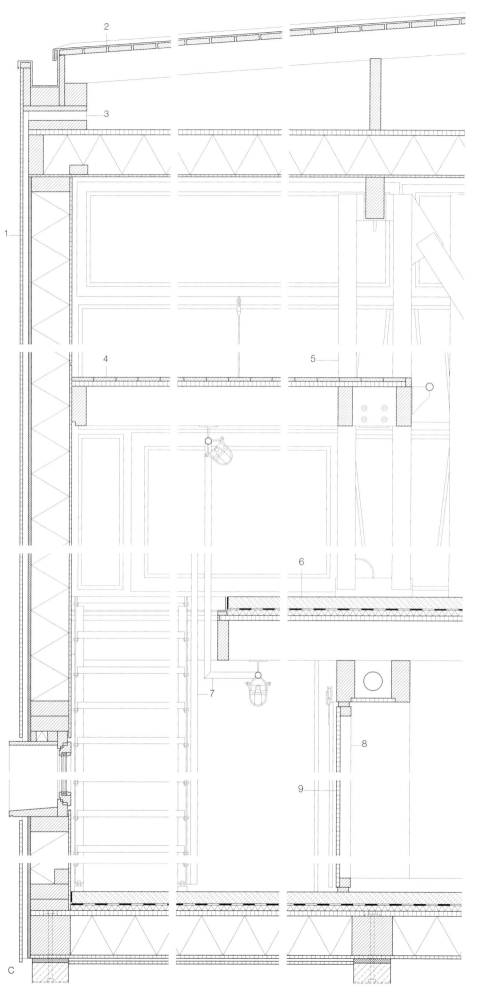

vertical sections
horizontal section
scale 1:20

1   facade construction:
    15 mm okoume plywood
    30 mm ventilation cavity
    18 mm fibreboard
    210 mm cellulose insulation
    12 mm birch plywood
    roof construction:
    metal sheeting on
    27 mm open-jointed timber boarding
    27 mm sandwich slab
    210 mm cellulose insulation
    12 mm birch plywood
3   ventilation opening
4   gallery floor construction:
    20 mm softwood strip flooring
    27 mm sandwich slab
    210 mm joists
5   pair of 100 mm Ø tubular steel columns
6   floor construction:
    70 mm screed
    separating layer
    40 mm impact-sound insulation
    27 mm sandwich slab
    210 mm joists
7   3.5 mm Ø tubular steel balustrade and lighting
8   internal wall construction:
    timber stud construction clad on one face with
    12 mm birch plywood
9   12 mm birch plywood sliding door
10 ventilation:
    20 × 30 mm timber louvers
11 wind bracing to facade:
    32 + 20 mm Ø galvanized steel tubes
12 20 mm laminated safety glass in
    thermally separated steel frames
13 40 mm timber strut
14 convector

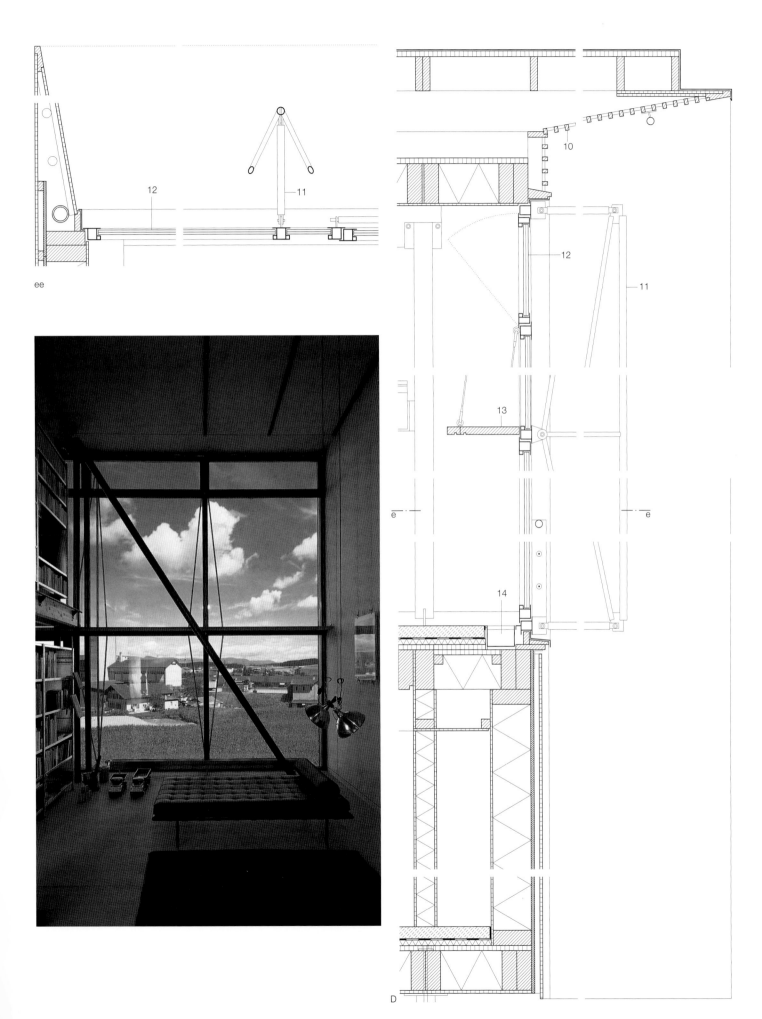

ee

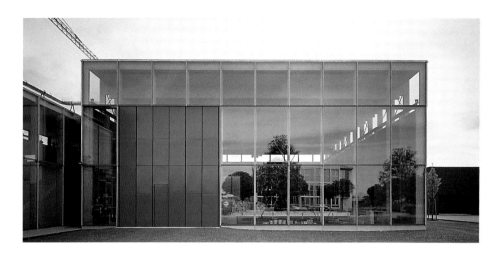

Carpentry Works in Feldkirch

This new timber manufacturing and administration building for a carpentry works in Austria can be seen as an expression of the environmentally friendly working methods of the firm itself. The individual buildings are compactly designed in order to maximise both functional and economic advantages and to ensure energy efficiency. Following the merger with another carpentry works, the southern wall was shifted – as provided for in the original concept – and the construction enlarged in order to cope with the increased demands for space. An attractive entrance situation, accentuated by a cylindrical silo bearing the company's logo, has been created at the junction between the production hall and the north-facing administration tract. The transparent north facade allows views into the working area as well as glare-free daylight conditions.

Visual links were created between the offices and the hall; and by opening the sound-insulating windows, aural contact is also possible. A glazed staircase leads to the offices on the upper floor.

The production hall is laid out on a 200 cm grid. All beams and columns are constructed of laminated timber, including those that bear the loads from the overhead crane. Neither steel nor concrete columns have been used and elaborate consoles have been done away with. Horizontal bracing is provided by the closed facade elements on the east and west sides, and the construction has the advantage that the crane is able to approach very close to the facade. The roof beams are cut out at the bearing points over the columns, creating an elegant transition between the two. This rebate also forms a space for continuous lighting strips and service runs above the crane track. The walls consist of composite timber panels and insulating glazing elements which rest on rubber bearers and are fixed to separate battens with aluminium clamps.

The office tract was built to passive energy standards and the visibility of the heating system clearly displays the sustainable recycling of timber; the predominant local building material.

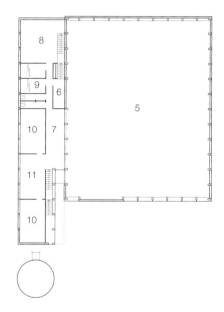

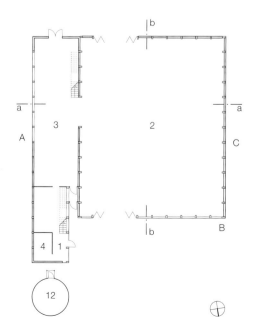

project team • building details

architects:	Walter Unterrainer, Feldkirch
structural engineers:	Merz/Kaufmann & Partner, Dornbirn
client:	LOT Holzbau
usage:	business
construction:	timber
system:	panel construction
internal ceiling height:	10.4 m
site area:	1800 m²
gross floor area:	680 m²
total construction cost:	€ 550,000 (gross)
date of construction:	2000
period of construction:	6 months

floor plans • sections
scale 1:500

1 entrance
2 production hall
3 machine hall
4 heating
5 void
6 archive
7 corridor
8 storage
9 changing room/WC
10 office
11 meeting room
12 silo

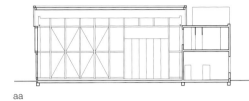

aa

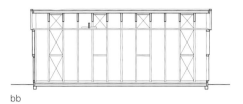

bb

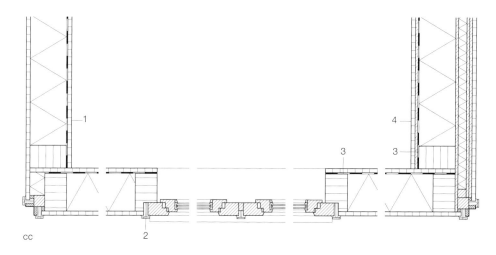

cc

2

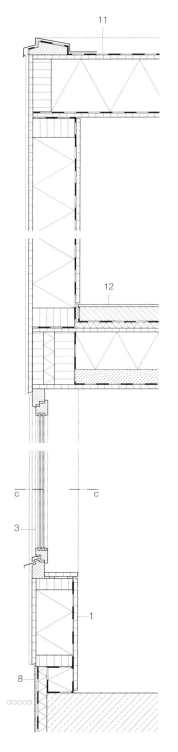

11

12

c — c

3

1

8

A

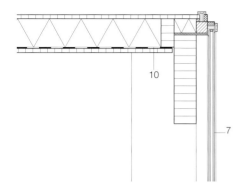

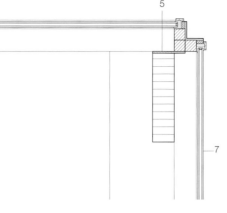

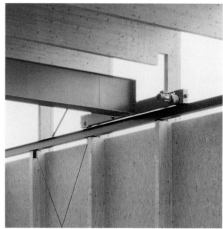

10

5

7

7

dd

ee

horizontal sections
vertical sections
scale 1:20

1 wall construction:
   22 mm oriented-strand board
   vapour barrier
   200 mm thermal insulation
   22 mm oriented-strand board
2 8 mm fibre-cement strip
3 laminated timber frame
4 wall construction:
   22 mm oriented-strand board
   15 mm fibre-cement sheeting
   vapour barrier
   200 mm thermal insulation
   15 mm fibre-cement sheeting
   45 mm thermal insulation
   2× 15 mm fibre-cement sheets
   22 mm oriented-strand board
5 10 mm steel plate
6 roof construction:
   sealing layer
   2× 100 mm thermal insulation
   vapour barrier
   timber boarding 35 mm
7 double glazing in aluminium frame
8 8 mm fibre-cement sheeting
   sealing layer
   50 mm thermal insulation
9 180 mm thermal insulation
10 150 mm thermal insulation
11 roof construction:
   sealing layer
   22 mm oriented-strand board
   280 mm thermal insulation
   vapour barrier
   22 mm oriented-strand board
12 intermediate floor construction:
   linoleum
   70 mm screed
   30 mm impact-sound insulation
   22 mm oriented-strand board
   200 mm sound insulation
   80 mm stone chippings on sealing layer
   22 mm oriented-strand board

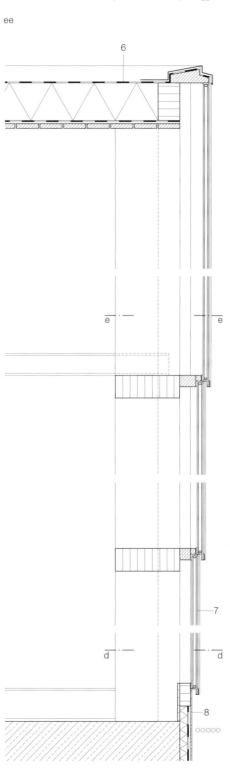

6

e   e

7

d   d

8

B

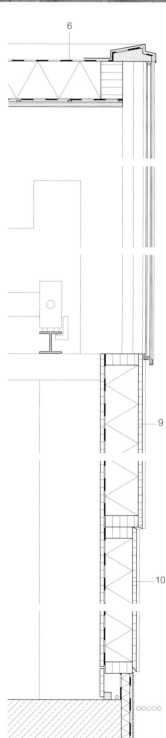

6

9

10

C

Technology Centre in Munich

Since hosting the Olympic Games in 1972, Munich has been considered a sporting venue of international standard. It is intended that the new technology centre for sport sciences at the Technical University of Munich will uphold this reputation and encourage an environment supportive of highly specialised research in the fields of health, sport and material sciences. The new centre is centrally located in the immediate proximity of the Olympic facilities, yet nestled in a natural landscape, at the intersection of the Central College Sports Grounds which stretch north-south, and the east-west orientated main axis of the former Olympic Village.

Based upon the client's brief, the building was designed as a flexible, yet function-specific, construction. The 13-metre-high and 67-metre-long building is constructed of reinforced concrete and based upon an internal finishing grid of 2.4 m with two end zones linked by a middle tract. The two end zones house spaces for various events, seminars and the internal access facilities. The centrally located high-secu-

rity tract accommodates four academic chairs with their associated administration and laboratory rooms; the two lower storeys benefit from internal ceiling heights of 4.2 and 3.6 m respectively in order to cater to different laboratory requirements, and the upper levels are given over to the offices and seminar rooms. Funding for the technical equipping of the laboratories and construction costs were combined in one budget with the result that financial scope for architectural ornamentation was extremely limited, even from the very start of the project. The demands placed on the standard of the fittings were so high that the constructional budget was restricted.

Thus, prefabricated concrete elements were utilised instead of in-situ concrete, and thermally insulating facade panels and a relatively low proportion of glass areas were decided upon. Only the two end-zones were constructed of in-situ concrete in order to provide the necessary bracing. 2.4-metre-wide, storey-high prefabricated reinforced concrete elements with integrated window openings

were specifically developed for the external walls of the 50 by 13 m central tract. The upper edges of the prefabricated elements are mortised to accommodate the floor slabs. These slabs are borne by pairs of columns located between the corridor and laboratories in order to ensure spatial flexibility. The partition walls are almost exclusively of lightweight construction and can be relocated as desired.

The pale green pigmented rendered facade blends into the surrounding landscape of meadows and sports fields. The allusion to a textile building skin of fabric layers is by no means accidental; the facade envelopes the building much as skin-tight sports clothing does an athlete. This concept was achieved by the application of a pale green finish, in swathes of different widths, up to four times. Rather than monotonously accumulating identical openings, the architects rhythmically articulated both facades and interiors alike by alternating wider and narrower window forms.

project team • building details

architects:	Hild and K, Munich
with:	Matthias Haber, Sandra Räder
structural engineers:	Herrschmann Engineers, Munich
client:	Free State of Bavaria
usage:	research
construction:	reinforced concrete
system:	panel construction
internal ceiling height:	4.2 m ground floor
	3.6 m first floor
	2.8 m second floor
gross floor area:	3100 m²
total internal volume:	12,400 m³
total construction cost:	€ 6.7 mill. (gross)
date of construction:	2004
period of construction:	18 months

sections · floor plans
scale 1:500

1 entrance
2 foyer
3 laboratory
4 storage
5 changing room
6 delivery
7 seminar room
8 services
9 meeting room
10 office

aa

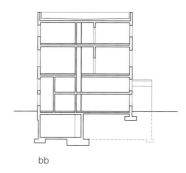

bb

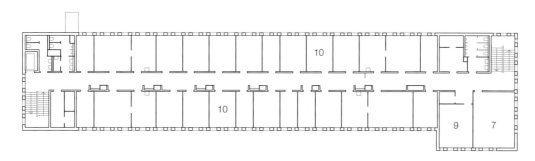

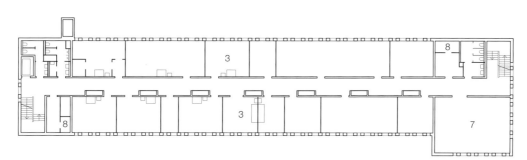

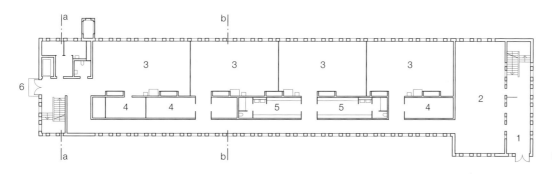

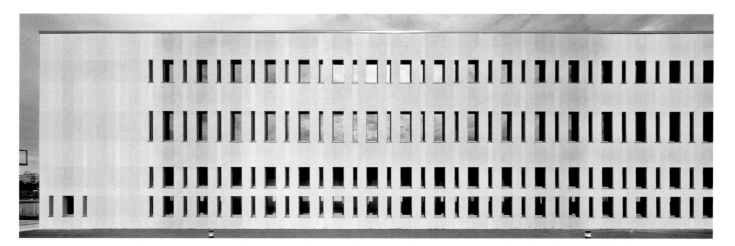

vertical section
horizontal section
scale 1:20

1 parapet construction:
   2 mm aluminium sheeting, powder coated
   40 mm sealing membrane
   100 mm thermal insulation
   vapour barrier
   180 mm reinforced concrete parapet
2 gravel edge strip
3 roof construction:
   80 mm vegetation layer
   filter mat, drainage with
   30–50 mm protective storage mat
   root protection membrane, separating layer
   60 mm rockwool insulation, with falls
   180 mm rockwool thermal insulation
   vapour barrier
   275 mm reinforced concrete
4 double glazing: 8 mm laminated safety glass +
   16 mm cavity + 16 mm toughened glass
   metal window frame
5 office floor construction:
   7 mm needle felt
   93 mm floating screed, separating layer
   20 mm impact-sound insulation
   275 mm reinforced concrete slab
6 adjustable cable duct, with convection grille
7 wall construction:
   varnish layer
   120 mm composite thermal insulation system,
   adhesive fixed
   250 mm exposed concrete
8 sport laboratory floor construction:
   16 mm elastic sports flooring
   0.5 mm synthetic ground mass
   0.5 mm glass roving fabric
   11 mm elastic layer
   64 mm reinforced screed
   polyethylene membrane separating layer
   2× 20 mm impact-sound insulation
   200 mm reinforced concrete slab

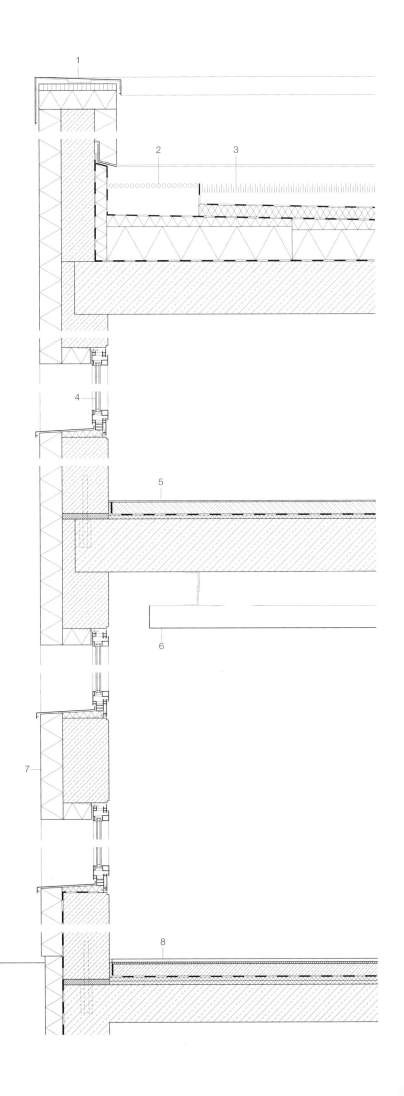

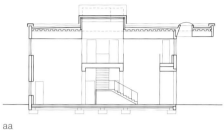

aa

Advertising Agency in Munich

A reinterpretation of commercial construction as an architectural challenge was one of the goals of the architects of this advertising agency in Munich. An easily recognisable building, with exceptional internal spatial qualities and the ability to assert itself within its heterogeneous surroundings, was created on a modest budget. A cantilevered canopy identifies the entrance and delivery areas. Visitors enter a two-storey hall, which is lit by four north-facing roof lights, and a curved staircase leads up to the offices on the first floor. The complexity of the interior is not decipherable externally. Two horizontal strips of rectangular windows encircle the building. The openings in the upper level are slightly larger than those in the lower level, differentiating between the office and factory floors. In order to create a presence capable of asserting itself within the spaciousness of the surrounding area, large format precast concrete elements were selected. Although B35 strength concrete would technically have sufficed for the wall elements, B45 was selected due to its shorter setting period and the panels were able to be transported sooner.

Large-scale sliding windows and the coherent frame structure of the building determine the spatial quality of the flexibly used rooms, while the horizontal line set by the underside of the beams is carried through to the plasterboard cladding as well as the window and door heights. The advantages of prefabrication and standardisation are self-evident; lower building costs, a shorter construction period and greater control of production under factory conditions. The use of entirely precast sandwich wall elements proved to be a more efficient solution than an in-situ concrete construction clad with precast panels. In spite of this standardisation, a range of individual solutions was possible, due to the highly detailed planning by the architects and coordination with the client in the early stages of planning.

Two further design aspects were of importance to the architects; the junctions between beams, walls and columns were to be executed without the use of visually intrusive consoles, and a distinctive facade finish. For clear abutment between the elements, the architects used an improved version of the socket-insert sys-

tem they had previously developed for a nearby hall structure. The green tone of the facade panels is intended to be reminiscent of the alpine streams in the mountains visible from the site. To achieve an individualised facade finish, the concrete panels were rotary-polished on the vibrating table before they were completely set. A wide range of effects can be achieved in this way, depending on the duration and intensity of the treatment and the degree to which the concrete has set. This method was also used to bring out the green pigment strewn into the surface layer of the elements. It was originally intended that the polished concrete panels be subsequently treated with wax or otherwise impregnated. Within the first few weeks, however, it became apparent that the panels demonstrated a vibrant range of effects from a reflective shine on rainy days to a soft, pale, almost cloudy, appearance when the weather was overcast – which lent the rigid form of the building the desired depth and complexity. The mitred corner details articulate the intellectual contrast between concrete as a solid material and its use as an external membrane.

project team • building details

architects:	Amann & Gittel Architekten, Munich
	Ingrid Amann, Rainer Gittel
with:	Christian Hartranft, Christopher von der Howen, Thomas Thalhofer
structural engineers:	Dorrer Bau AG, Neunburg v. Wald
client:	Walter Werbung GmbH, Munich
usage:	office
construction:	concrete
system:	panel construction
internal ceiling height:	3.0 m
site area:	1500 m²
gross floor area:	1060 m²
total internal volume:	5300 m³
total construction cost:	€ 1.3 mill (gross)
date of construction:	2002

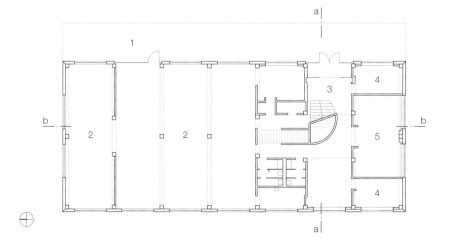

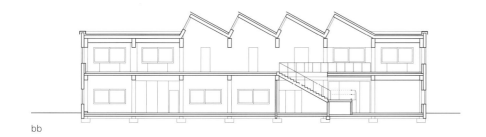

bb

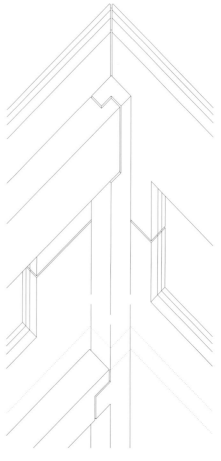

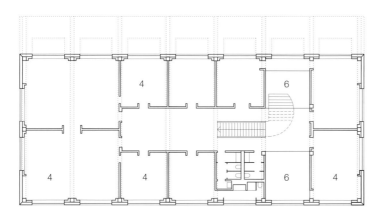

sections · floor plans
scale 1:400

axonometric
socket insert system with concealed consoles

1 deliveries
2 store
3 entrance hall
4 office
5 meeting room
6 void

A

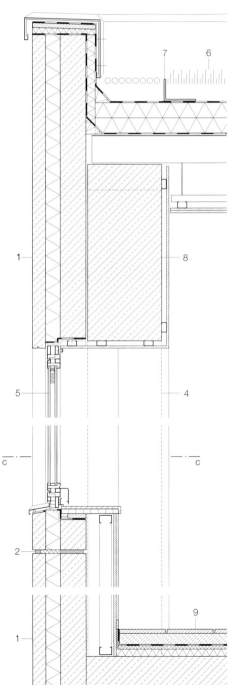

cc

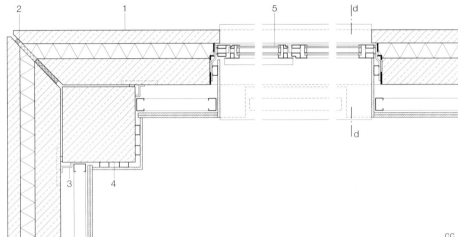

B

C

dd

horizontal section · vertical sections
scale 1:20

A large-format slabs being transported in inclined position
B, C rapid assembly of wall elements
D saw-tooth roof slabs are laid in rebates along the sloping top edges of the triangular side walls

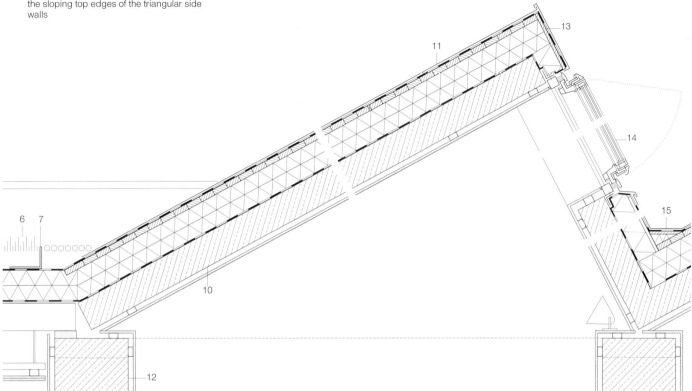

1 sandwich wall element:
   70 mm precast concrete element
   with green pigmentation, rotary planed finish
   80 mm polystyrene rigid-foam thermal insulation
   140 mm precast concrete element
2 coloured silicone elastic joint seal
3 channel section anchor between column and wall
4 400 × 400 mm precast concrete column
5 aluminium sliding window with double glazing:
   5 mm float glass + 32 mm cavity with 15 mm
   adjustable sun-shading louvers
   + 6 mm coated float glass (U = 1.1 W/m²K)
6 roof construction:
   80 mm topsoil layer with sedum, filter mat
   20 mm mineral substrate layer
   polyethylene separation layer,
   bituminous membrane
   160 mm polystyrene rigid-foam thermal insulation
   vapour barrier,
   150 × 0.9 mm ribbed steel sheeting
   2× 12.5 mm plasterboard suspended soffit
7 12 × 120 × 200 mm fibre-cement edge section
8 400 × 800 – 950 × 1935 mm precast concrete roof
   beam: upper surface with 2 % falls
9 floor construction:
   22 mm fumed oak block parquet
   68 mm screed, separation layer
   25 × 20 mm impact-sound insulation
   40 mm levelling insulation/cable ducts
10 160 mm precast concrete element
   on side walls to saw-tooth roofs
11 0.7 mm sheet-copper roofing
   bituminous roofing felt
   30 mm softwood boarding
   160 mm polystyrene rigid-foam thermal insulation
   between 80 × 160 mm rafters
12 400 × 800 – 900 × 1935 mm precast concrete roof
   beam: horizontal beneath roof light
13 24 mm formwork boarding
14 aluminium post-and-rail roof light with double
   glazing: 8 mm toughened glass + 16 mm cavity
   + 2× 6 mm lam. safety glass (U = 1.1 W/m²K)
   motorised opening light, set flush with glazing
15 sheet-copper gutter, heated

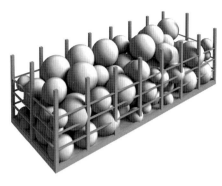

Winery Extension in Fläsch

Run by only three people, this exclusive wine estate in Fläsch, Switzerland, is a family concern in the truest sense. Situated at the edge of the gently sloping vineyards, these three buildings form a small courtyard. The two existing single-storey structures have been complemented by a new tract two storeys in height. A basement with eight broad-headed mushroom-shaped columns forms an extension to the fermentation cellar, which is half sunk into the ground. There is a hall, at courtyard level, where grapes are pressed while the stately rooms above provide space for tasting the select wines and the adjoining roof terrace affords guests a fine view over the Rhine Valley near Bad Ragaz.

The architects designed a pragmatic, yet aesthetically pleasing, building. The structure basically consists of a concrete frame with a simple, pitched roof covered with corrugated fibre-cement sheeting. During the construction of the carcass, the architects consulted two colleagues about the infill facade panels.

They had developed prototypical wall

elements, assembled by industrial robots belonging to the institute, in the context of a research project at the Department for Architecture and Digital Fabrication at the ETH Zurich. Inspired by the brief, the consultants interpreted the concrete frame structure as resembling an oversized basket. In a computer simulation, they allowed spheres of different diameters to fall like grapes into the virtual container. By turning the individual bricks – laid in stretcher bond with open vertical joints – they were able to make the facade resemble this image. Since the industrial robots were directly programmed with the design data, it was possible to prefabricate the facade elements at the ETH within two weeks. They were then brought to the site and put in position by crane. The open-jointed brickwork provides the requisite sun protection, while reducing the direct entry of light and ensuring an almost constant temperature for an optimal fermentation process. Internally, transparent polycarbonate sheeting provides protection against the intrusion of wind and moisture.

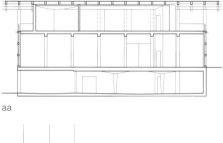

aa

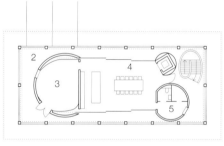

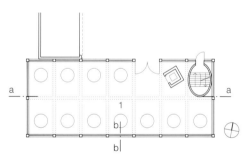

project team • building details

architects:	Bearth & Deplazes Architects, Chur/Zurich Valentin Bearth, Andrea Deplazes, Daniel Ladner
facade with:	Gramazio & Kohler Architects, Zurich Dept. Architecture and Digital Fabrication, ETH Zurich
structural engineers:	Jürg Buchli, Haldenstein
client:	Martha and Daniel Gantenbein, Fläsch
usage:	business
construction:	masonry concrete skeleton
system:	panel construction
internal ceiling height:	3.35–4.88 m
gross floor area:	924 m²
total internal volume:	4207 m³
date of construction:	2008
period of construction:	2007/2008

section
floor plans
scale 1:500

1 grape pressing
2 terrace
3 presentation room
4 tasting room
5 WC/cloakroom

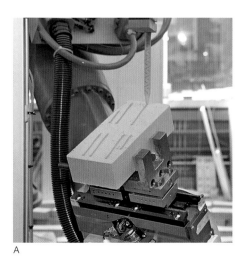

A

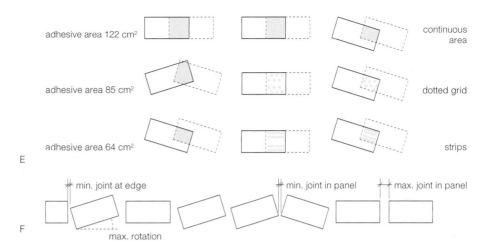

adhesive area 122 cm²   continuous area

adhesive area 85 cm²   dotted grid

adhesive area 64 cm²   strips

A   application of adhesive strips
B   placement of bricks by industrial robot
C   finished wall elements
D   delivery to site
E   bonding alternatives
F   open vertical joints between bricks

units:
3330–4570 × 1098–1464 mm
max. rotation: 16.96°
min. joint at edge: 2 mm
min. joint in panel: 2 mm
max. joint in panel: 50.5 mm

E

min. joint at edge   min. joint in panel   max. joint in panel

max. rotation

F

As part of their research work at the ETH in Zurich, Gramazio and Kohler are developing production processes for the manufacture of "intelligent", specialised architectural elements. For this purpose, they built their own CNC industrial robot plant, located in a process chamber measuring approximately three by six metres, with which students have been able to create prototypes of wall elements. The self-supporting infill units for the vineyard extension are a further development of these prototypes. The 400 m² facade area in the frame structure is divided into 72 segments and filled with some 20,000 engineering bricks. To achieve the applied "grapes in a basket" effect, the bricks were rotated about their own axes, creating an interplay of light and shade. Initially the variations in the grey tones of the graphics were analysed by computer: the areas without any curved image were evaluated as a middle grey tone and were constructed in classic stretcher-bond without rotation of the bricks. The more a brick is rotated, the greater the variation of tone between light and dark,

and the resultant plastic effect of the spheres is achieved.

In order to ensure stability, the bricks were only rotated by a maximum of 17° and were laid straight at the edges of the units. The infill panels were placed upon reinforced concrete bases to ensure ease of transportation. Instead of traditional mortar, the brick courses were bonded with a two component, epoxy-resin based adhesive, while the vertical joints were left open. The brick manufacturer was involved in the project in an advisory capacity; he was responsible for both the system guarantee and for providing the technical knowledge required for the calculation of the amount of adhesive necessary to ensure the load-bearing performance of the panels. Because the architects had only three months to complete the building, it was necessary to restrict all processes as much as possible. By feeding the design data directly into the robot (with a MAYA computer program) it was possible to produce the wall units within two weeks. The robot was capable of positioning a brick every 30

seconds. In order to automate the bonding process, a pneumatically controlled adhesive pistol was also integrated into the robot, whereby the trigger mechanism was connected by a bus-system to the control program. Since the bricks are turned at different angles, the overlapping areas vary greatly between courses. In collaboration with the manufacturer's engineer, a geometrical system was developed so that identical adhesive strength was achieved at each and every point. Four parallel adhesive strips, individually calculated for each brick, were extruded at predetermined intervals from the central axis in order to ensure an even, constant bonding force of approximately 8 kN/m². The initial performance tests carried out on the first prefabricated panels were so successful that no additional reinforcement was deemed necessary.

B

C

D

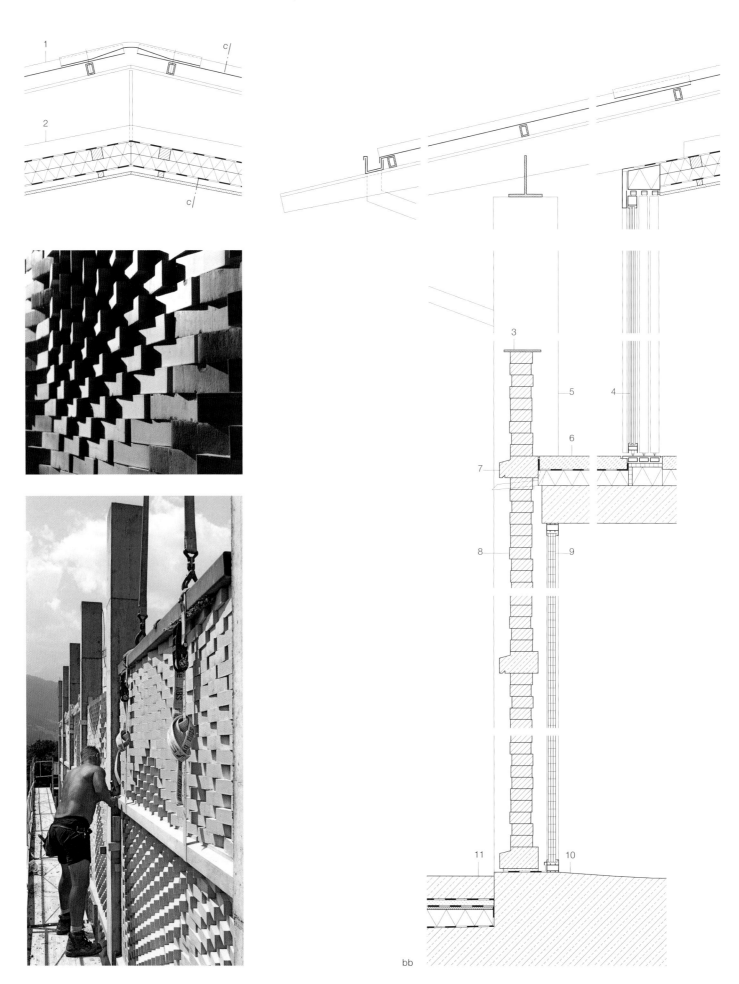

bb

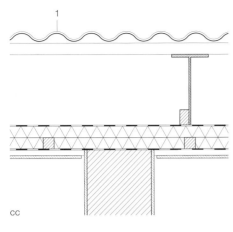

horizontal section
scale 1:20

1 55 mm corrugated fibre-cement sheeting
   40 × 60 mm steel RHS
   200 × 100–400 mm steel T-section rafters
   180 × 220 mm steel T-section eaves purlin
2 50 × 80 mm side battens
   micro-fibre felt
   2× 60 × 60 mm battens
   2× 60 mm mineral wool thermal insulation
   vapour barrier, 30 × 30 mm battens
   15 mm gypsum fibreboard
3 10 × 200 mm steel cover plate
4 double glazing: 8 mm float glass + 9 mm cavity +
   2× 5 mm lam. safety glass (U-value: 1.1 W/m²K)
5 350 × 350 mm reinforced concrete column
6 70 mm anhydrite screed

   polyethylene sheeting
   80 mm phenolic-resin rigid-foam insulation
   160 mm reinforced concrete floor slab
7 210 × 115 mm precast concrete frame
8 limestone-coloured brickwork
   in stretcher bond (240 × 115 × 61 mm)
   with two-component impregnating resin bond
   laid and bonded by robot
9 65 mm three-layer polycarbonate cellular
   sheeting
10 420 mm reinforced concrete
11 120 mm reinforced concrete pressure
   distribution layer, polyethylene sheeting
   30 mm protective chippings layer
   separation layer, 15 mm drainage layer
   100 mm polystyrene thermal insulation
   two-layer polymer-bitumen sheeting
   180–250 mm reinforced concrete, to falls

Hotel Management and Catering School in Nivillers

Only 10 km away from Beauvais dans l'Oise at the edge of Nivillers, an ensemble consisting of a 19th-century palace and a small 18th-century hunting lodge is set in its own park-like grounds. A new school for hotel management and two associated dwelling tracts have been integrated into this historic environment. The residences are located on the periphery of the site and accommodate 12 people each. The school was laid out at right angles to the palace creating an open courtyard, in the middle of which stands a 200-year-old cedar which dominates the complex. While the new facade overlooking the courtyard is fully glazed, the outer facade consists of a series of brick elements which reflect the built fabric of the existing ensemble. These panels are prefabricated, load-bearing, room-height monolithic slabs of perforated brickwork and require no supplementary surface treatment. This construction system is more economical than traditional brickwork and also reduces the site construction period. Complementing these basic elements is a range of specially designed connecting components,

such as corner units, lintels and balustrades, all of which are co-ordinated to form a modular building system which is normally only utilised for larger industrial or agricultural constructions. The brick panels have a standard height of 250–280 cm with a width a multiple of 15 cm; in this case 30 and 60 cm. This allows for a flexible facade grid, within which openings can be freely positioned. The panels are available with or without core insulation and can be used as both wall and roof elements. The brickwork panels are anchored to the foundations and other structural members with steel reinforcement rods. These rods can be inserted into the cavities of the panels either prior to delivery or on site, where they are subsequently fixed with concrete. This anchoring always occurs near the corners and towards the inner face of the panels. The outer cavities in the panels provide air circulation and serve to transport potential condensation away from the insulation. The short ends of the roof panels also cantilever sufficiently in order to allow air to circulate freely through these cavities.

project team • building details

architects:	Tectône, Paris
	Sabri Bendimérad and
	Pascal Chombart de Lauwe
assistant architect:	Yann Rault
structural engineers:	Becip, Beauvais
client:	J.C.L.T., Paris

usage:	education
construction:	brickwork
construction:	brickwork
system:	panel constructions
internal ceiling height:	classrooms 2.8 m
	bedrooms 2.5 m
site area:	32,690 m²
gross floor area:	school 1200 m²
	bedrooms 800 m²
total internal volume:	5378 m³
total construction cost:	school € 1.0 million (gross)
	bedrooms € 700,000 (gross)
date of construction:	2000
period of construction:	1999–2000

section • floor plans
scale 1:400

1 office
2 administration
3 library
4 classrooms
5 foyer
6 cloakroom
7 laundry
8 practical training room
9 store
10 dining room
11 existing building

aa

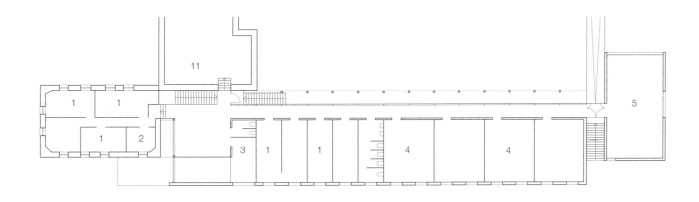

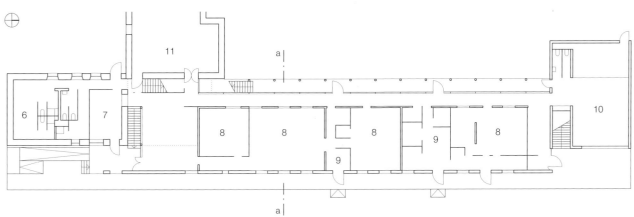

157

horizontal section
vertical sections
scale 1:20

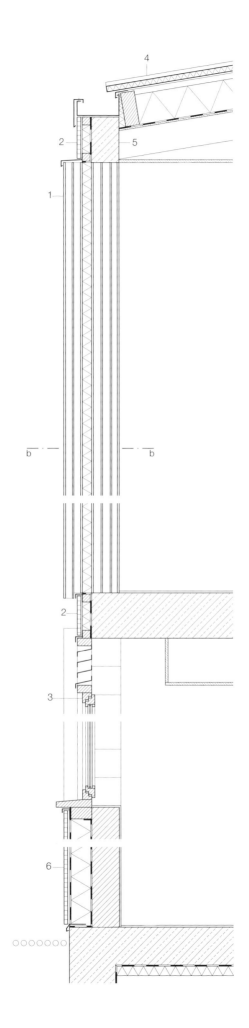

2

1

bb

3

4

2

5

1

b ———— b

2

3

6

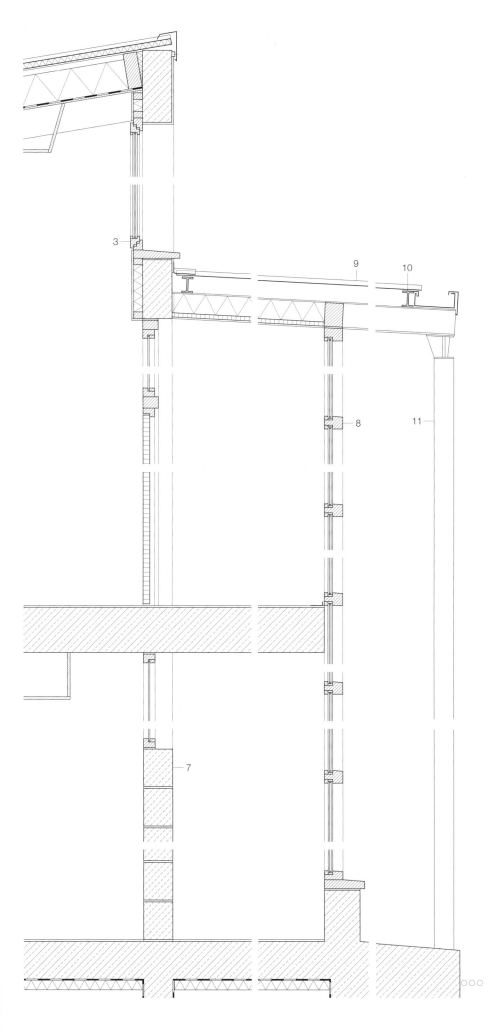

1   300 × 600 × 2500 mm brick panels with
    50 mm core insulation
2   19 mm plywood
3   50 mm softwood casement with
    double insulating glazing
4   sheet-steel roofing panel with
    65 mm polyurethane foam insulation
    160 mm thermal insulation between
    80 × 200 mm rafters
    vapour barrier, 10 mm plasterboard
5   150 × 280 mm reinforced concrete lintel
6   19 mm plywood
    20 × 40 mm battens on windproof paper
    120 mm thermal insulation, vapour barrier
    150 mm brick panel with tile finish
7   160 mm concrete block wall
8   200 mm pine frame with double glazing
9   30 mm corrugated metal sheeting
10 steel I-beam 140 mm deep
11 120 mm Ø steel tube

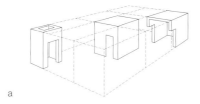
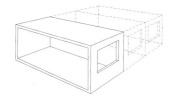

a

b

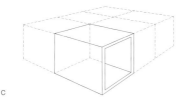
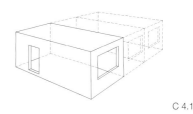

c

d

C 4.1

Room modul systems

Room modules are modular building units that can be interconnected on site to form a building and, according to the construction concept, are either load-bearing or non-load-bearing. With room modules, the structural system is prefabricated together with various elements of the internal fit-out. Depending on the intended function, the units can be manufactured with high levels of prefabrication with all the necessary service installations and built-in furnishings and fittings included. It is possible to insert windows and doors in the production plant. In this situation, however, it is necessary that all planning be fully completed prior to commencement of construction. With the assistance of modern fabrication techniques, it is possible to provide highly specialised, customised room modules to suit specific projects. When a more flexible layout is desired, room modules are produced that are closed on two sides only (fig. C 4.1).

Today, the load-bearing system for room modules is usually of steel, timber or concrete. The dimensions are determined by the methods of transport available. The high level of prefabrication enables rapid assembly of buildings on site.
In the 1960s and 1970s, visionary and utopian architectural design was dominated by buildings based on standardised, mostly plastic, room modules. The principles of these constructions were closed modular building systems that could be simply interconnected so that units could be added or removed as desired. The flexibility of this construction system, in conjunction with the progressive, new material plastic, was considered to be trend-setting in the construction industry and represented the vision of mobile and temporary architecture popular at that time.

Today, however, room module systems are predominantly employed when site assembly is to be completed as quickly as possible. Room module systems are suitable for both temporary and permanent buildings where the floor plan layouts are regular and can be organised into unified modules. The assembly of construction modules is carried out in both horizontal and vertical directions simultaneously. For example, facade systems for room modules can be of aluminium, timber steel or glass, or rendered facades in conjunction with a thermal insulation composite system.

Steel room module systems

Steel room module systems are suitable for both permanent and temporary construction projects, such as provisional solutions during building extension and renovation work, or structures for trade fairs. Depending on the type of element, it is possible to stack room modules up to six storeys high. The usual dimensions of the modules are dependent on the building function, transport alternatives and the

C 4.1 Room module construction systems
       a combined with large panels
       b with long sides open and load-bearing
          external walls
       c with one open transverse end
       d all sides closed
C 4.2 Backpackers hostel (steel room module as
       temporary sculptural addition to an existing
       housing block), Leipzig (D) 2004, Stefan Eber-
       stadt
C 4.3 Production of steel room modules in a factory
C 4.4 Thermal insulation infill to a steel module wall
C 4.5 Vertical section through a house wall built with
       steel room modules
C 4.6 Section through a steel room module, student
       accommodation, Cardiff (GB), Ove Arup &
       Partner
C 4.7 Alho Comfort Line, wall construction of a steel
       building module

C 4.2

C 4.3
C 4.4

1 floor construction
  insulation
2 steel frame section
3 render on insula-
  tion
  gypsum fibre-
  board
  stud section with
  insulation
4 particleboard
  insulation
  plasterboard
5 transverse steel
  IPE-beam

C 4.5

construction system selected. Standard sizes are 3 × 8 m, although a maximum dimension of 6 × 20 m is possible. Steel room modules usually measure 3.2 to 3.7 m in height.

Steel room modules are prefabricated in specialised works and transported to the building or assembly site. The primary construction consists of welded or bolted steel frames and steel sections or hollow sections which form a three-dimensional structure (fig. C 4.3). Structurally, this construction performs according to the principles of a frame structure and, when the individual modules are connected, is capable of forming the loadbearing structure of an entire building. Steel room modules, however, are normally available with the infill panels already incorporated by the manufacturers. The areas between the steel section frames are filled with fire-resistant insulation according to DIN 18165 and subsequently clad (fig. C 4.4). Standard cladding for the external envelope is often galvanised profiled steel panels or sandwich elements of steel sheet plus rigid foam insulation. Technically, however, a great variety of alternative cladding materials is possible. The internal lining consists of coated, wood-based panel products or plasterboard. The floor construction is usually composed of profiled steel sheeting with thermal insulation and a floor covering. Another alternative is or lay a screed or dry subfloor directly on the thermal insulation.

The prefabricated modules are transported to the site and positioned with lifting equipment; the building can be erected, storey by storey, in a very short period of time (fig. C 4.6). The individual modules are interconnected by bolts, welds, pins or clamps (fig. C 4.5). The low mass per unit area of the modules of 100 to 150 KN/m² is advantageous for transportation.

▶ ALHO Comfort Line
  (ALHO Systembau GmbH)

This system is based on a steel modular building technique for new constructions, extensions or extra storeys. The elements are structurally tested according to their type and function (fig. C 4.7).

A level of prefabrication of up to 90% is possible. Depending on the size of the building project, the modules can be ready for delivery in eight weeks.

These modules are adaptable; for example, if the function of the building changes or it has to be transferred to another location. Additional modules can be combined both vertically and horizontally as required, with a maximum height of six storeys.

• applications: facades, windows, roofs, canopies, parapets
• uses: office and administration buildings, laboratories, kindergartens, sports and recreational facilities, canteens, shops, clinics, nursing homes, etc.

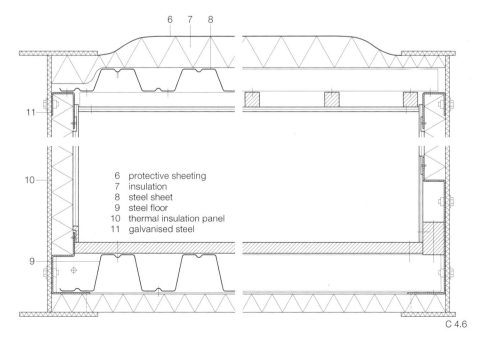

6 protective sheeting
7 insulation
8 steel sheet
9 steel floor
10 thermal insulation panel
11 galvanised steel

C 4.6

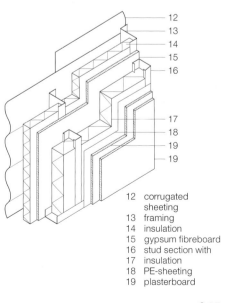

12 corrugated
   sheeting
13 framing
14 insulation
15 gypsum fibreboard
16 stud section with
   insulation
17 insulation
18 PE-sheeting
19 plasterboard

C 4.7

Legend C 4.10
1 birch veneer timber panel, hinged
2 mattress
3 solar cells
4 roof construction:
   edged aluminium sheeting
   timber fin, with fall
   impermeable membrane
   veneer plywood
   thermal insulation
   veneer plywood
   vapour barrier
   veneer plywood
5 wall construction:
   veneer plywood
   insulation between
   particleboard studs
   veneer plywood

C 4.8

floor construction
floor beams with insulation
double OSB panels
floor beams with insulation
vapour barrier
plasterboard on battens

external wall cladding
on sub-structure
timber posts
vapour barrier
battens with insulation
plasterboard

C 4.9

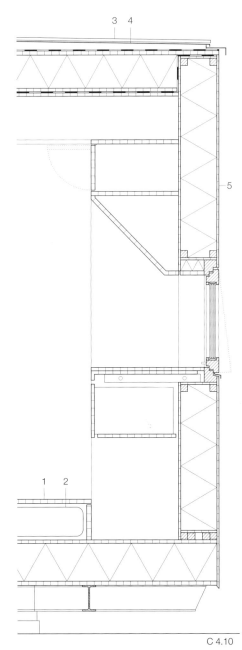

C 4.10

Timber room modul systems

Timber modular systems can also be used, depending upon the desired function, for temporary or permanent constructions. Generally, timber modular systems consist of vertical wall panels and horizontal roof panels that are combined according to the principles of modular arrangement. They can be constructed not only as cubic forms but also with gables or pitched roofs as desired. Timber room modul systems are particularly suitable for smaller building projects and housing construction due to the ease with which individual demands can be met by modern production techniques (figs. C 4.10 and C 4.11). Manufacturers offer prefabricated room modules, complete with all installations and internal fittings, which can be delivered to building sites. Due to their lower weight, the timber modules are prefabricated in specialised carpentry works and can be easily transported over greater distances than comparable concrete modules (fig. C 4.8). The dimensions of the timber modules depend on the restrictions of road transport and are usually in the range of 3 m in width by

8 m in length and 3.2 m high; the maximum dimensions are 6 × 20 × 3.7 m. Timber building modules are either constructed of clad timber frames or solid timber wall elements. Corresponding to the selected building method, a three-dimensional load-bearing frame structure of laminated timber elements is first erected. The spaces between the posts are then filled with insulation material to satisfy the thermal and sound protection requirements (fig. C 4.9). Bracing is often provided by double-sided cladding of the framework with panels of processed timber construction material or, alternatively, internally with plasterboard. When additional stabilising elements are to be avoided – for example, wall cladding – it is possible to brace the structure with rigid corner elements.

Timber modules are assembled in production facilities out of timber wall, slab and floor panels according to the principles of solid timber construction. The external faces of the walls receive additional insulation when required; the single-layer walls fulfil sound protection requirements with their material density.

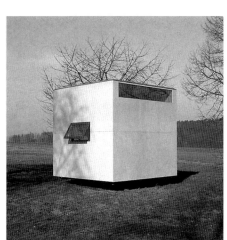

C 4.11

C 4.8 Fabrication, transport and assembly of timber building modules
C 4.9 Constructional section through a house built with timber modular construction techniques, Hilmersdorf (D) 1995, SPP Architects and Engineers
C 4.10 Constructional section through a timber building module, rotating living cube, Dipperz (D) 1996, Sturm and Wartzeck
C 4.11 Timber building module, rotating living cube
C 4.12 Production of concrete building modules in a factory
   a Striking of formwork
   b Concrete building module ready for assembly
C 4.13 Assembly of concrete building modules
C 4.14 Reinforced concrete modular multi-storey housing development, Habitat 67, Montreal (CDN) 1966–67, Moshe Safdie
   a Additional principle of U-shaped modules
   b Complete view of housing development

a

b
C 4.12

C 4.13

Both construction systems allow the application of wet or dry screeds to the floor panels as alternatives to the use of processed timber construction materials. For the erection of a building, hoisting equipment is used to set the timber construction modules on either strip or pad footings on site directly from the transport vehicle. After adjustment into the exact position, the modules are fixed with perforated metal nail plates.

The total allowable height of these structures is restricted, however, to three storeys due to fire protection and structural limitations. For buildings higher than three storeys, non-structural timber construction modules can be inserted into load-bearing steel or reinforced concrete frame structures.

Concrete room modul systems

Concrete building modules can be constructed of either normal or lightweight concrete. All walls, slabs and floors fulfil structural functions and should be dimensioned and reinforced accordingly. The manufacture is carried out in specialised

concrete facilities where the concrete modules can be produced free of joints, in a vertical steel formwork (fig. C 4.12). The steel formwork ensures that the concrete surfaces, both internally and externally, are of the highest quality and can be left as exposed concrete surfaces if so desired. Subsequent treatment of the internal faces is, therefore, unnecessary. The minimum thickness of the walls is 5 cm. In order to fulfil fire rating requirements, for example the German rating of F 90–A, the wall thickness must be increased to 10 cm. The combination of concrete modules at the site automatically creates double-layered walling – this is advantageous for both fire and sound protection levels.

The floor surfaces are of similar high quality and do not require any additional surface treatment. Specific requirements, such as falls in the floor construction or floor drainage in sanitary cells, are incorporated during production.

At the site, specialised hoisting equipment transfers the concrete modules directly from the transport vehicles to their designated position on the floor slab. The

structural strength of the modules makes multi-storey constructions feasible (fig. C 4.13). In order to avoid double elements in the horizontal plane, U-shaped modules can be manufactured (fig. C 4.14). The dimensions of the concrete modules are comparable with those of timber and steel modules. The finished sizes of the concrete modules should be limited so that transport by road is possible without special permission being required. The modules weigh, according to type and dimensions, between 20 and 70 t; thus, heavy-duty hoisting equipment is necessary for assembly [1].

Notes:
[1]   Detail 05/1998, p. 848

a

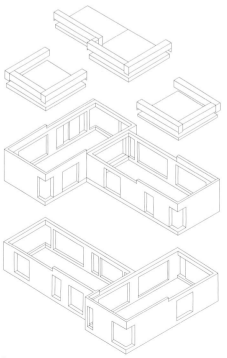

b
C 4.14

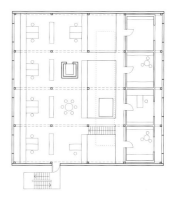

D

Office Block in Fellbach

Interdisciplinary activities characterize the sphere of work of this service company that is engaged in planning and executing automation processes for clients in industry. Analysis, planning and feasibility studies for the installation of these processes, in addition to the necessary experimentation, dominate the activities carried out; a continually changing network of functional and organisational processes which require openness and space in order to respond to the shifting interactions within the company. As a reflection of the customised services the company provides, the form of this office block was to be tailored to the individual needs of the staff. It contains a variety of spaces, from group working areas to individual offices and conference rooms. This, in turn, called for different aspects, forms of enclosure and lighting alternatives. The building was initially designed without a specific site in mind, but clearly defined parameters in terms of construction period, cost and required areas were set. The simply articulated outer envelope, consisting of two

closed and two glazed facades, accommodates four square floor levels linked by a continuous, vertical void that extends through the full height of the building. The three upper levels have the same system and layout, but are successively rotated by 90° in relation to each other, such that a spiral access route is created by the staircase. Although the levels have standardised layouts, they are differentiated by their relationship to each another, orientation and facade treatment.

The containers that house the conference rooms and sanitary facilities are contrastingly closed elements which were hoisted into position within the frame structure. The prefabricated floor, wall and stair elements were also inserted into this framework. The entire building is constructed of individual, independently produced, standard elements. Readily available materials were selected in order to satisfy structural, material and formal requirements to guarantee the high level of prefabrication necessary to cope with the specified cost and time restrictions.

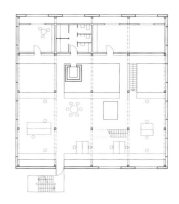

C

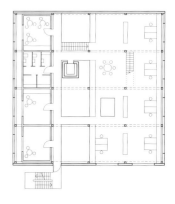

B

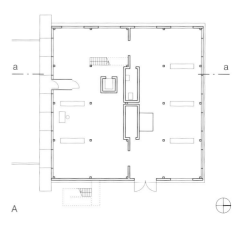

A

project team • building details

architects:	Dollmann + Partner, Stuttgart
with:	Stefan Rappold, Arno Freudenberge
structural engineers:	Heinz Kipp, Stuttgart
client:	IMT-Nagler GmbH, Fellbach
usage:	office
construction:	steel
system:	room cell construction
internal ceiling height:	3.5 m
site area:	1660 m²
gross floor area:	1717 m²
total internal volume:	6414 m³
total construction cost:	€ 1.9 mill. (gross)
date of construction:	1998
period of construction:	8 months

floor plans · section
scale 1:500

A ground floor
B first floor
C second floor
D third floor

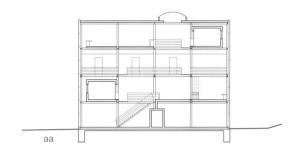

aa

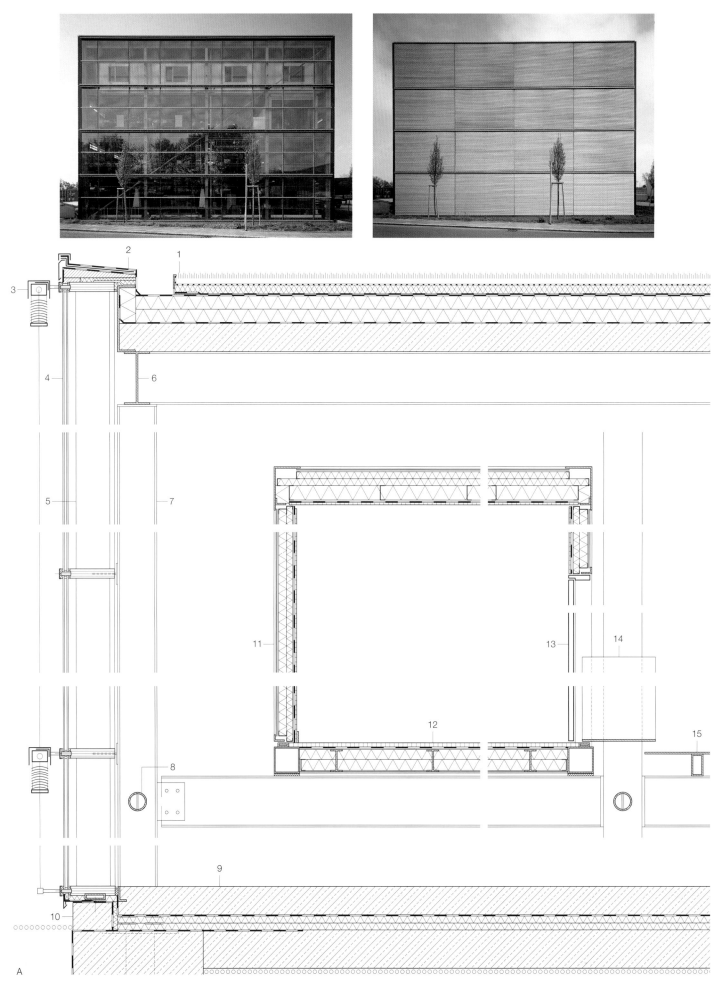

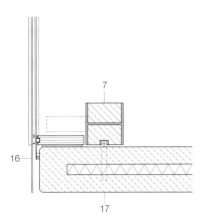

A section through north/south glazed facade
B vertical section through east/west facade
C horizontal section through corner
   scale 1:20

1 roof construction with extensive planting layer:
   60 mm substrate on filter mat
   50 mm drainage layer on protective matting
   root-resistant layer on 160 mm thermal insulation
   safety sealing layer, vapour barrier, reinforced
   concrete slab on trapezoidal metal sheeting
2 parapet flashing:
   roof sealing layer and sheet metal strip
3 aluminium louver sunblind
4 double glazing with aluminium cover strips
5 laminated timber posts and rails
6 270 mm steel I-beam
7 220 mm steel I-column, concrete filled
8 108 × 7.1 mm Ø tubular steel compression member
9 floor construction: reinforced concrete slab,
   smoothed, separating layer

   2× 50 mm compression-resistant
   thermal insulation slabs, waterproof membrane
10 exposed concrete plinth
11 container wall construction:
   galvanized trapezoidal steel sheeting
   60 + 40 mm mineral wool slabs between
   galvanised steel studding
   polyethylene vapour barrier
   12 mm Aleppo pine plywood, primed
12 black linoleum on composite wood board
13 door with sheet-steel lining and frame
14 8 mm steel plate
15 walkway: 8 mm sheet steel on
   120 × 60 × 5 mm steel RHS
16 laminated safety glass
17 240 mm pumice concrete facade element
   with core insulation, painted grey
18 unit joint with permanent elastic seal
19 galvanised steel sheet flashing
20 window louvers with double glazing
21 waterproof mortar

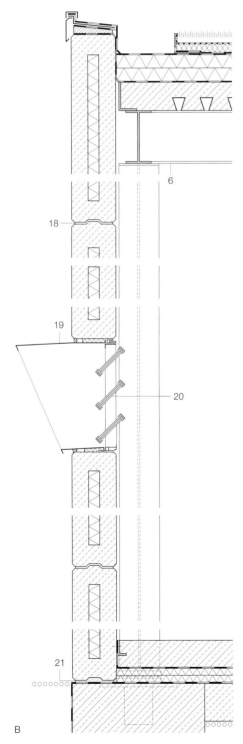

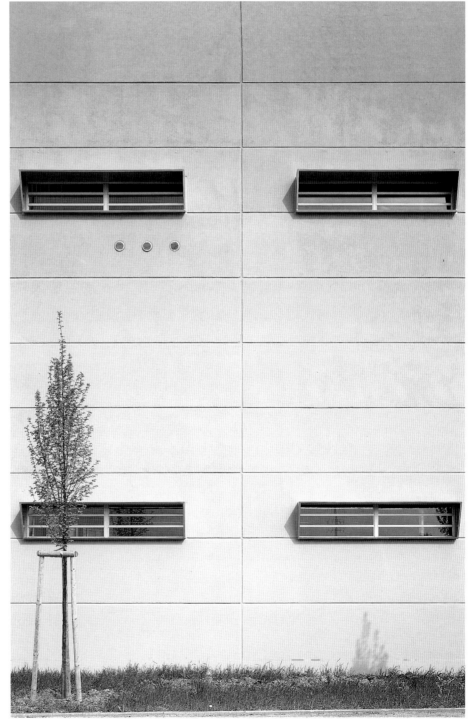

Housing and Commercial Block in Rathenow

The building is located in a quarter characterized by block constructions mixing residential, commercial and trade usages. Numerous constructions had been inserted into the courtyard of this roughly 100-year-old building and, over the course of time, had become so dilapidated that renovation could not be considered. All the sheds and garages in the courtyard were demolished and the space turned into a garden. In order to carry out the planned extension in the courtyard, the principle building was gutted, leaving only the load-bearing elements and the bracing staircase walls.

A renovation concept founded on prefabricated elements was developed for the existing building to achieve an economical, yet high quality, solution, compared with the more expensive alternative of a new construction using conventional building techniques.

The load-bearing structure consists of a precast concrete frame designed to support twelve prefabricated housing containers.

These were pre-assembled, complete with sanitary installations and other technical services, in a factory 500 km from Rathenow. The cells were executed in sizes not exceeding 2.5 m in width, in order to enable economical transport by standard trucks without the need for police escort.

On site, the containers were hoisted into position in the reinforced concrete framework by crane and slotted into the existing service systems. The containers were constructed of standard industrial materials, such as insulated wall and roof panels and anodised corrugated aluminium sheeting.

The base floor slabs were constructed of reinforced concrete in order to comply with fire regulations.

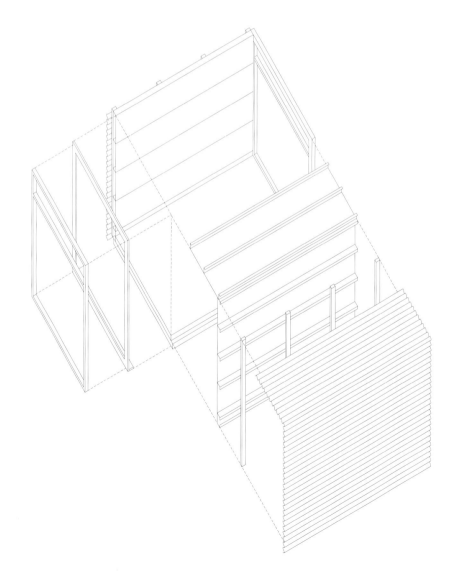

project team • building details

architects:	Klaus Sill with Jochen Keim, Hamburg
with:	Hannes Moser, Martin Marschner
structural engineers:	Rohwer Ingenieure, Rathenow
client:	Rohwer Ingenieure, Rathenow
usage:	residential/office
construction:	steel/reinforced concrete
system:	room cell construction
internal ceiling height:	2.5/2.3 m
site area:	1223 m²
gross floor area:	1058 m²
total internal volume:	3120 m³
total construction cost:	€ 1 mill. (gross)
date of construction:	1997
period of construction:	14 months

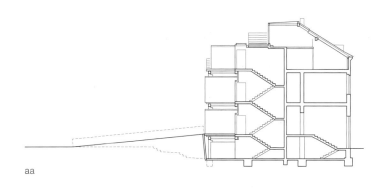

aa

exploded diagram

section · floor plans
scale 1:400

1 balcony
2 gallery
3 roof terrace
4 glass roof

5 void
6 self-contained flat
7 "container"
8 office area

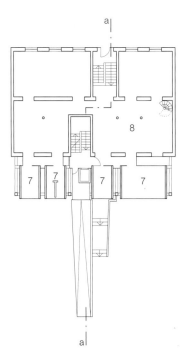

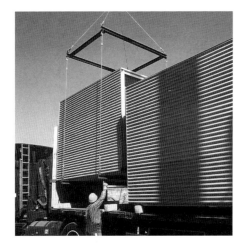

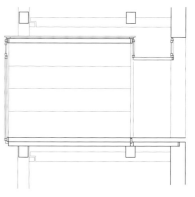

bb

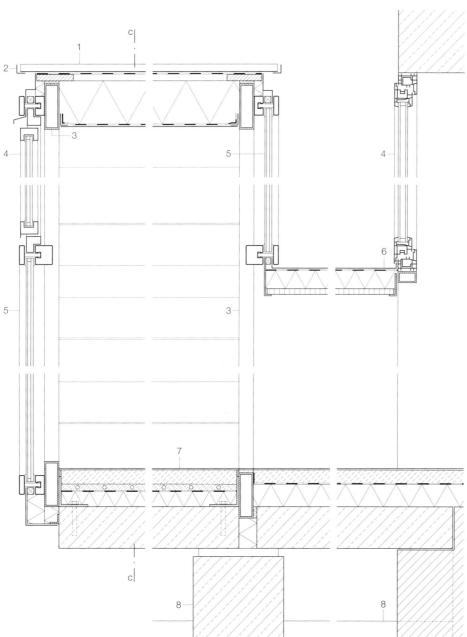

section · floor plan
container 1st floor
scale 1:100

detail section
scale 1:10

1   18 × 76 mm corrugated aluminium sheet
    0.2 mm polyethylene membrane on battens
    120 mm water-repellent, linen-covered,
    mineral-fibre insulation
    sheet steel panel: 600 × 120 mm galvanized,
    perforated, colour-coated channel section
2   angle edging for water run-off
3   120 × 40 mm steel RHS frame
4   opening pane
5   fixed glazing
6   0.7 mm zinc sheeting on roofing paper
    50 mm rigid-foam insulation
    15 mm construction board
7   2 mm linoleum on 2× 20 mm gypsum fibreboard
    underfloor heating in 20 mm mineral chippings
    0.2 mm polyethylene separating layer
    40 mm rigid-foam insulation
    110 mm reinforced concrete slab
8   reinforced concrete frame
9   existing building
10 electrical socket

170

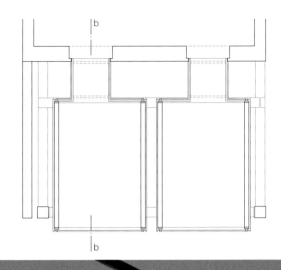

b

b

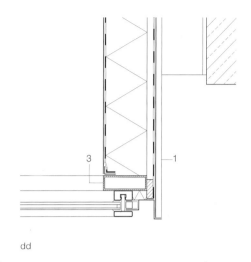

3   1

dd

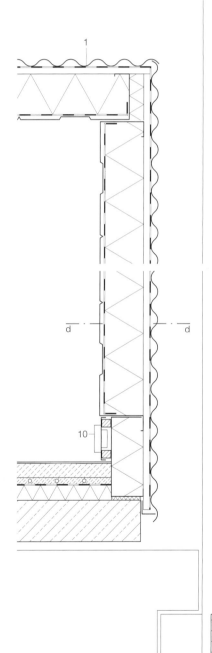

1

d ———— d

10

cc

Office Building in Munich

Originally planned as provisional space during the construction of new offices, this facility was created in two tracts set at a slight angle to each other. The three-storey, double-bay container buildings are accessed from a centrally located, single glazed, reinforced concrete stairwell. Open steel stairs, manufactured from prefabricated elements, provide the additional escape routes at each end of the building. The industrially produced, steel containers were prefabricated as much as possible in the factory and required little more than service connection following delivery. The sanitary cores have externally fixed services and are located immediately adjacent to the concrete stairwells; cutting ducts and channels through the floor slabs could therefore be averted. The discrete, single slope roof – cantilevering at both ends – was constructed as a ventilated structure of trapezoidal steel sheeting. It unites the individual containers and, in conjunction with the plant trellises on the facades, serves as a constructional thermal buffer in summer. The coloration of the facades is based on the official corporate colours of this municipal authority.

project team • building details

architects:	Guggenbichler + Netzer, Munich
	Josef Guggenbichler, Gabriele Netzer-Guggenbichler
with:	Michael Kandler, Gabriele Schambeck
structural engineers:	Ingenieurbüro Lettl, Straßlach
client:	Munich City Utilities
usage:	office
construction:	steel
system:	room cell construction
internal ceiling height:	2.5 m
site area:	12,600 m²
gross floor area:	4600 m²
total internal volume:	12,600 m³
total construction cost:	€ 3.78 mill. (gross)
date of construction:	1997
period of construction:	6 months

172

ground floor section • plan
scale 1:400
detail section
scale 1:10

1   0.75 mm trapezoidal ribbed steel sheeting
    (135 mm deep)
2   100 mm steel I-beam
3   60 × 60 × 4 mm steel SHS with lugs welded
    on both sides bolted to
4   60 × 60 × 4 mm steel SHS column
5   30 × 40 × 5 mm RHS frame
6   woven grating (25 × 25 mm mesh)
7   50 × 50 × 5 mm perforated angle as
    continuous fixing strip
8   5 mm Ø stainless steel cable
    for climbing plants
9   60 × 60 × 4 mm steel SHS bracing
    with lugs bolted to columns
10 steel container

aa

a

a

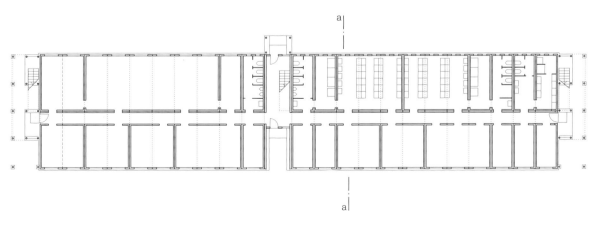

173

Tomihiro Art Museum in Azuma

The Japanese painter and poet Tomihiro Hoshino has been paralysed from the neck down since an accident in the 1970s and now paints with his mouth. His expressive interpretations of nature are underscored by his own original poetic texts. In 1991, a museum was opened in a former senior citizens' residence in his home village, Azuma, to display his work which is well known throughout Japan. The gallery proved to be a great success, attracting many visitors and becoming an important economic factor in the region. To present the artist's work in a fitting environment, the community – which is spread out around the edge of an artificial reservoir – decided to hold an international competition in 2002 for the creation of a new museum on the waterfront. The successful design is based upon an unusual concept; 33 single-storey cylindrical exhibition spaces of various diameters are compactly laid out on a single-storey square plan with light wells open to the sky in the cavities between them. Along the edges of the complex, the cylinders are simply cut in order to fit into the square. The architect was inspired by petals of water lilies floating in a pond which change their spatial composition according to the amount of sunlight falling on them. The villagers took an active part in planning as some of the space was to be made available for community events. Within the strict system, it was possible to divide these rooms flexibly and give them an individual atmosphere. The architect wanted autonomous spaces rather than neutral, sterile ones to be created. Different materials for the finishes and wall surfaces were selected for the individual cylinders, whereby the contrasts between open and closed, and warm and cool surfaces were accentuated. In consultation with the artist, a range of colour tones was decided upon for each space based on the surrounding landscape. Introverted halls dedicated to the small-scale works of the artist are juxtaposed with glazed walling which opens onto planted courtyards or to the nearby expanse of water.

The self-supporting cylinders consist of prefabricated sheet-steel elements constructed by a specialised silo manufacturer and subsequently interconnected. Uninterrupted by corridors or supporting columns, the spatial flow through the museum is not predetermined. Perforations in the walls afford glimpses of the intermediate courtyards which are planted with the same species as those interpreted by the artist in his works. From the surrounding hills, one can see the roof of the museum and the underlying constructional system revealed in an almost abstract form.

project team • building details

architects:	aat + Makoto Yokomizo architects, Tokyo
structural engineers:	Arup Japan, Tokyo
client:	Midori City, Gunma Prefecture
usage:	culture
construction:	steel
system:	room cell construction
internal ceiling height:	3.0 m
site area:	18,114 m²
gross floor area:	2463.5 m²
total internal volume:	7390.5 m³
total construction cost:	€ 7.7 mill. (gross)
date of construction:	2005
period of construction:	6 months

A

aa

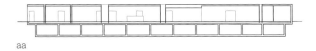

section · floor plan
scale 1:750

1 entrance
2 foyer
3 exhibition space
4 storage
5 services
6 lounge
7 lecture hall
8 cafe
9 museum shop
10 administration
11 director's office
12 deliveries
13 WCs
14 courtyard
15 library

B

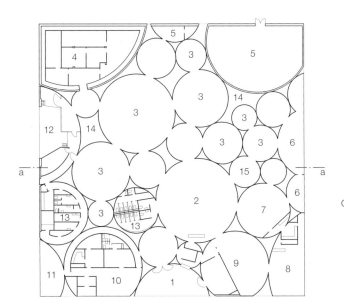

C

A delivery of prefabricated elements
B positioning of wall elements by crane
C connection of individual elements,
 closure of spaces with roof panels
D interior during construction

D

Pavilion in Venice

This pavilion, consisting of tubular steel sections, formed the entrance to the 50th Art Biennale in Venice 2003. Double-skinned segments of oxidized steel, reminiscent of oversized metal barrels or cross-sections of a giant pipeline, were interconnected by a similarly oxidized, coffered metal roof with peripheral tie beams. Light entered the pavilion via large circular perforations and illuminated the piazza below. One of the tubular elements served as the entrance tunnel; as in the "info tunnel", its internal walls were covered with information pertaining to the Biennale. The remaining modules – glazed at one end and more austerely fitted out – accommodated a ticket office, cloakrooms and a small police station. Internally, all the modules were painted in vibrant fluorescent colours.
The pavilion formed part of a temporary project entitled "The Cord", which comprised some 200 m of tubular sections inscribed internally and used to promote the Biennale in various Italian cities.

floor plan · section
scale 1:200

1 entrance tunnel
2 information tunnel
3 ticket office
4 cloakroom
5 police station

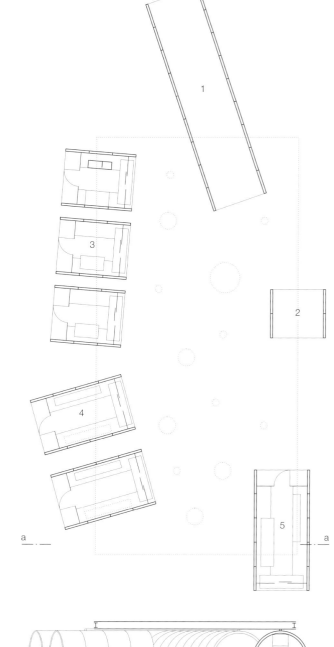

aa

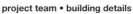

project team · building details

architects:	Archea Associati, Florence C+S Associati, Venice
with:	Laura Andreini, Marco Casa-monti, Silvia Fabi, Gianna Parisse, Giovanni Polazzi (Archea), Carlo Cappai, Maria Alessandra Segantini, Andrea Bondì (C+S)
structural engineers:	Favero & Milan Ingegneria, Mirano
client:	Pierre Mendès University, Grenoble
usage:	ticketing and entrance area
construction:	steel
system:	tubular sections construction

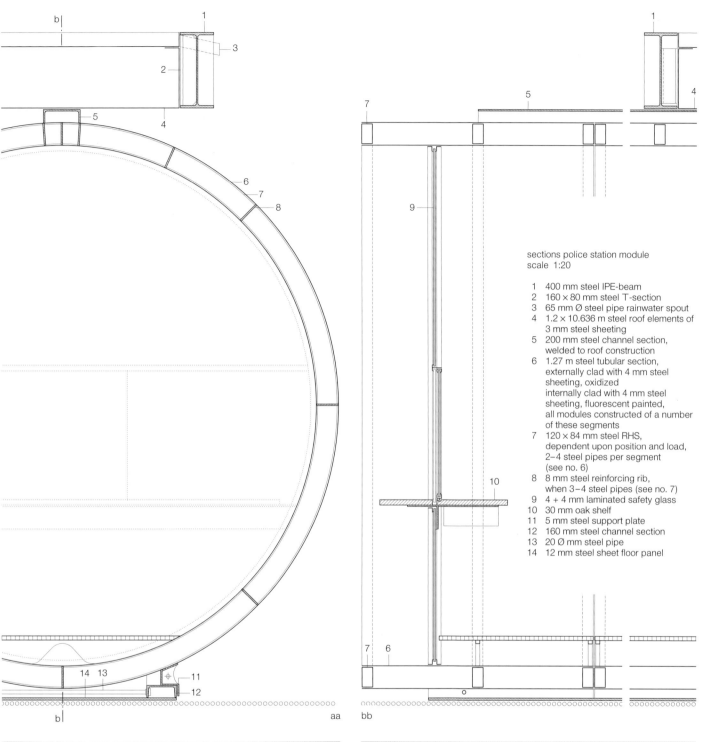

b|

1

3

2

5

4

6

7

8

14 13

11

12

b|

aa

7

5

1

4

9

10

7

6

7 6

bb

sections police station module
scale 1:20

1 400 mm steel IPE-beam
2 160 × 80 mm steel T-section
3 65 mm Ø steel pipe rainwater spout
4 1.2 × 10.636 m steel roof elements of
  3 mm steel sheeting
5 200 mm steel channel section,
  welded to roof construction
6 1.27 m steel tubular section,
  externally clad with 4 mm steel
  sheeting, oxidized
  internally clad with 4 mm steel
  sheeting, fluorescent painted,
  all modules constructed of a number
  of these segments
7 120 × 84 mm steel RHS,
  dependent upon position and load,
  2–4 steel pipes per segment
  (see no. 6)
8 8 mm steel reinforcing rib,
  when 3–4 steel pipes (see no. 7)
9 4 + 4 mm laminated safety glass
10 30 mm oak shelf
11 5 mm steel support plate
12 160 mm steel channel section
13 20 Ø mm steel pipe
14 12 mm steel sheet floor panel

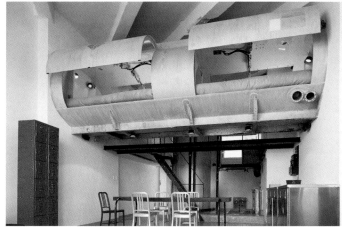

Loft in New York

This unconventional dwelling is located in a former parking garage in the West Village, New York. The conversion maintains the typical open-plan loft character of the former industrial space, offering the residents great flexibility and a feeling of openness. The design retains maximum open space while simultaneously providing well-screened private zones for bathrooms and bedrooms. The discarded cylindrical aluminium container of an oil tank vehicle was selected and retrofitted to contain these private areas.

Cut into two parts and delivered by crane, the tank is incorporated into the dwelling. One half is installed vertically and extends the full height of the internal space. It contains two sanitary spaces set above each other. All plumbing pipes are exposed and run vertically along the outside of the tank. The second half of the tank spans the living area horizontally like a bridge and contains two sleeping pods; these are accessible via a ring of steel walkways positioned at the mezzanine level.

Cut directly into the aluminium skin, top-hinged flaps open up on both sides of the sleeping pods; ventilation and illumination of the sleeping chambers is guaranteed by the motorized opening of these access flaps.

The mattresses are laid directly onto simple plywood sheets and the space beneath used for additional storage. The partition between the two sleeping chambers is formed by an existing division that used to stabilize the liquid contents of the tank during transport. The same kind of partition acts as a floor panel between the two sanitary cells, separating the upper and lower bathrooms.

The reuse of existing industrial objects in LOT/EK work is not just a recycling operation; it is more related to the huge potential that they recognize in existing objects, and their intention to transform them into amazing architecture.

The use of recycled objects is, in fact, of primary importance for the architects: existing objects are raw materials which assume new significance through the operations and processes they undergo. With changed practical functions, they become an integral part of the architecture – just like the discarded oil tank.

The result creates a strong dialogue and interaction between the practice of art and architecture.

project team • building details

architects:	LOT/EK architecture, New York, Ada Tolla & Giuseppe Lignano
structural engineers:	Katz Cader, New York
client:	private
usage:	loft living
construction:	Aluminium tank with steel supports
system:	room cell construction
internal ceiling height:	4.27 m
gross floor area:	93 m²
total internal volume:	397 m³
total construction cost:	€ 175,000 (gross)
date of construction:	2000
period of construction:	6 months

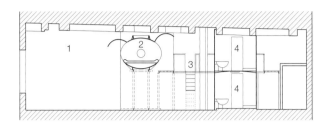

bb

section · mezzanine floor plan
scale 1:200

longitudinal section · transverse section
sleeping chamber
scale 1:50

1   void over living area
2   sleeping chamber
3   metal walkway
4   bathroom
5   void over kitchen
6   fitted cupboard
7   lounge
8   aluminium tank
9   hydraulic arm
10 base plate and supporting structure:
    220 mm steel I-beams at bearing points
    with 18.5 mm stiffening plates
11 76.2 mm Ø tubular steel columns
12 steel flat strap, welded
13 steel flat member
14 plywood sheet

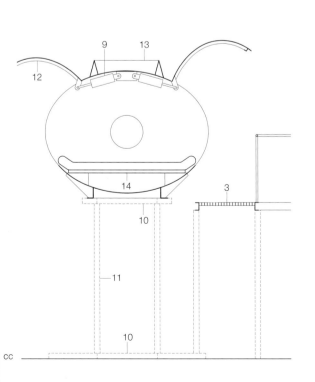

cc

Café in Helsinki

When Helsinki was the European Cultural Capital in 2000, this temporary summer café was erected between the city park on the Töölönlahti Bay and the Finlandia Hall. Although this timber-and-glass pavilion – the winning entry in a student competition held by the University of Technology, the Finnish Timber Council and the city of Helsinki – was originally planned as a temporary construction, it is now intended to open the café for visitors in the coming years. The solid timber "ring" enclosure that frames the view of the city and park is, in fact, the load-bearing structure and building envelope in one. The floor, walls, roof, and outside benches are constructed of 62 cm wide laminated timber panels that were delivered to the site and assembled there.

The name, "Hiili" (Café Carbon), refers to the black timber facades, which are flame-treated, impregnated with creosote and flame-treated again. Executed twice a year, this procedure ensures adequate resistance to rain. Internally, the timber is simply planed and left in its natural state. The interiors are also reduced to their essentials; the counter and oven are constructed of black steel. The café is furnished with tables and chairs as required.

floor plan • sections
scale 1:200

1 café
2 counter
3 veranda
4 services
5 storage
6 kitchen
7 terrace

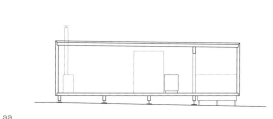

aa

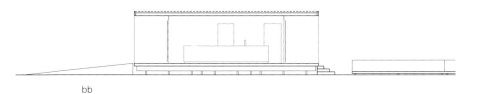

bb

project team • building details

architects:	Niko Sirola/Woodstudio 2000/Helsinki University of Technology
structural engineers:	Nuovo Engineering Ltd., Espoo
client:	The Helsinki City of Culture 2000 Foundation
usage:	café
construction:	timber
system:	room cell construction
gross floor area:	100 m²
date of construction:	2000
period of construction:	4 months

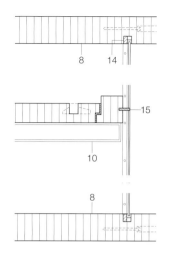

cc

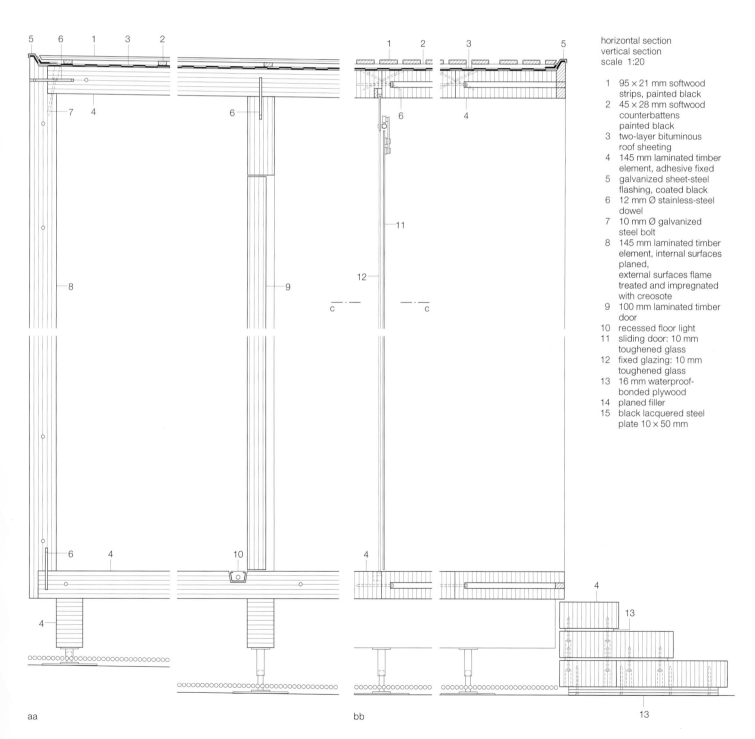

aa

bb

13

horizontal section
vertical section
scale 1:20

1 95 × 21 mm softwood
   strips, painted black
2 45 × 28 mm softwood
   counterbattens
   painted black
3 two-layer bituminous
   roof sheeting
4 145 mm laminated timber
   element, adhesive fixed
5 galvanized sheet-steel
   flashing, coated black
6 12 mm Ø stainless-steel
   dowel
7 10 mm Ø galvanized
   steel bolt
8 145 mm laminated timber
   element, internal surfaces
   planed,
   external surfaces flame
   treated and impregnated
   with creosote
9 100 mm laminated timber
   door
10 recessed floor light
11 sliding door: 10 mm
   toughened glass
12 fixed glazing: 10 mm
   toughened glass
13 16 mm waterproof-
   bonded plywood
14 planed filler
15 black lacquered steel
   plate 10 × 50 mm

Hotel Extension in Bezau

In 1970, Leopold Kaufmann, the architect's father, built a new hotel that was expanded over the years. The result is a heterogeneous accumulation of buildings; including the hotel, an indoor swimming pool and a tennis hall. The complex was to be extended by an additional bedroom tract with a hall for various functions. Since the hotel is continually in use, except for four weeks in the winter, it was necessary to devise a building system capable of conforming to an exceptionally short construction period. The solution was found in a series of prefabricated, fully installed, hotel-room containers that could be easily transported to the site and stacked on top of each other. The 7.5 × 4.0 m boxes are self-supporting, so that no primary structure or additional bracing was required. The external and internal surfaces, underfloor heating and bathroom facilities were already integrated. Services were laid in the voids between the cells and only the glass bathroom walls and the timber furniture had to be subsequently installed. The boxes and their roof – which was sealed with plastic roof sheeting – were erected within a mere two days.

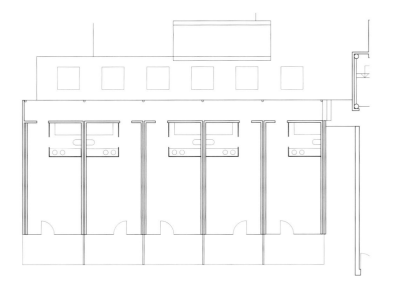

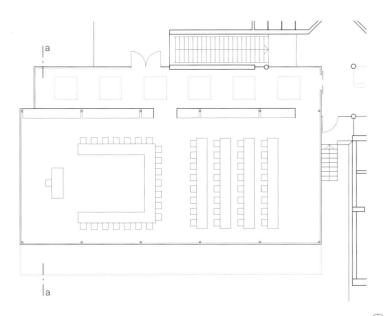

project team • building details

architects:	Kaufmann 96, Dornbirn
structural engineers:	Merz/Kaufmann & Partners, Dornbirn
client:	Kur und Sporthotel Post Susanne Kaufmann, Bezau
usage:	hotel
construction:	timber
system:	room cell construction
internal ceiling height:	2.5 m
site area:	12,000 m²
gross floor area:	420 m²
total internal volume:	1200 m³
total construction cost:	€ 840,000 (gross)
date of construction:	1998
period of construction:	5 weeks

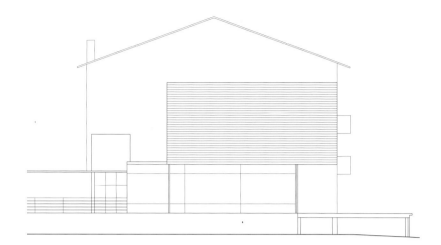

elevations
floor plans
scale 1:250

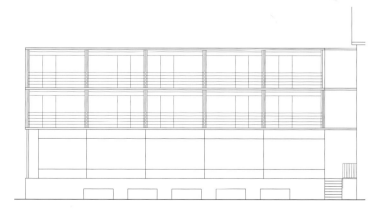

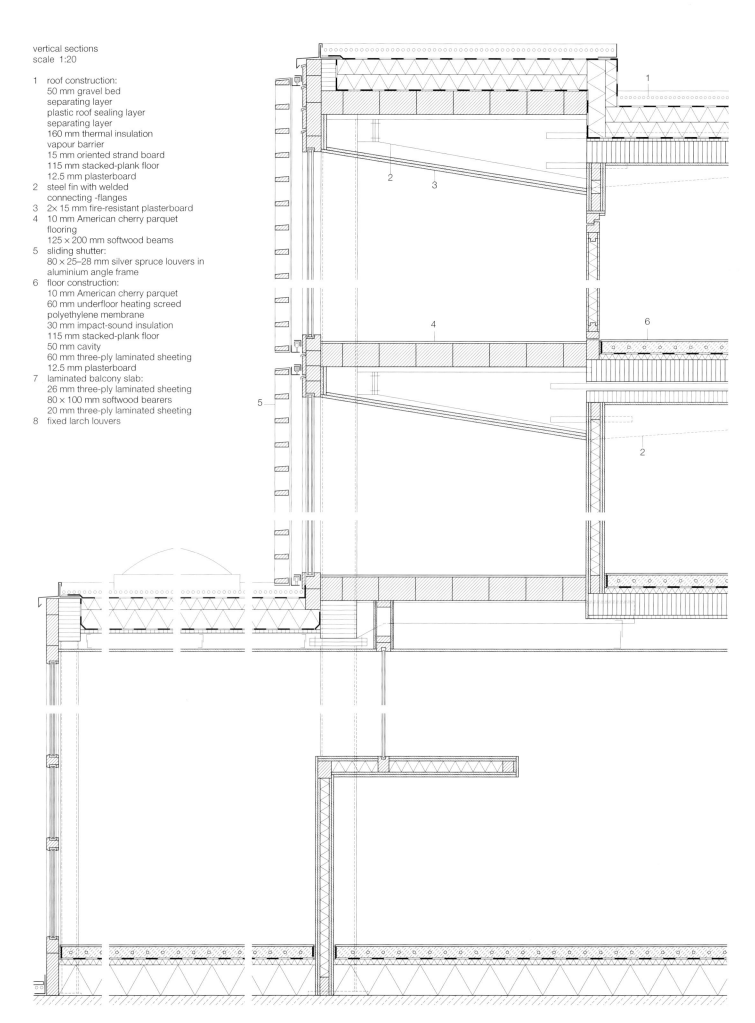

vertical sections
scale 1:20

1   roof construction:
    50 mm gravel bed
    separating layer
    plastic roof sealing layer
    separating layer
    160 mm thermal insulation
    vapour barrier
    15 mm oriented strand board
    115 mm stacked-plank floor
    12.5 mm plasterboard
2   steel fin with welded
    connecting -flanges
3   2× 15 mm fire-resistant plasterboard
4   10 mm American cherry parquet
    flooring
    125 × 200 mm softwood beams
5   sliding shutter:
    80 × 25–28 mm silver spruce louvers in
    aluminium angle frame
6   floor construction:
    10 mm American cherry parquet
    60 mm underfloor heating screed
    polyethylene membrane
    30 mm impact-sound insulation
    115 mm stacked-plank floor
    50 mm cavity
    60 mm three-ply laminated sheeting
    12.5 mm plasterboard
7   laminated balcony slab:
    26 mm three-ply laminated sheeting
    80 × 100 mm softwood bearers
    20 mm three-ply laminated sheeting
8   fixed larch louvers

184

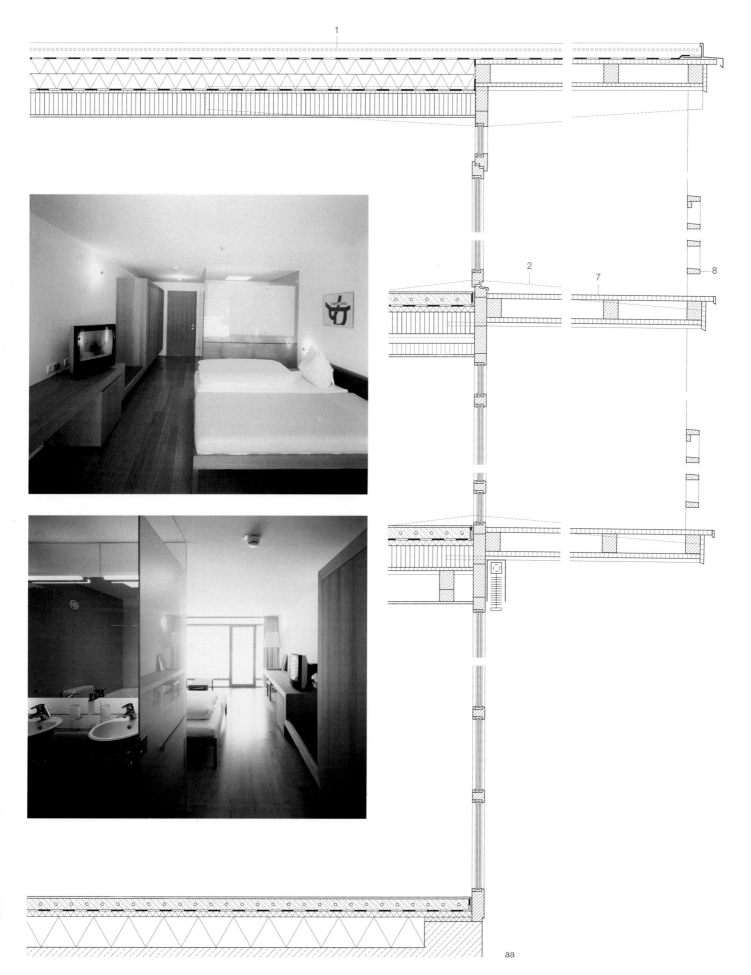

aa

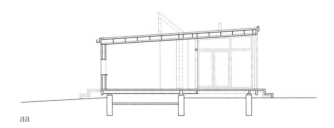

A

Prefabricated House from Denmark

While selecting living room or bedroom furniture from an international furniture manufacturer's catalogue, it is now possible to order the corresponding house at the same time. In contrast to similar concepts, this house, developed by the Danish architectural firm ONV, has attained high levels of design quality and flexibility. The minimalist residence is available in six basic variations that can be adapted to the clients' specific needs and expanded with additional prefabricated segments. Due to the high degree of prefabrication, the structure can be manufactured at a relatively low cost. The smallest version is produced entirely in the factory and can be delivered to site by a truck, while larger versions are made up of two to four modules. On site, these prefabricated modules are set on strip footings, then the roof sheeting is sealed, the skylights installed and, finally, the connections cleaned. The timber-framed external walls of this austere structure are clad in Siberian larch and the interior walls with gypsum fibreboard.

The layout is planned around a large communal space which accommodates living and dining areas, and an open kitchen which can be connected to a covered terrace as desired. The internal and external spaces are linked to each other via extensive glazing. The number of additional rooms remains flexible, circulation space is kept to a minimum and all the floor surfaces are finished in either high quality ash parquet or natural stone.

axonometric drawings of
the available versions

version A   60 m²
version B   86 m²
version C   103 m²
version D   138 m²
version E   160 m²

aa

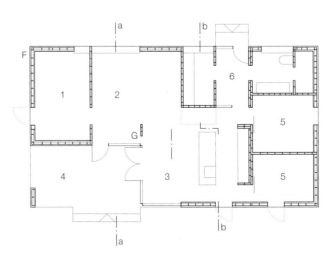

project team • building details

architects:	ONV architects, Vanløse
with:	Søren Rasmussen, Christian Hanak
structural engineers:	Jens Abildgård, Hjørring
usage:	single-family house
construction:	timber
system:	room cell construction
gross floor area:	60–169 m²
period of construction:	8–12 weeks

floor plan • section
scale 1:200

1   bedroom
2   living
3   dining
4   covered terrace
5   room
6   entrance

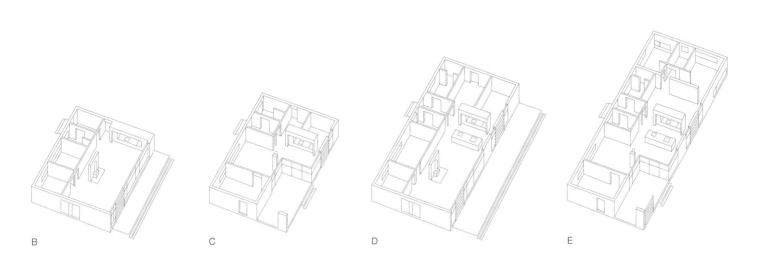

B   C   D   E

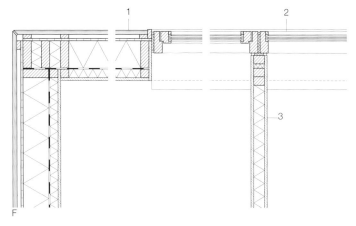

F

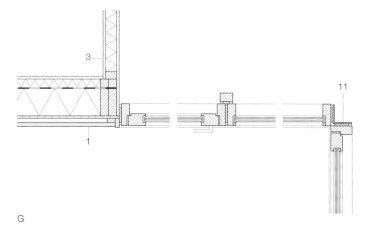

G

horizontal sections
vertical sections
scale 1:20

1 tongue-and-groove boarding, 22 mm
   transp. coated larch, 22 mm battens
   with ventilation cavity, 12 mm plywood,
   145 × 45 mm post-and-rail facade
   145 mm mineral-wool insulation,
   vapour barrier
   45 mm insulation between 45 × 45
   battens, 15 mm gypsum fibreboard
2 120 mm larch frame with
   double-glazing: 12 mm +
   6 mm cavity + 12 mm
3 15 mm gypsum fibreboard,
   70 mm thermal insulation between
   70 × 45 mm timber studs,
   15 mm gypsum fibreboard
4 65 × 233 mm laminated timber beam
5 14 mm parquet, vapour barrier,
   15 mm plywood, 195 mm mineral-wool
   insulation, 3 mm synthetic panel
6 timber member with ventilation outlet
7 100 mm reinforced concrete foundation slab with drainage opening
8 2-ply bituminous sheeting welded in-
   situ, 15 mm plywood,
   195 mm mineral-wool insulation,
   195 × 45 mm rafters, vapour barrier,
   45 mm insulation,
   45 × 45 mm battens,
   15 mm gypsum fibreboard
9 sliding element terrace:
   30 × 30 mm galvanized steel angle
   45 × 25 mm larch louvers,
   transparent coated
10 300 mm reinforced concrete strip
   foundation, filled on site
11 120 × 20 mm steel angle column

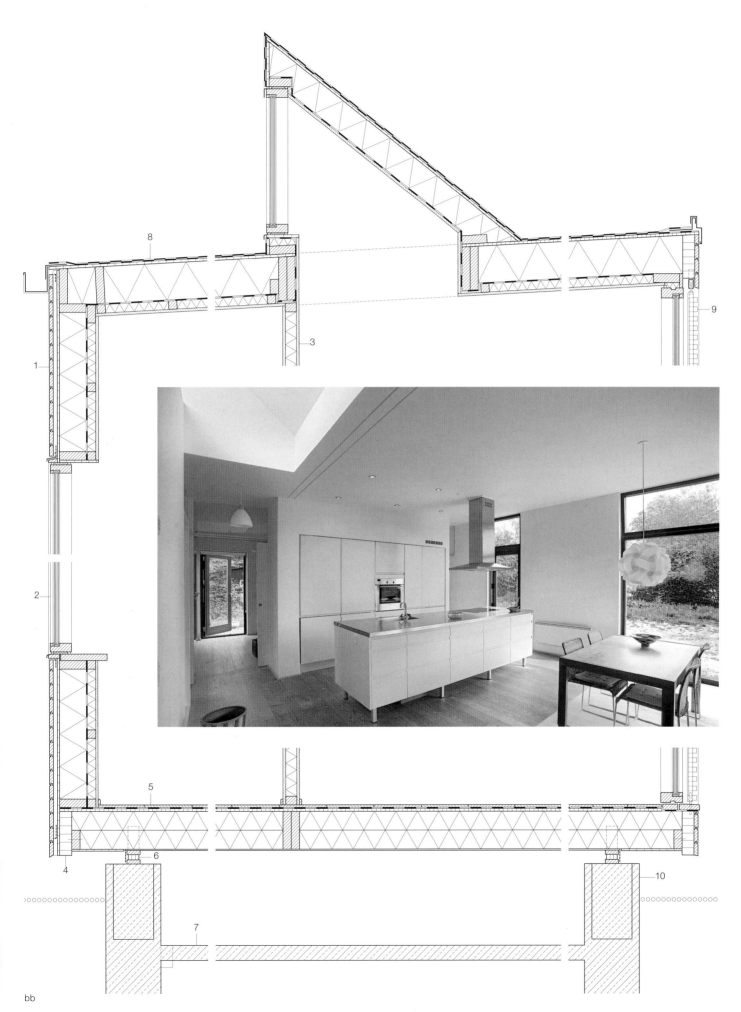

1

2

8

3

9

5

6

4

10

7

bb

189

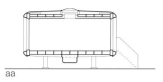

aa

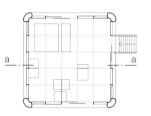

a — a

Transportable Living Unit

With its inner dimensions of 6.66 × 6.66 metres, the basic Loftcube unit provides a living area of roughly 39 square metres. The next larger unit, rectangular on plan, is 55 square metres in area and is also available with an internal ceiling height of 2.9 metres. Due to a flexible fit-out system, entire housing landscapes, linked by bridges, can be created according to the individual creative desires and functional demands of the clients.

The requisite mobility is ensured by restricting the size of all construction elements to container dimensions. The Loftcube, including all internal finishings, can be erected in six days. It can be dismantled and re-assembled in two to three days when another location is desired. If the desired location is 130 metres or more above the ground on top of a high-rise building, the cube can be transported in its entirety by helicopter.

The entire load-bearing frame is constructed of steel in order to minimise the weight applied to existing base structures. The floor is raised above the flat roof base on four inset tubular columns and consists – like the roof of the cube –

of four individually framed units joined together. The roof is borne by eight corner facade columns. Panels of glass-fibre reinforced plastic (GRP) are fixed to the structure by means of a quick-lock mechanism and can be easily replaced if damaged or when colour alternatives are desired by the client.

The column-free layout is based on a 125 cm finishings grid appropriate for both custom-built and standardised elements. Fixed and sliding functional partitions are inserted into guide tracks in the floor and ceiling in order to articulate and organise the internal space.

Electrical and water-supply modules, as well as those for communications, are also installed here and have flexible connection points. All sanitary fittings are manufactured of solid, moulded acrylic polymer with an integrated proportion of stone dust.

The marketing strategy for the serial production of the Loftcube is similar to that of the automobile industry; architecture, design, technical services and management are responsibilities of the core team while structural planning and marketing are tendered out.

project team • building details

architects:	Aisslinger + Bracht, and8, Hamburg
designers:	Studio Aisslinger, Werner Aisslinger, Berlin
structural engineers:	Stupperich + Partner, Hamburg
client:	Loftcube GmbH, Munich
usage:	living/office
construction:	steel/timber
system:	room cell construction
internal ceiling height:	2.51 m
gross floor area:	53 m²
total internal volume:	133 m³
total construction cost:	€ 99,000 (gross)
period of construction:	6 days (approx.)

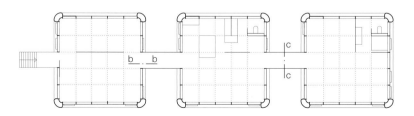

section
plans
scale 1:250

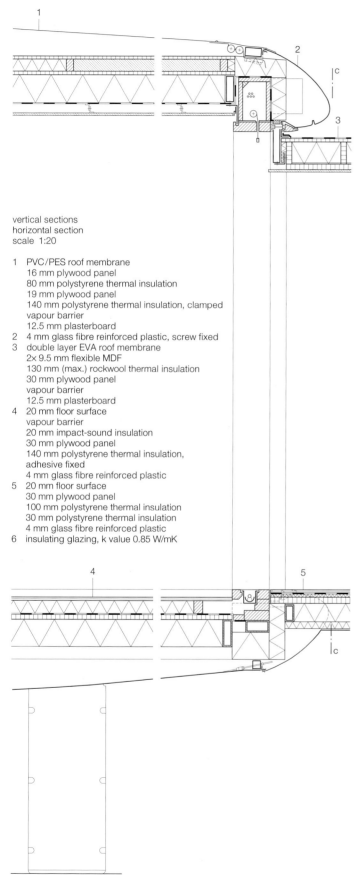
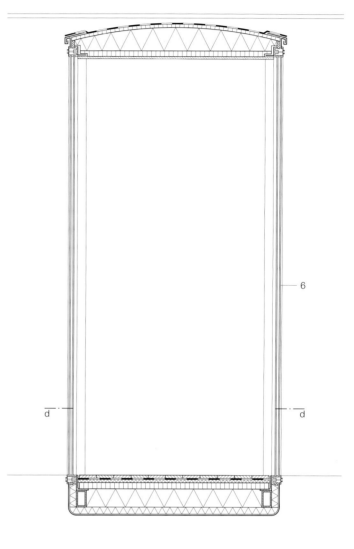
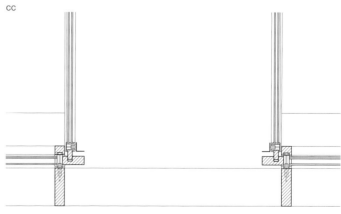

vertical sections
horizontal section
scale 1:20

1 PVC/PES roof membrane
    16 mm plywood panel
    80 mm polystyrene thermal insulation
    19 mm plywood panel
    140 mm polystyrene thermal insulation, clamped
    vapour barrier
    12.5 mm plasterboard
2 4 mm glass fibre reinforced plastic, screw fixed
3 double layer EVA roof membrane
    2× 9.5 mm flexible MDF
    130 mm (max.) rockwool thermal insulation
    30 mm plywood panel
    vapour barrier
    12.5 mm plasterboard
4 20 mm floor surface
    vapour barrier
    20 mm impact-sound insulation
    30 mm plywood panel
    140 mm polystyrene thermal insulation,
    adhesive fixed
    4 mm glass fibre reinforced plastic
5 20 mm floor surface
    30 mm plywood panel
    100 mm polystyrene thermal insulation
    30 mm polystyrene thermal insulation
    4 mm glass fibre reinforced plastic
6 insulating glazing, k value 0.85 W/mK

bb

cc

dd

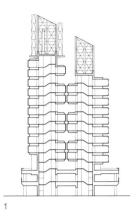

1

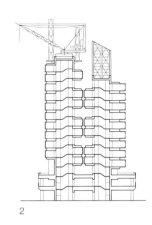

2

Nakagin Capsule Tower in Tokyo

Built in the 1970s, the Nakagin Capsule
Tower was the world's first capsule construction to be realised. Capsule architectural design – the establishment of the
capsule as a usable space and its inser-
tion into a mega-structure – can be linked
with other contemporary works of architecture of the late 1960's. This movement
addressed the challenge of whether
mass production was capable of generat-
ing diverse, yet high quality, architecture.
Kurokawa developed a technique whereby capsule units could be fixed to a concrete core using only four high-tension
bolts; the units were also detachable and
replaceable. The capsules were designed to accommodate individuals in an
apartment or studio space or, by inter-
connecting modules, families in larger
units.

The capsule interior is pre-assembled in
a factory off-site, complete with appliances and furniture – in fact, everything from
an audio system to the telephone. On
site, the capsule is then hoisted by crane
and fastened to the concrete core.

Due to the replacement or removal of individual capsules, the appearance of the
tower continuously evolves over time.

planned procedure for capsule
replacement
1   demolish rooftop equipment,
    demolish stack
2   assemble crane foundation and
    support, set crane on tower roof
3   remove capsules from central
    services in order of precedence
4   assemble scaffolding around core,
    renew fasteners for capsules
5   disassemble scaffolding,
    install new capsules and
    connect to central services
6   disassemble crane,
    rebuild rooftop equipment

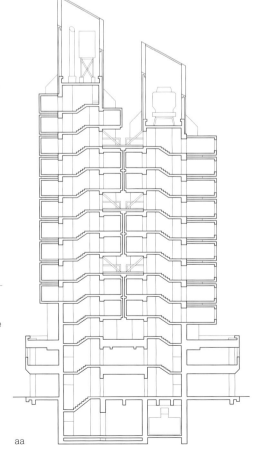

aa

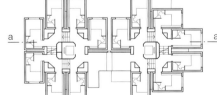

a   a

floor plan · section
scale 1:500

project team · building details

architects:	Kisho Kurokawa & Associates
with:	Nihon Sekkei, Inc., Tokyo
structural engineers:	Gengo Matsui + O.R.S Office Tokyo
client:	Nakagin Mansion
usage:	living
construction:	steel
system:	frame construction
internal ceiling height:	2.77 m
site area:	441.89 m^2
gross floor area:	3091.23 m^2
date of construction:	1972
period of construction:	15 months

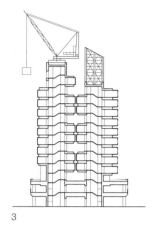
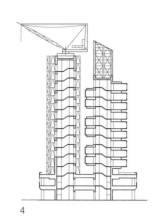
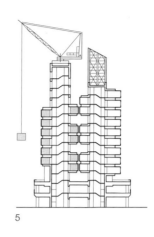
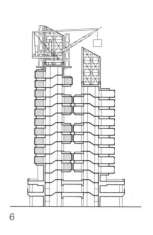

3

4

5

6

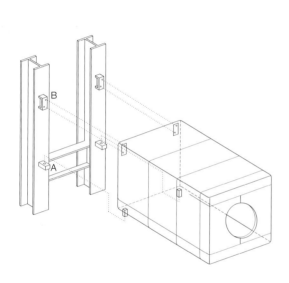

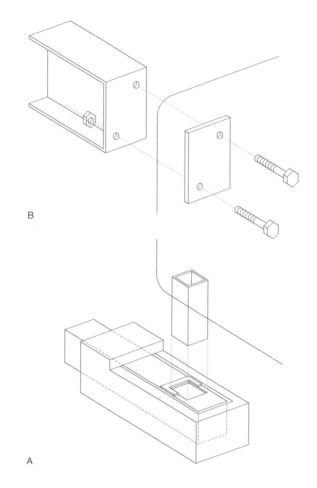

B

A

schematic
exploded diagram
capsule connection

A lower connection
  capsule to beam
B upper connection
  capsule to beam

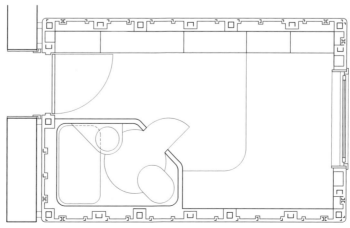

floor plan
capsule
scale 1:20

Part D   Building envelopes

Structural facades   196
Non-structural facades   196
  Post-and-rail facades
  Prefabricated facades
Glass facade systems   197
  Methods of fixing
  Jointing
  Types of glass in prefabricated
  construction
Multi-layer glass facade
and window systems   198
  Double-glazed windows in
  prefabricated construction
  Double window elements in
  punctuated facades
Metal facade systems   201
  Metal sheeting
  Formed elements
  Composite metal sheeting
Timber facade systems   203
  Substructure
  Methods of fixing
  Surface treatment
Concrete facade systems   204
  Surface quality
  Methods of fixing
Brickwork facade systems   205
Natural stonework facade
systems   205
Plastic facade systems   206
  Facade elements
  Panel facades and formed elements
  Pneumatic cushion facades

Glazed grid shells
Changes in the planning process   208
Glazed single-skin steel grid shells   209
  Westfield Shopping Centre
  PalaisQuartier

figure D

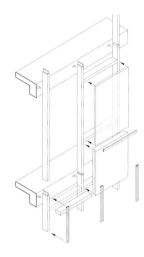

D 1.1

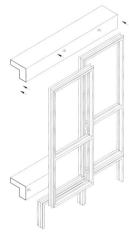

D 1.2

Building envelopes

The primary function of the building envelope is to provide weather protection and act as a filter between the interior and exterior. Simultaneously, the facade also conveys the outward image and character of the construction.

Material selection and choice of openings are not only decisive for the image of a facade, but also greatly affect the internal environment and energy consumption of a building.

Noticeable advancements have been made in recent years in the field of facade technology in unitised construction systems. The facade, as such, is no longer simply seen as a protective shell, but as an independent system with specific technical characteristics. Articulated into individual elements, the facade system can be combined with a great variety of different structural systems. Based on their constructional principles, facades can be subdivided into structural and non-structural facades.

Structural facades

Structural facades are usually solid wall constructions that transfer all loads from the roof and floor slabs and also fulfil the function of bracing the construction. They can either be single or multi-layered and should meet all the requirements of building physics. Structural facades, based on systemised construction techniques, are often executed in precast concrete elements or prefabricated solid timber wall panels.

The building elements in single-layer facades must not only fulfil the requirements of building physics, but also those of static stability. Multi-layer facades are usually made up of a triple-layer sandwich construction with a structural, insulating

and facing layer. It is possible that the discrete elements of the sandwich construction be independently optimised with regard to their functions; structural stability, thermal insulation and surface treatment. In cases of increased moisture penetration, an additional ventilation cavity can be included between the insulation layer and the facing layer.

During the assembly of prefabricated elements with butt joints, it is extremely important that the insulation layers continue unbroken throughout the facade and for the fireproof connections in the joints to be sealed with an appropriate material.

Non-structural facades

Non-structural facades, also known as curtain facades, are closed systems that form an independent entity, irrespective of the structural system. These two partial systems, facade and carcass, are coordinated with one another by means of a basic grid and modular organisation. Non-structural facades can either be single or multi-layer entities, dependent upon requirements, and are executed as either post-and-rail or panel constructions. It is necessary that the facades be built to coincide with the requirements of thermal insulation, noise protection and fire protection. The points of weakness here, with regard to building physics, are the junctions between the columns, walls and ceiling slabs. A moisture barrier can be guaranteed by using appropriate constructional connections and sealing materials. Connection joints between the discrete facade elements compensate for deviations of the individual elements, which result from static and dynamic loading, manufacture-related tolerances and dynamic wind loading.

D   Glass facade, administration building RWE, Essen (D) 1997, Ingenhoven Overdieck Kalen and Partner
D 1.1   Exploded isometry of a post-and-rail facade
D 1.2   Exploded isometry of a prefabricated facade
D 1.3   Prefabricated facade in fibre-reinforced concrete
         a layered construction
         b view of panel
D 1.4   Post-and-rail facade, Hogeschool, Rotterdam (NL) 2000, Eric van Egeraat associated architects
         a view of facade
         b exploded isometry of a post-and-rail facade with glazing bars
D 1.5   Prefabricated facade, bank extension, Budapest (H) 1997, Eric van Egeraat associated architects
         a isometry of a prefabricated facade
         b view of facade

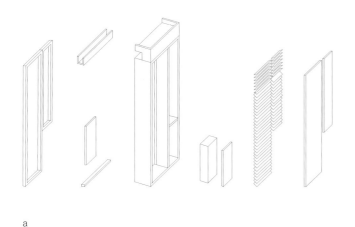

a

b   D 1.3

a

Based on their constructional principles, non-structural building envelopes can be subdivided into post-and-rail and panel facades.

Post-and-rail facades

The constructional building elements of this type of system consist of vertical posts and horizontal rails which provide the structural framework for infill elements of glass, plastic, timber or metal (fig. D 1.1). The framework elements, which are prefabricated in transportable sizes in production plants, are assembled on site and connected to the slabs, walls and columns of the carcass construction. The infill elements are fixed to the framework construction, either in the plant or on site, with point fixings or glazing bars. It is, of course, also possible that the posts, rails and infill elements be transported to the site as separate elements. Fixing systems, which are specifically developed for post-and-rail facades, enable simple and speedy assembly.

Prefabricated facades

Prefabricated facades consist of panels of glass, metal, timber masonry, natural stone or concrete that have been prefabricated in production plants. Due to their extreme modularity, they are particularly appropriate for regular, unified buildings. The facade elements can be conceived as either single or double-layered, and often incorporate environmental protection elements – such as sun-shading, glare louvers or coated glazing – in addition to integral thermal insulation (fig. D 1.3). On site, these fully prefabricated facade elements are mounted onto consoles or anchors on that have been secured to the rough carcass (fig. D 1.2) and where this type of element requires appropriate adjustment before height and position are

correct. Prior to assembly, all butt joints must be treated with flexible seals, which act as moisture barriers and absorb tolerances. The crossing points of the panels are the weakest areas of such a system and appropriate constructional measures must be taken [1].

Glass facade systems

Glass facades generally consist of structural frame, fixing, panes and joints. They can either be single or double-layered and are based on the same principles as the post-and-rail facade. When posts and rails provide the structural system, the glass panes are either fixed linearly with glazing bars or specially developed point fixing systems (fig. D 1.4).
In prefabricated facades, the glass pane, frame and fixings are assembled in the factory to create a single building element. The construction and the glass panes absorb loads – for example wind loads – and transfer these to the load-bearing structure of the building (fig. D 1.5). The bearing area of the fixing member must be sufficiently dimensioned within the glass pane to be able to equally transfer the vertical pressure loads. In order to avoid hard bearing areas it is necessary to include elastic layers within steel frames between different materials – for example, EPDM plastic or soft metals; these also permanently absorb friction loads.
Methods of fixing the glass elements are defined by their basic principles.

Methods of fixing
Glazing bar construction
Glazing bars are elements – made of steel, aluminium or timber for example – which fix two panes of glass to a sub-

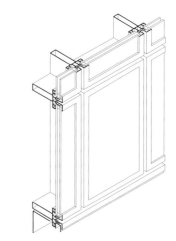

b   D 1.4

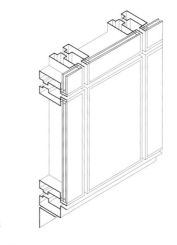

a

b   D 1.5

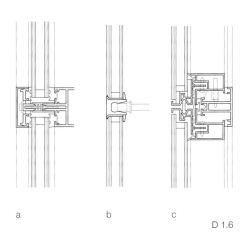

a   b   c
                                        D 1.6

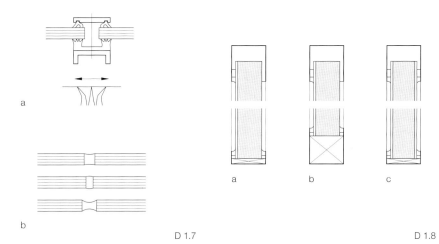

a

b
                                        D 1.7

a   b   c
                                        D 1.8

structure. The panes are fixed to the substructure via a screw connection under
pressure.

It is necessary to include a permanently
elastic material in the region between the
glazing bar, glass pane and substructure
to seal the connection. Glazing bars and
substructures can be of slender cross-
section because the forces to be transferred are linear and continuous. The
panes can be fixed on two or four sides;
with two-sided fixings the joint is sealed
flush with silicon on the open side of the
pane. It is necessary that both glazing
bars and substructure be thermally separated when the glass panes are employed
as insulating elements.

Glass panes can also be secured to the
substructure by way of a point-fixing
system under pressure.

The fixing elements are located either
centrally at the edge of the glass pane or
at its corners. Thermally pre-stressed
glass is used in order to equally transfer
all loads, which are applied to the glass
pane, across the entire bearing area. The
joints between the individual panes of
glass are subsequently sealed with silicon.

Drilled point fixing

A hole is drilled into the pane of glass
where the fixing elements, which are
responsible for load transfer, are
inserted. The fixing elements are usually
manufactured of stainless steel and are
adhesive-fixed to the glass pane in the
recess and sealed. Joints to adjacent
panes are similarly sealed.

Adhesive fixed connections

In this type of fixing, the pane of glass is
set into a frame and fixed using adhesives; the joints are automatically sealed.
The loads resulting from the dead weight
of the glass and externally applied wind

loads are transferred to the load-bearing
structure via the combined structure of
the glass pane and framework (fig. D 3.2).

Jointing

Jointing configuration in prefabricated glass construction elements

The joints between individual glass elements must be planned to enable them
to cater for possible deformations, yet
remain impervious to high winds and
driving rain. Joints are sealed either by
contact sealing or adhesive sealing (fig.
D 1.7). Adhesive sealing techniques,
using permanent elastic silicon, provide
flexible, elastic connections that are also
capable of withstanding tensile forces.
Contact sealing techniques rely on the
use of permanently elastic block-shaped
or lip-sealing elements applied between
the different contact surfaces of the building structure and the panes of glass [2].

Types of glass in prefabricated construction

Float glass

Float glass is the most commonly used
material in facade construction within the
building industry. It is high-quality glass
and, therefore, particularly appropriate for
the manufacture of multiple layered glazing (fig. D 3.3). Maximum dimensions of
float glass are 321 × 600 cm, with a thickness of 2 to 19 mm. By using additives of
special metal oxides, it is also possible to
attain light colour variations in float glass;
for example green, blue, bronze or grey.
Pigmentation is often decided upon to
provide glare and sun protection, or for
aesthetic reasons.

Figured glass

Figured glass building elements are particularly robust and were initially developed for industrial situations, but are
now used in all types of buildings (fig.

D 1.10b). During manufacture, the hot
malleable glass strips pass between special rollers and are formed into linear elements with U-shaped profiles. Figured
glass is available in the widths of 22, 25,
32 and 50 cm with a maximum length of
600 cm. The U-shaped cross-section of
the glass panels increases the buckling
stiffness of the glass and thereby ensures
a higher load-bearing capacity. Because
fixing is not necessary in the vertical
direction, this type of glass element is
particularly appropriate for glass facades
designed without intermediate members
(fig. D 1.10a). Should additional padding,
sealing or other construction elements
be required, they must be integrated in
accordance with manufacturer's latest
guidelines (fig. D 1.8).

Hollow glass blocks

Hollow glass blocks are manufactured by
fusing two half-blocks together. As the
blocks cool, negative pressure develops
in the hollow space between the two outer
surfaces, whereby the thermal insulating
properties of the blocks are considerably
increased. The hollow glass blocks are
laid end-to-end and fixed with mortar;
these mortar joints unfortunately provide
thermal bridges between the blocks.
Hollow glass blocks are only capable of
withstanding minor vertical loads, and as
such are more appropriate for non-load-
bearing constructions. The standard
dimensions are 15/15 and 30/30 cm with
a thickness of 8 to 10 cm (fig. D 1.11) [3].

Multi-layer glass facade and window systems

The principles of construction of multi-layered facades and facade systems determine the function and appearance of a

Legend D 1.10
1 edged aluminium sheeting
2 aluminium cover plate
3 angle
4 figured glass elements in aluminium
sections with thermal insulation
5 steel section
6 double-glazing
7 aluminium frame
8 external sun-shading

Legend D 1.11
9 reinforced concrete slab on permanent
metal framework
10 glass block
11 insulated steel panel
12 steel angle
13 steel section
14 steel rod with thread
15 steel tube
16 steel I-beam with fire-protective coating

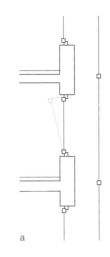

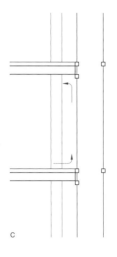

a   b   c

D 1.9

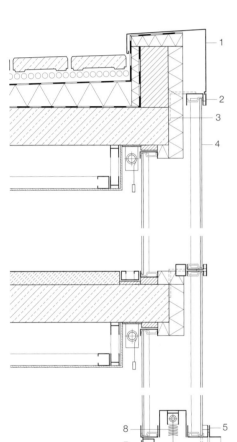

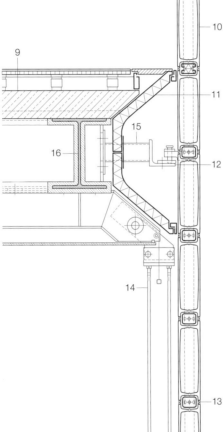
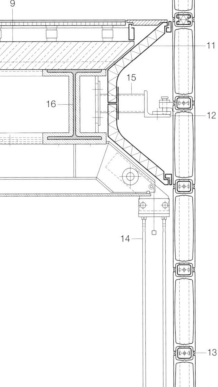

building envelope. One distinguishes between multi-layered glass facades and window systems, all-glass facade systems and perforated facades.

Double-glazed windows in prefabricated construction

When a glass facade consists of two layers of glass mounted one in front of the other, it is referred to as a double glazed facade. Compared with single glazed facades, higher standards of thermal and sound insulation can be achieved. Dependent upon the natural or mechanical ventilation system, the facades are distinguished as double-skin facades, mechanically ventilated facades or buffer facades (fig. D 1.9).

Double-skin facade
The principle of a double-skin facade is based upon a naturally ventilated layer of glass set in front of the main layer of glazing. The exchange of fresh air and exhaust air is controlled within the ventilated cavity. The cavity within this type of facade system can contain either vertically or horizontally arranged panes of glass.

D 1.6 Fixing techniques, glazing bars, point fixings, adhesive connections
D 1.7 Glass connections, contact sealant, adhesive sealant
D 1.9 Ventilation principles of double glazed facades
a double-skin facade,
b mechanically ventilated facade
c buffer facade
D 1.8 Method of fixing figured glass elements;
a single layer
b single layer "sheet pile wall" (interior wall)
c double layer
D 1.10 Facade with figured glass elements, police station, Boxtel (NL) 1997, Wiel Arets
a vertical section
b view of facade
D 1.11 Facade with hollow glass blocks, Hermès shopping centre, Tokyo (J) 2001, Renzo Piano Building Workshop
a vertical section
b view of facade

a   a

b   D 1.10   b   D 1.11

199

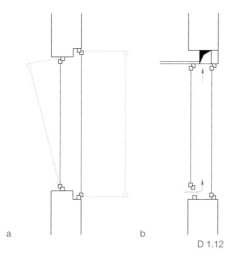

a   b

D 1.12

Legend D 1.13
1 window frame and light:
   extruded aluminium section
   thermally separated
2 sheet aluminium
3 toughened safety glass outer pane
4 grating over air inlet to void

Legend D 1.14
5 hinged, upward-opening sheet aluminium
6 outer facade, extra clear glass
7 stainless steel countersunk screw fixing
8 aluminium section facade post
9 inner facade, storey-high, heat-absorbing glass,
   extra clear glass in aluminium frame
10 insulating glazing
11 stainless steel countersunk screw fixing
12 aluminium facade post

This is referred to as a box-window facade (fig. D 1.13).

The individual double-layered facade elements are prefabricated in factories and can be modified to comply with a variety of functions; for example, ventilation, exhaust and sun protection. They are closed elements and remain independent of adjacent elements, in respect to ventilation. This separation is also advantageous in connection with fire protection and sound insulation (fig. D 1.14).

Compared with non-separated double-skin facades, the amount of natural thermal ventilation in box-window facades is insufficient to ventilate the entire facade. Natural ventilation is, however, possible via the integration of opening elements in both skins.

Mechanically ventilated facade
Mechanically ventilated facades employ the cavity between the facade skins to draw the warmed air from the building back to the air-conditioning system. The ventilation openings are located in the internal facade skin. The facade cavity is considered as being a ventilation ele-

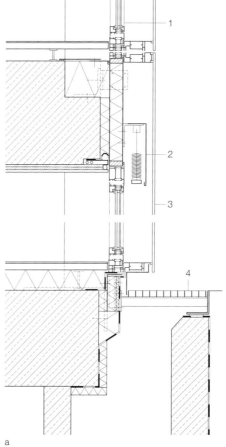

a

b   D 1.13

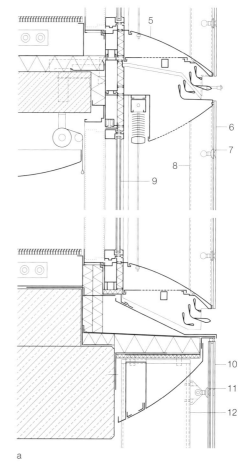

a

b   D 1.14

D 1.12 Mechanically ventilated window
D 1.13 Box-window facade, administration building, Kronberg im Taunus (D) 2000, Schneider and Schumacher
D 1.14 Box-window facade, RWE head office, Essen (D) 1997, Ingehoven Overdiek Kahlen and Partner
        a vertical section
        b view of facade
D 1.15 Facade of metal elements, Meteorite World, Essen (D) 1998, propeller z
D 1.16 Formed elements – external wall cladding
        a corner element
        b angle element

D 1.15

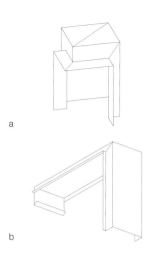

a

b

D 1.16

ment and, as such, a part of the entire ventilation system. Insulating glass panels are used for the external facade skin in order to reduce transmitted warmth.

Buffer facade
Buffer facades are conceived without ventilation openings in the two facade skins and function simply as thermal and sound insulators. The buffer zone is a closed entity and, as such, no air exchange occurs between the outside and inner space. The interior of the building is fully air-conditioned.

Double window elements in punctuated facades
Prefabricated double window elements are also employed in classic punctuated facades where the solid external walls are responsible for load transmission. Here, the window elements are differentiated as box windows, ventilated windows and double-glazed windows.
In box windows, both panes can be independently opened.
Ventilated windows consist of two fixed glazing elements, where the external pane is insulating glass and the internal pane is usually single glazed. The ventilation occurs in the cavity between the two panes and is mechanically controlled by an air-conditioning system. Sun protection elements can also be incorporated within this space, where they are unaffected by weather (fig. D 1.12).
Double-glazed windows consist of two window frames connected flush, immediately one in front of the other, and set into the facade.
There is no possibility of natural ventilation. This type of window is particularly appropriate for buildings located in areas with extreme sound or environmental pollution problems [4].

Metal facade systems

Steel, aluminium and copper are the most widely used metals for the manufacture of facade elements. They are available as semi-finished building materials in the form of metal sheeting and can be refined to create panels, formed elements and connection elements by way of stamping, folding, separating and coating. Due to their high expansion coefficients, it is necessary that heat-related deformation of these building panels be taken into account during facade planning.
Sheet metals are more resistant to weather over a long period of time than other building materials; their surfaces can acquire additional protection by way of galvanising, coating or deliberate pre-oxidisation. Some metals, such as iron and copper, develop corrosive coatings that impart natural patinas.
Metal sheeting is completely moisture proof; this makes the ventilation of their substructures absolutely essential.

Metal sheeting
Due to their light weight, metal sheeting is highly appropriate for large-format facade elements. Profiled, perforated and expanded metal sheeting are most frequently used for metal facade elements (fig. D 1.15).
The joints between discrete sheets are closed by way of flat or standing folded seams (fig. D 1.17). When metal sheeting is mounted onto a substructure without being completely joined, it is necessary that the substructure be adequately waterproofed.
An important factor for the external appearance of metal facades is, in addition to metal selection and the surface treatment, the manner of fixing the facade panels. When the substructure is a timber

construction, the metal panels are screw-fixed, while a steel framed substructure necessitates clamping onto fixing profiles.

Formed elements
Formed elements are known as coffered panels or angle elements, which have been produced by folding and stamping lightweight metals, steel sheeting or stainless steel (fig. D 1.16). They are available in a wide variety of standard sections, but can also be custom-made for specific facade requirements as necessary (fig. D 1.19, p. 202).
Formed elements are hung onto screw-fixed bolts on the substructures. Elongated screw-holes enable adjustment of the facade panels in both the horizontal and vertical directions (fig. D 1.18, p. 202).

Composite metal sheeting
Composite metal sheeting is a 3–6 mm thick composite element of 0.5 mm, surface treated, aluminium or steel enclosing a core of either plastic or a mineral material. Composite metal panels are available in widths from 1000 mm and in lengths of up to 8000 mm and can be manufactured with great surface uniformity. The panels can be produced in curves and hot-air welded as necessary. Composite metal elements can be further refined by stamping and edging in order to produce coffered facade elements.
Composite metal panels can be screw-fixed, riveted or fixed with clamps and fixing profiles to the steel substructures and are appropriate for both ventilated facades and roof cladding as desired [5].

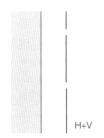

H+V

Panels with open (drained) joints

- fixings exposed or concealed
- second, water run-off layer required

H+V

with sheet metal folded around frame

- difficult to maintain tension
- second, water run-off layer required

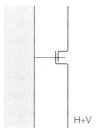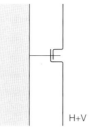

H+V

Pans

- peripheral folded edges stabilise the form
- detachable joints

D 1.17   Methods of fixing and joint configuration in metal panel facade elements
H = horizontal section
V = vertical section
D 1.18   Assembly of facade elements onto posts of substructure
D 1.19   Steel sheet profile facade cladding
1 hung fixing
2 substructure
3 perforated rainwater gutter
D 1.20   Solid timber facade in block construction technique
D 1.21   Facade of panel elements
D 1.22   Substructure for vertical boarding and large format panels
a vertical panelling, separated ventilation with drip profile
b large-format timber panels, continuous ventilation without drip profile

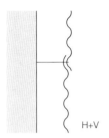

H+V

Overlapping planar elements with stable form

- formats depend on production
- stability not identical in both directions

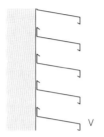

V

Louvers

- linear folds or extruded elements
- louvers spaced so that no water can penetrate
- butt joints require backing pieces

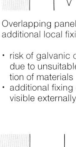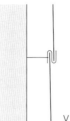

V

Overlapping panels with additional local fixing element

- risk of galvanic corrosion due to unsuitable combination of materials
- additional fixing element visible externally

H+V

Welted seam

- can also be combined with fixing
- welt formed *in situ*
- detachable

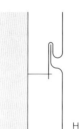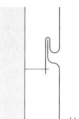

H+V

Standing seam

- also possible without fixing
- seam formed *in situ*
- forms very distinct pattern on surface
- detachable

H

Concealed fixing

- elements cannot be replaced individually

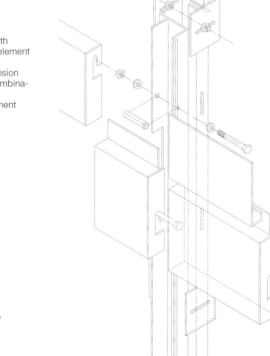

D 1.18

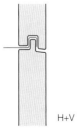

H+V

Sandwich elements with fixings in joints

- concealed fixings
- supporting construction only required in one direction
- elements cannot be replaced individually (erection sequence)

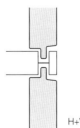

H+V

Sandwich elements fixed with third element concealing butt joint

- integrated into post-and-rail construction
- elements can be replaced individually

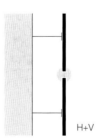

H+V

Panels with jointing by way of additional sealing element

- elements can be replaced individually if sealing element can be opened

D 1.17

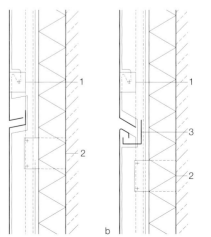

a   b

D 1.19

D 1.20

D 1.21

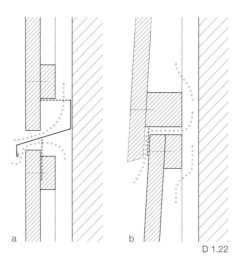
a   b   D 1.22

Timber facade systems

Timber facade elements can be divided into solid elements that simultaneously act as both structural external walls and facade elements and non-structural elements with which other structural wall elements are clad (fig. D 1.20).
Solid timber elements consist of either round or sawn constructional timber and are predominantly used in timber block constructions or timber panel constructions. They can be prefabricated in factories as structural timber panels with integrated window and door openings, as well as with internal and external cladding.

Non-structural timber facades include boarding and shingles, in addition to large-format prefabricated timber elements, which are more stable than solid timber products because the surface layer is manufactured of high-quality timber products. Due to the uniformity of manufacturing conditions, the danger of material deviation due to expansion and contraction of these prefabricated timber elements is also less than their solid timber counterparts.
Semi-finished timber panel elements can be subdivided into multi-layered plywood, timber fibre panels and particleboard (fig. D 1.21).

The application of timber facade elements is only authorised for low-rise constructions due to the fact that the individual elements cannot be sufficiently secured against wind suction loads and other factors under certain conditions.

Substructure
The substructure supports the facade and is connected to the structural system.

Usually constructed of timber battens, it determines whether the facade is ventilated or non-ventilated, dependent upon the system of fixing (fig. D 1.22). Non-ventilated facades require a rear coating of the timber elements in addition to a waterproof membrane which is, nonetheless, open to diffusion. When the risk of moisture penetration is high, a ventilated system between the facade envelope and insulation layer is highly recommended. The application of timber wedges or blocks in the substructure can assist in the equalising of facade surface irregularities.

Methods of fixing
Screws and nails are the visible methods of fixing planar timber facade elements. Although they are simple to use, incorrect application can lead to unnecessary material damage. Screw-fixings, for example Phillips head screws and Torx screws, are particularly appropriate when cladding the facades of temporary buildings, due to the ease with which they can be removed.

To assemble the facade, the panels are screw-fixed – with the help of metal spacers – to a substructure of main battens and counterbattens. The joint dimensions between the individual panels are usually in the region of 10 mm, but must not be less than 8 or greater than 12 mm.
The number of fixing points for timber boarding is dependent upon the width of the boards. For widths of up to 120 mm, one fixing point is adequate; for elements over 120 mm wide two fixing points are necessary. The standard spacing between fixing points in the length is 1000 mm. The distances to the edge of the boards are 15 mm when measured perpendicular to the grain and 50 mm when measured parallel to the grain.

Non-visible fixing methods for timber facade elements are clamps and hooks. During assembly, they are fixed to the substructure by way of screws or nails and can later be connected with the profiles of the facade elements; for example, in tongue-and-groove panels. Permanent corrosion protection is mandatory for all fixing elements in order to prevent unsightly discolouration of the building elements, particularly by rust. Stainless steel is an especially appropriate material for corrosion-protected fixings [6].

Surface treatment
The external surfaces of timber facade elements must be appropriately treated in order to resist the effects of precipitation, direct sunlight and pest infestation. Various paints and coatings, varnishes and impregnations are of great assistance here.
Preservative timber treatments are subdivided into biological and chemical treatments.

Biological timber preservatives
· Wax: fills pores and small cracks, remains open to diffusion
· Oils: e.g. linseed oil and plant-based oils provide good moisture protection

Chemical timber preservatives
· Varnish: film-forming, usually transparent coating
· Stains: special colouring of timber by the use of pigmentation, timber grain remains visible
· Impregnation: water repellent surface, open pores, is not film forming
· Water-emulsion paint: opaque coating, water soluble
· Paint: closed surface, water repellent
· Coatings: coating with membranes, laminates or linoleum

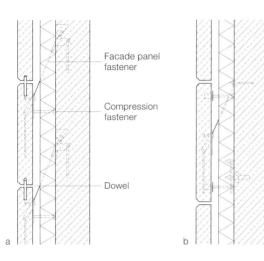
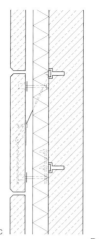

Facade panel
fastener

Compression
fastener

Dowel

a   b   c

D 1.23

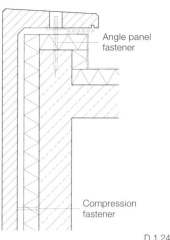

Angle panel
fastener

Compression
fastener

D 1.24

Concrete facade systems

Concrete facade elements consist not only of panels but also of sandwich elements of composite construction with thermal insulation where both the load-bearing wall and external envelope are constructed of concrete (fig. D 1.25). Concrete panels can also be mounted as non-structural facing wall elements. In this situation, reinforcement of the panels is indispensable (fig. D 1.26). Steel reinforcement requires a certain amount of material cover in order to prevent corrosion, which results in the elements being limited to a minimum width of about 7 cm. The usual contemporary solution to this problem is to reinforce the concrete facade panels with either glass fibres or textile fabrics (fig. D 1.28b). Thus, it is possible to manufacture concrete facade panels with a minimum thickness of 3 cm (fig. D 1.28a). Facade elements are available in both small and large formats (fig. D 1.27). Small panels measure between 0.2 and 1 m² while large format panels are confined by manufacture, assembly and transport considerations to a maximum length of 5 m. Specialised elements for parapets, corners and window reveals are manufactured in the form of angle panels (fig. D 1.24).

Surface quality

The surface treatment of the facade elements is, in addition to various other factors, of great importance to the visual appearance of a building. As a result of the manner of fabrication, in situ concrete elements are inevitably more limited in scope than those produced in the factory. On the other hand, prefabricated concrete elements can be manufactured with a wide variety of surface treatments and colouration; the desired effects being incorporated into the production process or after the setting of the concrete under controlled conditions.

In order to achieve different plastic effects on the surfaces of the facade elements, profiled panels are placed into the formwork prior to casting. These profiled panels are produced with the help of CNC technology.

High-quality exposed concrete surfaces are achieved by the use of extremely smooth formwork: for example, steel or plastic. The surfaces are subsequently polished or further treated by the application of a coating. Hardened concrete panels can be additionally refined by sand blasting, bush hammering, acidification or profiling.

Methods of fixing

Concrete facade elements can be fixed in a variety of ways; by hold-down clips or ties which are previously fixed to the substructure, by being supported on console brackets or by welded connections. Stainless steel ties are the most widely-used connection system for concrete facade panels in the building industry today. They carry the dead-load of the panels and transfer the loads evenly to the structural system as a result of their symmetrical layout (fig. D 1.23).

With frame structures, the facade elements are connected via ties that are either fixed to anchoring bars, which are clicked into the rails of the framework, or welded directly to the steel frame.

Generally speaking, the fixing elements must absorb and transfer the dead-loads of the facade panels, in addition to all applied tensile and wind loads, to the load-bearing construction.

D 1.25

D 1.26

D 1.27

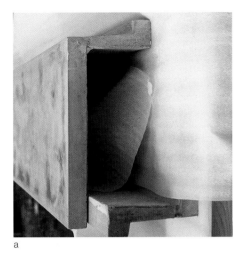
a

D 1.29

D 1.30

D 1.23 Fixing techniques for concrete facade elements
D 1.24 Specialised elements
D 1.25 Concrete sandwich elements
D 1.26 Assembly of a prefabricated concrete facade element, Phaeno Science Centre, Wolfsburg (D) 2005, Zaha Hadid
D 1.27 Facade of prefabricated concrete panels, house in Aargau Canton (CH) 2005, Schneider & Schneider
D 1.28 Facade of glass fibre reinforced concrete elements, housing and office block, Kassel (D) 1999, Alexander Reichel
       a specialised element (window sill)
       b facade elevation
D 1.29 Facade elements of face brickwork panels
D 1.30 Natural stone wall cladding, Barcelona Pavilion, Barcelona (E) 1930 (restoration 1989), Ludwig Mies van der Rohe
D 1.31 Facade element with face brickwork panels, high-rise on Potsdamer Platz, Berlin (D) 2000, Hans Kollhoff
       a horizontal section
       b elevation

Brickwork facade systems

Brickwork facade elements are non-structural building elements of concrete with frost-proof face-brickwork (fig. D 1.29). The elements are up to 8 m in length and 3.6 m high. In order to ensure dimensional accuracy and high quality, the panels are prefabricated in steel formwork in factories. It is possible to manufacture the panels complete with window openings and sun protection elements (fig. D 1.31).

During production, the bricks are first placed onto rubber matting (which later represents a negative of the joint patterning of the panels), which has been inserted into the formwork frame. The joints are then filled with a special mortar and reinforcement is laid in the mortar bed before the normal concrete is poured into the steel formwork. The bricks bond particularly well with the concrete, because they have been halved lengthwise and present a particularly absorbent surface. This process also offers the opportunity to include additional structural modelling in the panel.

The upper edges of the facade elements are fixed to the load-bearing structure and the undersides secured with stainless steel inserts to the rough concrete ledges. The facade panels are constructed with integrated continuous grooves for sealing joints, in which elastic rubber strips are incorporated, making it possible to avoid externally visible silicon joints. It is also feasible to plan the jointing system in such a way that the joints are camouflaged by the modelling of the masonry panels.

Natural stonework facade systems

Natural stone can be refined for facade panels by way of splitting, sawing and drilling. For facade construction these are usually thinly cut stone panels; for example, sandstone, granite, basalt or slate panels (figs. D 1.30 and D 1.33, p. 206). These panels must demonstrate the physical prerequisites of minimum compressive strength, bending strength and frost resistance.
Analogous to glass facades, thinly cut stone panels can also be employed as

b
D 1.28

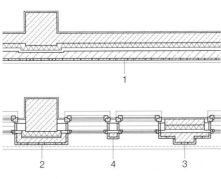
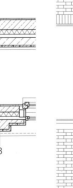

1 spandrel element
2 column cladding
3 pilaster
4 frame

a

b
D 1.31

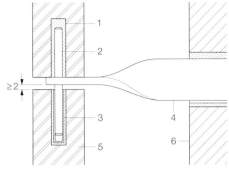

1 hole   4 fastener
2 dowel   5 stone panel
3 sleeve   6 masonry

a

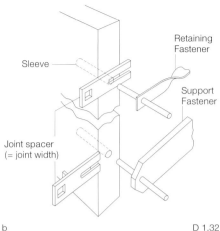

Sleeve

Retaining
Fastener

Support
Fastener

Joint spacer
(= joint width)

b   D 1.32

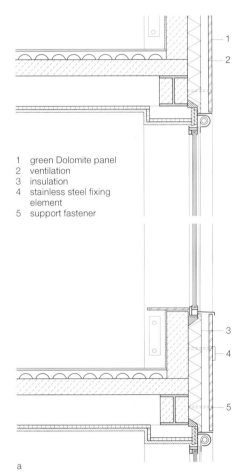

1 green Dolomite panel
2 ventilation
3 insulation
4 stainless steel fixing
   element
5 support fastener

a

b   D 1.33

semi-translucent, wind and rainproof panels mounted to substructures. Facing-stone facade elements can be fixed with supporting metal ties and clips, which absorb and transfer the vertical and horizontal loads to the structural system of the building (fig. D 1.32). The fixing system is usually located within the joints between the individual panels. The load transfer is conducted from each panel individually into the substructure, which is also responsible for the transference of all dead loads and wind loads to the load-bearing structure of the building. Each stone panel must be carried by at least three or four symmetrically located connection points in order to secure the stress-free transfer of loads.

Joints should measure between 8 and 10 mm and can be left open if the substructure is completely weatherproof. If the joints are closed, it is necessary to employ an elastic filling material, which can deal with maximum movement [8].

Plastic facade systems

Due to their individual chemical properties, plastics offer a variety of material properties, which can be applicable for different situations within the building industry.

Facade elements
High quality plastics are available today for the construction of facade elements. They are employed as semi-fabricated products in the forms of panels, pre-moulded elements and pneumatic cushions.

Plastic panels
Plastic panels are manufactured as flat, corrugated or webbed panels (fig. D

1.34). The most widely practised methods of productions are rolling (calendering), pressing and extruding whereby the malleable plastic passes through a profiled mould under pressure.

Popular plastic materials for the manufacture of smooth transparent panels are polymethylmethacrylate (PMMA) and polycarbonate (PC). Their properties are particularly appropriate with regard to impact resistance and water resistance. They are usually available in the dimensions of 205 by 305 cm.
Corrugated panels are particularly rigid as a result of their cross-section. They are available in sizes of up to 300 by 2000 cm. Glass fibre reinforced plastic panels are referred to as GFP – these panels present even more rigidity (fig. D 1.35).

Webbed panels can be manufactured out of two or more layers of the above-mentioned plastics (figs. D 1.36 and D 1.37). The stabilising bracing of the internal web elements allows the production of panels of up to 700 cm in length in

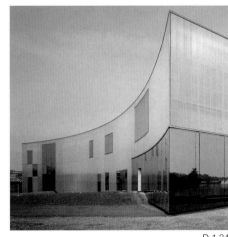

D 1.34

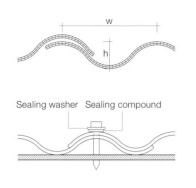

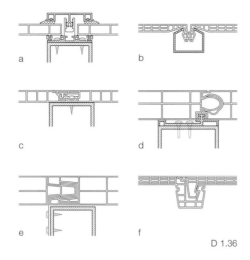

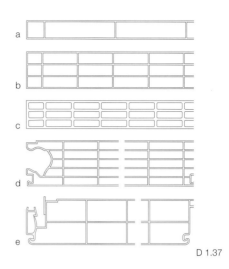

D 1.35

D 1.36

D 1.37

PMMA, 1100 cm in PC and 1400 cm in GFP. The hollow chambers between the webs contribute to the low thermal transmission coefficient of these panels. Their properties can be further enhanced by producing multi-layered panels.

Plastic moulded elements
Free-formed plastic elements for facades can be manufactured by moulding or laminating in almost any size and shape. Glass fibre fabrics and synthetic resins are layered to produce building elements. The result is a moulded element of glass fibre reinforced plastic with good material properties and high stability. The surface can be further refined by sanding, polishing or coating, for example, after the element has completely hardened.

Panel facades and formed elements
Due to the high coefficient of expansion of semi-finished plastic panels and moulded elements, it is possible that minimal deformation can occur as a result of heat absorption (fig. D 1.38). Non-rigid fixing with the substructure, in addition to flexible sealing profiles, can equalise tol-

erances at the critical connection points. It is usually the case that manufacturers provide appropriate connection elements and techniques in association with plastic building elements. Screws, clamps, adhesives and welding are all suitable for joining the plastic elements together (fig. D 1.39). The principles of connection for semi-finished plastic panels are the same as those governing the connections of timber, metal and glass facade constructions.

Pneumatic cushion facades
Due to their good static properties and minimal self-weight, semi-transparent pneumatic cushion constructions have become quite popular in the building industry in recent years (fig. D 1.40). PVC-P membranes, reinforced with polyester or aramid fibre fabrics, can even absorb tensile forces and are capable of spanning large spaces with minimal material outlay.
The pneumatic cushions become stabilised by the stresses, which result from the enforced surface curvature when fixed in curved metal frames [9].

D 1.32 Fixing of natural stone panels
  a mortar anchor with pin sleeve, horizontal section
  b axonometric view of load-bearing and retaining anchor
D 1.33 Facade with natural stone panels, office block, Berlin (D) 1997, Klaus Theo Brenner
  a vertical section
  b elevation
D 1.34 Facade of plastic web panels, Laban Centre, London (GB) 2003, Herzog & de Meuron
D 1.35 Cross-sections of corrugated panel profiles
D 1.36 Fixing systems for web panels with glazing bars (a) folding and screw connections (b–f)
D 1.37 cross-sections of semi-fabricated panel profiles
D 1.38 Facade with moulded plastic elements, Olivetti Training Centre, Haslemere (GB) 1973, James Stirling
D 1.39 Moulded plastic elements with point connections, spacelab, Graz (A) 2003, Peter Cook, Colin Furnier
D 1.40 Facade of pneumatic cushions, Allianz Arena, Munich (D) 2005, Herzog & de Meuron

Notes:
[1] Herzog, Thomas et al.: Facade Manual. Munich/Basle 2004, p. 53ff.
[2] Schittich, Christian et al.: Glass Construction Manual. Munich/Basle 1998, p. 91ff.
[3] ibid. [2], p. 62ff.
[4] ibid. [1], p. 233ff.
[5] Neumann, Dietrich et al.: Frick/Knöll. Baukonstruktionslehre 1, 33rd edition. Stuttgart 2002, p. 270ff.
[6] Hugues, Theodor et al.: Detail Practice, Timber Construction. Munich 2002, p. 73
[7] Deplazes, Andrea: Architektur konstruieren. Vom Rohmaterial zum Bauwerk. Ein Handbuch. Basle/ Berlin 2005, p. 54ff.
[8] ibid. [1], p. 65ff.
[9] ibid. [1], p. 212ff.

D 1.38

D 1.39

D 1.40

Glazed grid shells

Jan Knippers, Thorsten Helbig

Architects have been applying themselves to the concept of prefabrication since the beginning of modern times. During the course of the 20th century, they developed numerous systems applicable to different tasks: from the timber constructions of Konrad Wachsmann to the space frames of Max Mengeringhausen and the precast concrete constructions of the 1950s. The central starting point was always the utilisation of as many identical building elements as possible that could be interconnected on site as easily as possible. Up until the end of the 20th century, economical types of prefabrication meant the industrial production of identical building elements in large series. The production took place successively, in identical phases, with as much mechanical input as possible. However, this situation changed radically within the course of a few years in the late 20th century with the introduction of computer-operated fabrication processes. For CNC equipment, it is fundamentally irrelevant if the geometry of the elements to be produced is identical or not. Although fundamental construction principles must be predetermined – for example, the selection of connection techniques – the modular, geometric arrangements, which were the decisive themes for decades, are now less important. The organisation of information transfer has now come to the fore, i.e. the smooth, accurate flow of information from planning, through production and on to site logistics.
New planning and production techniques will be described in detail by way of examples of spatial steel structures production. Their production was always based on prefabrication and their appearance determined by the calculation and manufacturing procedures available. Recent developments in prefabrication

have, however, affected all other construction systems as well. For example, precast concrete walls for housing can be adapted to each individual building project by taking advantage of computer assistance for the production of walls with different geometries. A similar situation exists for timber panel construction methods.

Changes in the planning process

It was previously necessary that the number of struts of different length, and the connection nodes with different angles be kept to a minimum in grid shells and space frames in order to reduce the complexity of fabrication. Even the methods of structural calculation were only capable of determining the internal forces for a limited number of geometrical situations. These technical limitations led, necessarily, to repeated standard solutions for the design of domes and barrel vaults.

In the 1960s, Frei Otto, Heinz Isler and others developed methods for the structural optimisation of shell structures by experimenting with soap bubbles and suspension models. A short time later, these systems found their analytical parallels in the force density method and dynamic relaxation. The structural calculation of complex grid structures was then made possible using the finite element method, but production conditions still continued to have a decisive influence on the design of these structures.
When Jörg Schlaich and Hans Schober transferred Frei Otto's principles for timber grid shells forms to a steel-glass dome in Neckarsulm in the early 1990s, the determining criterion for the genera-

D 2.1 View of the building site from crane (top left, the palletes of nodes), Westfield Shopping Centre, London (GB) 2008, Benoy
D 2.2 Complete geometry of shopping mall roof, Westfield Shopping Centre
D 2.3 Mesh for FE calculations (western roof), Westfield Shopping Centre
D 2.4 Detail of node principle, Westfield Shopping Centre
D 2.5 Exploded drawing of node

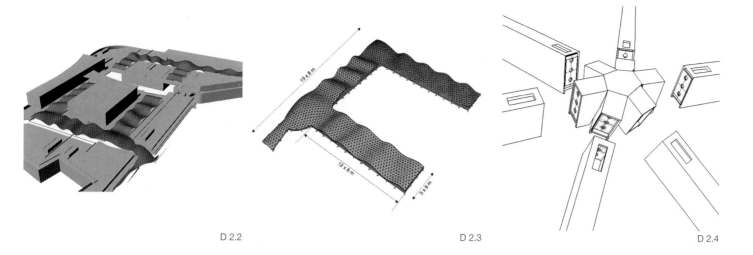

D 2.2   D 2.3   D 2.4

tion of the grid was a standard length of
1 m for all members. The connection
nodes were also developed in a way that
– despite the varying connecting angles –
they could be manufactured out of identical pieces. This was similar with the roof
of the "Museum of Hamburg History"
which was designed soon after [1]. It was
only necessary to design different elements for the edge of the roof.
In the mid-1990s, however, this construction technique changed completely.
Exhaustive comparative studies were carried out for the InterCity railway station in
Spandau, where a 410-metre-long barrel-
vaulted grid shell was planned to span
over three platforms, each of which was
different from the others and with different
curves [2]. It was shown that a cranked
grid, polygonal on plan and with as many
geometrically identical members as possible, offered only minimal economic
advantages over a homogeneous network
of approximately 12,500 geometrically different nodes that followed the line of the
platforms. A prerequisite for the successful accomplishment of the project was,
however, the appropriate computer-aided
technology.
Since then, of course, many free-formed
steel-glass grid shell structures have
been built. Apart from some particularly
inspiring projects, there are many examples where architectural aspirations could
not be successfully realised. Irregular
meshes where neither the flow of the
forces nor form are considered, in addition to details designed without thought
for appearance, had a negative effect the
architectural and constructional quality of
such grid shells.
The planning of free-form grid shell structures requires new dimensions in the
planning process, for which there are as
yet neither established, standardised

processes nor equipment; nor are they
factors in the customary planning process.
Architects generally use 3D modelling
software (Rhino, Maya) for the generation
of forms and structural calculations are
carried out using FE programs, which
usually have only interfaces with the CAD
software responsible for the construction
and fabrication drawings. In order to
achieve higher architectural and constructional quality for free-formed grid
shell structures, it is necessary to develop
a continuous, uninterrupted planning
process from the initial generated form to
the completed assembly on site. A continuous data model, which is the foundation of all planning and construction
stages, is an absolutely essential prerequisite for consistent planning. The production and maintenance of such a data
model is a new and independent facet of
the planning process. This also applies to
the generation of 3D network models,
where there are also no widely available
methods. The logical, digitally based
design of 3D structures requires new
developments in the planning process.

Glazed single-skin steel grid shells
Two examples will be used to demonstrate the changes in the planning processes and the effects on the architecture.

Westfield Shopping Centre, London White City
The new shopping mall in London White
City is covered by a partially transparent,
partially opaque grid shell, with standard
spans of 24 m (fig. D 2.1). The roof is
made up of eastern and western sections, with a total roof area of approximately 17,000 m². The longest wing
measures 124 m. The 8500 members
have welded cross-sections measuring

160 × 65 mm with an average length of
2.3 m. There are no joints in either roof
section and they are supported, free to
slide, on edge supports every 12 m. The
roof cladding consists of panes of insulating glass and insulated panels of metal
sheeting.
First, a two-dimensional mesh was generated in order to project it subsequently
onto a three-dimensional area. The mesh
shown in D 2.3 was the foundation of
both the structural calculations and the
fabrication. The member and node identi-
fication system was coordinated with the
demands of the various stages of the
process and carried through the entire
project from the structural calculations
right up to final assembly.

The production technology was consistently coordinated with the digital planning and fabrication processes. A bolted
construction, set into a hollow section,
connects the nodes and members via a
vertical contact plate (fig. D 2.4); a total
of 3000 nodes were developed for the
entire system. Each node has an individual geometry, in accordance with the
concept of a free-form roof (fig. D 2.5,
p. 210). The nodes are welded together
out of 26 different panels, which accommodate the forms of the incoming
member ends. The thickness of the node
plates, in addition to the number and
diameter of the bolts, was optimised for
each node individually, dependent upon
the forces to be expected. The nodes
were only complete after the accurate
mechanical milling of the welded plates
and the electronic checking of the node
geometry (fig. D 2.6). The nodes and
members were bolted together on site.
Adjusting tolerances on site was unnecessary as a result of the rigorous accuracy of the bolted connections. Due to

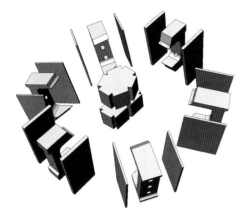

D 2.5

D 2.6 Production of nodes
  a Milling of elements
  b Checking accuracy
  c View of members awaiting erection, showing metal thicknesses and bolted connections
D 2.7 Assembly of nodes on site

the exceptionally precise prefabrication techniques, deviations in size between the manufactured product and its calculated geometry were able to be kept to a minimum: a deviation of just 15 mm over the assembled length of 164 m (fig. D 2.7). The high level of prefabrication also meant great precision in the on-site connections, in addition to speedy assembly procedures, independent of the weather conditions. It was also possible to apply corrosion protection to the prefabricated elements in the production plant.

One of the most important achievements of this construction was the development of a fully automated planning process, with coordination between structural calculations, factory planning and fabrication. The structural models of the mesh structure served as databases for the fabrication planning, whereas the geometric data for the detail checks of the node points and their connections was, in turn, drawn from this data. The information obtained from the detail checks regarding metal thickness and the number and diameter of the

bolts, was subsequently incorporated into the fabrication planning and then transferred directly to the production plant. In spite of the highly automated processes used, assembly drawings generated for the individual nodes also sufficed for the monitoring of the fabrication process (fig. D 2.8).

PalaisQuartier, Frankfurt
The second project will demonstrate a construction based on the application of strongly curved geometry. Currently, a

a

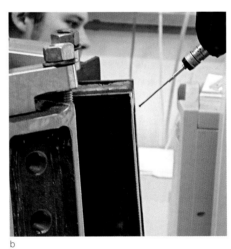

b

c   D 2.6

D 2.7

a

b   D 2.8

D 2.8 Completed roof, shopping mall
    a Entire internal view
    b Close-up internal view
D 2.9 Star-shaped node principle
    PalaisQuartier, Frankfurt/Main (D)
    (under construction), Massimiliano Fuksas
D 2.10 PalaisQuartier, Zeilforum
D 2.11 Development of glass roof geometry
    a architect's initial form concept
    b geometry of optimised roof

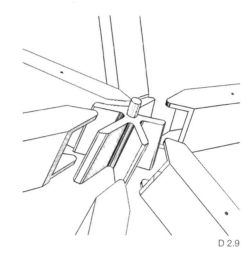

D 2.9

complex of buildings – the "Palais-Quartier" – is being constructed in the centre of Frankfurt. It consists of two high-rise buildings, the renovated Thurn und Taxis Palace and a five storey shopping centre, the so-called "Zeilforum", and was designed by the Italian architect Massimiliano Fuksas. The Zeilforum is covered by a free-form roof structure of rods that rests like a glazed carpet above the shopping levels (fig. D 2.10). The glazed shell construction has a total area of 13,000 m².

Illustration D 2.11a demonstrates the architect's first conceptual ideas. The form consists of flat areas that merge with one another by way of curves of small radii. The so called canyon, which covers the central shopping passage, was designed to remain free of columns. The first phase of the process was the optimisation of the three-dimensional sketches. The elements the architect called the trumpets, and initially only considered to be decorative design objects, were redefined to act as statically effec-

tive columns. One of these columns is supported by the ground floor level while the other is supported by the facade. The geometry was further modified in a way that the load-bearing effect of the shell structure could be utilised by increasing the curvature of the canyon (fig. D 2.11b). This benefited the design in that not only columns, but also other reinforcing members (trusses and girders), could be avoided in and above the shopping passage. The flatter zones of the strut system above the upper levels could be sup-

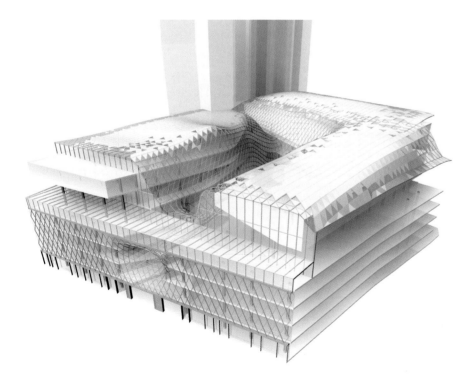

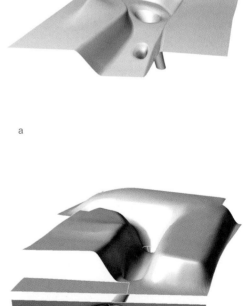

a

b

D 2.10

D 2.11

211

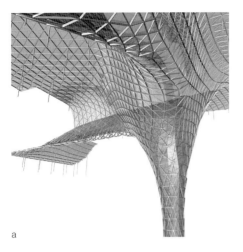

a

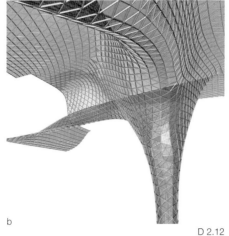

b

D 2.12

D 2.13

ported by columns at regular intervals and act as a structural grid.

One of the next steps in the development of this project was the transformation of the 3D areas into statically effective networks of struts. Due to the complex geometry, it was not possible to work with the projection principle as in the London project described previously. No satisfactory standardised processes are available for the generation of complex geometrical networks. Automatic network generation systems simply start at the edge of the form and interconnect independently-created partial networks; this often leads to irregular strut lengths and node geometry (fig. D 2.14a). This, in turn, results in unsatisfactory solutions both in architectural and constructional terms.

At the outset of this project, orientation lines or guide lines were determined, in collaboration with the architect, for the network. The locations of the nodes were also fixed at certain important positions; for example, at the connection points on the vertical facades. This fulfilled the essential architectural prerequisites for network generation (fig. D 2.14b).

Based on these assumptions, it was then possible to divide the three-dimensional area into large triangular forms. As a result of the automatic network generation system, the nodes were simple five-point solutions, which leads to irregularity in the network. Each large triangular form was further optimised by subdividing it into regular networks with six-point nodes that could subsequently be interconnected to build a complete network. The average strut length was 2.3 m.

This process is based upon the methods Walther Bauersfeld and R. Buckminster Fuller used for the development of their geodetic shell structures. Numerous intermediate steps were necessary before the network, which is portrayed in figures D 2.12b and D 2.14c, was achieved. This network then became the basis for static calculations, workshop planning and production of the individual construction elements.

The transfer from a data model to a built structure is, necessarily, greatly dependent upon the experience of the individual manufacturer and the available fabrication methods. There is no standardised solu-

tion for network nodes [3]. The usual situation is for the manufacturing company to recommend node constructions that have been employed on other projects, and which are then discussed in relation to the new, specialised situation with regard to geometry, static loading and the architect's design expectations.

In contrast to his design for the roof of the new trade fair centre in Milan [4], the architect planned as (visually) reserved a node detail as possible for this project; one which could be manufactured as a welded node construction. Cut from a single piece of metal sheeting, the star-shaped form is the central element of the node construction upon which the struts are later welded. The struts are individually manufactured, according to required form and angle, from box elements and usually measure 120 by 60 mm. The thickness of the material is dependent upon the static demands applied to each element (fig. D 2.9, p. 211). The box elements were so constructed that the webs were extended making any further refinement of the seams between web and flange unnecessary. These extended

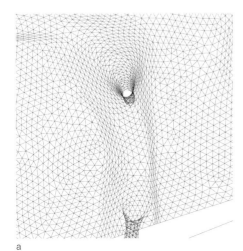

a

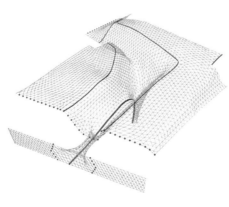

b

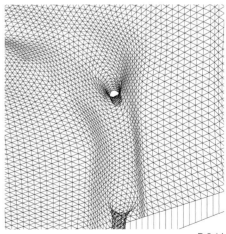

c

D 2.14

212

D 2.15

D 2.12   Visualisation of network alternatives
         a Internal view of the first network
         b Internal view of the definitive network
D 2.13   Mock up of node
D 2.14   Network optimisation
         a First automatically generated network
         b Definition of the edge conditions for gen-
           eration of the network
         c definitive automatically generated network
D 2.15   Welding of nodes on side
D 2.16   Construction of roof

webs were conceived as dividing elements, which continue out onto the star-shaped node elements (fig. D 2.13).

The true challenge for the creativity of the engineers of both projects lays in the organisation of an efficient and accurate exchange of information between static calculations, workshop planning and fabrication.

Project associates
Westfield, London White City
Client: Westfield Shoppingtowns Ltd.
Architect: Benoy, London, Buchanan Group, London
Construction: Seele GmbH & Co KG, Gersthofen

Zeilforum Frankfurt Hoch Vier, Frankfurt
Client: Bouwfonds MAB Frankfurt HochVier GmbH
Architect: Massimiliano Fuksas Architetto,
Rome/Frankfurt
Construction and working drawings: Waagner-Biro
AG, Vienna

Structural engineering for both projects:
Knippers Helbig Consulting Engineers, Stuttgart
Prof. Dr.-Ing. Jan Knippers, Dipl.-Ing. Thorsten Helbig
With: Fabian Friz, Florian Kamp, Sven Wörner, Florian
Scheible, Markus Gabler

Authors
Prof. Dr.-Ing. Jan Knippers and Dipl.-Ing. Thorsten
Helbig were both employed by Schlaich Bergmann
and Partners from 1993 to 2000 and are now partners
in an engineering office.
Jan Knippers is also head of the Institute for Construction and Design at the University of Stuttgart.

Notes:
[1]   Schlaich, Jörg et al.: Verglaste Netzkuppeln. In:
      Bautechnik 69, issue 1. Berlin 1992, p. 3ff.
[2]   Schlaich, Jörg et al.: Bahnsteigüberdachung
      Fernbahnhof Berlin-Spandau.
      In: Stahlbau 68, issue 12. Berlin 1999, p. 1022ff.
[3]   Stephan, Sören et al.: Stabwerke auf Freiform-
      flächen.
      In: Stahlbau 73, issue 8. Berlin 2004, p. 562ff.
[4]   Schober, Hans et al.: Neue Messe Mailand –
      Netzstruktur und Tragverhalten einer Freiform-
      fläche. In: Stahlbau 73, issue 8. Berlin 2004,
      p. 541ff.

D 2.16

Westhafen Tower in Frankfurt/Main

The cylindrical Westhafen Tower was the first skyscraper in Frankfurt to be erected directly on the banks of the River Main. The almost 100-metre-high tower has a diameter of roughly 38 metres.

The appearance of the green glass facade is dominated by the triangular arrangement of the pigmented external glazing elements. Since the elements are flat, the circumference is, in fact, articulated into a polygonal form with the points of the triangles leaning alternately slightly inwards and outwards. The alternation of the different angles of reflection lends the external cylindrical envelope an almost diamond-like, facetted quality. The facade is divided into 116 prefabricated glazed triangular framed elements per floor.

During the assembly process, pairs of 2.03-metre-wide and 3.54-metre-high triangular facade elements were joined together to form rhombus-shaped units. These were brought into position by a travelling crane on a peripheral monorail assembly track and suspended from the floor slabs by means of cast-aluminium

brackets. It was possible for the cast-aluminium brackets to compensate for assembly tolerances on site. The brackets were fixed to the concrete slabs via anchor rails precisely positioned for the assembly of the facade elements. At their bases, these facade elements are connected to sliding stainless-steel bolts that can absorb movements originating in the load-bearing structure, as well as those resulting from expansion in the facade elements themselves.

In the conservatory zones (a), the facade brackets are fixed to curved tubular steel members set in front of the recessed edges of the floor slabs parallel to the outer line of the facade arc. The facade elements are suspended from the upper floor slabs by means of four-storey long, 16 mm diameter tension rods and supported against the set-back edges of the slabs with horizontal struts.

The frames of the triangular facade elements were manufactured from continuous, thermally separated, powder-coated aluminium sections.

The insulating double-glazing consists of outer panes of green-toned toughened safety glass and inner panes of laminated (partially toughened) safety glass that are coated in various areas. The combination of toned external panes, with coating on the internal surfaces of τ/g 68/34, markedly increases solar protection.

The large, triangular opening elements, which are a special feature of the Westhafen Tower façade, are motor-operated and open outwards. They allow natural ventilation of the conservatory spaces and corner offices. The offices are divided from the conservatory spaces by a second, internal facade layer consisting of rectangular framed elements of laminated safety glass panes with side and bottom hung opening panels.

project team • building details

architects:	schneider + schumacher architecture GmbH, Frankfurt/Main
facade planner:	IFFT Institute for Facade Technology, Karlotto Schott, Frankfurt/Main
structural engineers:	SPI Schlüsselplan, Frankfurt/Main
client:	Westhafen Tower GmbH & Co Project Development KG
usage:	office
construction (facade):	aluminium/glass
system:	panel construction
internal ceiling height:	3.0 m/2.75 m (ground floor)
site area:	5021 m²
gross floor area:	46,300 m²
total internal volume:	184,600 m³
total construction cost:	€ 80 mill. (gross)
date of construction:	2003
period of construction:	2000–2003

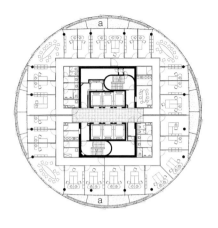

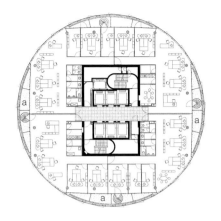

floor plans
scale 1:750

A schematic section vertical   scale 1:20
B schematic section horizontal   scale 1:20

1 8 mm toughened glass + 16 mm cavity +
   6 mm partially toughened glass in alum. frame
2 lam. safety glass (2× 6 mm) in alum. door frame
3 cast-aluminium facade-fixing element
4 fire-resisting closing piece (90 min.):
   sheet steel and rockwool

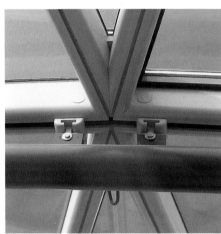

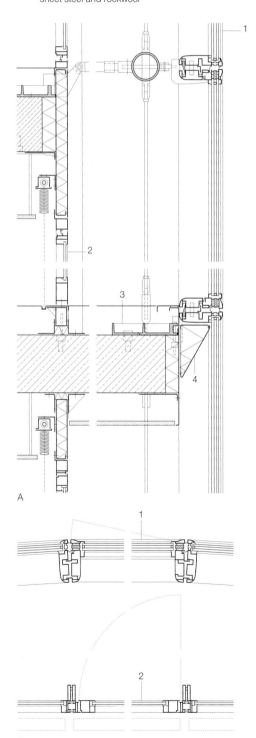

A

B

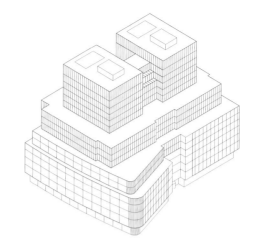

Office Block in London

This 15-storey office building, situated in the centre of London close to the Thames, has a facade area of approximately 22,000 m². The two main facade types, the so-called "A wall" and "B wall", both include small curved areas and essentially have either fixed glazing, casement or casement/tilt windows. The "A wall" is a storey-high, unitised, curtain facade of natural stone elements linked together by stainless steel connections to form chains, and with rigid solar protection panels clamped between. This facade type covers extensive areas of levels one to seven. The "B wall" is a double-skin facade with anodised, pressed aluminium floor grilles located in the trafficable cavity between the skins; the inner facade is equipped with integrated sunscreen elements. Arranged in a scale-like pattern, the clear outer glazing is transparent and each pane is held by four cast aluminium fixings. Some of the elements of the "B wall" facade have set-in terrace doors and the emergency exit and access ladders are mounted to the inner facade.

project team • building details

architects:	Arup Associates Ltd., London
structural engineers:	Arup Associates Ltd., London
facade consultant:	Arup Facade Engineering, London
facade construction:	Josef Gartner GmbH, Gundelfingen
client:	The British Land Company PLC, London
usage:	office
construction (facade):	steel/glass
system:	panel construcion
date of construction:	facade: 2002–2003
period of construction:	15 months (facade)

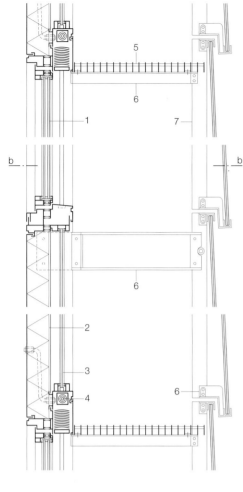

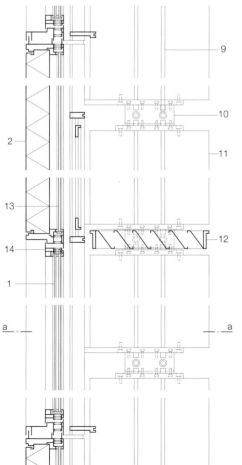

axonometry
schematic section horizontal
schematic section vertical
scale 1:20

1 double glazing in aluminium sections
2 thermal insulation

B wall (double skin glazed facade)

3 glass spandrel elements
4 solar protection louvers
5 anodised, pressed aluminium floor grille
6 cast aluminium cantilever
7 RHS flat aluminium bar
8 casement/tilt glazing

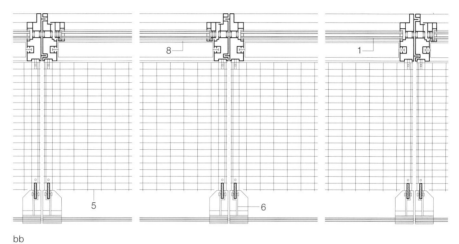

bb

A wall (storey-high, unitised facade)

9 stainless steel tension rod
10 stainless steel bracket
11 Jurassic limestone fin
12 aluminium solar protection elements
13 glass spandrel elements
14 casement glazing

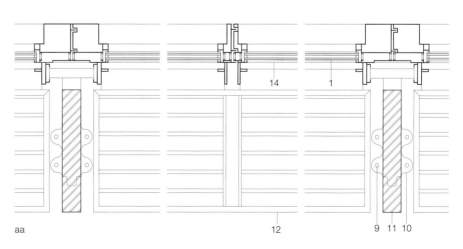

aa

floor plans
section
scale 1:1000

A ground floor
B standard floor
C 37th floor: conference level

Uptown Munich

This 38-storey administration building was erected in a prominent position in close proximity to the Olympic Park, the television tower and the BMW high-rise building in the north of Munich. With a height of 146 metres, the new development is the tallest office block in the city to date and is situated on the middle ring road, one of Munich's main traffic arteries, exactly on the edge of the inner city. In a local referendum held in 2004, it was decided that no buildings of more than 100 metres in height should be allowed within this zone. The new high-rise block is flanked by a "campus" of four seven-storey office tracts. These are linked to each other by a structure with a curved louvered roof and glazed walls that form a protective screen against noise. The development includes a further building containing 139 dwellings. This ensemble is complemented by a central boulevard, with pine trees planted in the open areas. A single skin of double glazing covers the entire face of the tower block. The individual facade panels, laid in a 1.4 metre grid, were interconnected to form panels of 5.8 metres in width prior to assembly on site. This made it possible to construct

one storey in five to seven days. The rounded glass corners, with radii of 2.8 metres, form a distinctive architectural feature. The smooth surface of the facade is enlivened by a grid of circular ventilation elements that can be opened outwards parallel to the face of the building. When open, they form an irregular pattern over the facade. Specially developed for this building, these motor-operated window units can be independently activated to provide additional natural ventilation. The solar-control facade glazing assists in preventing overheating of the interior and internal blinds protect against glare, giving the staff the ability to individually control the entry of light. The load-bearing structure, which consists of a reinforced central core with concrete columns and floor slabs, transmits loads down to a solid foundation slab. A spacious foyer with a lift access area, in addition to a reception area and information counters, is located on the ground floor. A generously designed space at the top of the building affords breathtaking views of the Alps, which – on a clear day – seem to be almost close enough to reach out and touch.

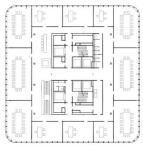

C

B

project team • building details

architects:	Ingenhoven Architects, Düsseldorf
project architect:	Christoph Ingenhoven, Barbara Bruder
structural engineers:	Burggraf, Weichinger & Partner, Munich
client:	Hines Immobilien GmbH
usage:	office
construction:	aluminium/glass
system:	panel construction
internal ceiling height:	6.0/3.0 m
total internal volume:	450,000 m³
date of construction:	2005
period of construction:	2002–2005

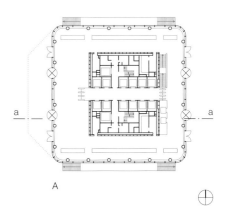

A

218

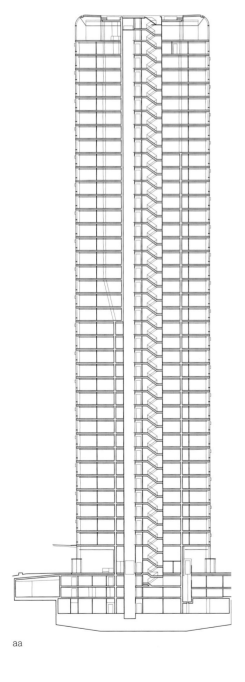

aa

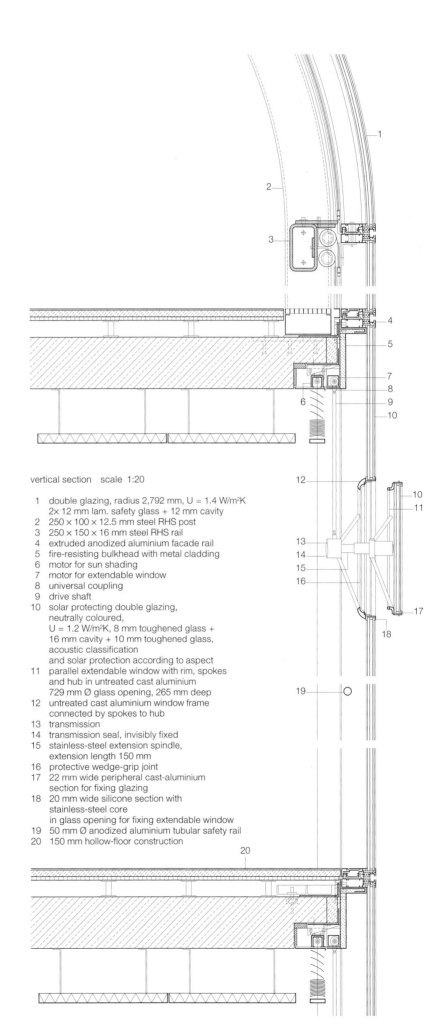

vertical section   scale 1:20

1 double glazing, radius 2,792 mm, U = 1.4 W/m²K
   2× 12 mm lam. safety glass + 12 mm cavity
2 250 × 100 × 12.5 mm steel RHS post
3 250 × 150 × 16 mm steel RHS rail
4 extruded anodized aluminium facade rail
5 fire-resisting bulkhead with metal cladding
6 motor for sun shading
7 motor for extendable window
8 universal coupling
9 drive shaft
10 solar protecting double glazing,
   neutrally coloured,
   U = 1.2 W/m²K, 8 mm toughened glass +
   16 mm cavity + 10 mm toughened glass,
   acoustic classification
   and solar protection according to aspect
11 parallel extendable window with rim, spokes
   and hub in untreated cast aluminium
   729 mm Ø glass opening, 265 mm deep
12 untreated cast aluminium window frame
   connected by spokes to hub
13 transmission
14 transmission seal, invisibly fixed
15 stainless-steel extension spindle,
   extension length 150 mm
16 protective wedge-grip joint
17 22 mm wide peripheral cast-aluminium
   section for fixing glazing
18 20 mm wide silicone section with
   stainless-steel core
   in glass opening for fixing extendable window
19 50 mm Ø anodized aluminium tubular safety rail
20 150 mm hollow-floor construction

Hotel in Tokyo

This 24-storey hotel, The Peninsula Tokyo, is situated in a business district in close proximity to the Imperial Palace.
The hotel was the first building in Tokyo to be constructed with a facade of mill-finish brass profiles. It is mounted upon a six storey high glazed brass podium which is the showcase of this luxurious hotel tower. The brass facade on the north, east and south that covers a total area of 1,800 square metres was developed as a unitised glass and metal curtain wall structure of 16 vertical bays, each measuring 5.5 metres in width and 25 metres in height. The bays were assembled of 5.5 × 2.5 metre units and feature distinctive 49 cm deep decorative brass columns.
Horizontal, extruded brass lattice louver panels allow the necessary access for maintenance and cleaning. They are incorporated into the facade structure between the top and bottom units.

project team • building details

architects:	Mitsubishi Jisho Sekkei Inc., Tokyo
with:	Kazukiyo Sato, Tetsuya Okusa, Koki Miyachi
structural engineers:	Ichiro Ogawa, Kazuhiko Higashi
facade construction:	Josef Gartner GmbH, Gundelfingen
client:	Mitsubishi Real Estate Co., Ltd. Peninsula of Tokyo Limited, Tokyo
usage:	hotel
construction (facade):	brass
system:	panel construction
internal ceiling height:	8.2 m (main lobby)
	6.0 m (ball room)
	6.0 m (swimming pool)
	2.6/2.9 m (standard guest room)
	3.0/3.3 m (suite)
	3.2 m (restaurant)
site area:	4343.62 m²
gross floor area:	2287.09 m²
total internal volume:	58,571.57 m³
date of construction:	2004–2007
period of construction:	32 months

ground floor plan
section
scale 1:1000

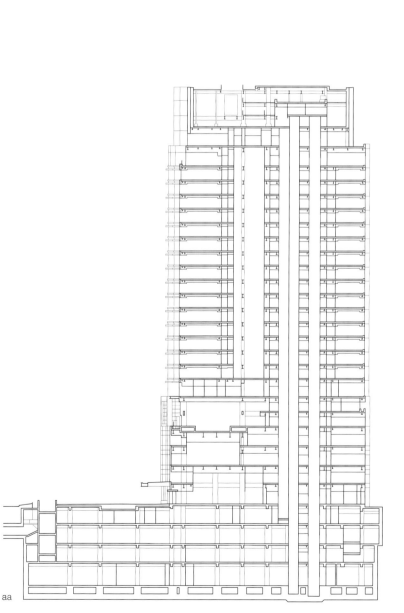

aa

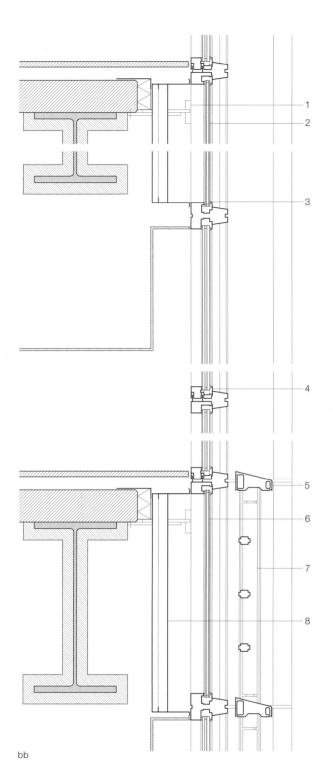

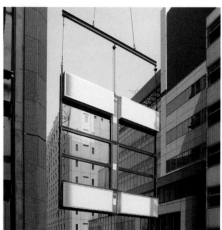

schematic section vertical
schematic section horizontal
scale 1:20

1 cast facade fixing bracket
2 double glazing in brass
  profile:
  15 mm toughened glass +
  12 mm cavity +
  12 mm toughened
  glass
3 EPDM gasket
4 brass profile
5 window sill
  tubular steel sub-
  structure
6 spandrel element, double
  glazing in brass profile:
  8 mm toughened glass
  + 15 mm cavity
  + 8 mm toughened glass
7 brass lattice louvers
8 spandrel panels
9 2× 60 mm thermal
  insulation

bb

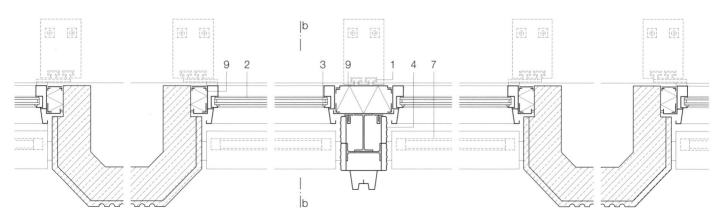

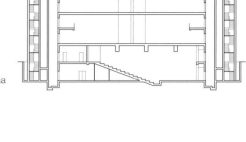

aa

b

a — — a

section
plan of 2nd floor
scale 1:1000

Museum of Contemporary Art in Chicago

The museum is located on Mies van der Rohe Way on a site halfway between the city and Lake Shore Park and the building's axis creates a physical connection between the two. The central elements of the design are simplicity and openness, as well as the interplay of transparent and closed elements and the contrast between internal and external spaces. The square forms the basis for the design proportions; not developed out of the layout of the building but as a structuring element of the grid of bands that determined both the site and the arrangement of the facade.

The entire facade is clad with panels made from cast aluminium elements embossed with pyramid-shaped indentations. The panels were blasted with iron filings to change their surface structure. An irregular patina was thus created by the corrosion of the small iron particles which remained embedded in the soft aluminium surface after the blasting process.

Kleihues refers to local building traditions by fixing the facade elements with exposed, stainless steel screws to create the curtain wall construction.

vertical section · horizontal section
scale 1:20

1 facade panel:
  square cast aluminium panels with
  textured surface finish, fixed with exposed
  specially fabricated, stainless-steel screws
  ventilation cavity
  galvanised steel sheet
  extruded rigid-foam,
  polystyrene thermal insulation
  mineral fibre thermal insulation
  sheet steel
2 65 × 65 mm SHS steel
  sub-construction
3 steel flats for fixing the steel sub-construction
  to the primary load-bearing structure

4 heating cover panels:
  anodised aluminium in wooden frame
5 aluminium window frame with double glazing:
  16 mm toughened safety glass +
  12 mm cavity +
  6 mm toughened safety glass
6 electrically operated roller blind
7 plasterboard suspended ceiling
8 fire stop
9 EPDM sealing strip in open (drained) joint
10 plinth: calcium silicate panels, fixed with
  exposed, specially fabricated,
  stainless-steel screws
11 plasterboard partition on metal framing

project team • building details

architects:	Josef P. Kleihues, Berlin
with:	Johannes Rath, Marc Bastian, John DeSalvo, Pablo Diaz, Arden Freeman, Haukur Hardason, Richard McLoughin, Greg Sherlock
structural engineers:	Ove Arup & Partners
client:	Museum of Contemporary Art
usage:	culture
construction (facade):	aluminium
system:	panel construction
gross floor area:	10,000 m²
total internal volume:	72,000 m³
total construction cost:	€ 29 mill. (gross)
date of construction:	1996
period of construction:	24 months

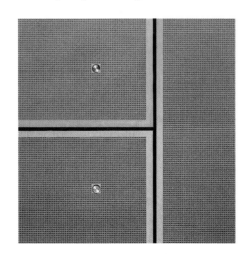

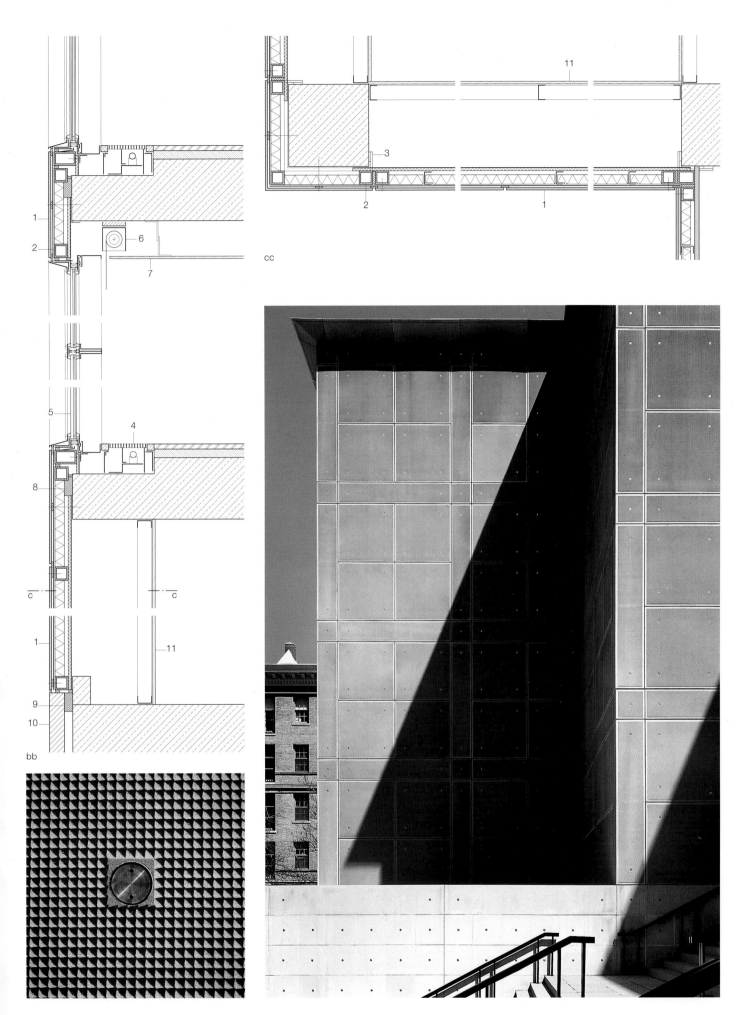

cc

bb

c — — c

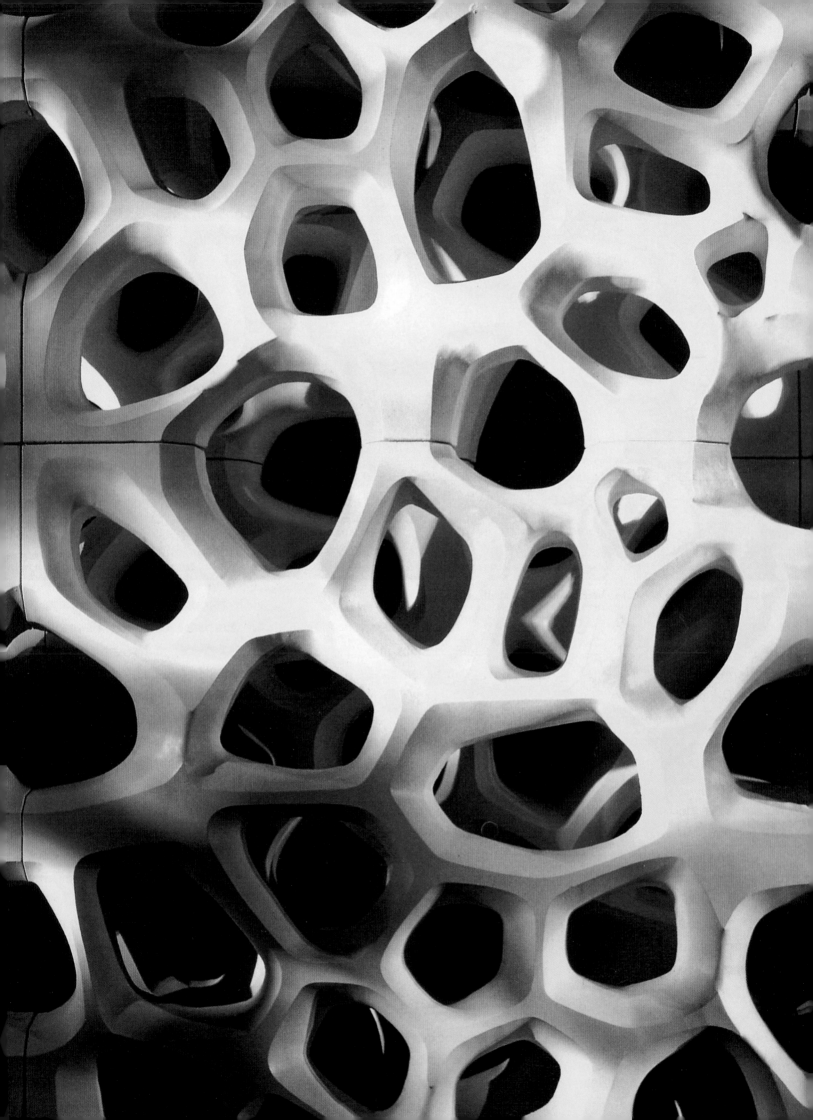

Part E   Developments

From industrial mass production
to customised prefabrication   226
Computer-assisted design   226
Computer-assisted
production processes   227
Computer Numerical Control
Computer Aided Manufacturing
Construction robots   228
User-specific customisation   228
Digital construction systems   229

figure E

Developments

From industrial mass production to customised prefabrication

Construction is a cost-intensive process due to the necessary levels of manual labour. Experimentation with the alternatives of industrial prefabrication has been carried out since the beginning of the 20th century in order to build more economically and more efficiently. In this process, the manual production of building elements is gradually being replaced by mechanical fabrication techniques. The prerequisite for this transfer is the meticulous dimensional coordination of the elements that serves as the basis for their standardisation.

Although construction systems have become widely used in multi-storey housing and for the construction of industrial buildings, industrially prefabricated houses are less readily accepted by their clients. Particularly in housing, where individual desires have to be accommodated, the expression "industrial" is still associated with mass production and monotony. Many products in the building industry, however, are based on automatic production methods – windows and doors, for example, would be prohibitively expensive without these processes. Although there are countless construction systems on the market today, due to their system-based dimensional coordination they are incompatible with one another and, therefore, limited in their range of application.

Future developments in industrialised construction should enable the economical implementation of individual ideas for individual building projects. Contemporary computer-controlled fabrication methods – in the automotive industry for example – are capable of manufacturing both standardised and customised elements for the same production costs as traditional production techniques. In the construction industry, however, the majority of projects are still being manually erected in the conventional manner.

New approaches to industrial construction, based on the application of computer-based production methods, promise an increase in the amount of creative freedom associated with the end product. Particularly for architects, the combination of industrial fabrication and manual building techniques presents an interesting aspect for high-quality, economical construction.
With the use of digital planning and production methods, which are already standard procedure in the aeronautical and space industry, architects are presented with great opportunities for dealing with new construction challenges – especially when one considers that the technical demands for buildings are lower than those for vehicles and aircraft. The optimisation of industrial building processes, in association with innovative production concepts, is of paramount importance (fig. E 1).

Computer-assisted design

While it is already standard procedure for the development of design drawings to be based on CAD software in almost all architectural practices, the future of industrial construction lies in the development of computer-based fabrication methods. Building components for geometrically complex structures are already being produced using these techniques; even entire construction systems, which

E   Close-up view of a precast concrete wall cast in polyurethane formwork, Cocoon Club, Frankfurt (D) 2004, AG Dietz Joppien
E 1   Layout of glass elements, rendering of roof shell, Hungerburg Station, Innsbruck (A) 2007, Zaha Hadid
E 2   Construction of a timber load-bearing structure with CNC-manufactured elements, ESG Pavilion (CH) 2003, ETH Zurich
E 3   CNC-produced dovetail and mortise-and-tenon joints for secondary beam, ESG Pavilion
E 4   Prototype of a structure constructed of CNC-manufactured units, ESG Pavilion
E 5   Machining of steel sheeting with a CNC laser cutter, bus shelter, Landshut (D) 1998, Hild & Kaltwasser
E 6   Producing formwork with a CNC milling machine
E 7   Production of a precast concrete wall elements with formwork inlays produced with CNC technology for the Cocoon Club

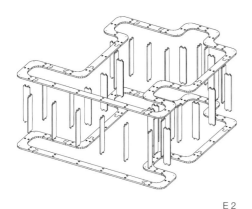

E 2

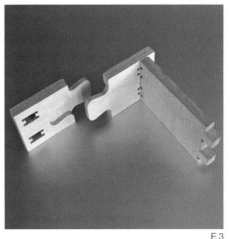

E 3

E 4

present unlimited scope for design, have been developed.

The idea of assisting the building process with computers was conceived in the middle of the 20th century. The computer program Euclid was developed in 1969 for the design of wings for supersonic aircraft. It was the first CAD program with which solid volumes could be modelled. Programs capable of calculating the configuration of a building composed of prefabricated elements, from three-dimensional models, were already in existence in the 1970s. During that same period, digital planning and production methods were being applied for machine and vehicle construction. Today, computer-generated 3D models provide the necessary information on specific building elements which is required for their fabrication using CNC milling technology. Computer-based fabrication techniques are used for both timber and steel construction, while comparable techniques for concrete and masonry construction are still being developed. Variable pneumatic or hydraulic formwork systems would be conceivable for the production of complex concrete forms.

Computer-assisted production processes

Computer Numerical Control (CNC)

The application of CNC production processes means the computer-based control of cutting and milling machines. The new production methods based on this system enable variable and differentiated serial manufacturing techniques. Many building materials, such as timber and plastics, can be particularly well machined with the assistance of CNC technology (figs. E 2 and E 4).

Traditional carpentry work, like the timber joints in frame construction, can now be executed in the factory with the help of CNC machines (fig. E 3). Metal sheeting is cut by laser cutters and arbitrary forms in glass and stone can be achieved using water-jet cutters (fig. E 5).

The data that defines elements designed for particular building functions is imported via the standardised CAD drawing exchange format DXF into control software for CNC machines. This represents a new challenge for architects and engineers to design and implement constructions with this modern technology.

For example, building elements could be

constructed with CNC milling machines for prefabricated houses. The three-dimensional digital model generated is then converted into two dimensions and translated into the program paths of the CAD software. Based on these paths, a three-axis milling machine produces a mould that determines the final shape of the desired building element (fig. E 6). Thus, complex formwork for concrete constructions becomes a real possibility. Particularly in combination with glass-fibre and textile reinforcement techniques, filigree – yet stable – concrete building elements can be produced [1] (fig. E 7).

Computer Aided Manufacturing (CAM)

In contrast to the so called subtractive techniques of building component production, where amounts of material are removed by way of milling, turning, drilling and sawing, there are also 3D digital fabricators – so called fabbers – where production is based on additive processes. This type of production is known as Computer Aided Manufacturing (CAM) and facilitates the direct fabrication of components. In additive processes, bind-

E 5

E 6

E 7

E 8

E 9

ing agents are injected into cellulose powder with great accuracy; the cellulose stabilises and, layer by layer, three-dimensional solid objects are formed. One major disadvantage of this system is that the objects can only be formed out of materials appropriate for the 3D digital fabricators, i.e. materials suitable for modelmaking (fig. E 10). There are, however, hopes that, through the use of nanotechnology, these additive processes can be transferred to various other materials.

Construction robots

The majority of industrially manufactured products – for example, cars and electronic appliances – are already produced by robots. At the University of South California and the ETH Zurich, research is being carried out on the development of construction robots that are independently capable of erecting the carcass of a single family house within 24 hours (fig. E 11). In the industrialised western nations, this type of technology is still viewed rather critically. Although acceptable in the automotive industry, the house is still considered to be a place for individuals; housing construction is linked with traditions of craftsmanship. In Japan, however, the use of robots has been standard practice in housing construction for over thirty years. Companies from the car manufacturing industry – Toyota is one example – offer construction systems for houses that can be assembled from a range of twelve different modular room sizes. The customer can design his house from a catalogue and have it built by robots.

User-specific customisation

In order to comply with individual client requests, parametric design and computer controlled machines have made customisation a standard procedure in the furniture and clothing industries; this trend is known as "mass customisation" (fig. E 12).
Parametric building elements are units which have been designed and manufactured based on computer controlled geometry. Software optimises the organisation of the units and determines the necessary parameters for the production machine. It is possible that these parameters alter slightly during the fabrication process.
Stanford University in California promoted research, in collaboration with Frank O. Gehry, into the flexible prefabrication and control of building processes. The methods developed for the efficient creation of unusual building forms were based upon the initial deconstruction of the building or load-bearing structure into individual elements during the design phase in order to, subsequently, digitally parameterise them for serial production in the factory (fig. E 8). A rational assembly of complex elements then becomes ultimately possible.
The potential of these new methods lies in the accurate and rapid production of units, specific to a particular building, by way of automatic fabrication techniques (fig. E 9). The goals of these developments are the considerable reduction of building costs, an extended range of designs based on identical modules and the efficient fabrication of the individual objects themselves. This would make it possible to economically construct, pro-

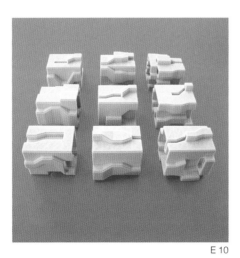

E 10

E 11

E 8 Processing of individual units of a parametrically developed building system, NDS Pavilion, Zurich (CH) 2002, ETH Hönneberg
E 9 Example of a load-bearing system of parametrically developed building elements, NDS Pavilion
E 10 Scale plaster model produced in a 3D printer at 1:100, ESG Pavilion
E 11 Masonry robot
E 12 Individual customisation of a sports shoe in the clothing industry
E 13 Configurable, prefabricated house from the Streif company
E 14 Example of a curved timber load-bearing structure with computer based fabrication of unit elements, look-out tower, Helsinki Zoo (FIN) 2002, Ville Hara

E 12

E 13

E 14

duce and sell buildings in small series. These possibilities can be transferred to the prefabricated housing industry that developed in the USA at the beginning of the 20th century. Prefabricated houses could be conceived for individual building projects, then either manufactured as single houses or serial reproductions thanks to digital planning and computer based fabrication methods. Each client would then be able to adapt the house to satisfy his individual desires and the topography, climate, materials and functions.

Digital construction systems

In spite of the existence of the necessary technology, the application of digital design processes, where communication between the client and architect occurs via the internet, is not yet standard procedure. Programs where the architect can create a digital building model out of virtual units have existed since the 1980s.
The generation of interactive designs for a specific building project is based upon the programming, rather than the drawing, of the developed alternatives. The architect transfers the three-dimensional geometry of his design to the client via the internet. The client can then view the external form and internal layout on the project web site in addition to presenting suggestions for variation (fig. E 13). The preferred alternative is selected based upon these virtual construction kits.
The next stage requires that a detailed construction and unitisation concept be developed for the individual building elements. Suitable manufacturing processes are the basis for economical elements produced in series. It is therefore of para-

mount importance that production-specific restrictions be incorporated into the design as early as possible.
The units of a design, for which rational production techniques make economic sense, are defined in the next phase. Thus the planning of individual building projects can be achieved by utilising the available parametric building elements; a list of the components to be manufactured is made prior to production. For a curved strut framework roof construction, for example, the struts and nodes could be automatically fabricated as parametric building elements with the help of computer based techniques. Each unit has its specific, predetermined role to play in the construction. Each individual strut and node can be exactly described and the precise assembly position prescribed (fig. E 14).
This combination of digitalised design and computer based machines enables the fabrication of differently designed units without additional expenditure [2].

Thanks to contemporary techniques, prefabricated unitised systems are no longer strictly bound to clear geometric arrangements and series of numerous identical units. Technical production and assembly systems no longer limit potential or dictate planning within a predetermined framework; rather, they bring the product, as determined by the planner, to fruition. New possibilities and freedom are thus available to planners today.
The term "system" no longer refers to a combination of countless identical units and the resultant forms, but to a connection of numerous individual elements which can be interrelated based on specific predetermined rules.
The different systems of a building are all,

either directly or indirectly, associated with each other. The number of these associations is continually increasing due to more highly refined expectations and conditions; that means that the specialisation of systems increases in equal measure with their networking and interaction.

Technology originating in various different fields of expertise, the discrete elements and systems of a construction, and even the techniques of building itself, are continually being developed and refined. Nowadays, there are resources available that present enormous freedom and enable the development of greatly improved solutions.
This not only creates new opportunities but also new types of problems. The greater the amount of freedom and range of opportunities available in planning and production techniques, the more important it is to determine unified and widely applicable fundamental guidelines. The exchange of data and information requires cautious and rational interaction, via the communication interfaces, between all parties concerned with the building process.

We should certainly take advantage of the opportunities presented to us but, at the same time, not forget that techniques and building systems present an important feature of construction which is, nonetheless, linked to other aspects within the framework of architectural concepts. Only the balanced interplay of all components can produce good architecture.

Notes:
[1] Detail 12/2007, p. 1494 ff.
[2] Fritz, Oliver: Digitale Technologien in der Vorfabrikation. In: Archithese 2/2003, p. 46 ff.

Authors

Gerald Staib
Born 1950
Studied architecture at Darmstadt Technical University
and the Swiss Federal Institute of Technology (ETH) Zurich
Subsequently in professional practice with Behnisch & Partner until 1993
Since 1992 Professor for Building Construction and Design
at Dresden Technical University
Since 1993 self-employed architect in Stuttgart

Andreas Dörrhöfer
Born 1976
Studied architecture at Kaiserslautern Technical University
Subsequently 2 years in professional practice
Since 2005 technical assistant at the Chair of Building Construction
and Design, Dresden Technical University

Markus J. Rosenthal
Born 1978
Studied architecture at the Dresden Technical University and the Stockholm
Royal Institute of Technology
Since 2007 technical assistant at the Chair of Building Construction
and Design, Dresden Technical University

Statutory instruments, directives, standards

The EU has issued directives for a number of products, the particular aim of which is to ensure the safety and health of users. These directives must be implemented in the member states in the form of compulsory legislation and regulations. The directives themselves do not contain any technical details, but instead only lay down the requisite, underlying requirements.

The corresponding technical values are specified in associated sets of technical rules (e.g. codes of practice) and in the form of EN standards harmonised throughout Europe.

In general, the technical rules provide advice and information for everyday activities. They are not statutory instruments, but rather give users a decision-making aid, a guideline for implementing technical procedures correctly and/or practical information for turning legislation into practice. The use of the technical rules is not compulsory; only when they have been included in government legislation or other statutory instruments do they become mandatory (e.g. in building law), or when the parties to a contract include them in their conditions.

In Germany the technical rules include DIN standards, VDI directives and other publications such as the Technical Rules for Haz-ardous Substances.

The standards are divided into product, application and testing standards. They often relate to just one specific group of materials or products, and are based on the corresponding testing and calculation methods for the respective materials and components. The latest edition of a standard – which should correspond with the state of the art – always applies. A new or revised standard is first published as a draft for public discussion before (with revisions) it is finally adopted as a valid standard.

The origin and area of application of a standard can be gleaned from its designation:
- DIN plus number (e. g. DIN 4108) is essentially a national document (drafts are designated with "E" and preliminary standards with "V").
- DIN EN plus number (e. g. DIN EN 572) is a German edition of a European standard – drawn up by the European Standardisation Organisation CEN – that has been adopted without amendments.
- DIN EN ISO (e. g. DIN EN ISO 18064) is a standard with national, European and worldwide influence. Based on a standard from the International Standardisation Organisation ISO, a European standard was drawn up, which was then adopted as a DIN standard.
- DIN ISO (e. g. DIN ISO 21 930) is a German edition of an ISO standard that has been adopted without amendments.

DIN 105-5. Clay bricks; lightweight horizontally perforated bricks and lightweight horizontally perforated brick panels.

DIN 1025-1. Hot-rolled I-beams – Part 1: Narrow flange I-beams, I-series – Dimensions, masses, sectional properties.

DIN 1052/A1. Design of timber structures – General rules and rules for buildings; Amendment A1.

DIN 1053-4. Masonry – Part 4: Prefabricated masonry compound units.

DIN 4074-1. Strength grading of wood – Part 1: Sawn coniferous timber.

DIN EN 10027-1. Designation systems for steels – Part 1: Steel names; German version EN 10027-1:2005.

DIN 18000. Modular coordination in building.

DIN 18203-1. Tolerances in building construction – Part 1: Prefabricated components made of concrete, reinforced concrete and prestressed concrete.

DIN 30798. Modular systems, modular coordination.

The manufacturers named in this publication and those listed below represent only a selection of possible suppliers. All details given should not be understood as recommendations, but rather as examples and do not make any claim as to completeness.

Alho Systembau GmbH, Friesenhagen (D)
Cocoon Systemleichtbau AG, Basle (CH)
Dyckerhoff & Widmann AG, Munich (D)
Glunz AG, Meppen (D)
Haas Fertigbau GmbH, Falkenberg (D)
Hansen & Detlefsen GmbH, Heide (D)
induo Systemholztechnik GmbH & Co. KG, Korschenbroich (D)
Lignatur AG, Waldstatt (CH)
LIGNOTREND AG, Waldheim (D)
Merk Holzbau GmbH & Co. KG, Aichach (D)
MERO-TSK International GmbH Co. KG, Würzburg (D)
MiTek Industries GmbH, Cologne (D)
SIMPSON STRONG-TIE GmbH, Frankfurt am Main (D)
Steko-Holzbausysteme AG, Attelwil (CH
Trus Joist sprl, Planegg (D)

Bibliography

Part A

Ackermann, Kurt: Tragwerke in der konstruktiven Architektur. Stuttgart 1988

Adan, Amina: African nomadic architecture. Washington 1995

Architecture et industrie: passé et avenir d'un mariage de raison. Exhibition catalogue, Centre Georges Pompidou, Paris 1983

Exhibition catalogue: Fritz Haller – Bauen und Forschen. Kunstmuseum Solothurn 1988

Banham, Reyner: Megastructure: Urban Futures of the Recent Past. London 1976

Bauen + Wohnen 11/1970

Behrens, Peter: Vom sparsamen Bauen. Ein Beitrag zur Siedlungsfrage. Berlin 1918

Bill, Max: Wiederaufbau. Dokumente über Zerstörungen, Planungen, Konstruktionen. Zurich 1945

Binding, Günther et al.: kleine Kunstgeschichte des deutschen Fachwerkbaus. Darmstadt 1989

Brands, Gunnar et al.: Bautechnik der Antike. Mainz 1991

Bruce, Alfred; Sandbank, Harold: a history of prefabrication. New York 1944

Buchanan, Peter: Renzo Piano building workshop, Vol. 1. Stuttgart 1994

Buekschmitt, Justus: Ernst May. Bauten und Planungen Vol.1. Stuttgart 1963

Chemetov, Paul; Marrey, Bernard: Architectures à Paris 1848–1914, Paris 1980

Couchaux, Denis: Habitats nomades. Paris 2004

Das Fertighaus. Exhibition catalogue, Stuttgart 1947

db 1/1969

db 8/1975

Deutscher Werkbund (Ed.): Bau und Wohnung, Stuttgart 1927

Diamand, R. M. E.: Industrialized Building – 50 International Methods. London 1965

Diedrich, Richard: Metastadt – Idee und Wirklichkeit. In: db 8/1975

Downes, Charles: the building erected in Hyde Park for the great exhibition of the works of industry. London 1852

Durth, Werner: Gutschow Niels: Architektur und Städtebau der fünfziger Jahre. Bonn 1987

Ehrenkrantz, Ezra: The Modular Number Pattern: Flexibility through Standardization. London 1956

Elliott, Cecil C.: Technics and architecture. Cambridge 1992.

Engel, Heino: Measure and Construction of the Japanese House. Rutland/Vermont/Tokyo 1985

Faegre, Torvald: Zelte, die Architektur der Nomaden. Hamburg 1980

Frampton, Kenneth: die Architektur der Moderne. Stuttgart 1983

Fritz Haller: Werk, Bauen + Wohnen 7–8/1992

Fuller, Richard Buckminster: Bedienungsanleitung für das Raumschiff Erde. Dresden 1998

Fuller, Richard Buckminster: Inventions: The Patented Works of R. Buckminster Fuller. New York 1983

Gayle, Margot; Gillon, Edmund: Cast-Iron Architecture in New York. New York 1974

Gerner, Manfred: Fachwerk: Entwicklung, Instandsetzung, Neubau. Munich 2007

Gropius, Walter; Moholy-Nagy: Ein Versuchshaus des Bauhauses in Weimar. Weimar 1997

Großmann, Ulrich G.: der Fachwerkbau in Deutschland. Cologne 1998

Gschwend, Max: Schweizer Bauernhäuser. Berne 1971

Guidoni, Enrico. Architektur der primitiven Kulturen. Stuttgart 1976

Habraken, N. John: die Träger und die Menschen. The Hague 2000

Hänseroth, Thomas: Der Aufbruch zum modernen Bauwesen: Zur Geschichte des industriellen Bauens, dargestellt am Beispiel der Entwicklung des Montagebaus von der industriellen Revolution bis zu den frühen dreißiger Jahren des 20. Jahrhunderts. Doctoral/Professional dissertation, Dresden 1982

Hassler, Uta; Schmidt, Hartwig: Häuser aus Beton. Vom Stampfbeton zum Großtafelbau. Tübingen/Berlin 2004

Herbert, Gilbert: The Dream of the Factory-Made House: Walter Gropius and Konrad Wachsmann. Cambridge 1984

Herbert, Gilbert: Pioneers of Prefabrication. The British Contribution in the 19th Century. Baltimore 1978

Hirdina, Heinz (Ed.): Neues Bauen Neues Gestalten. Das neue Frankfurt/eine neue Stadt. Eine Zeitschrift zwischen 1926 und 1933. Dresden 1984, p. 222

Hitchcock, Henry-Russsell: Early Cast-Iron Facades. In: Architectural Review 109/1951

Hix, John: the Glass House. London 1996

Hütsch, Volker: der Münchner Glaspalast 1854–1931. Geschichte und Bedeutung. Berlin 1985

Exhibition catalogue: Jean Prouvé constructeur. Centre Pompidou, Paris 1990

Junghanns, Kurt: Das Haus für alle. Berlin 1994

Kelly, Burnham: the Prefabrication of Houses. Cambridge/New York 1951

Kistenmacher, Gustav: Fertighäuser, Tübingen 1950

Klotz, Heinrich: Vision der Moderne. Das Prinzip Konstruktion. Frankfurt/Main. 1986

Klotz, Heinrich: Von der Urhütte zum Wolkenkratzer. Munich 1991

Kohlmaier, Georg; von Sartory, Barna: Das Glashaus – ein Bautypus des 19. Jahrhunderts. Munich 1988

Krausse, Joachim; Lichtenstein, Claude (Ed.): Your Private Sky. R. Buckminster Fuller, Baden 1999

L'esprit nouveau – Le Corbusier und die Industrie. Zurich 1987

Landau, Royston: New Directions in British Architecture. New York 1968

Le Corbusier: Ausblick auf eine Architektur. Gütersloh 1969

Lüchinger, Arnulf: Herrmann Hertzberger 1959–1986. Bauten und Projekte. The Hague 1987

Marks, Robert W.: The Dymaxion World of Buckminster Fuller. New York 1960

Mengeringhausen, Max: Raumfachwerke aus Stäben und Knoten. Wiesbaden 1975

Meurer, Bernd; Vincon, Hartmut: Industrielle Ästhetik. Zur Geschichte und Theorie der Gestaltung. Giessen 1983

Meyer-Bohe, Walter: Vorfertigung. Atlas der Systeme. Essen 1967

Nerdinger, Winfried: Konstruktion und Raum in der Architektur des 20. Jahrhunderts. Munich 2002

Nerdinger, Winfried: Vision der Moderne. Das Prinzip Konstruktion. Frankfurt/Main 1986

Nerdinger, Winfried: Walter Gropius, Frankfurt/Main 1985/1996

Ogg, Alan: The Australien Context. Red Hill 1987

Pawley, Martin: Theorie und Gestaltung im zweiten Maschninenzeitalter. Brunswick 1998

Peters, Tom F.: Building the nineteenth century. Cambridge 1996

Pfeifer, Günter. et al.: der neue Holzbau. Munich 1998

Phleps, Hermann: Alemannische Holzbaukunst. Wiesbaden 1967

Phleps, Hermann: Holzbaukunst. Der Blockbau. Karlsruhe 1981

Piano, Renzo; Rogers, Richard: Du Plateau Beaubourg au Centre Pompidou. Paris 1987

Rasch, Heinz: Wie bauen? : Materialien und Konstruktionen für industrielle Produktion. Stuttgart 1928.

Rüegg, Arthur: Konstruktive Konzepte der Moderne. Zurich 2001

Russell, Barry: Building Systems, Industrialisation and Architecture. London 1981

Sack, Manfred: Otto Steidle. Brunswick 1985

Schädlich, Christian: Das Eisen in der Architektur des 19. Jahrhunderts. Ein Beitrag zur Geschichte eines neuen Baustoffes. Weimar 1967

Schulitz, Helmut C.: Bauen mit Teilen. In: db 3/1973

Schulitz, Helmut C.: Ein Haus – ein Stahlskelett – ein offenes System. In: db 11/1976

Schulitz, Helmut C.: Stahlkonstruktionen für den Wohnungsbau. In: Das Bauzentrum 1/1999

Schulitz, Helmut; Bauen mit Systemen. In: db 3/1973

Smith, Elizabeth A. T.: Case Study Houses 1945–1966 Der kalifornische Impuls. Cologne 2006

Smith, Terry: Making the Modern: Industry, Art, and Design in America. Chicago 1993

Spiegel, Hans: der Stahlhausbau Bd.1. Berlin 1929

Spieker, Elisabeth: Günter Behnisch – Die Entwicklung des architektonischen Werkes. Doctoral dissertation. TU Stuttgart 2005

Sulzer, Peter: Jean Prouvé oeuvre complète. Volume 1: 1917–1933. Basle 1995

Sulzer, Peter: Jean Prouvé oeuvre complète. Volume 2: 1934–1944. Basle 2000

Sulzer, Peter: Jean Prouvé oeuvre complète. Volume 3: 1944–1954. Basle 2005

Wachsmann, Konrad: Wendepunkt im Bauen. Stuttgart 1989

Wiel, Leopold: Baukonstruktionen des Wohnungsbaues. Leipzig 1990

Yoshida, Tetsuro: Das japanische Wohnhaus. Tübingen 1969

Part B

Bock, Thomas: Leichtbau und Systeme. In: Detail 07/08 2006, p. 769ff.

Cheret, Peter et al.: Informationsdienst Holz. Holzbausysteme. Issue 1, part 1, series 4 Dusseldorf/Bonn 2000

Döring, Wolfgang et al.: Fassaden. Architektur und Konstruktion mit Betonfertigteilen. Cologne/Bonn 2000

Herzog, Thomas et al.: Fassaden Atlas. Munich/Basle 2004

Koncz, Tihamér: Bauen industrialisiert. Wiesbaden 1976

Prochiner, Frank et al.: Automatisierungssysteme im Wohnungsbau. Stuttgart 1999

Weller, Konrad: Industrielles Bauen 1. Grundlagen und Entwicklung des industriellen, energie- und rohstoffsparenden Bauens. Stuttgart/Berlin/Cologne/Mainz 1986

Part C

Materials in system buildings

Cheret, Peter et al.: Informationsdienst Holz. Holzbausysteme. Issue 1, part 1, series 4 Dusseldorf/Bonn 2000

Herzog, Thomas et al.: Fassaden Atlas. Munich/Basle 2004

Kind-Barkauskas, Friedbert et al.: Beton Atlas. Munich/Dusseldorf 2001

Kolb, Josef: Holzbau mit System. Basle 2007

Neumann, Dietrich et al.: Frick/Knöll. Baukonstruktionslehre 1. 33rd edition, Stuttgart 2002

Ruskin, John: Seven Lamps of Architecture. London 1849

Schulitz, Helmut C. et al.: Stahlbau Atlas. Munich/Basle 1999

Spring, Anselm et al.: Holz. Das fünfte Element. Munich 1999, p.14

Stahlbau Zentrum Schweiz: Steeldoc 01/06 Bauen in Stahl. Konstruktives Entwerfen. Grundlagen und Praxis. Zurich 2006

Steinle, Alfred et al.: Bauen mit Betonfertigteilen im Hochbau. Berlin 1995

TU Dresden, Lehrstuhl für Baukonstruktion und Entwerfen: Vorlesungsskript: Beton – das Material. Dresden 2003

TU Dresden, Lehrstuhl für Baukonstruktion und Entwerfen: Vorlesungsskript: Der Baustoff Holz. Dresden 2004

Frame systems

Cheret, Peter et al.: Informationsdienst Holz. Holzbausysteme. Issue 1, part 1, series 4 Dusseldorf/Bonn 2000

Deplazes, Andrea: Architektur Konstruieren. vom Rohmaterial zum Bauwerk. ein Handbuch. Basle/Berlin 2005

Fachvereinigung Deutscher Betonfertigteilbau e.V.: www.fdb-wissensdatenbank.de, Bonn 2008

Herr, Roland et al.: Beton + Fertigteiljahrbuch 2003. Gütersloh 2003

Hugues, Theodor et al.: Detail Praxis. Holzbau. Munich 2002

Kolb, Josef: Holzbau mit System. Basle 2007

Landsberg, Heike et al.: Holzsysteme für den Hochbau. Grundlagen, Systeme. Beispiele. Stuttgart/Berlin/Cologne 1999

Natterer, Julius et al.: Holzbau Atlas Zwei. Dusseldorf 1991

Neumann, Dietrich et al.: Frick/Knöll. Baukonstruktionslehre 1. 33rd edition. Stuttgart 2002

Schulitz, Helmut C. et al.: Stahlbau Atlas. Munich/Basle 1999

Stahlbau Zentrum Schweiz: Steeldoc 01/06 Bauen in Stahl. Konstruktives Entwerfen. Grundlagen und Praxis. Zurich 2006

Stahl-Informations-Zentrum: Merkblatt 115. Stahlgeschossbauten Grundlagen für Entwurf und Konstruktion. Dusseldorf 1989

Steinle, Alfred et al.: Bauen mit Betonfertigteilen im Hochbau. Berlin 1995

Weller, Konrad: Industrielles Bauen 2. Industrielle Fertigung und Anwendung von Montagebauweisen aus Stahlbeton, Stahl, Holz und Entwicklung zum umweltbewussten Bauen. Stuttgart/Berlin/Cologne/Mainz 1989

Panel sytems

Arbeitsgemeinschaft Ziegeldecke: Auszug aus der Broschüre Planen und Bauen mit Ziegeldecken

Cheret, Peter et al.: Informationsdienst Holz. Holzbau-systeme. Issue 1, part 1, series 4 Dusseldorf/Bonn 2000

Deplazes, Andrea: Architektur Konstruieren. vom Rohmaterial zum Bauwerk. ein Handbuch. Basle/Berlin 2005

Detail 04/2003

Detail 07+08/2006

Döring, Wolfgang et al.: Fassaden. Architektur und Konstruktion mit Betonfertigteilen. Cologne/Bonn 2000

Fachvereinigung Deutscher Betonfertigteilbau e.V.: www.fdb-wissensdatenbank.de, Bonn 2008

Hugues, Theodor et al.: Detail Praxis. Holzbau. Munich 2002

Kolb, Josef: Holzbau mit System. Basle 2007

Koncz, Tihamér: Bauen industrialisiert. Wiesbaden 1976

Neumann, Dietrich et al.: Frick/Knöll. Baukonstruktionslehre 1. 33rd edition. Stuttgart 2002

Pfeifer, Günter et al.: Der neue Holzbau. Aktuelle Architektur, alle Bausysteme, neue Technologien. Munich 1998

Pfeifer, Günter et al.: Mauerwerk Atlas. Munich/Basle 2001

Stahl-Informations-Zentrum: Dokumentation 558. Bausysteme aus Stahl für Dach und Fassade. Dusseldorf 2000

Steinle, Alfred et al.: Bauen mit Betonfertigteilen im Hochbau. Berlin 1995

Syspro-Gruppe Betonbauteile e.V. (Ed.): Die Technik zu Decke und Wand. Erlensee 2005

Weber, Helmut et al.: Porenbeton Handbuch. Planen und Bauen mit System. 5th edition, Gütersloh 2002

Weller, Konrad: Industrielles Bauen 1. Grundlagen und Entwicklung des industriellen, energie- und rohstoffsparenden Bauens. Stuttgart/Berlin/Cologne/Mainz 1986

Weller, Konrad: Industrielles Bauen 2. Industrielle Fertigung und Anwendung von Montagebauweisen aus Stahlbeton, Stahl, Holz und Entwicklung zum umweltbewussten Bauen. Stuttgart/Berlin/Cologne/Mainz 1989

Room module systems

Deplazes, Andrea: Architektur Konstruieren. vom Rohmaterial zum Bauwerk. ein Handbuch. Basle/Berlin 2005

Detail 05/1998

Karutz, Holger et al.: Beton. Jahrbuch 2005. Architektur Hochbau Tiefbau. Gütersloh 2004

Koncz, Tihamér: Bauen industrialisiert. Wiesbaden 1976

Landsberg, Heike et al.: Holzsysteme für den Hochbau. Grundlagen, Systeme. Beispiele. Stuttgart/Berlin/Cologne 1999

Weller, Konrad: Industrielles Bauen 1. Grundlagen und Entwicklung des industriellen, energie- und rohstoffsparenden Bauens. Stuttgart/Berlin/Cologne/Mainz 1986

Weller, Konrad: Industrielles Bauen 2. Industrielle Fertigung und Anwendung von Montagebauweisen aus Stahlbeton, Stahl, Holz und Entwicklung zum umweltbewussten Bauen. Stuttgart/Berlin/Cologne/Mainz 1989

Alho Raumfabrik – Im Systembau zu Hause. Company broschure. Alho Systembau GmbH

Part D

Deplazes, Andrea: Architektur Konstruieren. vom Rohmaterial zum Bauwerk. ein Handbuch. Basle/Berlin 2005

Döring, Wolfgang et al.: Fassaden. Architektur und Konstruktion mit Betonfertigteilen. Cologne/Bonn 2000

Herzog, Thomas et al.: Fassaden Atlas. Munich/Basle 2004

Hugues, Theodor et al.: Detail Praxis. Holzbau. Munich 2002

Neumann, Dietrich et al.: Frick/Knöll. Baukonstruktionslehre 1. 33rd edition. Stuttgart 2002

Schittich, Christian et al.: Glasbau Atlas. Munich/Basle 1998

Steinle, Alfred et al.: Bauen mit Betonfertigteilen im Hochbau. Berlin 1995

Watts, Andrew: Moderne Baukonstruktion. Neue Gebäude, neue Techniken. Vienna 2001

Glazed grid shells

Schlaich, Jörg et al.: Verglaste Netzkuppeln. In: Bautechnik 69, issue 1. Berlin 1992

Schlaich, Jörg et al.: Bahnsteigüberdachung Fernbahnhof Berlin-Spandau. In: Stahlbau 68, issue 12. Berlin 1999

Schober, Hans et al.: Neue Messe Mailand – Netzstruktur und Tragverhalten einer Freiformfläche. In: Stahlbau 73, issue 8. Berlin 2004

Stephan, Sören et al.: Stabwerke auf Freiformflächen. In: Stahlbau 73, issue 8. Berlin 2004

Part E

Fritz, Oliver: Digitale Technologien in der Vorfabrikation. In: Archithese 2/2003, p. 46 ff.

Detail 12/2007

Illustration credits

The authors and publishers would like to express their sincere gratitude to all those who have assisted in the production of this book, be it through providing photos or artwork or granting permission to reproduce their documents or providing other information.
All the drawings in this book were specially commissioned. Photographs not specifically credited were taken by the architects or are works photographs or were supplied from the archives of DETAIL magazine. Despite intensive efforts we were unable to establish copyright ownership in just a few cases; however, copyright is assured. Please notify us accordingly in such instances. The numbers refer to the figures or to the page numbers.

Introduction

p. 8   Serge Brison, Brussels

Part A History of prefabrication

A	Christian Schittich, Munich
A 1	Christian Schittich, Munich
A 2	Christian Schittich, Munich
A 3	Rykwert, Joseph: Adams Haus im Paradies. Berlin 2005, p. 42
A 4	Hirmer Fotoarchiv Munich
A 5	Gschwend, Max: Schweizer Bauernhäuser. Basle 1971
A 6	Christian Schittich, Munich
A 7	see A 5
A 8	Elliott, Cecil C.: Technics and architecture, Camebridge 1992, p. 18
A 9	Yoshida, Tetsuro: Das japanische Wohnhaus. Tübingen 1969, p. 71
A 10	Christian Schittich, Munich
A 11	Ogg, Alan: The Australien Context. Red Hill 1987, p. 122
A 12	see A 11, p. 123
A 13	Herbert, Gilbert: Pioneers of Prefabrication, Baltimore 1978, p. 16
A 14	Jesberg, Paulgard, Die Geschichte der Ingenieurbaukunst, Stuttgart 1996, p. 130
A 15	Crystal Palace Exhibiton, Illustrated Catalogue, London 1851, New York 1997, p. 19
A 16	Stadtmuseum, Munich (Josef Albers)
A 17	Werner, Ernst: der Kristallpalast zu London, 1851, Dusseldorf 1970
A 18	Schittich, Christian et al.: Glasbau Atlas. Munich/Basle 1998, p. 147
A 19	Waite, John G., Iron Architecture in New York City – Two Studies in Industrial Archeology, New York 1972
A 20	Peters, Tom F.: Building the nineteenth century. Cambridge 1996, p. 44
A 21	see A 11, p. 75
A 22	Bayerische Staatsbibliothek, Munich
A 23	Roger-Viollet, Documentation Photographique, Paris
A 24	Pawley, Martin: Theorie und Gestaltung im zweiten Maschninenzeitalter. Brunswick 1998, p. 108
A 26	see A 8, p. 194
A 27	Kind-Barkauskas, Friedbert et al.: Beton Atlas. Munich/Dusseldorf 2001, p. 12
A 28	see A 27, p. 28
A 29	Dreysse, Dietrich-Wilhelm: May-Siedlungen. Frankfurt/Main 1987, p. 21
A 30	Deutsche Bauzeitung 47/1926, p. 392
A 31	Junghanns, Kurt: Das Haus für alle. Berlin 1994, p. 126
A 32–34	Spiegel, Hans, Der Stahlhausbau, 1 Wohn bauten aus Stahl, Leipzig 1928, p. 133
A 35–36	Voigt, Wolfgang: Paul Schmitthenner. 1884–1972. Tübingen 2003. p. 21
A 37	see A 31, p. 207
A 38–39	Krausse, Joachim; Lichtenstein, Claude (Ed.): Your Private Sky. R. Buckminster Fuller, Baden 1999. p. 134
A 40	see A 31, p. 197
A 41	Nerdinger, Winfried: Der Architekt Walter Gropius. Berlin 1996, p. 205
A 42	see A 24, p. 114
A 43	The Estate of R. Buckminster Fuller, Santa Barbara
A 44	see A 38, p. 234
A 45	MacCoy, Esther: Wohnbau auf neuen Wegen. Ravensburg 1964
A 46	Julius Shulman, Los Angeles
A 47	Klotz, Heinrich: Vision der Moderne. Munich 1986, p. 293
A 48	Hellwig, Jean-Marie/Prouvé-Archiv Peter Sulzer, Gleisweiler
A 49–50	Kistenmacher, Gustav: Fertighäuser, Tübingen 1950
A 51–52	Werner, Durth, Gutschow Niels: Architektur und Städtebau der fünfziger Jahre. Bonn 1987, p. 70
A 54	Ito, Miwako: Renzo Piano Building Workshop. Tokyo 1992, p. 132
A 55–56	Theresa Beyeler, Berne
A 58	Schulitz, Helmut C. et al.: Stahlbau Atlas, Munich/Basle 1999, p. 268
A 59	Mengeringhausen, Max: Raumfachwerke aus Stäben und Knoten. Wiesbaden 1975, p. 65
A 60	Harry Callahan, Chicago
A 61	Karl J. Habermann, Munich
A 62–63	Nerdinger, Winfried: Konstruktion und Raum in der Architektur des 20. Jahrhunderts. Munich 2002, p. 122
A 64	see A 62, p. 123
A 65	Weil, Leopold: Baukonstruktion des Wohnungsbaues. Leipzig 1990, p. 25
A 66	Winfried Reinhold, Südwestdeutsches Archiv für Architektur und Ingenieurbau Karlsruhe
A 67	Bauen + Wohnen 9/1964
A 68	K. Kinold, Munich
A 69	Drew, Philip: Die dritte Generation. Stuttgart 1972, p. 29
A 70	Verlag Bau + Technik, Dusseldorf
A 71	see A 27, p. 38
A 72	see A 58, p. 68
A 74	see A 47, p. 313
A 75	Frank Kaltenbach, Munich

Part B Fundamentals

B	Matthias Weissengruber, Kennelbach
B 1	Luckenbacher; Roth; Zöllner: Das Buch der Erfindungen, Gewerbe und Industrien. Vol. 4, 7th edition. Leipzig and Berlin 1877
B 2	Weller, Konrad: Industrielles Bauen 1. Stuttgart 1986, p. 22
B 5	Lluis Casals, Barcelona
B 7–8	Nerdinger, Winfried: Konstruktion und Raum in der Architektur des 20. Jahrhunderts. Munich/Berlin 2002, p. 105
B 9	see B 2
B 12	Therese Beyeler, Berne
B 14	DIN 18 000. 1984
B 16	Bussard, Pierre: Die Modulordnung im Hochbau, Stuttgart 1963
B 18	Girsberger, Hans (Ed.): ac panel, Asbestzement-Verbundplatten und -Elemente für Aussenwände, Zurich 1967
B 21	Weller, Konrad: Industrielles Bauen 1. Stuttgart/Berlin/Cologne/Mainz 1986
B 22a	2be_die Markenmacher, Nurnberg
B 22b	Syspro-Gruppe Betonbauteile e.V. (Ed.): Die Technik zu Decke und Wand. Erlensee 2005, p. 26
B 23	Döring, Wolfgang et al.: Fassaden. Architektur und Konstruktion mit Betonfertigteilen. Dusseldorf 2002, p. 63

Part C Structural systems

Materials in system building

C	David Franck, Ostfildern
C 1.1	Friedemann Zeitler, Penzberg
C 1.2	Susanne Stauss, Zurich
C 1.3	Robert Mehl, Aachen
C 1.4	Reid, Jo & Peck, John, Newport

Frame systems

C 2.1	Bauen mit Stahl e.V. (Ed.): Stahlbau Arbeits-hilfe 23
C 2.2	Stahlbau Zentrum Schweiz (Ed.): Steeldoc 01/06, Konstruktives Entwerfen (Sonderheft tec01). Zurich 2006, p. 9
C 2.3–4	Stahl-Informations-Zentrum (Ed.): Doku-mentation 532. Dusseldorf 2000, p. 19
C 2.5	Kay Fingerle, Berlin
C 2.6	Weller, Konrad: Industrielles Bauen 2. Stuttgart/Berlin/Cologne/Mainz 1989, p. 57
C 2.7	Stahl-Informations-Zentrum (Ed.):

Merkblatt 115. Dusseldorf 1989, p. 18
C 2.8 see A 58, p. 195
C 2.9 Reichel, Alexander et al.: Bauen mit Stahl. Munich 2006
C 2.10 see C 2.2, p. 13
C 2.11 see C 2.2, p. 24
C 2.12 see C 2.7, p. 13
C 2.13 see A 58, p. 128
C 2.14 see C 2.7, p. 12
C 2.15 see C 2.7, p. 15
C 2.16 see C 2.2, p. 23
C 2.17 see C 2.7, p. 16
C 2.18 Deplazes, Andrea: Architektur konstruieren: Vom Rohmaterial zum Bauwerk. Ein Handbuch. Basle/Berlin 2005. p. 128
C 2.19 see C 2.18, p. 139
C 2.20 see C 2.18, p. 132
C 2.21a Stahl-Informations-Zentrum (Ed.): Dokumentation 548. Dusseldorf 1998, p. 21
C 2.21b see C 2.21a, p. 19
C 2.22 s. A 58, p. 214
C 2.23 Kolb, Josef: Holzbau mit System. Basle 2007, p. 103
C 2.24 Cheret, Peter et al.: Informationsdienst Holz. Reihe 1 Teil 1 Folge 4. Dusseldorf/Bonn 2000, p. 16
C 2.25 see C 2.24, p. 17
C 2.26 Natterer, Julius et al.: Holzbau Atlas Zwei. Dusseldorf 1991, p. 111
C 2.27 Hugues, Theodor et al.: Detail Praxis. Holzbau. Munich 2002, p. 74
C 2.28 see C 2.27, p. 75
C 2.29 see C 2.23, p. 103
C 2.30a see C 2.26, p. 150
C 2.30b see C 2.26, p. 151
C 2.31a see C 2.26, p. 131
C 2.31b see C 2.26, p. 164
C 2.32a see C 2.26, p. 129
C 2.32b see C 2.26, p. 174
C 2.33 Landsberg, Heike et al.: Holzsysteme für den Hochbau. Stuttgart/Berlin/Cologne 1999, p. 103
C 2.34 MiTek Industries, Cologne
C 2.35 Herzog, Thomas et al.: Holzbau Atlas. 4th edition , Munich 2003, p. 52
C 2.36 Pfeifer, Günter et al.: Der neue Holzbau. Munich 1998, p. 140
C 2.37 see C 2.36, p. 120
C 2.38 based on: Schulitz, Helmut C. et al.: Stahlbau Atlas. Munich/Basle 1999, p. 214
C 2.39 see C 2.33, p. 105
C 2.40a see C 2.24, p. 20
C 2.40b see C 2.23, p.103
C 2.41 see C 2.33, p.111
C 2.42 see C 2.23. Basle 2007, p. 59
C 2.43 Natterer, Julius et al.: Holzbau Atlas Zwei. reprint, Munich 1999, p. 62
C 2.44–45 see C 2.35, p. 53
C 2.46a see C 2.24, p. 19
C 2.46b see C 2.24, p. 18
C 2.47 Florack Bauunternehmung GmbH, Heinsberg
C 2.48 Koncz, Tihamér: Bauen industrialisiert. Wiesbaden 1976, p. 59
C 2.49 see C 2.48, p. 61

C 2.50–51 Klebl AG, Neumarkt
C 2.52 Kind-Barkauskas, Friedbert et al.: Beton Atlas. Munich/Dusseldorf 2001, p. 122
C 2.53 Kaspar Röckeleien KG: Hochbau Stahlbeton-Skelettbau, company brochure, p. 6
C 2.54 Steinle, Alfred et al.: Bauen mit Betonfertigteilen im Hochbau. Berlin 1995, p. 98
C 2.55 see C 2.54, p. 99
C 2.56 see C 2.54, p. 114
C 2.57 based on: Herr, Roland et al.: Beton + Fertigteil Jahrbuch 2003. Gütersloh 2003, p. 142
C 2.58 see C 2.48, p. 51
C 2.59 Fachvereinigung Deutscher Betonfertigteilbau e.V.: www.fdb-wissensdatenbank.de, Bonn 2008

Examples
S. 72–73, 75   Arnaud Rinuccini, Paris
S. 76, 77 top   s. A 58, p. 233
S. 77 bottom   see A 58, p. 234
S. 78–79 bottom,
80–81   Bill Timmermann, Arizona
S. 82–83   Shinkenchiku-sha, Tokyo
S. 86–88   Tomio Ohashi, Tokyo
S. 89   Hiro Sakaguchi/A to Z, Tokyo
S. 90   Paul Ott, Graz
S. 92–93   Ignazio Martinez, Dornbirn
S. 96–97   Andrea Helbling, Zurich
S. 100 top, 101   Shinkenchiku-sha, Tokyo
S. 100 bottom   Fa. Todo Co., Tokyo
S. 102, 104–105   Philippe Ruault, Nantes
S. 107–109   Christian Richters, Münster

Panel systems
C 3.1 see C 2.6, p. 16
C 3.2 Rautaruukki, Oyi, Helsinki
C 3.5 db 11/2002
C 3.6 Neumann, Dietrich et al.: Frick/Knöll. Baukonstruktionslehre 1. 33. Aufl. Stuttgart 2002, p. 187
C 3.7–8 Cocoon Systemleichtbau AG, Basle
C 3.9 Stahl-Informations-Zentrum: Dokumentation 588. Dusseldorf 2007, p. 15,
C 3.10 Thyssen Krupp Bausysteme, Kreuztal
C 3.12 Alcan Singen GmbH, Singen
C 3.13 Luís Ferreira Alves, Oporto
C 3.14 see C 2.24, p. 18
C 3.15 Firma Merk, Aichach
C 3.17 see C 2.23, p. 132
C 3.18 see C 2.23, p. 113
C 3.19a see C 2.23, p. 121
C 3.19b see C 2.23, p. 127
C 3.19c see C 2.23, p. 123
C 3.20a see C 2.24, p. 30
C 3.20b see C 2.24, p. 31
C 3.21 see C 2.24, p. 24
C 3.22 see C 2.24, p. 22
C 3.23–24 see C 2.36, p. 203
C 3.25 see C 2.23, p.46
C 3.26 see C 2.18, p. 103
C 3.27 see C 2.24, p. 16
C 3.28 see C 2.23, p. 53
C 3.29 Lucia Degonda, Zurich/Sumvitg
C 3.30 see C 2.23, p. 52
C 3.31 Steko-Holzbausysteme AG, Attelwil

C 3.32a see C 2.23, p. 134
C 3.32b see C 2.23, p. 135
C 3.33 see C 2.23, p. 126
C 3.34 see C 2.23, p. 122
C 3.36 see C 2.48, p. 54
C 3.37 see B 23, p. 56
C 3.38 see B 23, p. 61
C 3.39 see B 23, p. 63
C 3.40 see B 23, p. 62
C 3.41 Feldmann, Heinz et al.: Beton-Bauteile für den Wohnungsbau. Dusseldorf 1993, p. 29
C 3.42a Schwerm, Dieter et al.: Deckensysteme aus Betonfertigteilen. Bonn 1997, p. 27
C 3.42b see C 3.42a, p. 26
C 3.43 C 3.41, p. 23
C 3.44 see B 23, p. 72
C 3.45 Weber, Helmut et al.: Porenbeton Handbuch. Planen und Bauen mit System. 5th edition, Gütersloh 2002, p. 193
C 3.46 see C 3.45, p. 195
C 3.47 Schwerm, Dieter et al.: Deckensysteme aus Betonfertigteilen. Bonn 1997
C 3.48 Thomas Mayer Archive, Neuss
C 3.50 Xella International GmbH, Duisburg
C 3.52 Arbeitsgemeinschaft Ziegeldecke (Ed.): Informationsbroschüre Planen und Bauen mit Ziegeldecken, Recklinghausen
C 3.53 Pfeifer, Günter et al.: Mauerwerk Atlas. Munich/Basle 2001, p. 120
C 3.54 C 3.52
C 3.55 Hugues, Theodor et al.: Detail Praxis. Großformatige Ziegel. Munich 2003, p. 28
C 3.56 see C 3.56, p. 29

Examples
S. 127   Ralph Feiner, Malans
S. 128–131   Bruno Klomfar, Vienna
S. 132–133   Hiroyuki Hirai, Tokyo
S. 134   Anthony Vizzari, Chicago
S. 136–137, 139   Picture Press/Thurmann, Hamburg
S. 140–142   Mathias Weissengruber, Kennelbach
S. 144 bottom,
145–147   Richard Heinrich, Munich
S. 148–151   Frank Kaltenbach, Munich
S. 152 top left,
154 top, 155:   Ralph Feiner, Malans
S. 156–157   Serge Demailly, Saint-Cyr-sur-Mer

Room module systems
C 4.1 see C 2.48, p. 55
C 4.2 Claus Bach, Weimar
C 4.3 Stahl-Informations-Zentrum (Ed.): Dokumentation 080. Dusseldorf 2001, p. 2
C 4.4 see C 2.21a, p. 25
C 4.5 see C 4.3, p. 4
C 4.6 Stahl-Informations-Zentrum (Ed.): Dokumentation 532. p. 35
C 4.7 ALHO Holding GmbH & Co. KG, Friesenhagen
C 4.12 Sachers, Thomas: Beton Jahrbuch 2005. Gütersloh 2005, p. 105
C 4.14a see A 69, p. 61
C 4.14b see A 69, p. 60

Examples
p. 165–167   Dietmar Strauß, Besigheim
p. 169, 171   Christoph Gebler, Hamburg
p. 172–173   Wofgang Haug, Eichenau
p. 174 top,
right middle   Christian Richters, Münster
p. 176–177   Pietro Savorelli, Florence
p. 178–179   Paul Wachol, New York
p. 180–181   Marko Huttunen, Lahti
p. 182–183, 185   Ingnazio Martinez, Hard
p. 186–187, 189   Per Johansen, Copenhagen
p. 190   Steffen Jänicke, Berlin
p. 192–193   Tomio Ohashi, Tokyo

Part D Building envelopes

D   Holger Knauf, Dusseldorf
D 1.1–2   Hart, Franz et al.: Stahlbau Atlas.
           Brussels 1982, p. 338
D 1.3   xia Intelligente Architektur 01–03/2008,
           p. 58
D 1.4a   Christian Richters, Münster
D 1.4b   Watts, Andrew: Moderne Baukonstruktion.
           Vienna 2001, p. 71
D 1.5a   see D 1.4b, p. 73
D 1.5b   Christian Richters, Münster
D 1.6   see A 18
D 1.7   see A 18, p. 92
D 1.8   see A 18, p. 64
D 1.9   Herzog, Thomas et al.: Fassaden Atlas.
           Munich/Basle 2004, p. 236
D 1.10b   Hisao Suzuki, Barcelona
D 1.11a   see D 1.9, p. 201
D 1.11b   Chrisitan Schittich, Munich
D 1.12   see D 1.9, p. 233
D 1.13a   see D 1.9, p. 251
D 1.13b   Jörg Hempel, Aachen
D 1.14a   see D 1.9, p. 257
D 1.14b   Holger Knauf, Dusseldorf
D 1.15   Margherita Spiluttini, Vienna
D 1.16   C 3.6, p. 272
D 1.17   Jan Cremers, Munich
D 1.18–19 see D 3.6, p. 272
D 1.20   Schlorhaufer, Bettina et al.: Cul zuffel e l'aura
           dado – Gion A. Caminada. Lucerne 2005, p. 50
D 1.21   Christian Richters, Münster
D 1.22   Informationsdienst Holz, Dusseldorf 1992
D 1.23   see D 1.9, p. 107
D 1.24   see B 23, p. 27
D 1.25   see B 23, p. 57
D 1.26   Fehling, Ekkehard et al.: Beton + Fertigteil-
           jahrbuch 2007. Gütersloh 2007, p. 10
D 1.27   Heinrich Helfenstein, Zurich
D 1.28a   Alexander Reichel, Munich/Kassel
D 1.29   see D 1.26, p. 10
D 1.30   Eloi Bonjoch, Barcelona
D 1.31   see C 2.18, p. 55
D 1.32   see D 1.9, p. 66
D 1.33a   see D 1.9, p. 69
D 1.33b   Christian Gahl, Berlin
D 1.34   Christian Richters, Münster
D 1.35   Kaltenbach, Frank (Ed.): Transluzente
           Materialien. Munich 2003, p. 50
D 1.36   see D 1.35, p. 54
D 1.37   see D 1.35, p. 48
D 1.38   Richard Einzig/Arcaid, Kingston upon
           Thames
D 1.39   Frank Kaltenbach, München

Glazed grid shells

D 2.1–16   Jan Knippers, Stuttgart

Examples
p. 214 left top   Christian Schittich, Munich
p. 214 right   Waltraud Krase, Frankfurt/Main
p. 215 left,
right top   Christian Schittich, Munich
p. 215 right
bottom   MM Video-Photographie adverti-
                  sing, Kaufungen/Josef Gartner
                  GmbH, Gundelfingen
p. 216 left   Gardin & Mazzoli, Treviso
p. 217 top,
bottom   Gardin & Mazzoli, Treviso
p. 218 bottom   Andreas Gabriel, Munich
p. 220   Kawasumi Architectural Photo-
                  graph office, Tokyo
p. 222, 223   Hélène Binet, London

Part E Developments

E   Robert Mehl, Aix-la-Chapelle
E 4   Bernhard Friese, Pforzheim
E 5   Michael Heinrich, Munich
E 6   Archithese 2/2003, p. 54
E 7   see D 1.26, p. 46
E 8–9   Archithese 2/2003, p. 50
E 12   Archithese 2/2003, p. 46
E 13   Archithese 2/2003, p. 48
E 14   Jussi Tiainen, Helsinki

Index of persons

A

aat+Makoto Yokomizo Architects 174
Aillaud, Emile 34
Amann & Gittel Architekten 148
and8 Architekten, Aisslinger + Bracht 190
Anderson Anderson Architecture 134
Archea Associati 176
Archigram 37
Arets, Wiel 199
Arn + Partner 136
Arup Associates 216

B

Badger, Daniel 21
Bage, Charles 19
Ban, Shigeru 132
Barkow Leibinger Architekten 51
Bauersfeld, Walter 31
Bearth & Deplazes Architekten 126, 152
Beaudoin, Eugène 28, 29
Behnisch, Günter 33, 34, 37
Behrens, Peter 23, 25
Benoy architects 213
Bessemer, Henry 19
blank studio 78
Bofill, Ricardo 34, 35
Bogardus, James 20, 21
Brenner, Klaus Theo 207
Brodie, John 22

C

Caminada, Gion A. 117
CAS Chappuis Aregger Sloèr 51
Christoph, Christian Ferdinand 17
Coignet, François 22
Conzelmann, John E. 22
Cook, Peter 207

D

Darby, Abraham 18, 19
Dietrichs, Richard 32, 33
Dietz-Joppien Architekten 226
Dollmann + Partner 164
Doecker 17

E

Eames, Charles and Ray 28, 29
Eberstadt, Stefan 160
Egeraat, Eric van 196
Ehrenkrantz, Ezra 35
Entenza, John 29
Eyck, Aldo van 35

F

Fairbairn, William 20, 21
Ford, Henry 23, 25
Foster, Norman 10, 11, 35, 37
Fox and Henderson 20
Fuksas, Massimiliano 211, 213
Fuller, R. Buckminster 11, 26, 29, 30, 37, 212
Furnier, Colin 207

G

Gangoly & Kristner Architekten 90
Gehry, Frank O. 54
Gigante, José Manuel 113
Gohm & Hiessberger 128
Graser, Jürg 96
Gropius, Walter 23, 24, 25, 27, 34
Guggenbichler + Netzer 172

H

Habraken, Niklas 35
Hadid, Zaha 205, 226
Haller, Fritz 30, 42, 43
Hamonic + Masson 72
Hara, Ville 228
Hennebique, François 22
Hertzberger, Herman 35
Herzog & de Meuron 207
Hild & Kaltwasser 123, 226
Hild und K. 50, 144

I

Ingenhoven Overdieck Kahlen 196, 200, 218
Ito, Toyo 86

K

Kaufmann 96 182
Kaufmann, Hermann 46
Kaufmann, Johannes 92
Kaufmann, Oskar Leo 92
Keim, Jochen 168
Kikutake, Kiyonoru 32
Kishi, Waro 54
Kisho Kurokawa & Associates 192
Kleihues, Joseph Paul 222
Kollhoff, Hans 205
Kurokawa, Kisho 32, 192

L

Labrouste, Henri 20
Lacaton & Vassal 102
Le Corbusier 11, 22, 23, 25, 29, 34, 51
Lods, Marcel 28, 29
LOT/EKarchitecture 178

M

May, Ernst 23, 24, 25
Mengeringhausen, Max 30, 31, 61, 208
Messerschmidt, Willy 29
Mies van der Rohe, Ludwig 41, 56, 205
Mitscherlich, Alxander 37
Mitsubishi Jisho Sekkei 220
Moneo, José Rafael 41
Monier, Joseph 21

N

Neutra, Richard 29

O

Otto, Frei 11, 31, 208, 209
ONV architects 186

P

Paxton, Joseph 11, 20, 28
Piano, Renzo 10, 29, 35, 37, 199
Pritchard, Peter Thomas 18
propeller z 200
Prouvé, Jean 28, 51

Q

Quinke, Albrecht 115

R

Reichel, Alexander 106, 205
Rice, Peter 11, 30
Rocha, Joao Alvaro 113
Rogers, Richard 10, 35, 36, 37

S

Saarinen, Eero 29
Safdie, Moshe 32
Saulnier, Jules 20
Schlaich, Jörg 31, 208, 213
Schmitthenner, Paul 26
Schneider & Schneider 205
schneider + schumacher 200, 214
Schulitz, Helmut C. 37, 76
Sill, Klaus 168
Sirola, Niko 180
Snow, George W. 16
SPP Architekten und Ingenieure 162
Steidle, Otto 36
Stirling, James 34, 35, 207
Sturm und Wartzeck 162

T

Takamatsu Architects and Associates 100
Taylor, Frederick Winslow 23, 25
Tectône architectes 156
Thomas, Sidney Gilchrist 19
Thompson, Peter 18

U

Urnammu 15
Unmack, Axel 17
Unterrainer, Walter 140
Utzon, Jorn 36

V

Vinoly, Rafael 51
Viollet-le-Duc, Eugène Emmanuel 15
Vitruv 15
Voit, August 18

W

Wachsmann, Konrad 20, 26, 27, 30, 208
Wagner, Christian 96
Wagner, Martin 23
Wilkinson, John 18

Y

Yamamoto, Riken 82

Index

A

adhesive fixed connections	198
assembly	47
axial grid	45

B

balloon frame construction systems	16, 111
Beech Aircraft Company	26, 27
brickwork	14
brickwork facade systems	205
buffer facade	201
building methods	41
building system	42

C

CAD software	209
Case Study House Programme	29
Case Study Houses	28, 36
cast masonry panels	124
ceiling and floor slabs	122
cement-bonded particleboard	118
Christoph & Unmack	17, 25, 27
CIAM	23
clay hollow pot floor elements	125
closed systems	42
CNC milling machine	227
Coalbrookdale	19
colonial expansion	17
composite masonry panels	125
composite metal sheeting	201
computer aided manufacturing (CAM)	227
computer numerical control (CNC)	227
computer-assisted	
- design	226
- production processes	227
concrete	
- lightweight	25
- columns	23
- construction – prefabricated	21
- elements – porous	121
- elements – special	123
- flat slabs	23
- panels	23
- room modul systems	163
- sandwich elements	120
concrete facade elements	
- porous	122
- methods of fixing	204
- surface quality	204
construction elements – concrete	120
construction grid	45
construction materials and elements – timber	118
construction robots	40, 41, 228
copper house	25
crosswall construction	110
Crystal Palace	19, 20, 30
customised prefabrication	226
cut stone panels	205

D

Diagoon Houses	35
digital construction systems	229
dimensional coordination	45
domes – geodesic	31
domes	31

Dom-ino house	23, 25
Dornier	29
double wall elements	121
double window elements in punctuated facades	201
double-glazed windows in prefabricated construction	199
double-skin facade	199
drilled point fixing	198
dymaxion house	26, 27
dynamic relaxation	209

E

elements	42

F

fabbers	227
facade system	50, 160, 196, 200
- brickwork	205, 31
- concrete	204
- glass	197
- metal	201
- natural stone	205
- plastic	206
- timber	203
FE program	209
fibreboard – wood	118
figured glass	198
finite element method	208
float glass	198
formed elements	201
frame construction	45, 54, 55, 67
- American	16
- timber	15, 16, 17
- systems	40, 41
frame systems	54, 55, 67
- concrete	68
- steel	55
- timber	61
framework	35, 37
- planar	31
- timber	15, 16
framework construction	
- steel	111
- timber	116

G

General Panel	
- Corporation	26
- System	27, 28, 43
- Units	28
geodesic domes	31
geodetic shell structures	212
geometric positioning elements	45
glass construction elements	198
glass facade systems	197
Glass Palace	19
glasshouses	19
glazed single-skin steel grid shells	209
glazing bar construction	197
glue-laminated timber panels (glulam)	119
gothic cathedrals	15
grid	44, 209
- axial	45
- installation	45
- internal fit-out	45

- modular	45
- construction	45
- services	45
grid shell structures	209, 211

H

Habitat	32
hand-laid masonry panels	124
heavy gauge laminated timber elements	119
high-rise iron construction	20
Holig-Homogen-Holzwerk	29
hollow glass blocks	198
- section	209
- slabs	123
housing experiment Genter Straße	35

I

IBM travelling pavilion	30
industrial fabrication	33
industrial prefabrication	40
industrial revolution	18
installation grid	45
internal fit-out grid	45
iron – the first systems	18
iron construction – high-rise	20
iron frame construction	19

J

Japanese house – traditional	17
joint treatment	121
jointing	47
jointing configuration in prefabricated	

L

laminated veneer timber panels	119
large span structural systems	31
large-panel construction	110
laser cutter	227
lightweight steel sections	113

M

main system	45
Maison du Peuple	28
MAN ready-built house	28
mass customisation	228
mass housing construction	22
mechanically ventilated facade	200
Mega-structures and visions	31
MERO-System	30, 31, 43
meta-city Wulfen	32, 33
metal facade systems	201
metal sheeting	201
methods of fixing	197
military expansion	17
MINI, MIDI or MAXI system	30, 43
mobilar Structure	30, 31
mobile production plants	41
modular arrangement	17, 20
- building systems	25, 26
- building unit	160
- construction	17, 22, 29, 30
- construction	42
- construction systems	43
- grid	45
- organisation	196

module 44
modules – timber 118
multi-layer glass facade 198

N
Nakagin Tower 32
natural stonework facade systems 205
network optimisation 212
nodes 208, 210, 211, 212
nomads 14
non-structural facades 196

O
occident process 23
open structures 34
open systems 43
OSB panels 118

P
Packaged House 26, 27
panel building methods – steel 111
panel construction 28, 114
  - timber 114
  - system 24, 27, 29, 34
panel facades and formed elements 207
panel systems 40, 42, 110, 116, 122
  - concrete 119
  - masonry, brickwork 124
  - steel 111
  - timber 114
particleboard 118
  - cement-bonded 118
planar framework 31
planetarium dome 31
plastic
  - facade elements 206
  - facade systems 206
  - moulded elements 207
  - panels 206
platform construction systems 111
platform framing 16
pneumatic cushion facades 207
Pompidou Centre 34, 35
porous concrete
  - elements 121
  - facade elements 122
portland cement 25
post-and-rail facades 197
prefabricated
  - concrete construction 21
  - facades 197
  - house 25
  - masonry building elements 124
projection principle 212

R
rationalisation 22
reinforced concrete wall elements 120
robots 40, 41, 228
rods 210
room module sytems 41, 52, 160
  - concrete 163
  - steel 161
  - timber 162
room-high brickwork elements 125

S
Sander house 26
sandwich elements
  - concrete 120
  - steel 113
SCSD program 35
sectional sheet panels 112
semi-finished
  - elements 43
  - plastic panels 207
serial production 22
services grid 45
settled dwellers 14
sheeting – steel 113
shell structure 208
site logistics 208
site prefabrications 41
small panel construction 110
solid slabs 122
solid timber panels 114
special concrete elements 123
St. Andrew's University 34
stacked-plank panels 119
steel
  - frame construction 41, 42
  - framework construction 111
  - panel building methods 111
  - room module systems 160
  - sandwich elements 113
  - sections – lightweight 113
  - sheeting 113
stone 14
structural facades 196
struts 208, 211, 212
sub-system 45
sumerian 14
System Behnisch 34
System Jespersen 34
systems
  - building 42
  - closed 42
  - MERO 30, 31, 43
  - open 43

T
T.E.S.T. Group 35
timber 15
timber block construction 117
timber block panels 114, 115
timber facade elements 203
timber facade systems
  - methods of fixing 203
  - substructure 203
  - surface treatment 203
timber facades elements
  - non-structural 203
  - solid 203
timber framed construction 15, 16, 17
timber framework 15, 16, 116
timber modules 118
timber panel construction 114
timber panels – solid 114
timber preservatives
  - biological 203
  - chemical 203

timber room modul systems 162
tolerances 47
transport 45
type standardisation 22, 42
types of glass in prefabricated construction 198

U
unitised slabs 123
user-specific customisation 228

V
visions 31

W
water-jet cutter 227
WBS 70 34
web panel slabs 123
Weißenhof 25
Wichita House 26, 27
window systems 198
wood fibreboard 118
Wulfen 32, 33